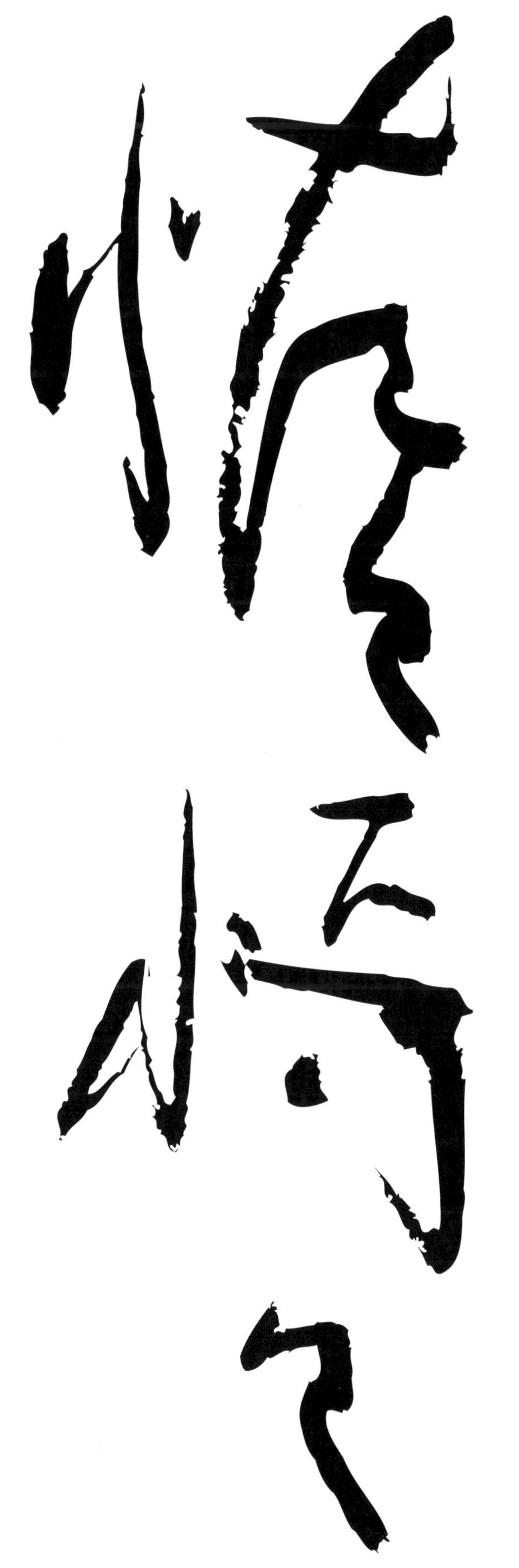

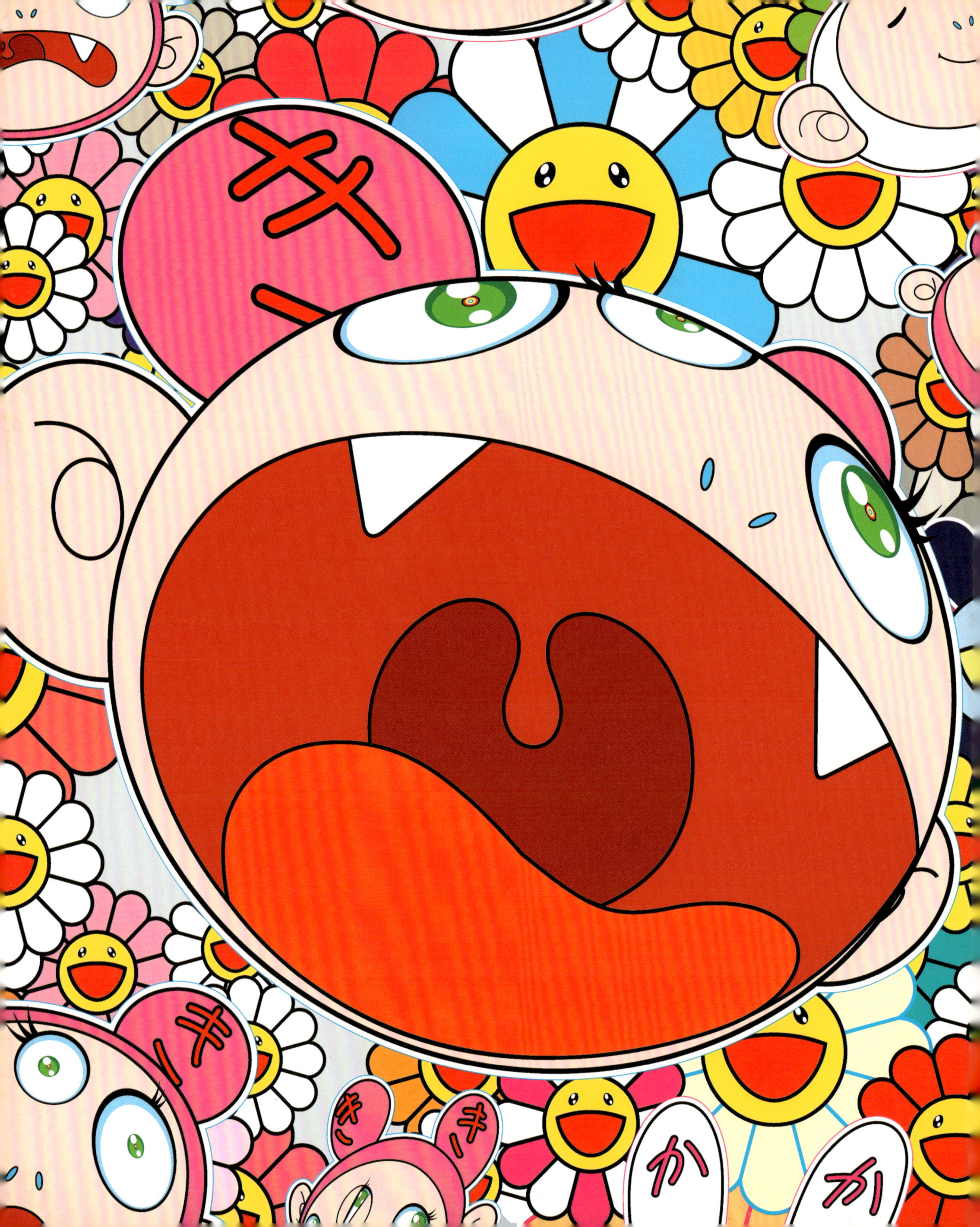

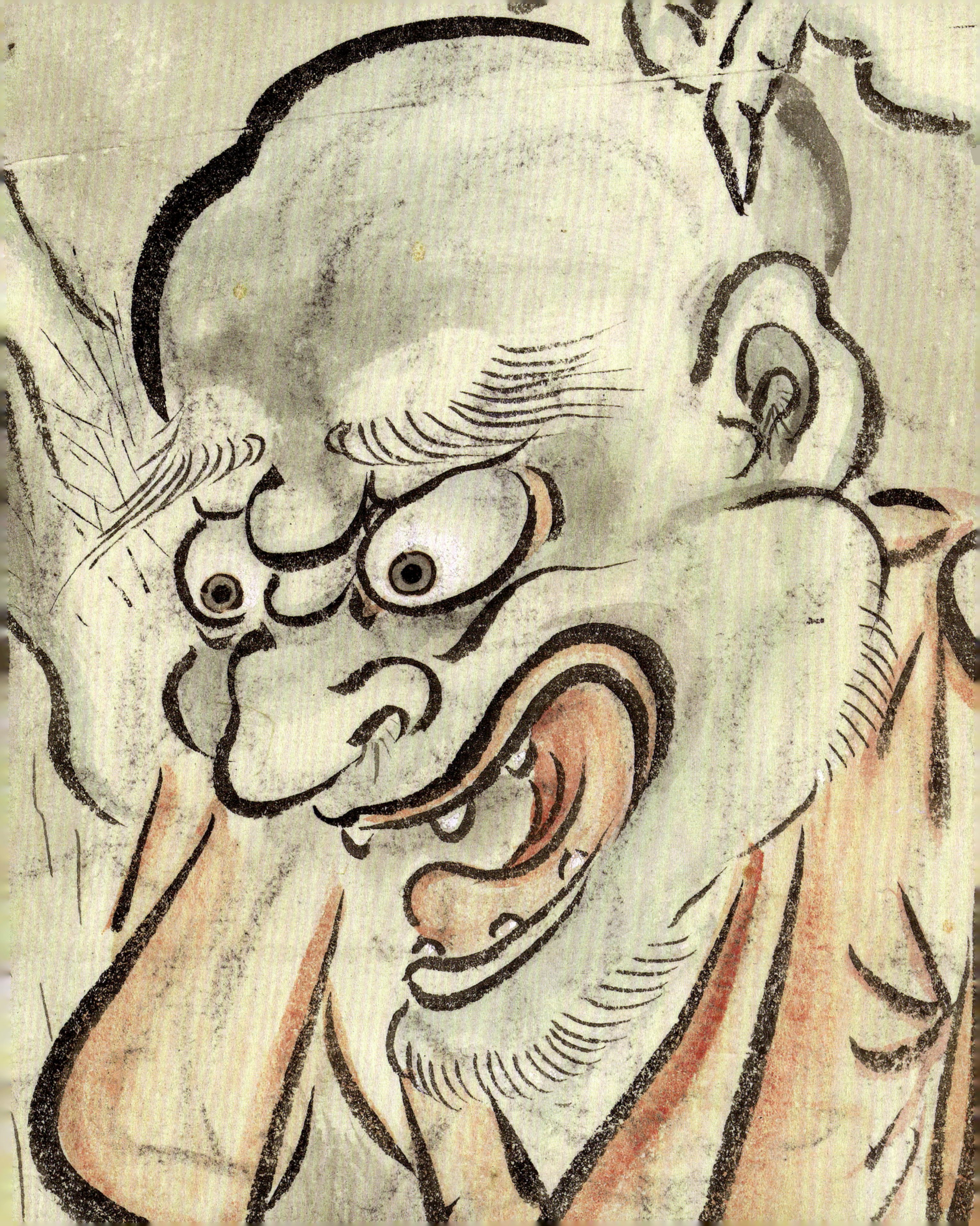

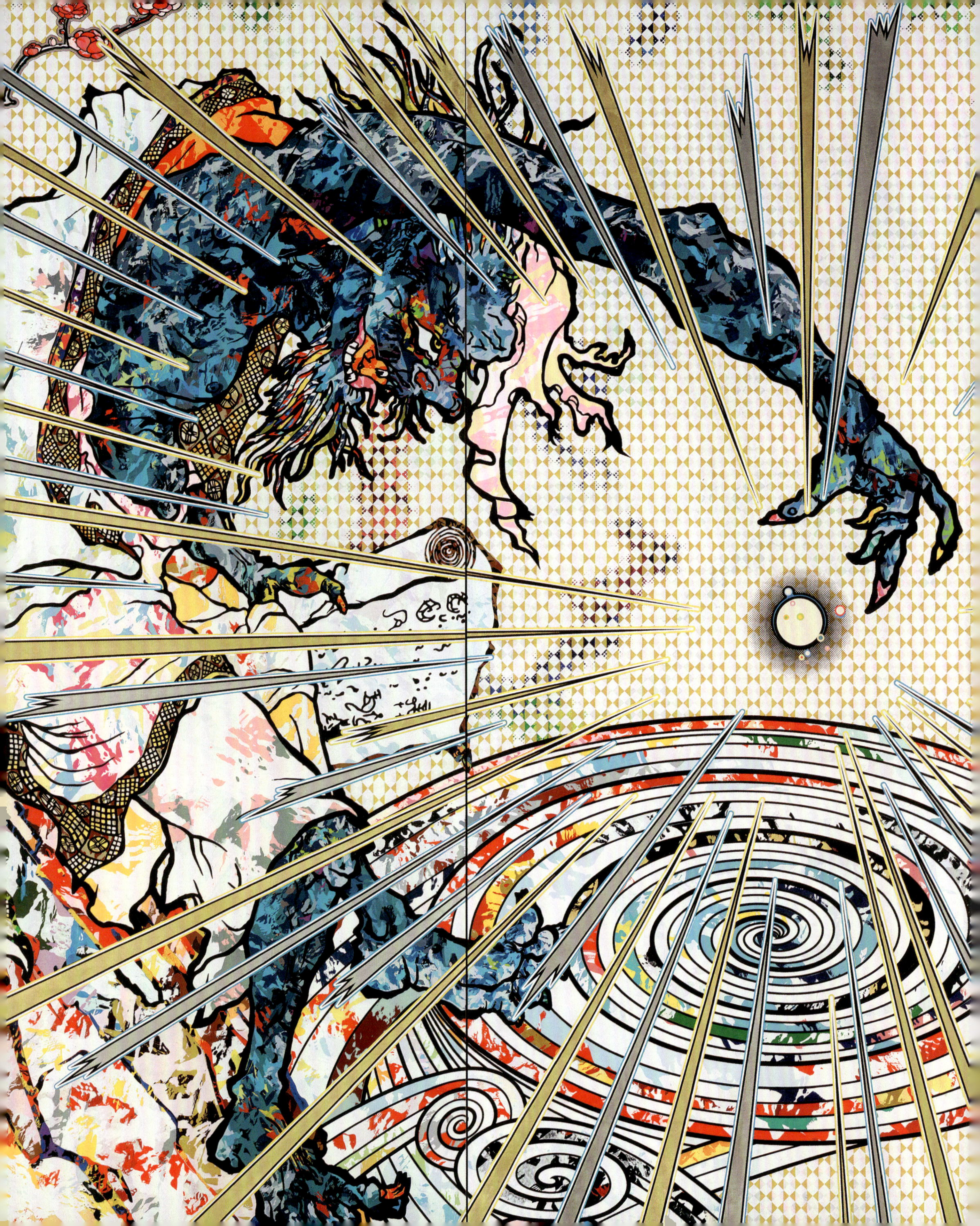

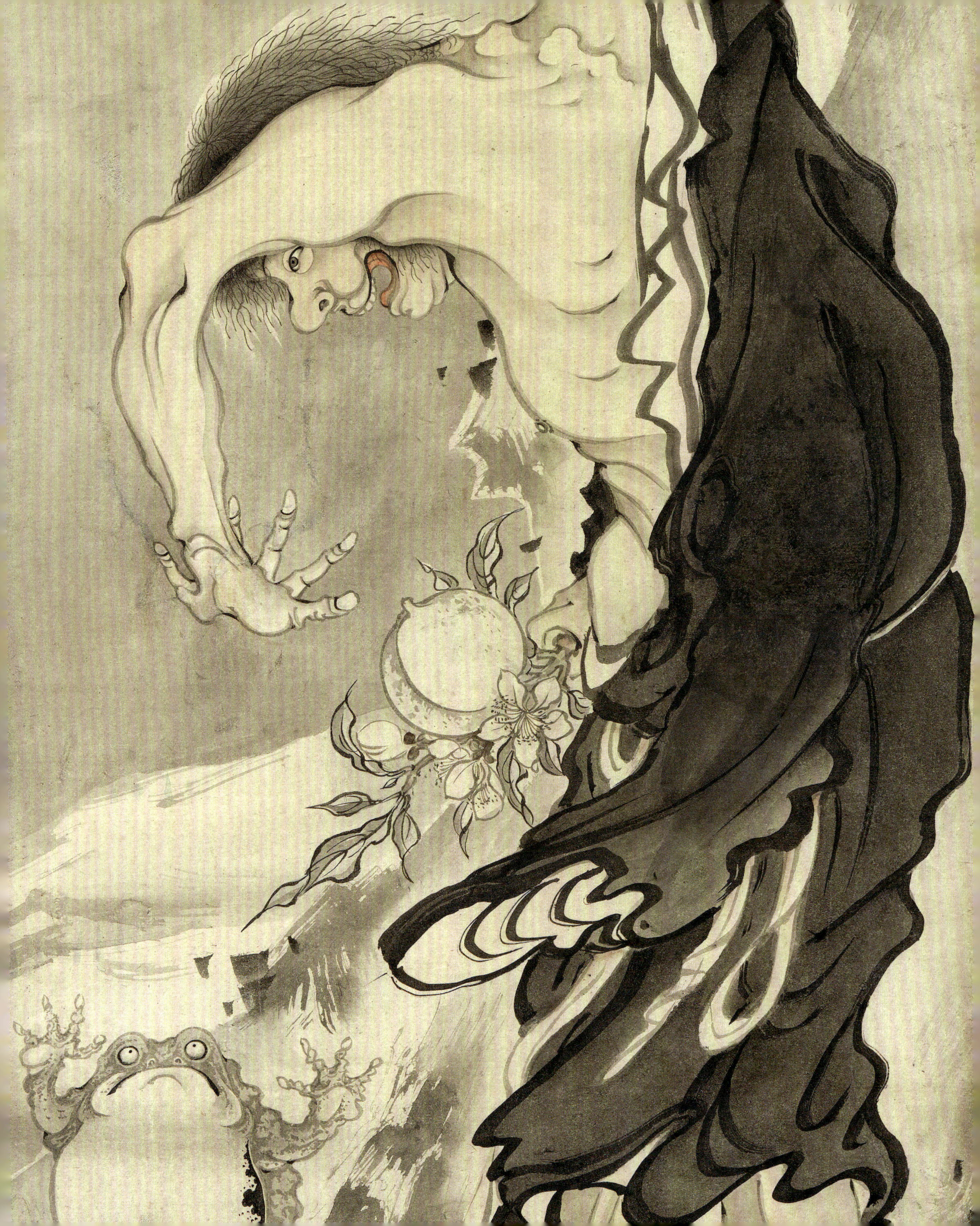

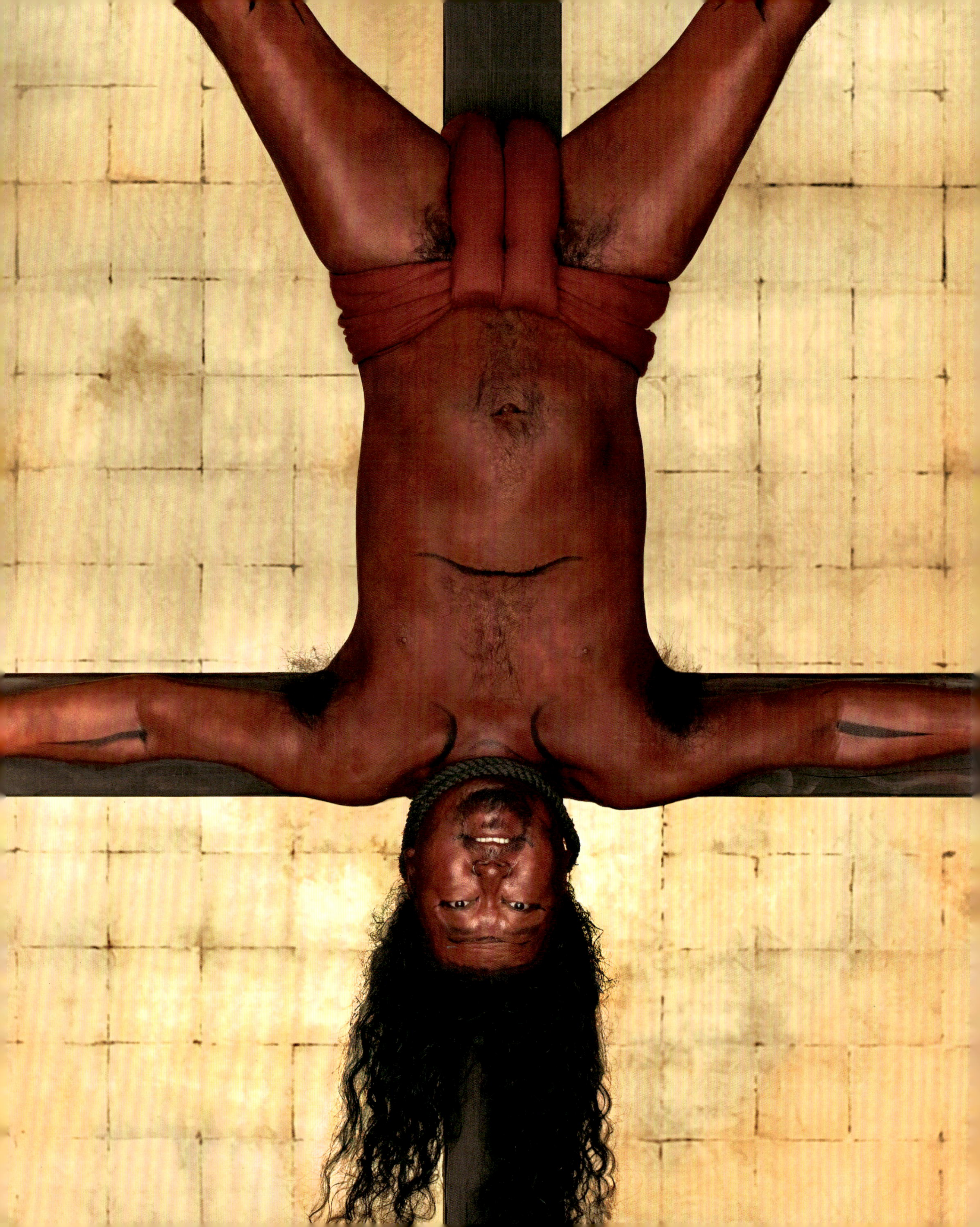

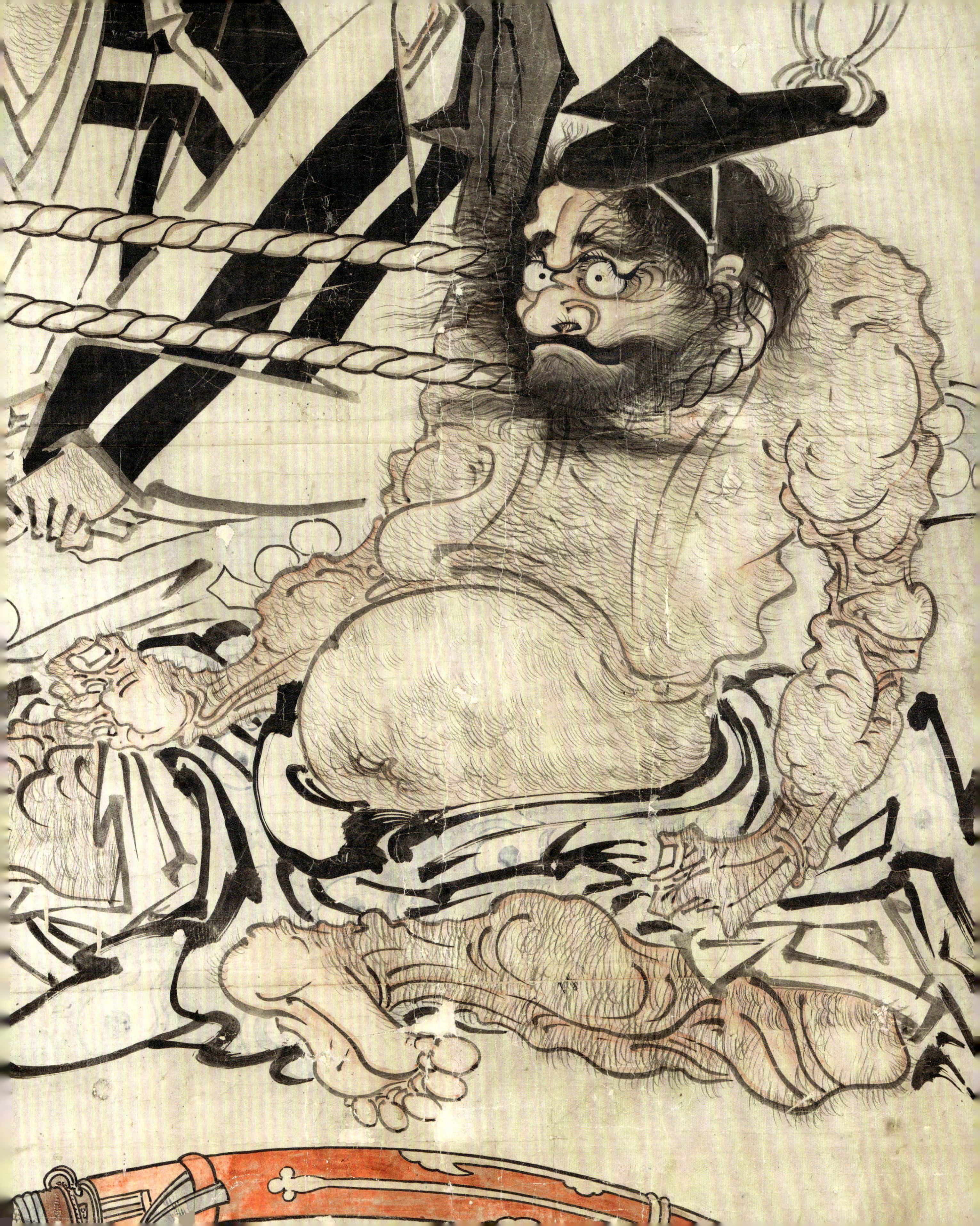

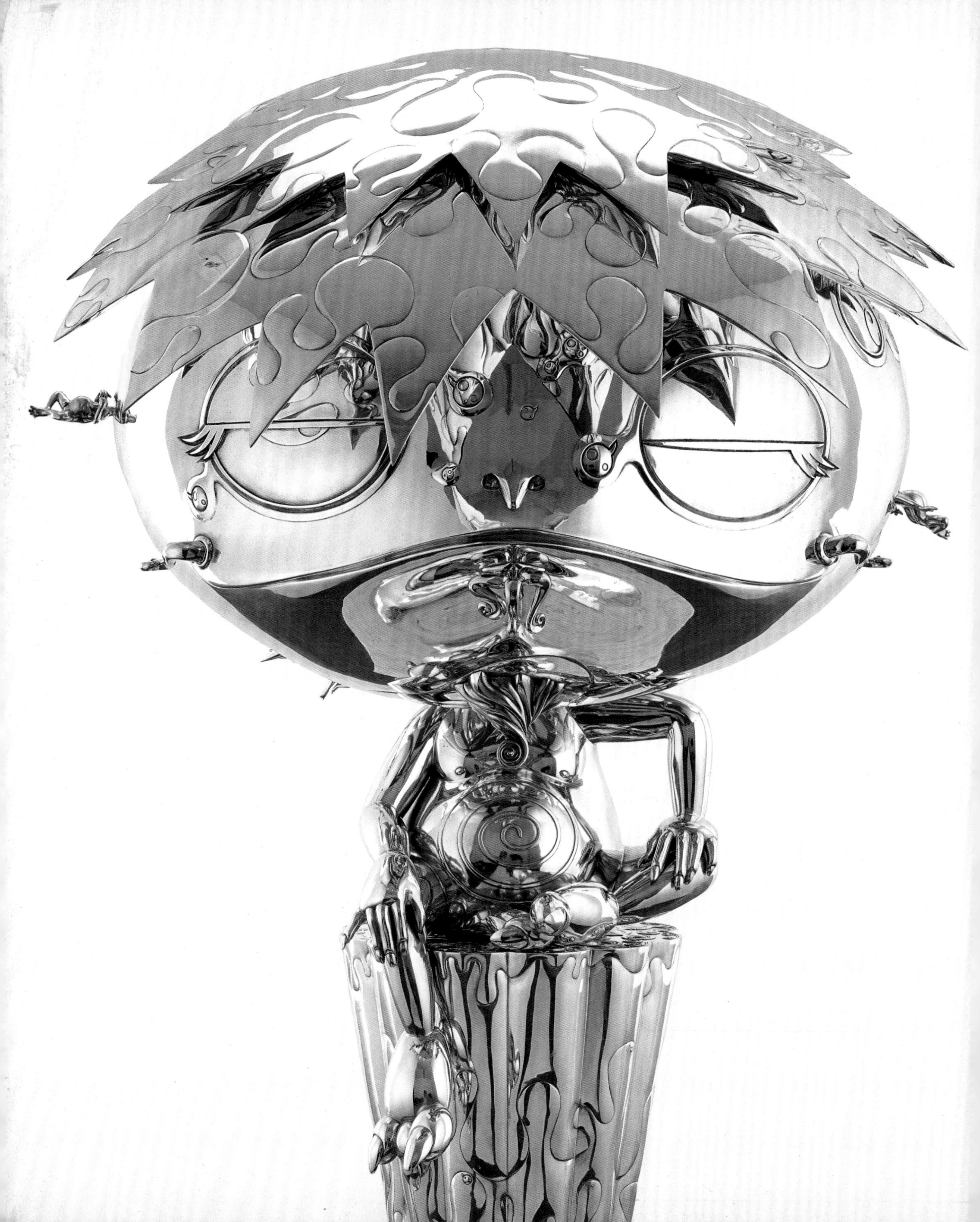

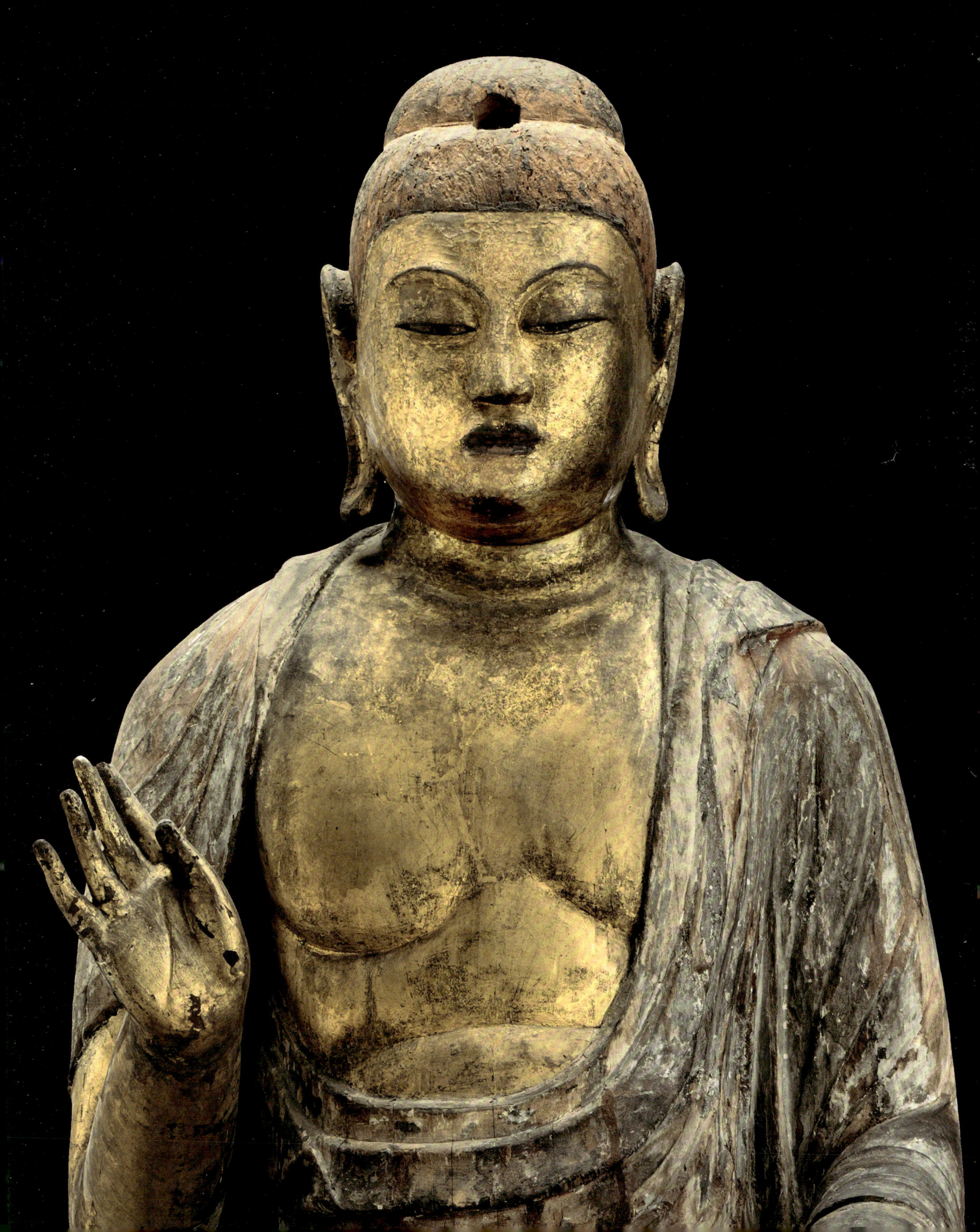

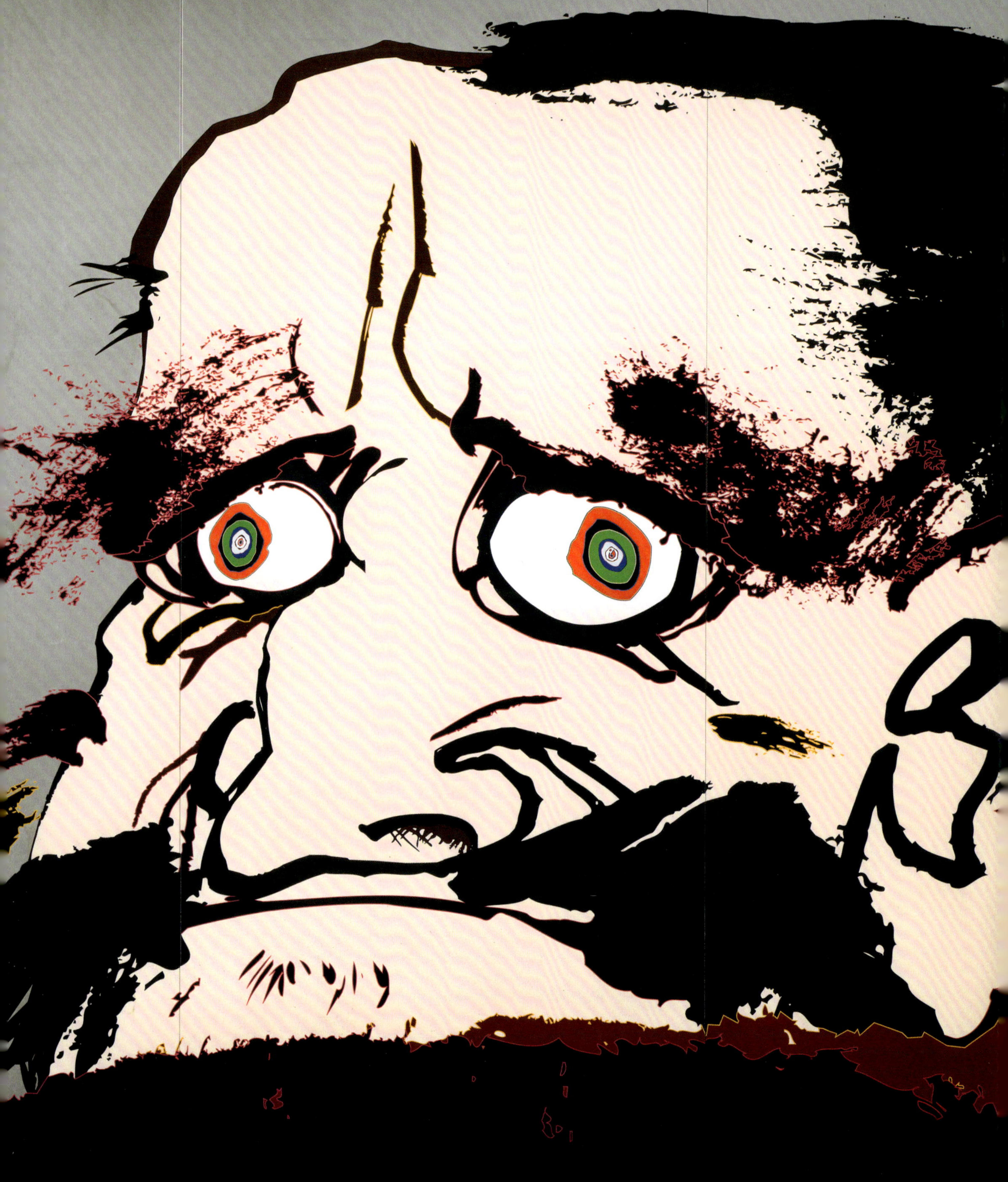

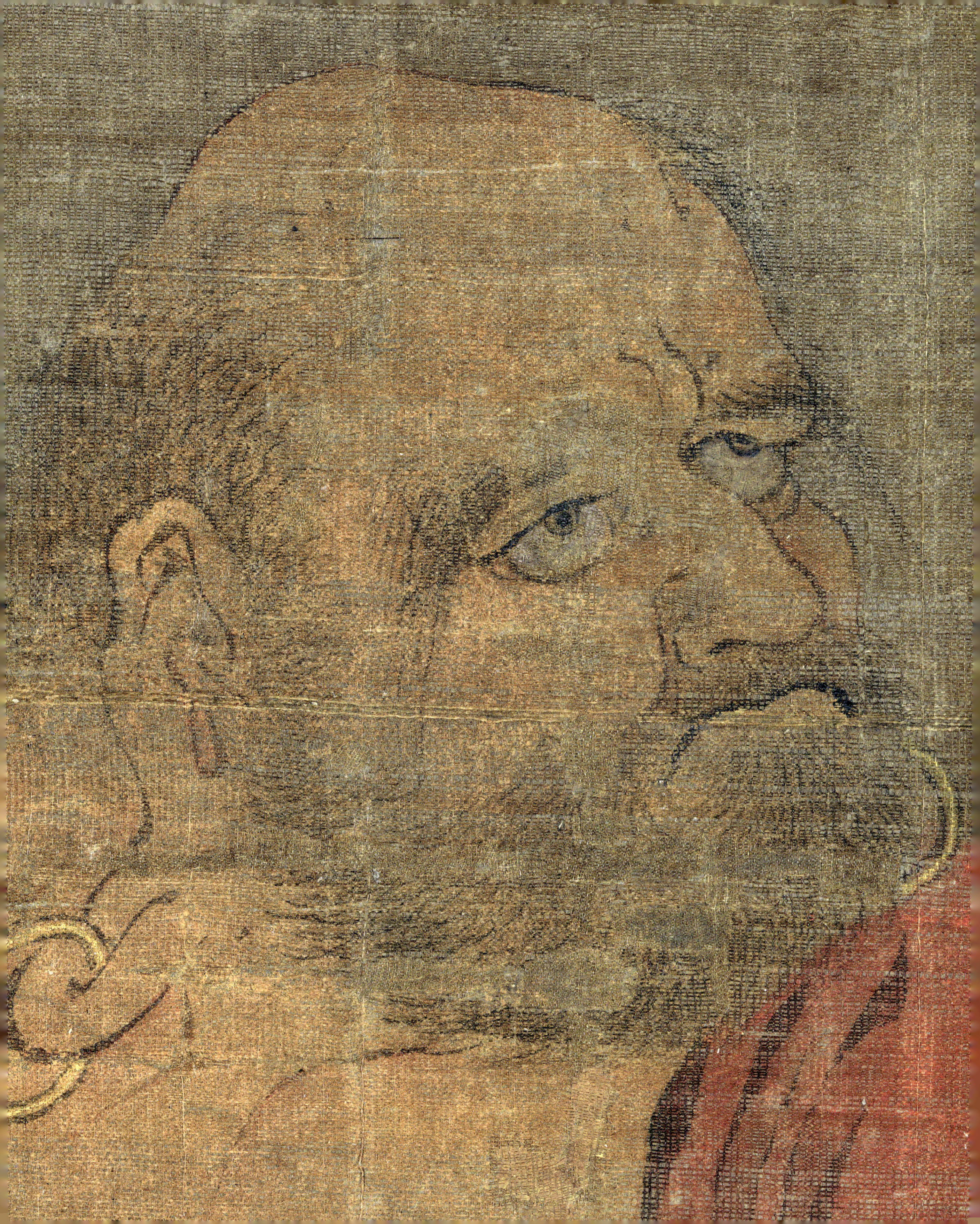

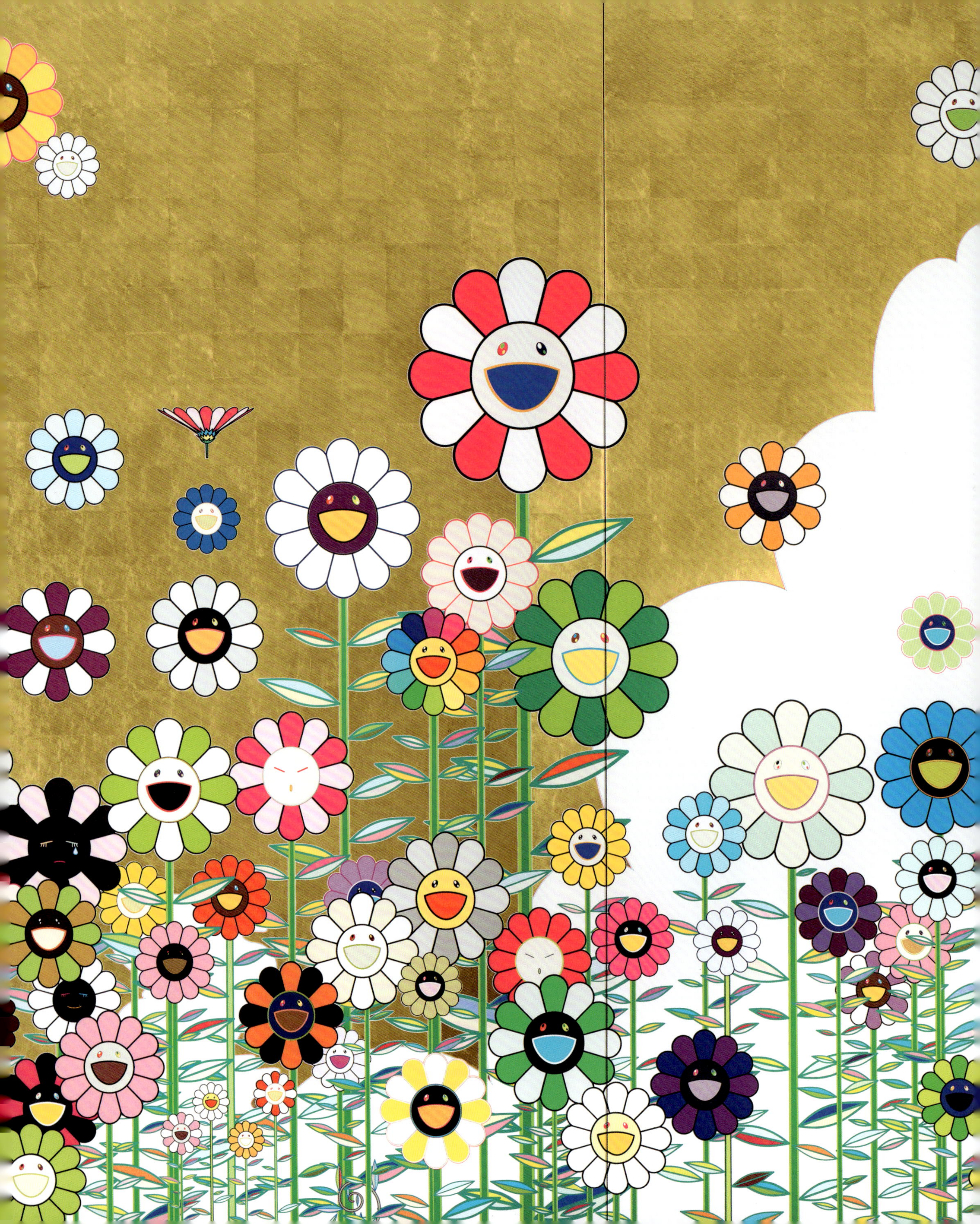

TAKASHI MURAKAMI
LINEAGE OF ECCENTRICS

A COLLABORATION WITH
NOBUO TSUJI
AND THE MUSEUM OF FINE ARTS, BOSTON

EDITED AND WITH AN INTRODUCTION BY
ANNE NISHIMURA MORSE

MFA PUBLICATIONS
MUSEUM OF FINE ARTS, BOSTON

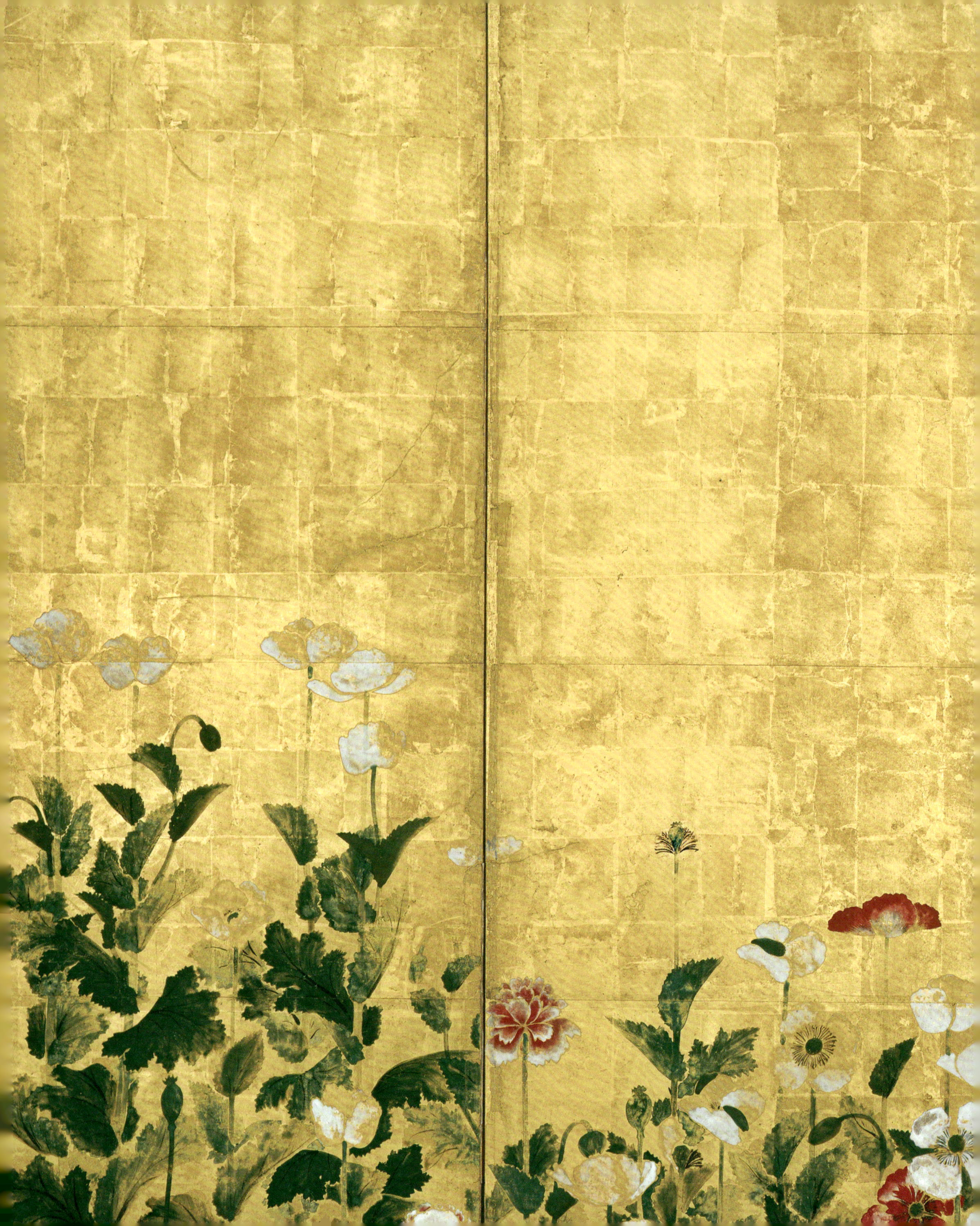

CONTENTS

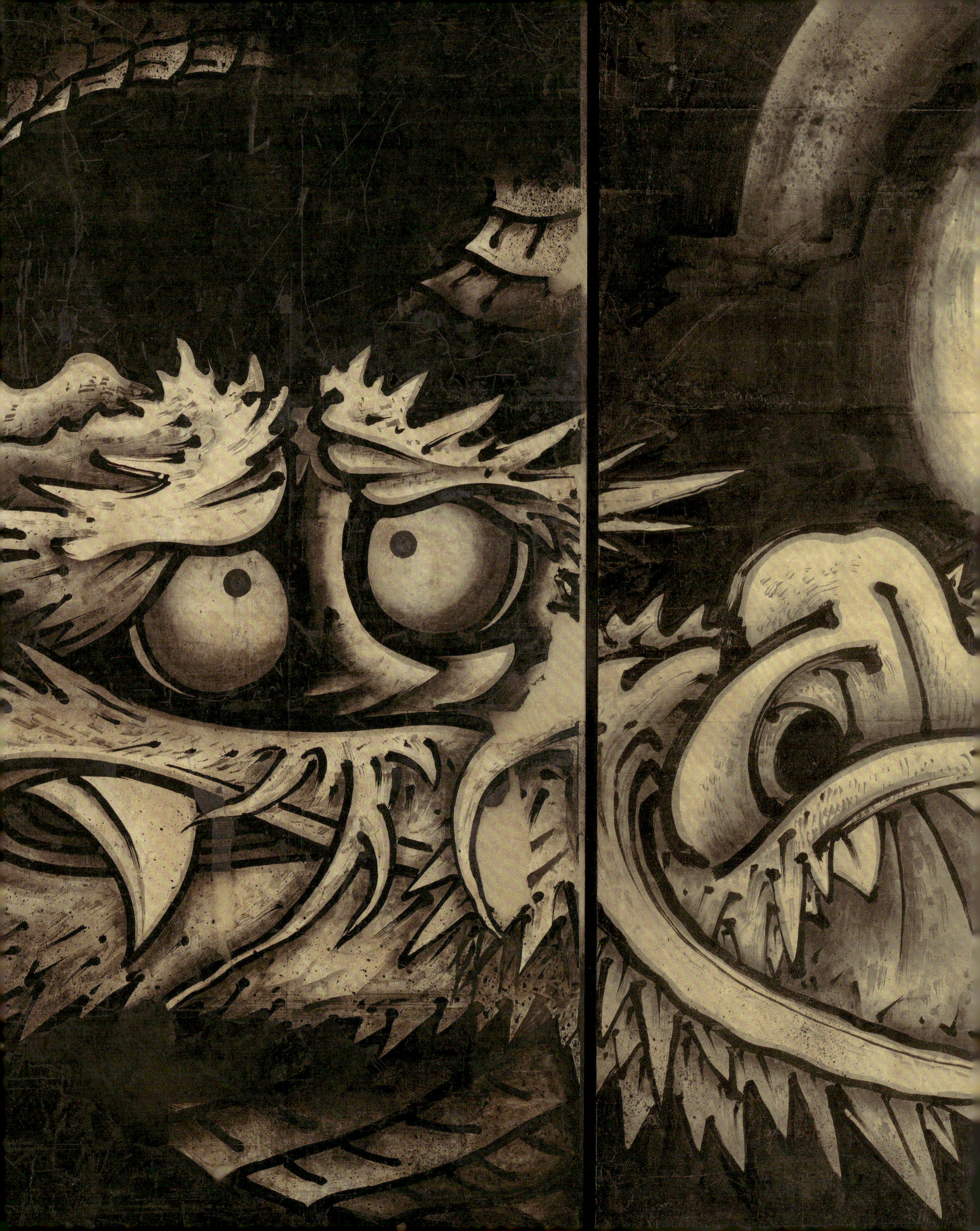

DIRECTOR'S FOREWORD

Where do friendship and commitment take us? Professor Nobuo Tsuji has known both Takashi Murakami and Anne Nishimura Morse, William and Helen Pounds Senior Curator of Japanese Art, for more than twenty-five years. To see them together is to see trust, respect, and the ease of true engagement. When invited to consider selecting work to show alongside his own at the MFA, Murakami asked to include his mentor, Professor Tsuji. Why? To share a journey, to explore side by side, to use the past to animate creativity in the present, to exchange in mutual learning. Anne Morse joined them, encouraged conversation, and made connections that had resonance and meaning in and for Boston. To see them stand alongside one another in this exhibition and publication is to see them share the pleasures of having brought together some sixty works—recent paintings and sculpture by Murakami and historic touchstones from the MFA's unparalleled collection of historical Japanese paintings and sculpture. And what of the narrative they have created? That there is value in tradition, value in the very act of remembering the past as a signpost for the creation of contemporary values. Friendship creates the basis of trust; commitment encourages a rigor and a discipline in the selection of objects and the connections made across time.

It has been sixteen years since the exhibition *Takashi Murakami: Made in Japan* opened here at the MFA. We are pleased to work with Takashi again—a creative and thoughtful artist in our midst. We thank him for his commitment. *Takashi Murakami: Lineage of Eccentrics, A Collaboration with Nobuo Tsuji and the Museum of Fine Arts, Boston* was generously supported by the Carl and Ruth Shapiro Family Foundation. Additional support was provided by Davis and Carol Noble, and Peggy Koenig. The media sponsor was *The Boston Globe*. Generous support for this publication was provided by the Andrew W. Mellon Publications Fund.

MATTHEW TEITELBAUM
ANN AND GRAHAM GUND DIRECTOR
MUSEUM OF FINE ARTS, BOSTON

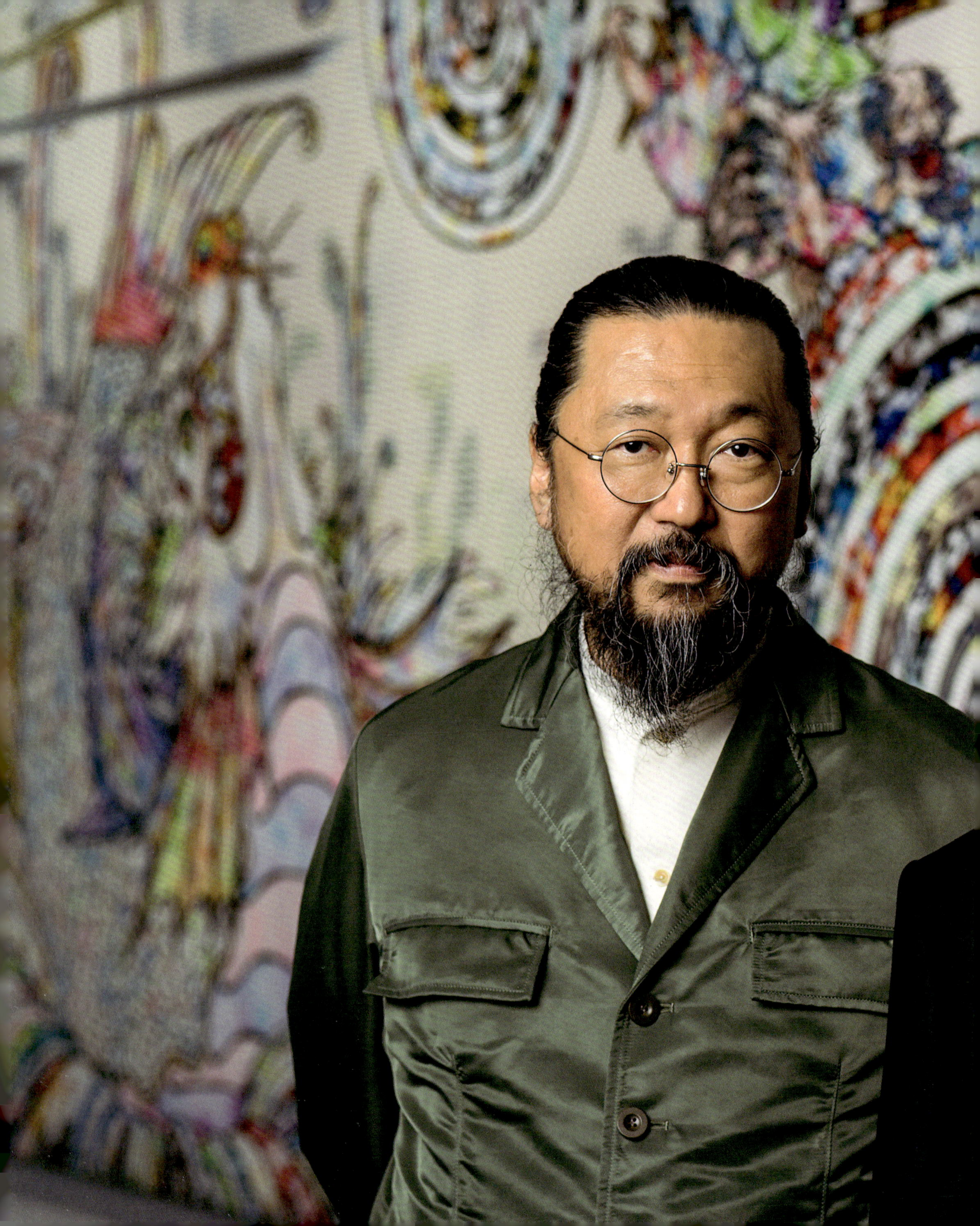

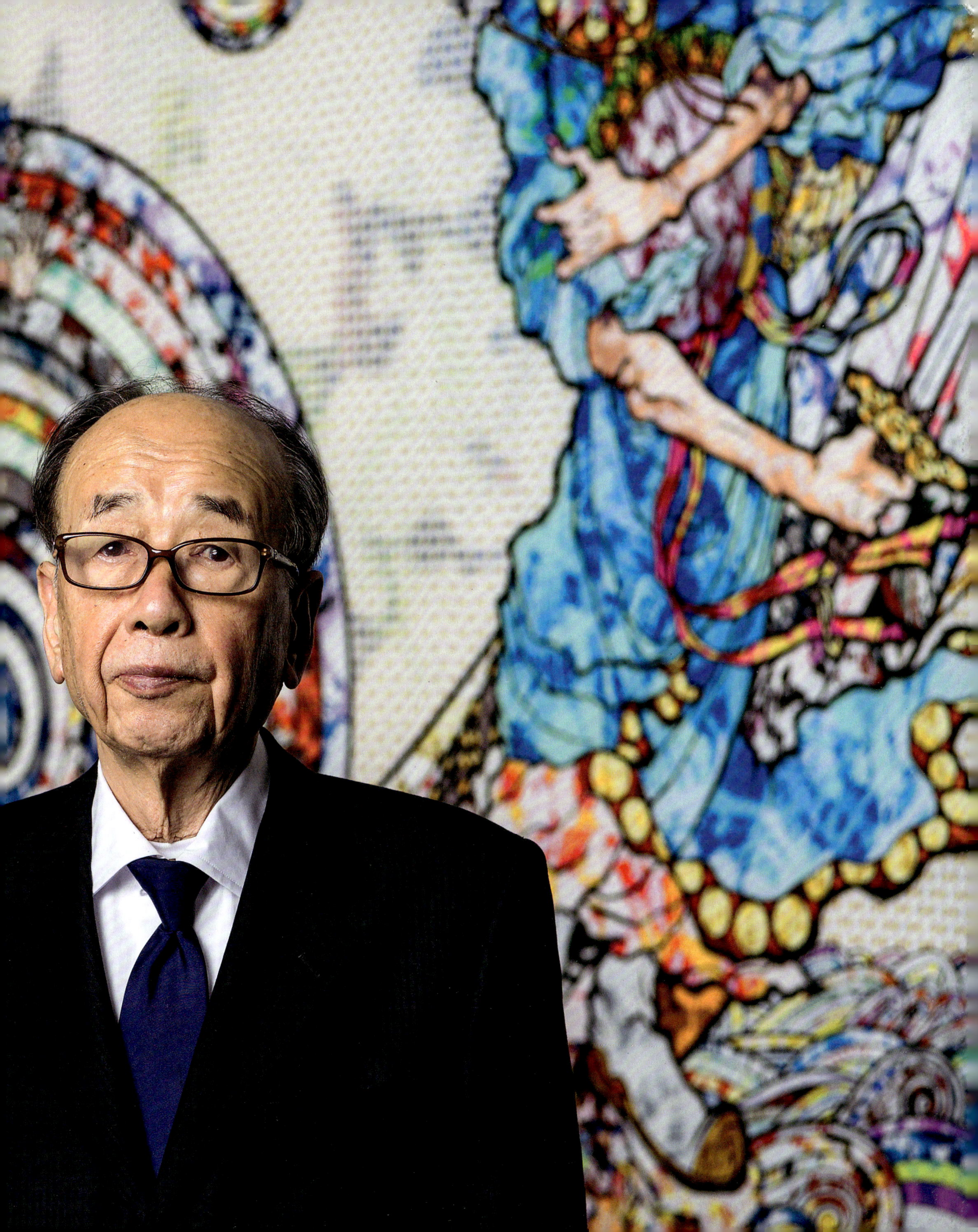

ARTIST STATEMENT

TAKASHI MURAKAMI

Takashi Murakami: Lineage of Eccentrics, A Collaboration with Nobuo Tsuji and the Museum of Fine Arts, Boston makes me keenly feel the role of fate between Professor Nobuo Tsuji, the Museum of Fine Arts, Boston, and myself. I understand that MFA curator Anne Nishimura Morse and Professor Tsuji have had a long-standing, profound relationship in the world of Japanese art history. On my part, I was led by a powerful intuition of karma in the interconnected relationships among us to realize this project.

Since around the time of my debut, I have been developing my career through works that objectively examine Japan. In contemporary art especially, comparative assessment of localized issues and phenomena with local culture and global art history is extremely important. With this in mind, I have been studying Japanese postwar culture, including anime and manga, as well as earlier Japanese art from the Heian period (794–1185) and the Momoyama period (1568–1615). Furthermore I have focused on the artists from the seventeenth through the nineteenth centuries whom Professor Tsuji has brought together in his book *Lineage of Eccentrics* (fig. 1). I have been contemplating how such a bizarre and eccentric artistic ecosystem came to be, and exploring its relationship to the present.

The MFA is known for the contributions of Ernest Francisco Fenollosa, William Sturgis Bigelow, and Edward Sylvester Morse in establishing its collection of Japanese art. The MFA also has strong ties to the Japanese scholar Okakura Kakuzō (founder of Tokyo Art School, the current Tokyo University of the Arts) and the artist Yokoyama Taikan (first graduating class of Tokyo Art School), both with a profound affiliation with the Department of Japanese Painting (Nihonga) in which I studied. I visited the MFA out of a sense of affinity while I was studying in New York for the first time, after graduating. Later, Anne Morse kindly invited me to do an exhibition there, and I visited the Museum again. On that occasion, I saw a sculpture of Shaka, the Historical Buddha. It depicted the Buddha sitting on a lotus pedestal. All the petals had fallen off from the pedestal, yet it was absolutely beautiful. I could not get the shape of the stripped pedestal out of my mind and later created a sculpture of my own called *Oval Buddha Silver* inspired by that very form.

I believe that the major highlight of the exhibition has been the presentation of *Dragon and Clouds* by Soga Shōhaku, the artist for whom I have utmost admiration, in juxtaposition with my own clumsy version of the painting, *Dragon in Clouds—Red Mutation: The version I painted myself in annoyance after Professor Nobuo Tsuji told me, "Why don't you paint something yourself for once?"* When I saw Shōhaku's painting, I felt as if I had found a savior, because the default setting for the Nihonga department at the university, when I was studying, was misguided tradition worshiping backed by Japan's negative complex against the West; its delusive idleness made it a very difficult place to be. And I realized that among the old masters there were people who would break through that kind of confinement to be free in their artwork, so that was very hopeful for me. Now I can see that after a couple of hundred years, that artwork has come over the ocean, and in Boston it has power and energy enough to be revived here.

1

Original 1970 cover of *Kisō no keifu* (*Lineage of Eccentrics*) by Nobuo Tsuji featuring Soga Shōhaku's *Dragon and Clouds*

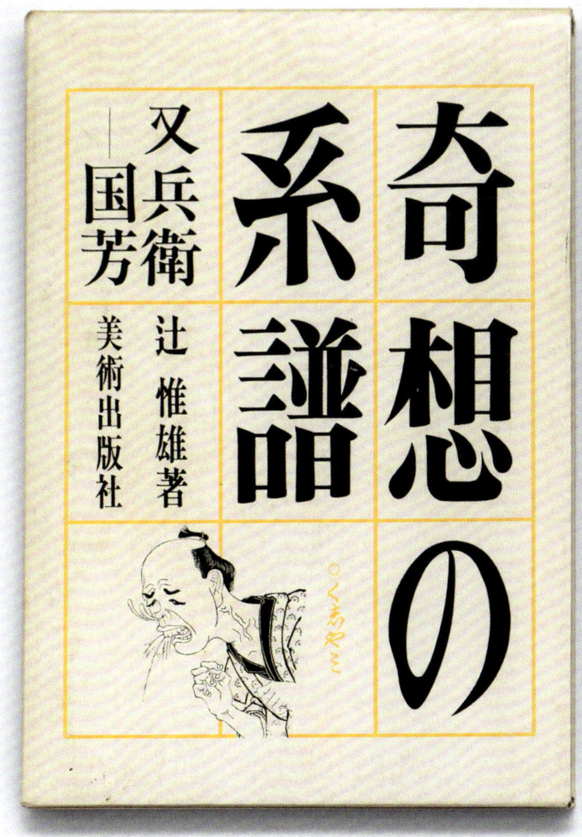

奇想の系譜
又兵衛
—国芳
辻 惟雄著
美術出版社
くゎらや

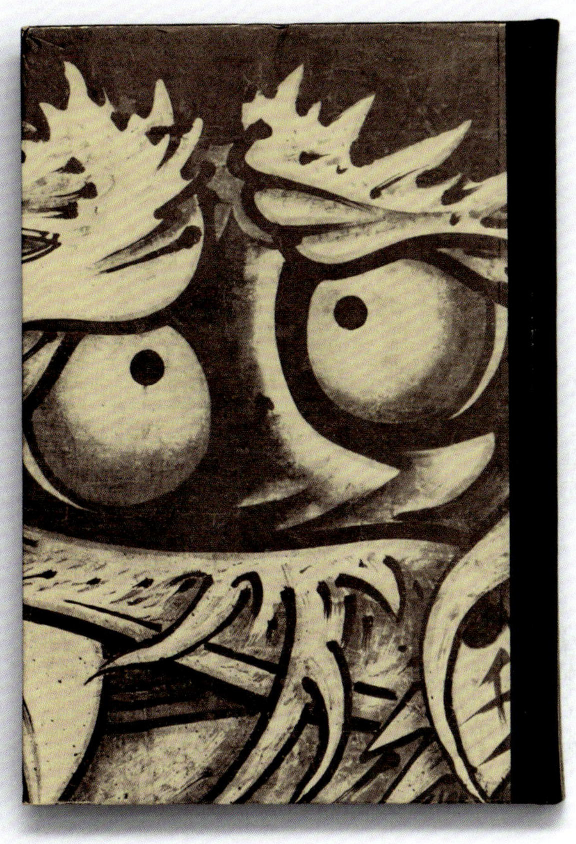

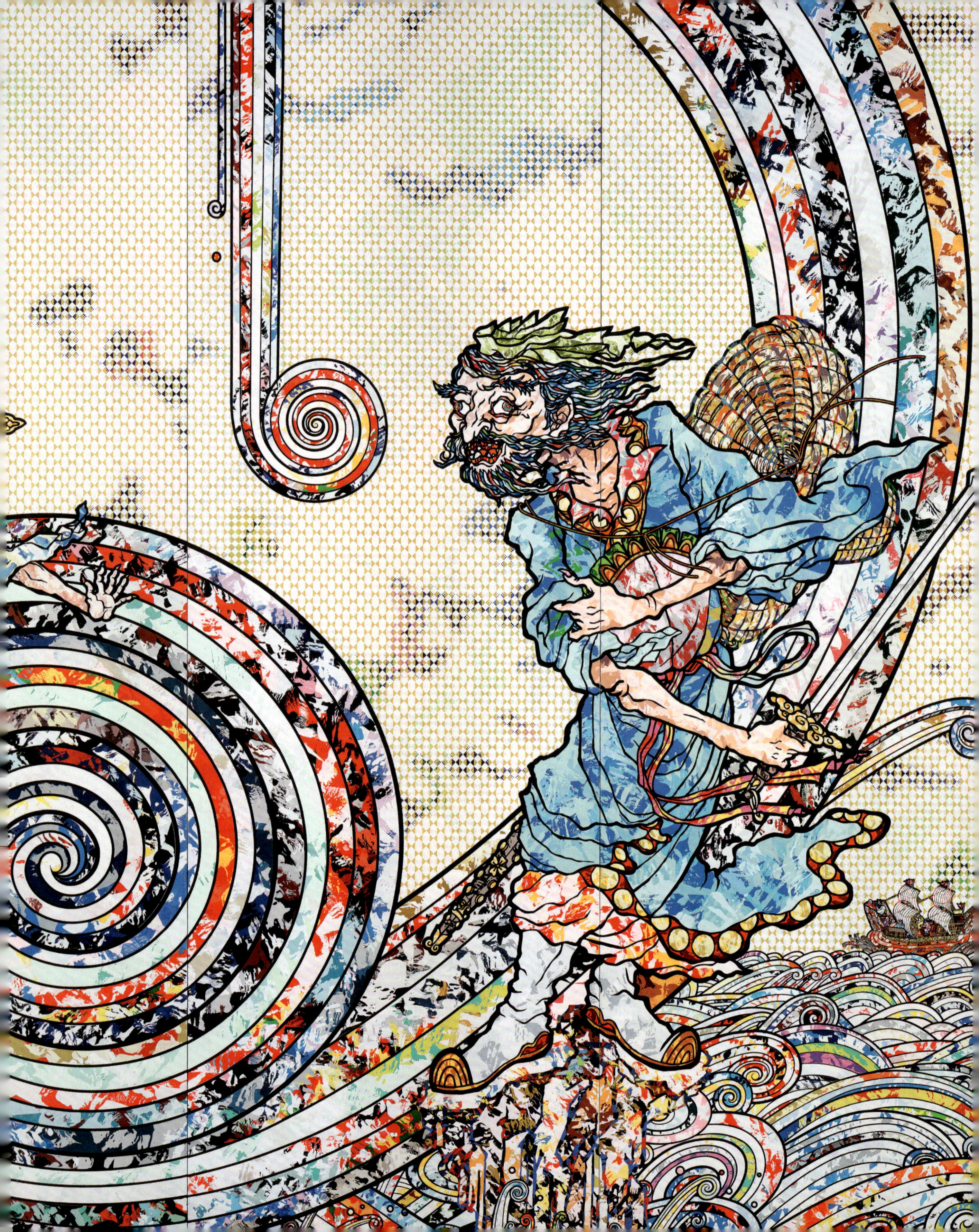

NEGOTIATING THE GLOBAL, ENGAGING WITH THE LOCAL

ANNE NISHIMURA MORSE

NOTE

In standard Japanese word order, the surname is given first, followed by the personal or artist name. Here, the Japanese word order is followed for people born before 1868; but for modern artists and writers, names are in Western word order, with the surname last.

Traditional Japanese multipart works and handscrolls are meant to be viewed right to left.

The giving to art objects a cultural significance is always a local matter.
—Clifford Geertz, *Local Knowledge*.[1]

Creator, social critic, entrepreneur, and media star Takashi Murakami (born in 1962) is one of the most celebrated artists of our day. Although his works have achieved their highest critical acclaim in the United States and Europe and have also been collected and exhibited primarily in the West, Murakami has been at the forefront of articulating a non-Western vision for contemporary art. Central to his thinking about his identity as a Japanese artist in the context of a global art market has been his recognition of the importance of American and European contributions to his production but also of the legacies of Japan's own past. This formulation has been greatly informed by the experiences of his undergraduate and graduate studies at Tokyo University of the Arts (formerly Tokyo National University of Fine Arts and Music) and his ongoing consultations with the preeminent art historian Nobuo Tsuji (born in 1932, fig. 2). Over the last forty years, Tsuji—in groundbreaking exhibitions, lectures, and writings—has constructed new narratives that have made it possible for audiences to bridge the historical and the contemporary in the art of Japan.

Since 2000, when Murakami issued his *Superflat Manifesto* outlining his own approach to image making and acknowledging the contributions of Tsuji's heralded book *Lineage of Eccentrics* (1970) in the development of his ideas, scholars and critics alike have frequently commented on Murakami's relationship with the art of the past, but often without detail. This book and the exhibition that inspired it, *Takashi Murakami: Lineage of Eccentrics, A Collaboration with Nobuo Tsuji and the Museum of Fine Arts, Boston*, juxtapose Murakami's works with those from the Museum's traditional Japanese collections. In today's museums, transhistorical explorations have often been promoted as a means to engage audiences in new ways of seeing that transcend the standard investigations of connoisseurship, iconography and iconology, and social history. By juxtaposing works from different periods, cultures, and genres they challenge audiences with unorthodox questions suggested by the inherent formative powers of the art itself.[2]

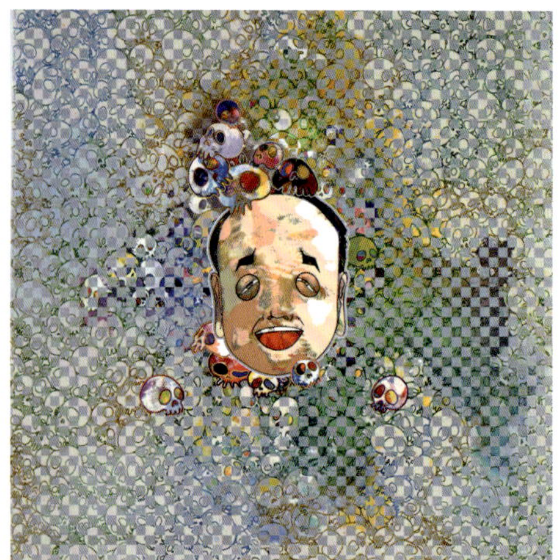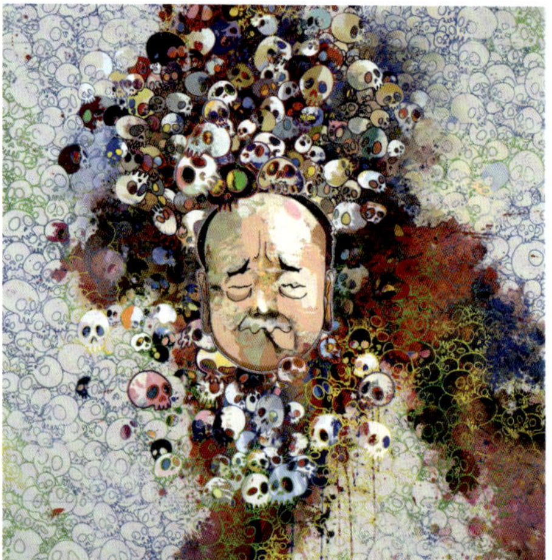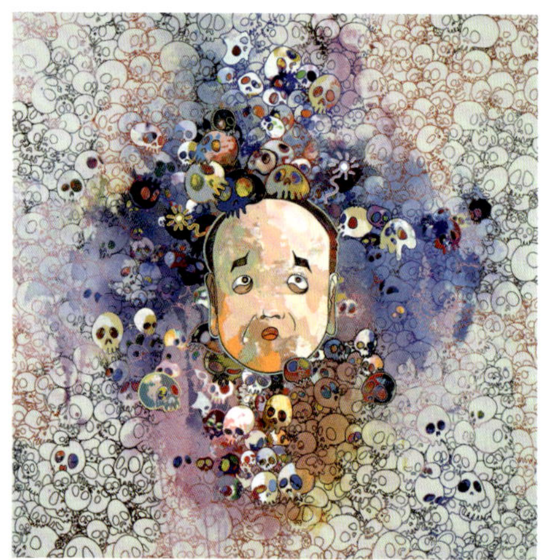

In fact, engagement by contemporary artists with objects from historical collections has been a long-accepted and, when well conceived, a successful curatorial strategy. However, the conversations represented by this book are tripartite ones, among an artist, an art historian, and the curators of a collection who have over many years been collectively engaged in conversations about past and present, tradition and innovation, the local and the global.

Takashi Murakami and the Legacy of the Early MFA Curators

Murakami's *Superflat Manifesto* has been widely hailed for its prescient articulation of a new approach to contemporary global image-making, grounded in a non-Western tradition, and responsive to the startling changing realities of the world's entangled economies brought on by the digital age. At the beginning of the millennium Murakami had emerged as one of the new, exciting voices, known for his works with their neo-Pop presentation that readily appealed to audiences in the United States, but with their *kawaii* (cute) inflection of signature characters and happy-faced flowers that commented on the dystopian *otaku* (geek) subculture of post-bubble-economy Japan.

Although Murakami, perhaps more than any other artist of his generation, has been attuned to the trials and opportunities presented by globalization, the issues that he addresses are far from new. In fact the early history of the Japanese collections at the Museum of Fine Arts, Boston, and its curators provides precedents of sometimes contentious negotiations of East and West—precedents that have had enormous implications for Murakami's establishment of his own artistic identity.

The Japanese holdings at the MFA, which now number nearly one hundred thousand objects from Neolithic to contemporary, in all genres, were largely formed by a group of far-sighted Bostonians resident in Japan, Edward Sylvester Morse (1838–1925), Ernest Francisco Fenollosa (1853–1908), and William Sturgis Bigelow (1850–1926) and their Japanese colleague Okakura Kakuzō (1863–1913) in the late nineteenth century (fig. 3). In 1853 Japan had been forced to open its doors to the West with the arrival of the black ships of Commodore Matthew Perry in Edo Bay. Rather than acceding to colonization, the country embarked upon an unprecedented campaign of modernization

2
Takashi Murakami, *The Severe Art Critic Redefined: Delighted! Difficult…and Dazed*, 2010

As part of the *Battle Royale* project, Murakami created these portraits of his mentor Nobuo Tsuji set against a background of skulls, a reference to the "impermanence of things."

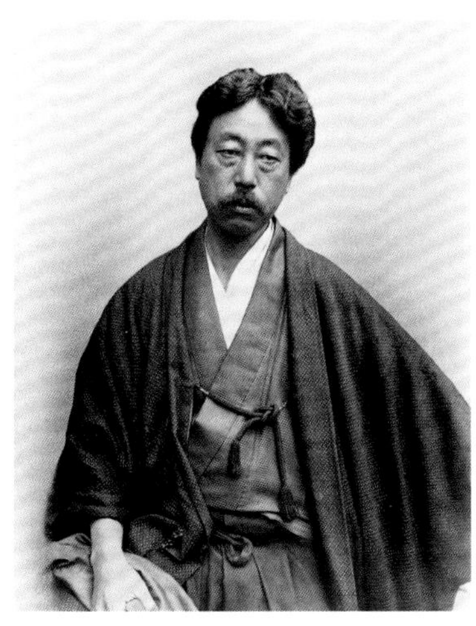

3
Portrait of Okakura Kakuzō (1863–1913)

and Westernization in the name of the newly enthroned Emperor Meiji (1852–1912; r. 1867–1912). Emissaries were sent across the United States and Europe to study political, technological, military, educational, and cultural institutions that could inform the establishment of a constitution, industry, the army and navy, fields of study at the imperial university, and museums and art education. In short, Japanese society as a whole rethought its identity as mediated by its understanding of the West.

Morse, Fenollosa, Bigelow, and Okakura were at the center of the discussions to define Japanese art, when the concept of and the word *art* itself had only just recently been introduced from the West. A member of a government-sponsored art commission that inventoried temple holdings and of societies that promoted the appreciation and preservation of traditional painting, Fenollosa, and then later Okakura, helped institute a canon of Japanese art that drew heavily from religious icons created for aristocratic temples and paintings by academic artists from well-established lineages. In his *Epochs of Chinese and Japanese Painting* (1907) Fenollosa outlined a history of Japanese art.[3] Although based on Western ideas of periodization, Fenollosa's history attempted to present Japanese art from what he perceived to be a "more authentic" Japanese, rather than a European orientalizing, Japoniste perspective. It was this insistence on a Japanese point of view together with advice from some of Japan's leading connoisseurs that also informed the collections that were acquired for Boston.

Fenollosa and Okakura had been part of a government-sponsored commission that studied art education in the United States and Europe. They drew upon their findings in establishing the Tokyo Art School (Tokyo bijutsu gakkō) in 1893, although Fenollosa departed to become Curator of Japanese Art at the Museum of Fine Arts before the school opened. The school immediately became embroiled in discussions about the definition of a national art, and during Okakura's tenure offered a curriculum in Nihonga, a style based on Japanese models using traditional materials. In time this school became Tokyo National University of Fine Arts and Music, which Takashi Murakami entered in 1981, after giving up his aspirations to become an anime artist.

Since its founding the school has been the center for debates about the competing artistic ideologies of East and West and the role that each should play in training Japanese artists. Nihonga, with its adherence to time-honored techniques but its introduction of Western chiaroscuro and vanishing-point perspective, was promoted as an art that could negotiate a place for traditional art in a modernizing world. However, as the debates continued about the production of art in this new Japan, a Japan whose artists had even entered the French Salon, in 1896 the school introduced, much to Okakura's disapprobation, a competing curriculum in Yōga, a style based on Western principles utilizing oils and canvas.

Contrary to what one would expect, Murakami, who now executes his monumental compositions in acrylic on canvas and who has looked to American and European contemporary artists as diverse as Andy Warhol and Anselm Kiefer for inspiration, elected to enter the Nihonga curriculum (fig. 4).[4] There he readily grasped the technical requirements of his classes—the mastery of which is very much in evidence in the consummate craftsmanship of his work today. Despite his claims to the contrary, he also acquired a deep understanding of the principles of Japanese art history. However, Murakami chafed at the university's division of the curriculum into the binary fields of Nihonga and Yōga, a curriculum that continued to be informed by Meiji-era premises about formats and materials. Therefore, when he decided to write his doctoral dissertation entitled "Imi no muimi no imi" ("The Meaning of the Meaninglessness of Meaning"), he explored the Japanese inferiority complex toward the West and Japan's

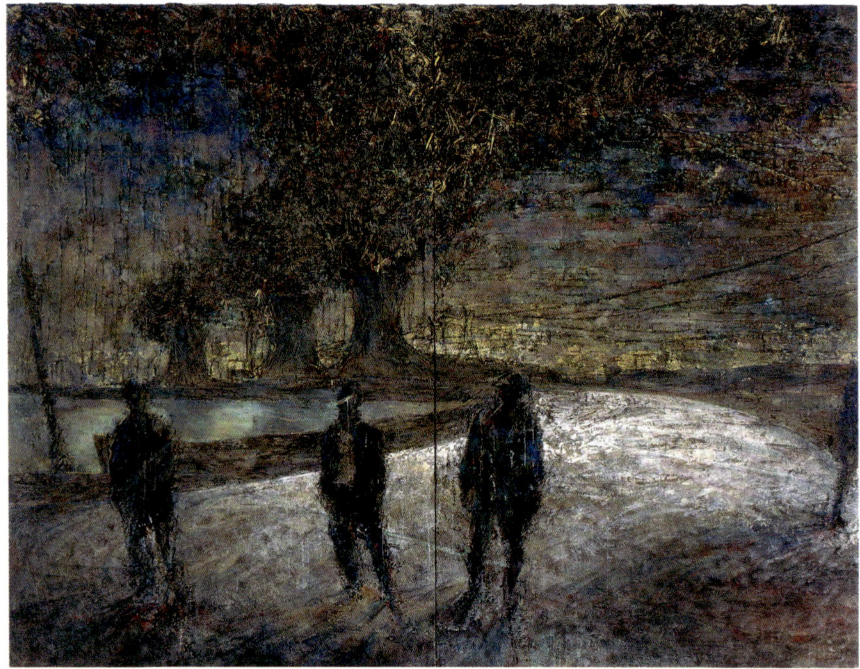

preoccupation with Western institutions, which had pervaded all cultural enterprises since the Meiji Restoration, and he analyzed the ways in which the Japanese had not been able to establish their own position.[5]

While Murakami has frequently dismissed his classes at Tokyo National University of Fine Arts and Music as providing him with little useful instruction, the legacy that he and all graduates of the school have received from Fenollosa and Okakura is one of a dichotomous and at times polarizing discourse about the relationship between the art of Japan and that of the West. Although the two men underlined the importance of Western art and its institutions, they also emphasized the primacy of national identity. These foundational premises have continued to raise profound questions for the school's members about how best to establish their own artistic character in a globalized environment—questions that they have been unable to escape. Already by the 1930s the tension between national and international aesthetics led the oil painter and poet Kōtarō Takamura, for example, to state in his essay "Midori no taiyō" ("Green Sun"):

> Just as a fish can't live out of water, even I remain silent, my identity is inextricably bound up with my being Japanese.... What this means is that my mental attitude when I create something is that of an individual human being. I give absolutely no thought to Japan. I merely go into action regardless, just as I think, just as I see, just as I feel.... [However,] anything that's produced by a Japanese person will inevitably be or turn out to be intrinsically Japanese. It will be intrinsically Japanese even if the artist doesn't deliberately set out to make it so. There's an inseparable bond here that simply can't be severed.[6]

Murakami has made similar declarations: "[A]t its core the standard of 'beauty' is one cultivated by the Japan that has been my home since my birth in 1962. It is a core that is not easily shaken."[7]

Even today Okakura has remained a somewhat legendary presence at the university. His ease with the English language and comfort with American intellectuals as well as grandes dames are well known. Okakura's insights on how a foreigner should present himself in the West to greatest effect, be it the way he structured his lecture or the particular style of dress he adopted, have given Murakami and other graduates models to navigate the expectations of their external and internal audiences. More importantly Okakura has provided an example of how a Japanese national can achieve success in the international community by being thoroughly conversant in the constructs of Western culture and yet insistent upon a Japanese perspective.

Takashi Murakami and Nobuo Tsuji

In 1994 Nobuo Tsuji, a renowned professor of Japanese art who had just retired from the University of Tokyo, attended an exhibition at SCAI the Bathhouse, a contemporary art gallery set in a renovated Edo-period (1615–1868) public bath near Tokyo's Ueno Park. He was there at the urging of an editor who wanted him to see the work of an up-and-coming artist who had just completed the PhD program at nearby Tokyo National University of Fine Arts and Music. That artist was the thirty-three-year-old Takashi Murakami. On display in the gallery, a long, horizontal panel entitled *Impossible Aim* with a small cartoon-like figure (Mr. DOB) drawing a bow at one end and another rendition of the same figure dodging an arrow at the other, across a span of silver leaf, immediately clarified for Tsuji the reason that he had been invited to attend the opening. The young Murakami clearly had been inspired by a humorous twelfth-century anecdote recounted in one of Tsuji's groundbreaking books.

In Tsuji's *Kisō no keifu* (1970, later published in English as *Lineage of Eccentrics*) and its companion volume, *Kisō no zufu* (The Album of Eccentric Painting, 1989), Murakami had found not only stories of delight but also a conceptual framework on which to structure his evolving artistic vision. The artist has since proclaimed: "These two books have saved me time and time again!"[8] In Tsuji, Murakami would also find a mentor and collaborator, who would subsequently have a profound effect on the development of his art.

Like generations of artists who had preceded him, Murakami had found it necessary to leave the confines of Japan in order to connect directly with the work of contemporary Western artists. Prior to the outbreak of World War II Japanese painters had often traveled to Paris to study in the academy and to experience the European landscape. For his part, feeling that New York was the center of contemporary art, Murakami made a brief trip to the city in the 1980s that was followed by a yearlong residency at the P.S.1 International Studio Program in 1994. For Murakami the conflation of fine art and commercial art exemplified by Andy Warhol and his Factory became models for study. Jeff Koons and his elevation of the clichéd and Jean-Michel Basquiat and his street art offered him new approaches to image making. But if Murakami found qualities worthy of emulation in these artists, he also immediately recognized the need to distinguish himself or face the risk that Japanese artists have faced since the Meiji era of being seen as mere imitators. For this he had to articulate what the architect Arata Isozaki has called "Japan-ness," the creation of something Japanese in response to the external artistic pressures from the West in the twentieth century.[9] "Following my hypothesis that New York tastes are the standard for the West, I established my own base of operations there, and in the process had the opportunity to show off quite a bit of my own culinary creation. If you are going to match the tastes of the West … some avant-garde spices are indispensable."[10] However, Murakami also noted that what would be exciting to the West (the United States and Western Europe) did not necessarily conform to contemporary Japanese expectations. In order to navigate between both worlds, what was needed was "an ambivalent flavor and presentation."[11] Critical to that "ambivalent" flavor was Tsuji's *Lineage of Eccentrics*.

Lineage of Eccentrics explored the careers and contributions of six artists of the Edo period: Iwasa Matabei, Kano Sansetsu, Itō Jakuchū, Soga Shōhaku, Nagasawa Rosetsu, and Utagawa Kuniyoshi. Tsuji's masterful and often humorous prose introduced the idea that though not formally related through school affiliation, style, or even subject matter, these six artists came to represent a line of creative image makers who, with their bizarre figures and unorthodox expressionistic techniques, flouted the conventions of academic circles patronized by the ruling military elites. Today Tsuji, who has taught at Tōhoku University and the University of Tokyo and led leading cultural institutions such as the government-sponsored International Research Center for Japanese Studies (Nichibunken), Tama Art University, and the Miho Museum, has become perhaps the most authoritative voice for Japanese art in Japan. However, when he wrote *Lineage of Eccentrics*, Tsuji, employed by the Tokyo National Research Institute for Cultural Properties, found himself conducting research somewhat furtively on these six little-known artists, while producing other essays such as his widely cited series on the more orthodox Kano Motonobu, the sixteenth-century master who headed the school of painters that dominated painting production for over three hundred years. Although several of these eccentric artists were ranked among the most influential in eighteenth-century listings of Kyoto painters, the contemporary art historical establishment considered Shōhaku a disgusting artist, with his grotesque and sometimes uncomfortable imagery, and felt that he merited no more than three lines in any survey history.[12]

Lineage of Eccentrics clearly represented an abrupt departure from the standard history of Japanese painting, a canon that had been articulated by Ernest Fenollosa in his *Epochs of Chinese and Japanese Painting* and other Meiji-era intellectuals who had been determined that Japan's hegemony could be firmly established through the gravitas of its religious and academic artistic traditions. This canon had been reinforced by the system of national treasures and important cultural properties established by the Japanese government. Written shortly after the student protests of 1968 against the sustained US military presence in Japan, *Lineage of Eccentrics* has been considered by some to be a critique of contemporary Japanese conformist, salary-man culture.[13] Although the book has had a profound effect upon the reception of the art of the Eccentrics today, it did not attract a wide readership when it was first published. However, several artists in the 1970s found inspiration and Takashi Murakami, who read the book more than a decade later, discovered immediate kinship with Tsuji's Eccentrics. One passage in the book that particularly resonated for him was:

> I would like to place these works by the Eccentrics—with which the public has little familiarity, but which have peculiar parallels with the most powerful cutting-edge contemporary art in media like manga, posters, and murals—on view in places where everyone can see them and gauge their response to them.[14]

When Murakami issued his *Superflat Manifes*to in 2000 he cited Tsuji's *Lineage of Eccentrics* as being central to the crystallization of his ideas. Observing congruences between the disposition and delineation of the images on the screen in the anime of Yoshinori Kanada and the paintings of Tsuji's Eccentrics, Murakami articulated an approach to composition that he identified as being specifically Japanese and placed it in contradistinction to that of the West. "All of the 'eccentric' artists shared a certain structural methodology, in which they created surface images that erased interstices and thus made the observer aware of the image's extreme planarity."[15] Although acutely aware of the need to "craft [his] expression according to the syntax of Western art," Murakami's theory of Superflat identified a local means of picture making relevant to global art production of the present day.[16] In Tsuji's reference to manga as a contemporary art Murakami found a profound kinship with his own evocations of popular culture. And though it was primarily a discussion of the careers of eighteenth-century artists, *Lineage of Eccentrics* became a critical component of Murakami's statement of his own artistic vision.

Nobuo Tsuji and the Legacy of the Early MFA Curators
Following his publication of *Lineage of Eccentrics* and its companion volume, *Album of Eccentric Painting*, Tsuji continued to explore new ways of looking at Japanese art that contrasted with the standard histories organized since the Meiji era according to the Hegelian conventions of periodization favored by Ernest Fenollosa. Asked to collaborate in the development of a television program for adult education, Tsuji focused on the characteristics of Japanese art from the Jōmon period (about 14,000–300 BCE) to the present. This type of conceptualization, which deviated from standard chronological displays centered on particular artists and schools and often intersected with observations that he had made in *Lineage of Eccentrics,* resulted in a series of lectures on *Playfulness in Japanese Art* at the University of Kansas in 1986.[17] Tsuji's theories about the importance of *kazari* (ornamentation) were first given expression in an exhibition, *Japanese Aesthetics: The World of Ornament*, at Mitsukoshi department store in Tokyo in 1988.[18] While heading the International Research Center for Japanese Studies, after retiring from the University of Tokyo, he explored animism, the belief that natural forms possess their own spiritual presence, as the underlying principle of Japanese religiosity with a group of resident scholars.[19] Studies of the relationship between animation and traditional narrative handscrolls (*emaki*) were the result of collaboration with Isao Takahata of Hayao Miyazaki's Studio Ghibli for an exhibition at the Chiba Museum of Art.

In identifying certain characteristics or keywords, including kazari, *asobi* (playfulness), animation, and religiosity, Tsuji looked to Japan's pre-Meiji era past to give voice to ways of conceptualizing Japanese art. Consistently he sought to employ a vocabulary that was in concert with a pre-modernized, pre-Westernized view of Japan, giving emphasis to an exuberance and earthiness that he found had often been suppressed by self-censoring Japanese seeking parity with the "more serious" and formal United States and Europe.[20] Tsuji's project to bring renewed attention to unconventional Edo-period artists, however, must also be viewed as a nostalgic search for a time in a pre-modern past when supposedly unlimited creativity abounded despite the social restrictions placed on the populace by the Tokugawa government.[21] Although Murakami himself has not explicitly identified his works with these additional concepts in the way that he has with eccentricity, critical accounts of his art frequently make reference to them and Tsuji has described Murakami's installations at Versailles (2010) as reminiscent of kazari and commented on the playfulness of the works (fig. 5).[22]

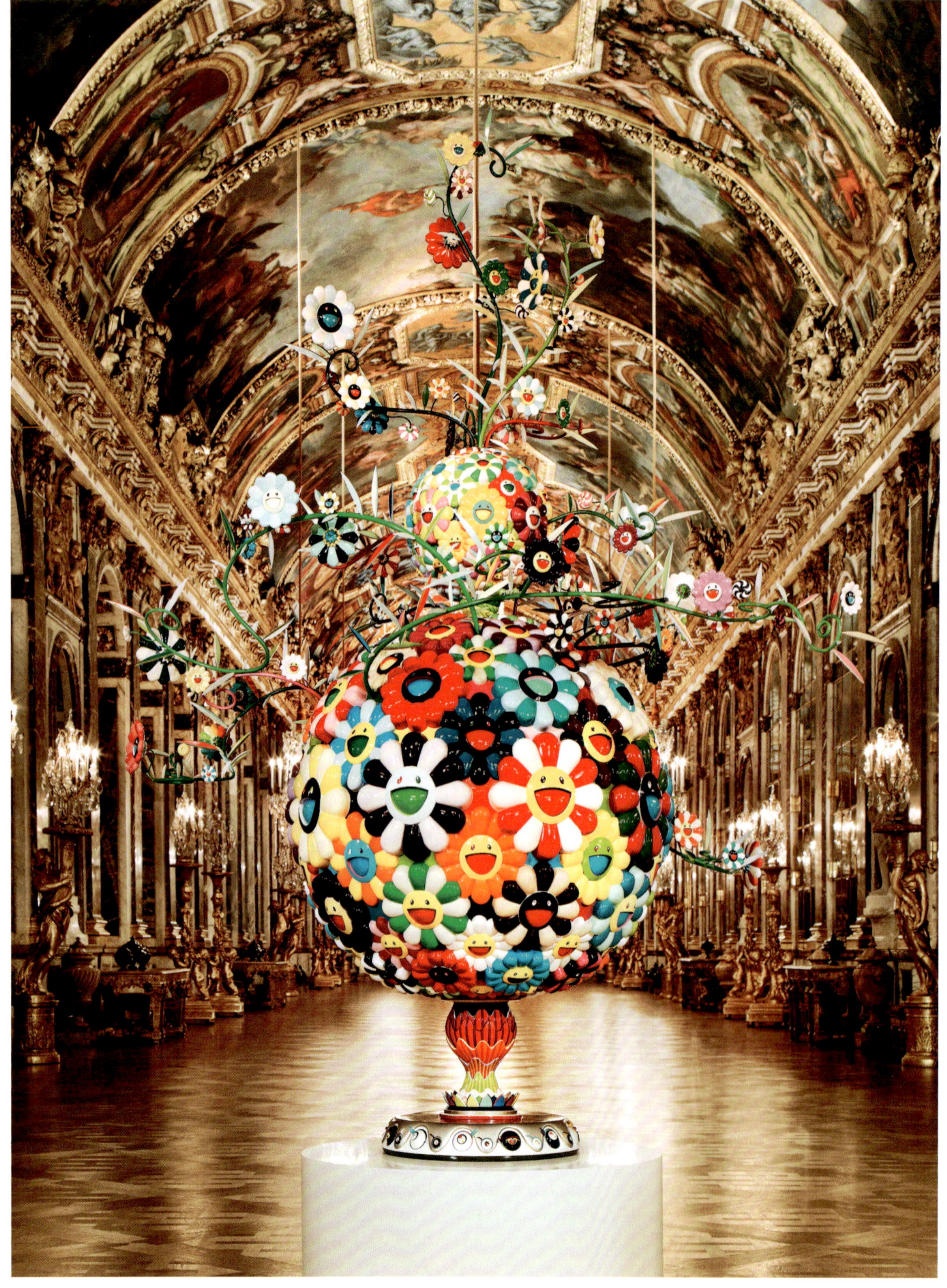

While Tsuji's conceptual categories have engaged the ideas of early curators of the MFA in a theoretical way, from 1991 through 2004 he worked closely with the current curators at the Museum in organizing a comprehensive survey underwritten by the Kajima Foundation for the Arts of the Museum's Japanese painting, sculpture, textiles, and lacquer collections.[23] In successive years leading Japanese specialists collaborated with the MFA curatorial and conservation staffs in examining the works that had not been catalogued since Okakura Kakuzō made an assessment of the collection when he first arrived in Boston as a consultant to the Department of Chinese and Japanese Art in 1904. Tsuji personally took the greatest satisfaction from the survey of Soga Shōhaku's paintings, making impromptu sketches of the compositions and assigning enthusiastic five-star grades to many of the works. Many of the paintings featured in this book were high on his list, among them *Kume the Transcendent* (1759), *Dragon and Clouds* (1763), and *The Four Sages of Mount Shang* (about 1768). Others were found to be later-school works or forgeries. However, upon the conclusion of that particular survey the MFA was found to still have the largest collection of Shōhaku works, with twenty-seven confidently attributed to the master. Over the last twenty years the surveys of the collection have made possible innumerable publications and exhibitions, including *Japanese Masterpieces from the Museum of Fine Arts, Boston*, which opened at the Tokyo National Museum in 2012; it was for this occasion that Shōhaku's *Dragon and Clouds* was put on view in Japan for the first time since the nineteenth century.[24]

Takashi Murakami, Nobuo Tsuji, and the MFA Collections

During Murakami's early career, elements of traditional Japanese art such as the begging bowl from the twelfth-century narrative handscroll *Legends of Mount Shigi* (*Shigisan engi emaki*) had been captured in a series of panel paintings, *The King's Seat of Two-Dimensional Perspective* (1997), or allusions had been made in the artist's statements about his work. However, the focus of Murakami's production had been on neo-Pop riffs on branded *kawaii* figures such as his Mr. DOB (fig. 6), Kaikai and Kiki or his happy-faced flowers and Jellyfish-eyes that could be marketed in galleries as multipaneled paintings, in convenience stores as miniature plastic toys, or at Louis Vuitton as much-in-demand handbags.[25] These elements, while of a totally different aesthetic in their sugar-loaded appeal, were also distinctly Japanese. Murakami's debut exhibition at the highly prestigious Gagosian Gallery in New York, *Tranquility of the Heart Torment of the Flesh—Open Wide the Eye of the Heart, and Nothing Is Invisible*, in 2007 was a dramatic restatement of his Japaneseness. It marked the first time that the iconography and even elements of the execution were directly informed by recognizable Japanese paintings from the past. In this case the monumental portraits of Bodhidharma, the first patriarch of the Zen sect, had been inspired by an oversize scroll by Kawanabe Kyōsai in the collection of Joe and Etsuko Price. At the time of the opening in May 2007 Murakami invited Sō-oku Sen, a descendant of the famed sixteenth-century tea master Sen no Rikyū, to preside over gatherings for select guests.

Since the 1950s, largely through the teachings of D.T. Suzuki, Zen had entered the parlance of East and West Coast cognoscenti as a rigorous rejection of conventional Western lifestyles and an understated aesthetic. John Cage had embraced its reverence for silence in his explorations of "non-intention"; the Museum of Modern Art in New York had presented an exhibition of abstract Japanese calligraphy (1954).[26] Throughout the 1960s, '70s, and '80s, Zen inspired poets and painters such as Gary Snyder and Robert Rauschenberg. Thus, Zen immediately introduced an already accepted cool "Japan-ness" to the exhibition offerings of the scowling Bodhidharmas executed with calligraphic

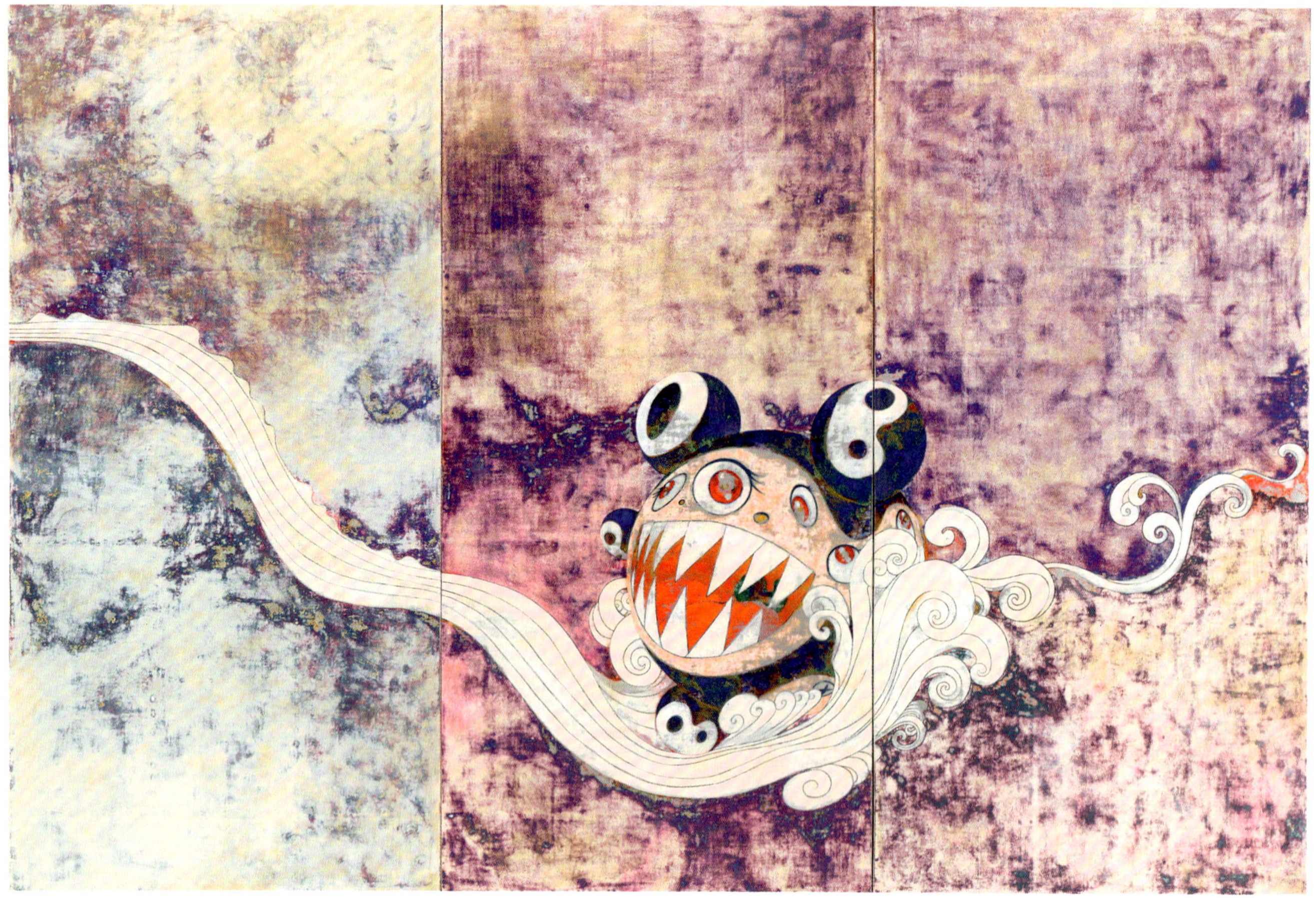

strokes and set against metallic grounds (see pp. 124–25). The kimono-garbed Murakami
at the opening and the formal offerings of tea added a new "authentic" element of
Murakami's "local" to an already globalized, almost clichéd understanding of Zen
culture.[27] As he himself described the occasion, "With [the musician] Hiroshi Fujiwara
kindly visiting my show in New York from Japan, Sō-oku Sen coming to perform tea
ceremonies, and the king of hip-hop, Jay Z, loving and drinking three consecutive bowls
of the *matcha* tea at one of the said ceremonies, I presented the Asian spirit by fully
unleashing its exoticism."[28] In the context of the history of the reception of Japanese art
in the West, it is worthwhile to draw an analogy between Murakami dressed in a kimono
orchestrating a tea ceremony and Okakura Kakuzō, who insisted on wearing Japanese
clothing during his lectures on tea at Fenway Court in Boston.

Spirited intellectual jousts between Murakami and Tsuji, which appeared in
a twenty-one-installment series in the monthly art journal *Geijutsu shinchō* from 2009
to 2011, marked a new level of engagement by Murakami with Japan's traditional art.
The two men had been in informal contact since 2001. In that year Murakami had an
exhibition at the Museum of Fine Arts, Boston, entitled *Takashi Murakami: Made in
Japan* (fig. 7). This show primarily presented Murakami's then current work informed by

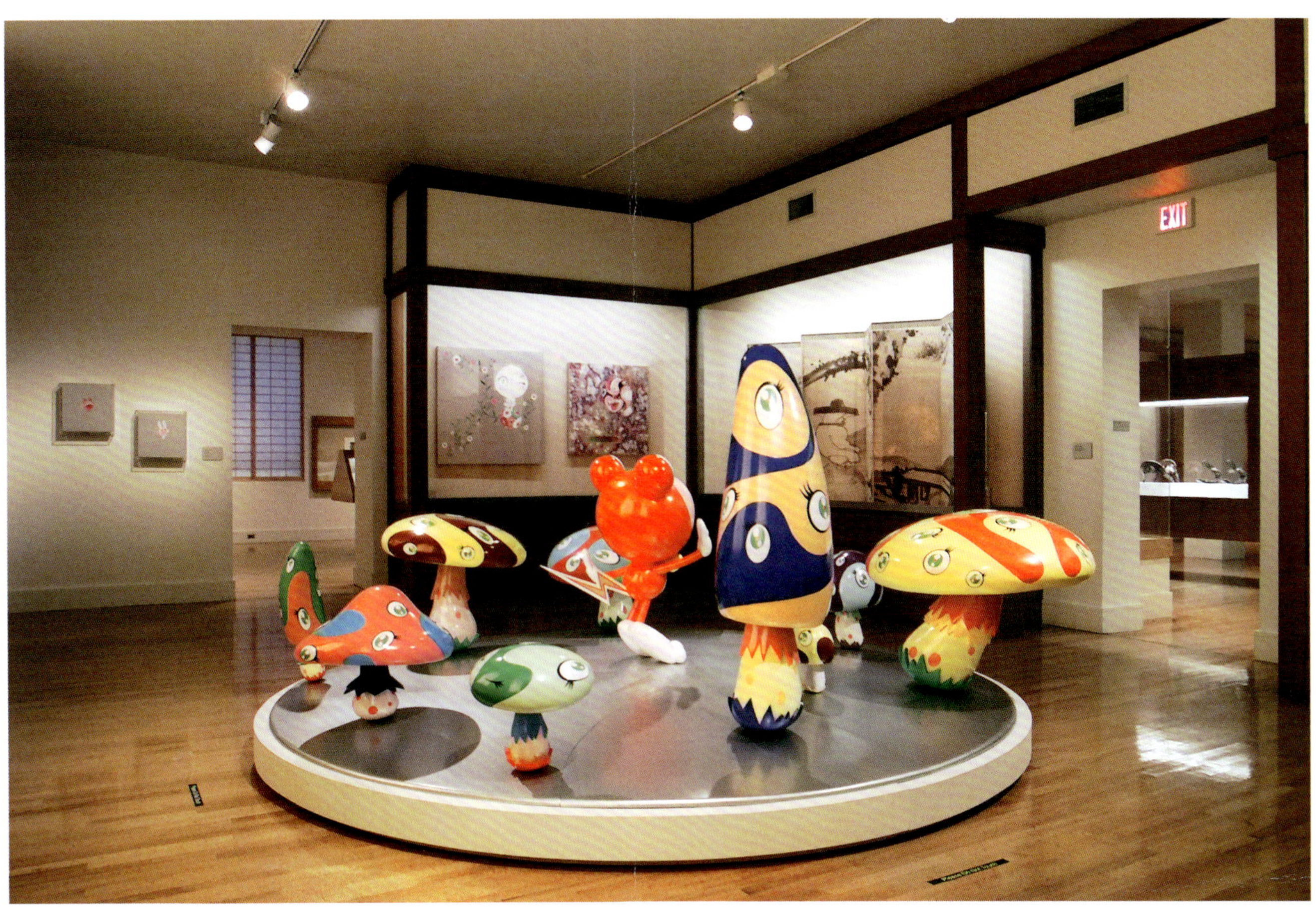

7
View of the exhibition
Takashi Murakami: Made in Japan,
Museum of Fine Arts, Boston
(April 25–September 3, 2001)

Japanese popular culture in the contemporary galleries. However, at the urging of the Japanese curators the exhibition also took the unprecedented approach of juxtaposing some of Murakami's works with a small number of paintings by Soga Shōhaku in the historical Japanese galleries. In the same year Tsuji had been a resident scholar at the Museum, but the *Geijutsu shinchō* series, recently published in book form as *Battle Royale!*, was their first true collaboration.

For each Tsuji provided a painting, object, or idea to which Murakami was obliged to respond by producing his own work of art. Tsuji furnished art historical background and pointed challenges and critiques; Murakami shared his thinking and angst. Some of the exchanges, such as that of the upside-down crucifixion, in which Murakami donned costuming and makeup and suspended himself upside down on a cross in imitation of a sixteenth-century banner with the image of the captured warrior Torii Sune'emon, were primarily for entertainment (figs. 8 and 9). However, others were meant by Tsuji to goad Murakami into reexamining his own artistic practice. In the fourth installment, Tsuji presented a pair of screens, *Elephant and Whale* (1795), by Itō Jakuchū that he had recently acquired for the Miho Museum. He also sent a pointed note: "I would rather like to hear your own voice. Why do you not pick up color pencils or something and

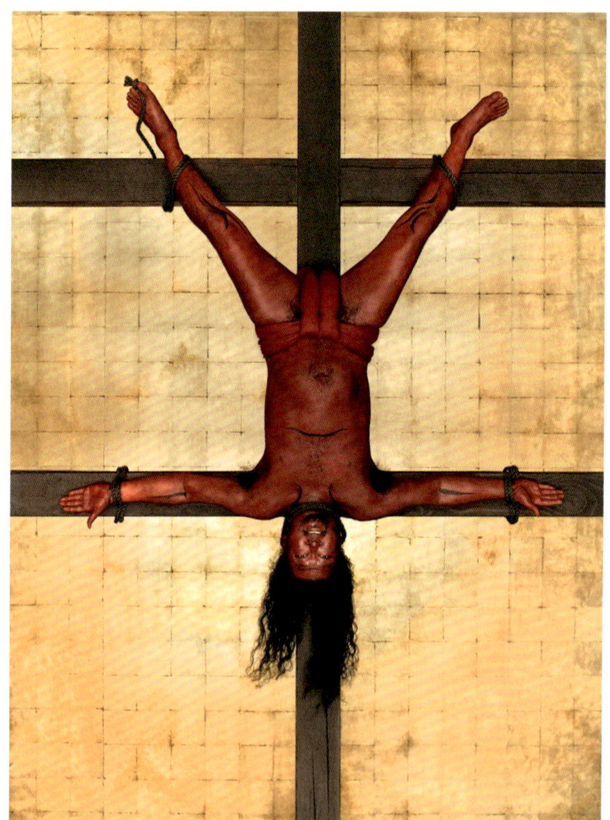

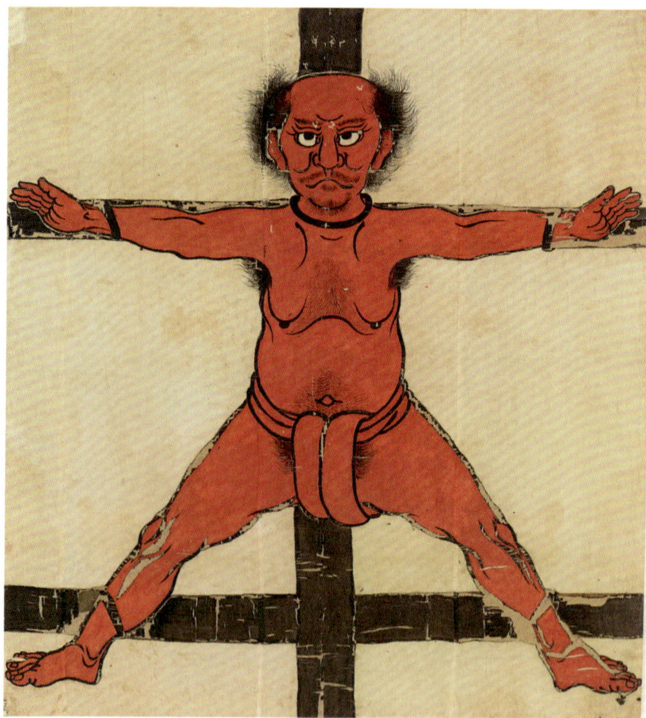

doodle more freely?"[29] Then in the sixth installment, Tsuji submitted *Dragon and Clouds* by Soga Shōhaku. For both men the thirty-five-foot *fusuma* (sliding door) paintings in ink with a ferocious, yet comical dragon had a special hold. Tsuji remembered his own reaction upon seeing the work for the first time: "The word 'sublime' did not do it justice; it was mind-boggling stupendous!"[30] Murakami responded: "It was in fact the image of this very *Dragon and Clouds* that made me give myself over entirely to the world of Professor Tsuji's *Lineage of Eccentrics* at the time when I first picked up the book."[31]

Although Murakami, like many postmodern artists, has disclaimed any historical study before producing his pieces, the essays and resulting artworks clearly indicate otherwise (unlike many of his Western counterparts, however, Murakami has insisted the reasons for his appropriation of motifs are purely ones of visual interest). Murakami has long identified with the bohemian Shōhaku, who embarked on bravura painting performances using highly unconventional techniques (sometimes after bouts of drinking). Like Murakami's, Shōhaku's figures are humorous and sometimes even grotesque, and his brushwork can be wildly expressionistic. On the other hand Shōhaku was well versed in classical Chinese literature and painting styles as well as Japan's ink painting traditions. Murakami has always admired Shōhaku's bravado; the son of a Kyoto dyer, Shōhaku claimed himself variously to be the descendant of the Soga school, which had been founded in the fifteenth century, and of the Chinese Ming emperor.

8
Takashi Murakami, *Crucified Upside Down*, 2010

9
Battle pennant of Ochiai Saheiji Michitsugu, Momoyama period, 16th century

Responding to a sixteenth-century banner with an image of the captured warrior Torii Sune'emon bound to a cross, Murakami donned makeup and costuming in one of the *Battle Royale!* challenges. Trying to resolve the question of the original orientation of the image, the artist had himself suspended upside down.

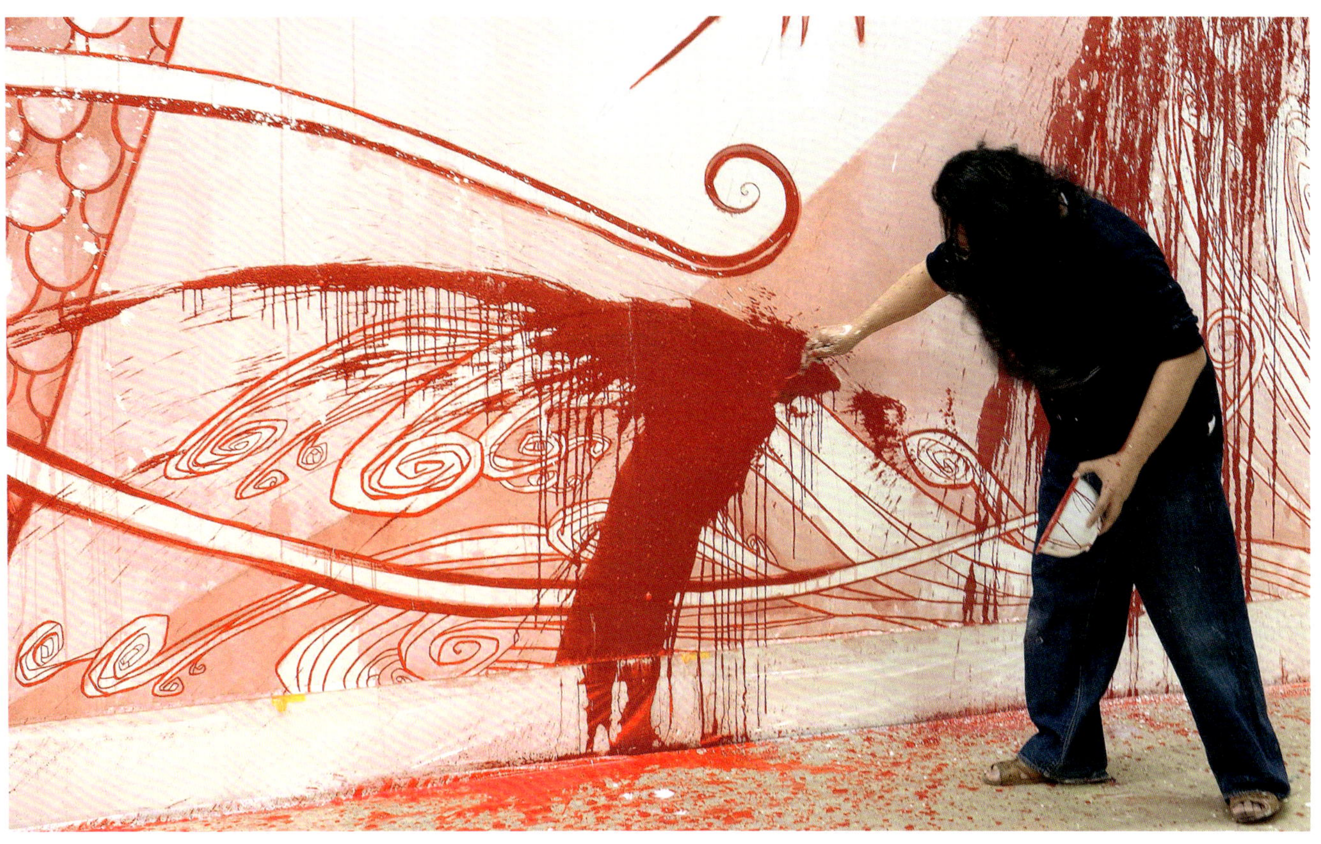

10
Takashi Murakami painting
*Dragon in Clouds—Red Mutation:
The version I painted myself in
annoyance after Professor Tsuji
told me, "Why don't you paint
something yourself for once?"*
in 2010

The *Battle Royale!* exchanges reveal, however, that although Shōhaku's painting in the MFA collection provided the primary inspiration for Murakami's rendition, the Tokyo artist also drew upon diverse premodern and contemporary sources, some Japanese and some Western, including paintings by Katsushika Hokusai and Kawanabe Kyōsai, as well as a drawing by William Blake that had figured in a novel in the series including *Silence of the Lambs* and a record jacket by the British rock group King Crimson. The resulting sixty-foot composition reflects Murakami's internalization of the Shōhaku work, an unprecedented investment of his actual physical being in the canvas, and a confidence of scale that would influence later projects (fig. 10). It is this internalization of the art historical past that separates this undertaking from what had preceded it and contributes to the framework of two later projects—the *500 Arhats* (2012), a commission for the exhibition *Murakami-Ego* in Doha, Qatar, and *In the Land of the Dead, Stepping on the Tail of a Rainbow* (2014) now in The Broad in Los Angeles.

Murakami claims to put no narrative content into his paintings, yet the complex arrangement of figures with long-established iconographies in both the *500 Arhats* and *In the Land of the Dead* demand a narrative reading. Created as the ultimate response to Tsuji's *Battle Royale!* challenges, *500 Arhats* draws upon some of the earlier compositions that Murakami developed for the contest, including the Miho Museum's *Elephant and Whale* and the Boston *Dragon and Clouds*. Studies were also made of

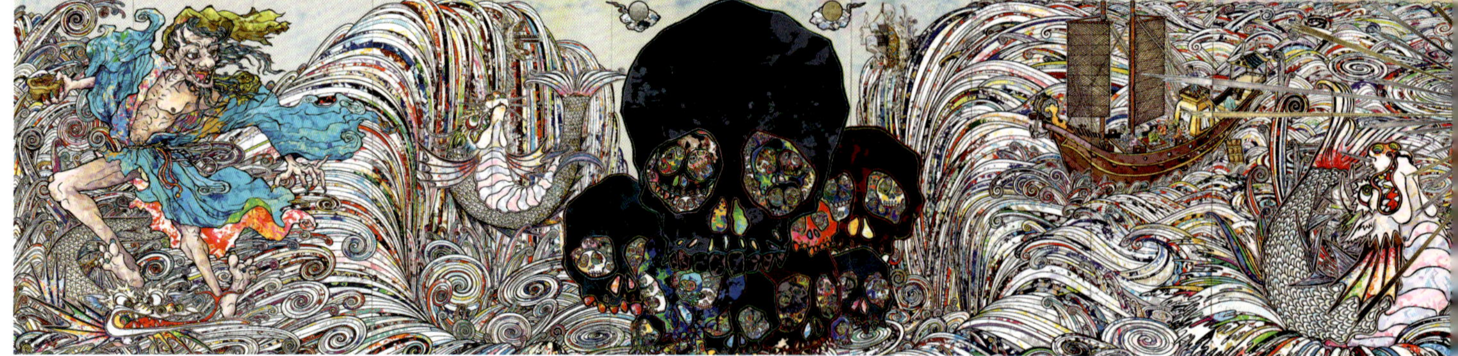

Buddhist paintings of arhats, including the scrolls by Kano Kazunobu, now housed at Asakusa Sensōji in Tokyo. The resulting 328-foot canvas, divided into quadrants representing the four cardinal directions symbolized by the Blue Dragon, White Tiger, Vermillion Bird, and Black Tortoise, serves as a powerful elegy to the victims of the earthquake, tsunami, and nuclear disaster that befell the Tōhoku region of Japan on March 11, 2011. Similarly *In the Land of the Dead* integrates elements from paintings by Shōhaku such as a pair of screens of the *Chinese Immortals* (1764) in the collection of the Agency for Cultural Affairs, a thirteenth-century narrative handscroll, *Legends of the Kegon Sect* (*Kegon engi*), belonging to Kōzanji, Kyoto, and the Miho Museum's *Elephant* screen by Jakuchū to create a fantastic watery landscape populated by transcendents and mythical creatures, another memorial to those who were lost on 3-11 (fig. 11). These incorporations of studies from the past can no longer be categorized as "exotic flavorings" or "ambivalent feeling" to pique the interest of a Western collector; they are integral to the vision of an artist who has been able to master the lessons from his artistic and spiritual mentors. Murakami commented to Tsuji, "I invested everything I learned from you, sensei, and wove in the *Lineage of Eccentrics* that existed in myself, the whole thing into it. It's a painting like a piece of knitting that one."[32] Most recently Murakami created a tribute to Tsuji and his *Lineage of Eccentrics* called *Transcendent Attacking a Whirlwind*, inspired by a Shōhaku painting of the same title (figs. 12 and 13). This new painting incorporates not only the sword-wielding immortal, the calligraphic whirlwind, and the upturned bystanders from the Boston screen, but also the figures on the left appropriated from a two-panel screen by Shōhaku in the collection of the museum of Tokyo University of the Arts. Murakami reinterpreted these figures in monumental scale and in a layered display of brilliant color against a shimmering background of glittered lozenges. Much in the same way Shōhaku was able to assert title to membership in the Soga school after displaying a mastery of ink, so Murakami can now stake his claim to be a member of the Lineage of Eccentrics.

The MFA's early curators and collectors shared a vision for the Museum, that through its holdings it could illustrate the entire evolution of Japanese art for the West. Critical to this ideal, of course, is a constant reevaluation of the collection and an engagement with the art of today. Through *Takashi Murakami: Lineage of Eccentrics*, we have turned to Nobuo Tsuji and Takashi Murakami so that we could see Japanese art and our collections through their eyes. In this project, Murakami has not only presented

11
Takashi Murakami, *In the Land of the Dead, Stepping on the Tail of a Rainbow*, 2014

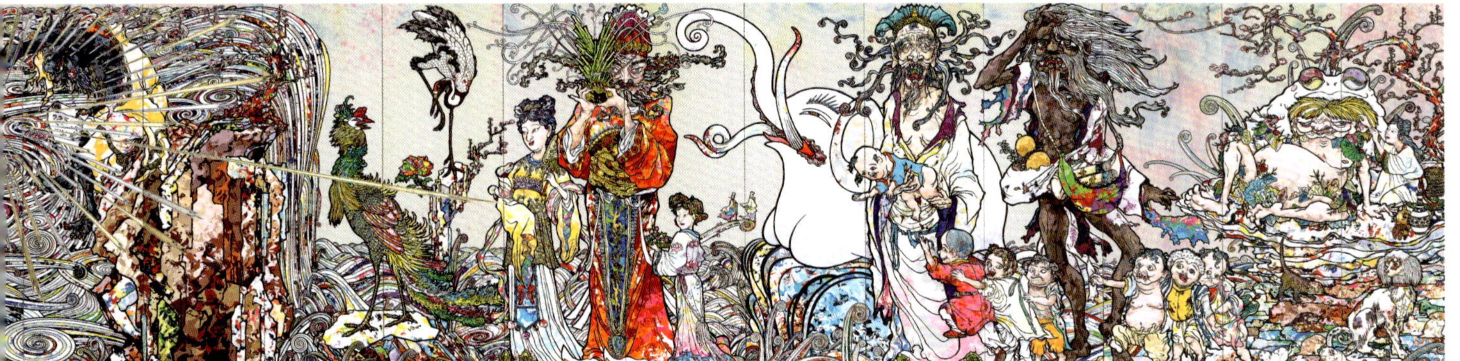

a selection of his own works and allowed us to contextualize them according to the principles of Japanese art history that Tsuji has propounded, but through his own close examination of the works in the collection, particularly those of Soga Shōhaku, allowed contemporary audiences to look at Japanese art in ways that certainly would have been unforeseen by the Meiji-era curators and collectors. Tsuji's insistence on an art history that illuminates the human spirit and exults in playfulness and individuality suggests ways to exhibit Japanese art that can immediately connect with audiences of today. Although the nineteenth-century "founding fathers" may have had the foresight to form the collection, it is through the interpretation and reinvention by Tsuji and Murakami and others to follow that the collection of Japanese art can continue to tell a vital story of Japanese art, now no longer just for the West, but for the global community.[33]

The author would like to express her deepest gratitude to Niko Vicario and Samuel C. Morse of Amherst College for their invaluable advice in the development of this essay and to Edward Saywell for his support throughout this project. Yuiko Hotta and Tomoko Nagakura have provided much appreciated research assistance in the production of this book.

1   Clifford Geertz, "Art as a Cultural System," in *Local Knowledge: Further Essays in Interpretive Anthropology* (New York: Basic Books, 1983), 97.

2   Paul Crowther, *The Transhistorical Image: Philosophizing Art and Its History* (Cambridge: Cambridge University Press, 2002), 2–3.

3   For further information about the roles of Ernest Fenollosa and Okakura Kakuzō in the development of Meiji-era thinking about the visual arts and the establishment of institutions, see Karatani Kōjin, "Japan as Museum: Okakura Tenshin and Ernest Fenollosa," trans. Sabu Kohso, *Japanese Art after 1945: Scream Against the Sky*, ed. Alexandra Munroe (New York: Harry N. Abrams, 1994), 33–39.

4   Acrylic pigments were introduced to Japan in the 1960s and then were widely used as Japanese manufacturers began to produce their own pigments.

5   Chelsea Foxwell provides an excellent analysis of the context for Murakami's training in Nihonga and his larger ambitions for an integration of Western and Japanese art in "The Total Work of Art: Takashi Murakami and Nihonga," in *Takashi Murakami: The Octopus Eats Its Own Leg*, ed. Michael Darling (New York: Skira Rizzoli, 2017), 40–50.

6   Kōtarō Takamura, "Green Sun," trans. Robin Thompson, *Art in Translation* 7, no. 3 (2015): 407–8.

7   Takashi Murakami, "Life as a Creat[o]r," in *Takashi Murakami: Summon Monsters? Open the Door? Heal? Or Die?* (Tokyo: Museum of Contemporary Art, 2001), 130.

8   Nobuo Tsuji and Takashi Murakami, *Battle Royale! Japanese Art History: Nobuo Tsuji vs. Takashi Murakami*, trans. Christopher Stephens and Yuko Sakata (Tokyo: Kaikai Kiki, 2017), 20.

9   Arata Isozaki, *Japan-ness in Architecture*, trans. Sabu Kohso and ed. David B. Stewart (Cambridge, MA: MIT Press, 2006), 3–21.

10   Murakami, "Life as a Creat[o]r," 130.

11   Murakami, "Life as a Creat[o]r," 131.

12   Yūji Yamashita and Nobuo Tsuji, "'Kisō no keifu' izen igo," in *Nihon bijutsu no hakkenshatachi*, ed. Arata Yajima et al. (Tokyo: Tokyo daigaku shuppan kai, 2003), 154.

13   Yukio Lippit, *Colorful Realm: Japanese Bird-and-Flower Paintings by Itō Jakuchū* (Washington, DC: National Gallery of Art, 2012), 167.

14   Tsuji and Murakami, *Battle Royale!*, 192–93.

15   Takashi Murakami, "A Theory of Superflat Japanese Art," in *Superflat* (Tokyo: Madra Publishing, 2000), 9.

16   Soyeon Ahn, "The Meaning of Superflat Always Remains Mysterious," in *Takashi in Superflat Wonderland* (Seoul: Plateau, 2013), 59.

17   Nobuo Tsuji, *Playfulness in Japanese Art*, The Franklin D. Murphy Lectures 7 (Lawrence, KA: Spencer Museum of Art, 1986).

18   Nobuo Tsuji, ed., *Nihon no bi "kazari no sekai"* (Tokyo: NHK Service Center, 1988). Tsuji also presented a lecture on kazari at Harvard University and Amherst College, which was published in "Ornament (*Kazari*)—An Approach to Japanese Culture," ed. John M. Rosenfield, *Archives of Asian Art* 47 (1994): 35–45, and organized an exhibition and catalogue with Nicole Coolidge Rousamaniere, *Kazari: Decoration and Display in Japan, 15th–19th Centuries* (New York: Japan Society, 2002).

19   Tsuji credits the philosopher Takeshi Umehara with guiding his thinking on animism. Nobuo Tsuji, *Asobu shinbutsu: Edo no shūkyō bijutsu to animizumu* (Tokyo: Chikuma gakugei bunko, 2015).

20   In his writings about ornamentation Tsuji has deliberately abandoned the word *sōshoku*, a word of Chinese origin that was adopted in the Meiji era to describe ornamentation, in favor of the more widely used *kazari*. In an informative essay Gennifer Weisenfeld discusses Murakami's evocation of a pre-Meiji past in "Reinscribing Tradition on a Transnational Art World (2007)," in *Contemporary Art in Asia*, ed. Melissa Chiu and Benjamin Genocchi (Cambridge, MA: MIT Press, 2011), 371–90.
      Ernest Fenollosa and Okakura Kakuzō's determination to privilege the "elevated" arts of Japan, for example, had meant that with the exception of Japanese prints and decorative arts (works of art that they largely ignored) there has been little humor or playfulness represented in the MFA collection; their primary interest in painting and sculpture—works of "fine art'"—has left the Museum with few decorative works.

21   Marilyn Ivy, in *Discourses of the Vanishing: Modernity, Phantasm, Japan* (Chicago: University of Chicago Press, 1995), discusses the Japanese nostalgia for the past in times of instability.

22   Nobuo Tsuji, "The Journey of Murakami's Art," trans. Aaron M. Rio, in *Murakami by Murakami* (Oslo: Astrup Fearnley Museet, 2017), 126.

23   Anne Nishimura Morse and Nobuo Tsuji, eds., *Japanese Art in the Museum of Fine Arts, Boston*, 2 vols. (Tokyo: Museum of Fine Arts, Boston, and Kodansha, 1998).

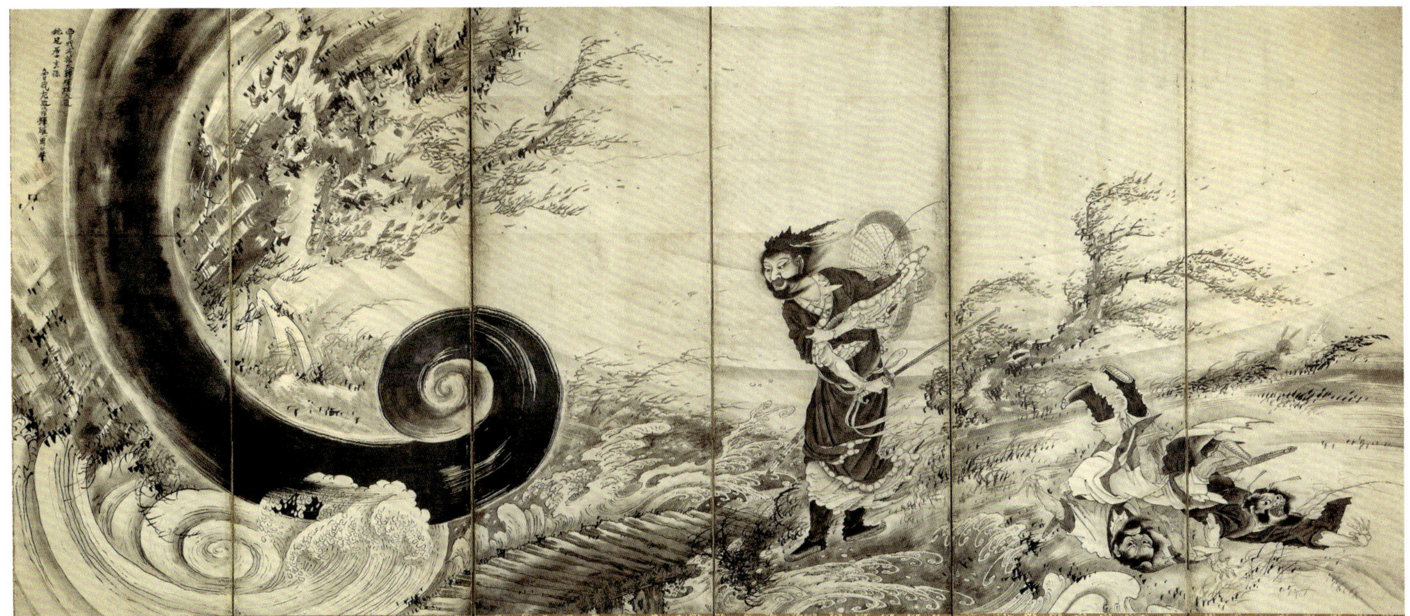

12
Soga Shōhaku (1730–1781),
*Transcendent Attacking
a Whirlwind*, Edo period,
about 1764

24   Tokyo National Museum et al., eds., *Bosuton bijutsukan Nihon bijutsu no shihō* (Tokyo: Tokyo National Museum, 2012).

25   For an excellent analysis of the commodification of Murakami's work, see Pamela M. Lee, "The World Is Flat/The End of the World: Takashi Murakami and the Aesthetics of Post-Fordism," in *Forgetting the Art World* (Cambridge, MA: MIT Press, 2012), 39–68.

26   John Cage, "John Cage: An Autobiographical Statement," *Southwest Review* (1991), reproduced at *John Cage Trust,* accessed October 30, 2017, http://johncage.org/autobiographical_statement.html.

27   After writing this essay, the author was informed of a similar discussion in Gregory P. A. Levine, *Long Strange Journey: On Modern Zen, Zen Art, and Other Predicaments* (Honolulu: University of Hawai'i Press, 2017), 94–95.

28   Tsuji and Murakami, *Battle Royale!*, 103.

29   Tsuji and Murakami, *Battle Royale!*, 60.

30   Tsuji and Murakami, *Battle Royale!*, 83.

31   Tsuji and Murakami, *Battle Royale!*, 85.

32   Takashi Murakami and Nobuo Tsuji in conversation with the author, June 28, 2017.

33   In *Modern Painters, Old Masters: The Art of Imitation from the Pre-Raphaelites to the First World War* (New Haven: Yale University Press, 2017), Elizabeth Prettejohn provides an insightful analysis of how the Pre-Raphaelites, through their "generous imitation" of fifteenth-century Italian artists, led to the introduction of now well-recognized masters such as Botticelli into the Western canon.

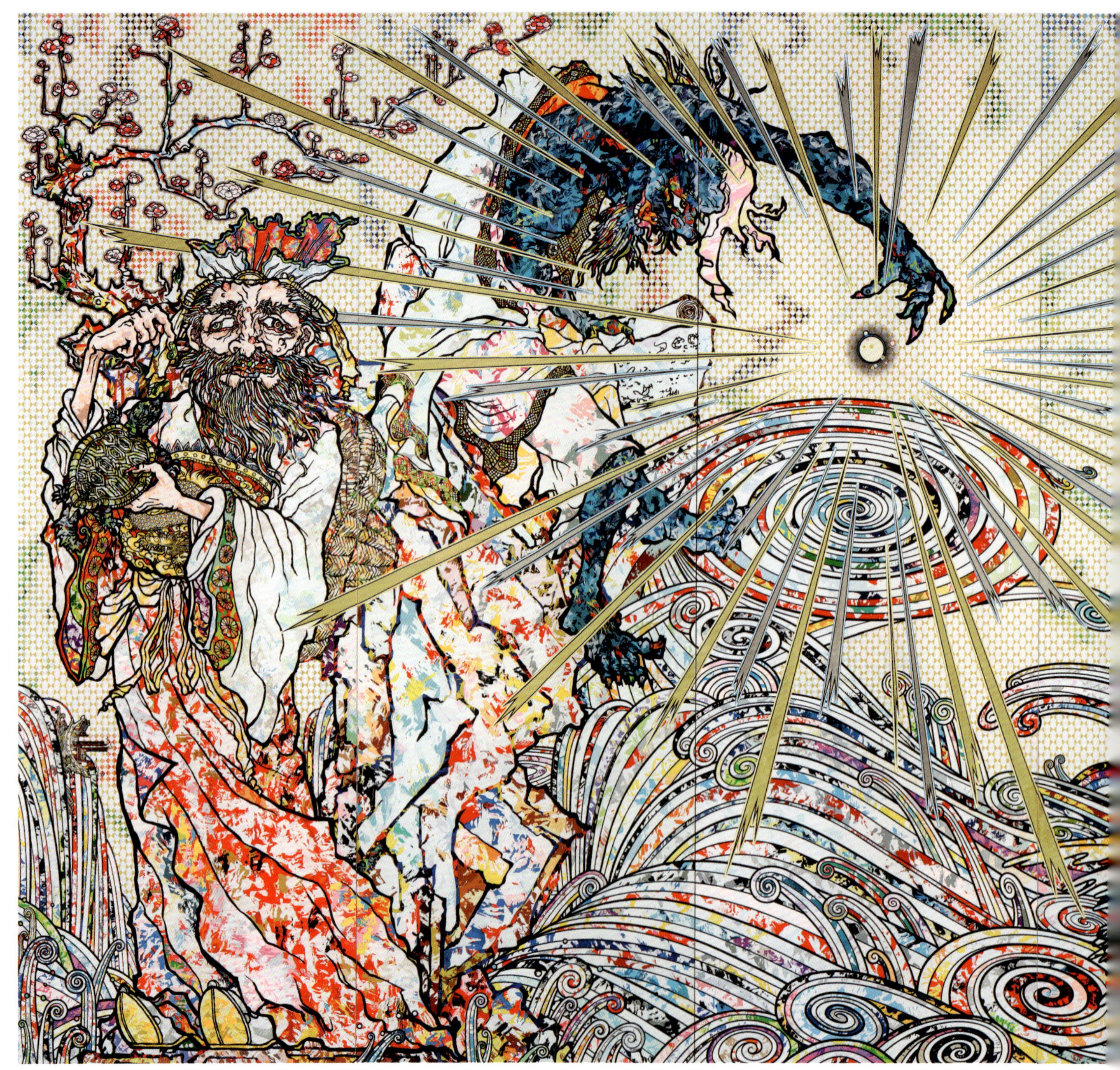

13
Takashi Murakami,
*Transcendent Attacking
a Whirlwind*, 2017

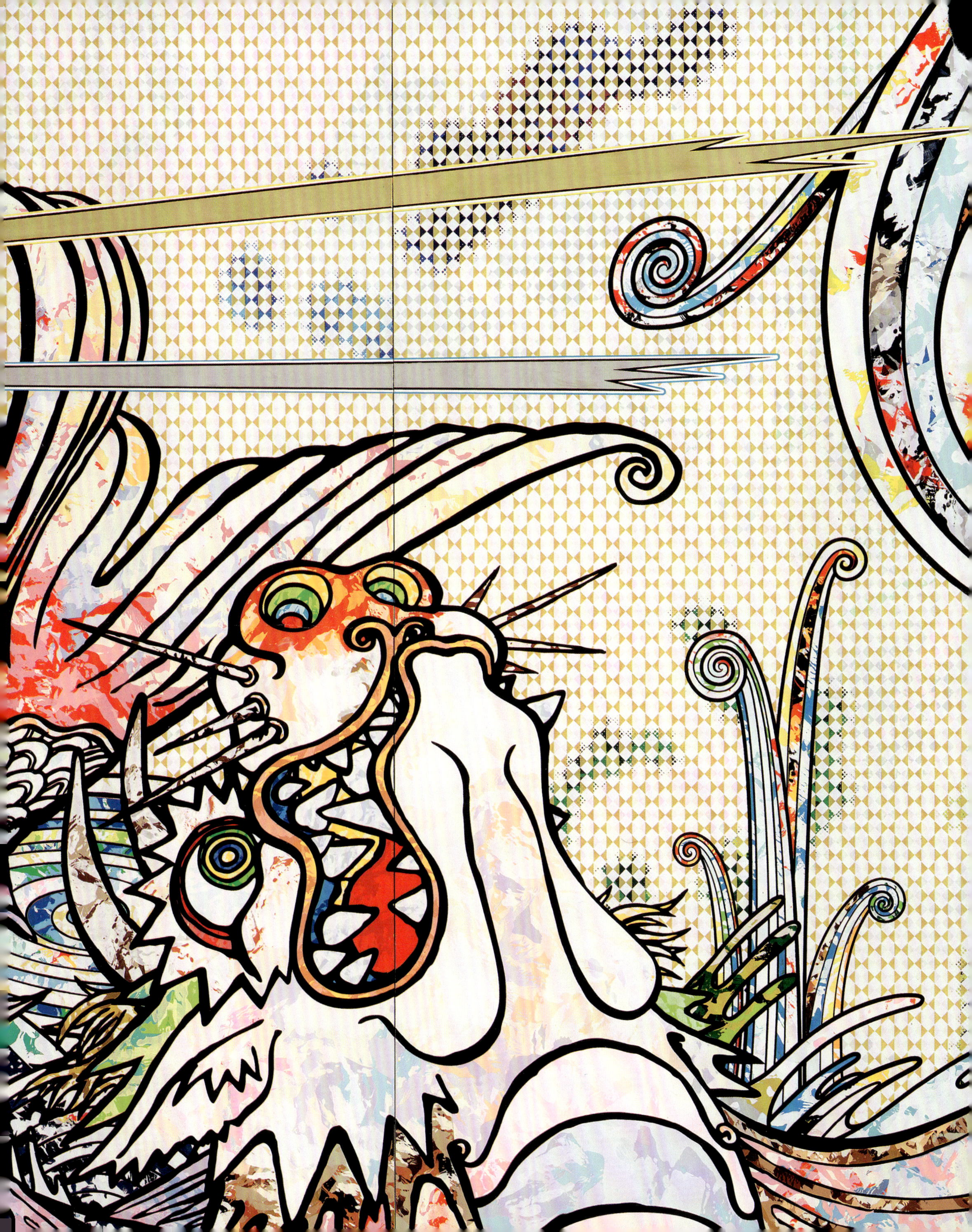

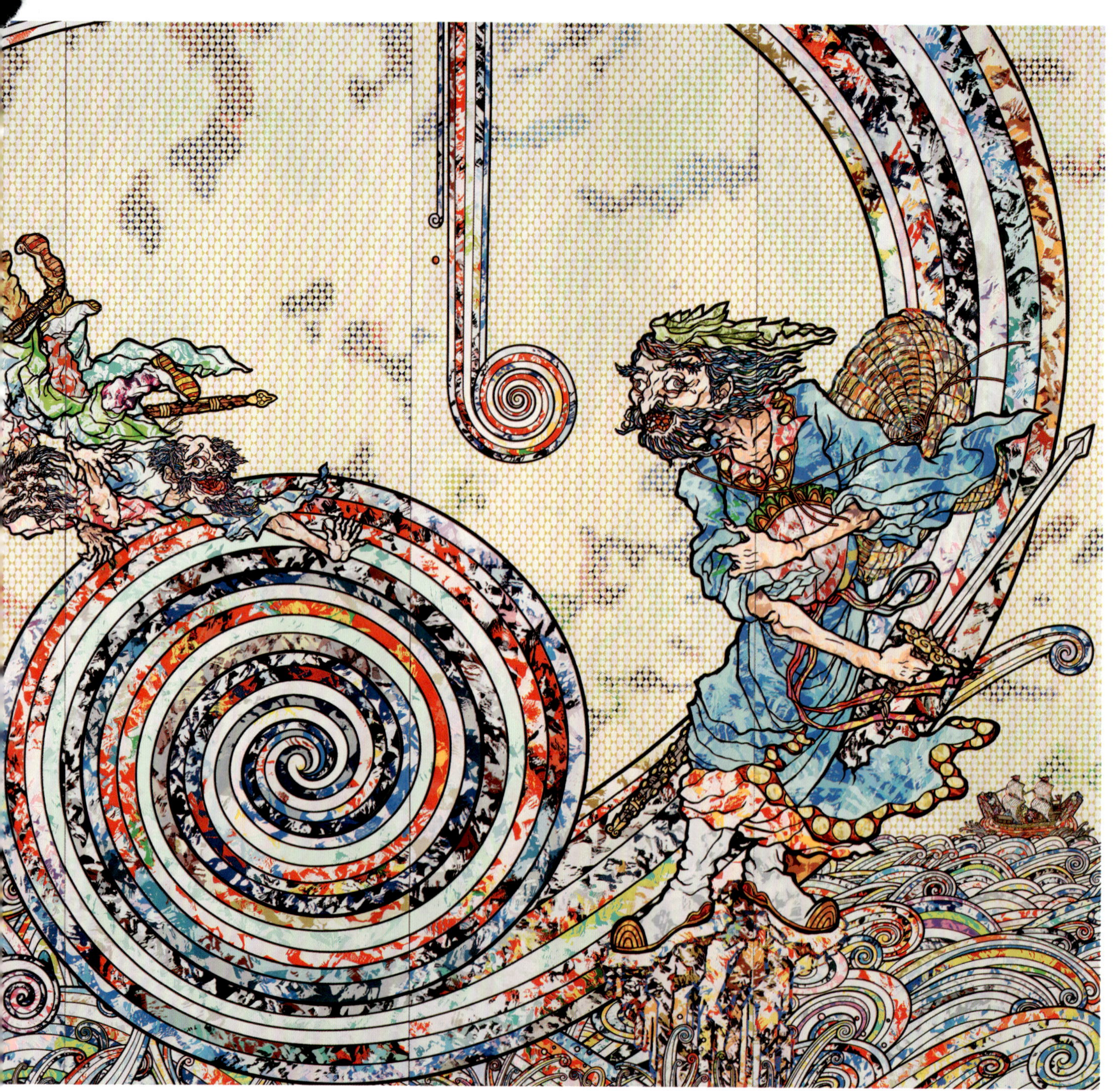

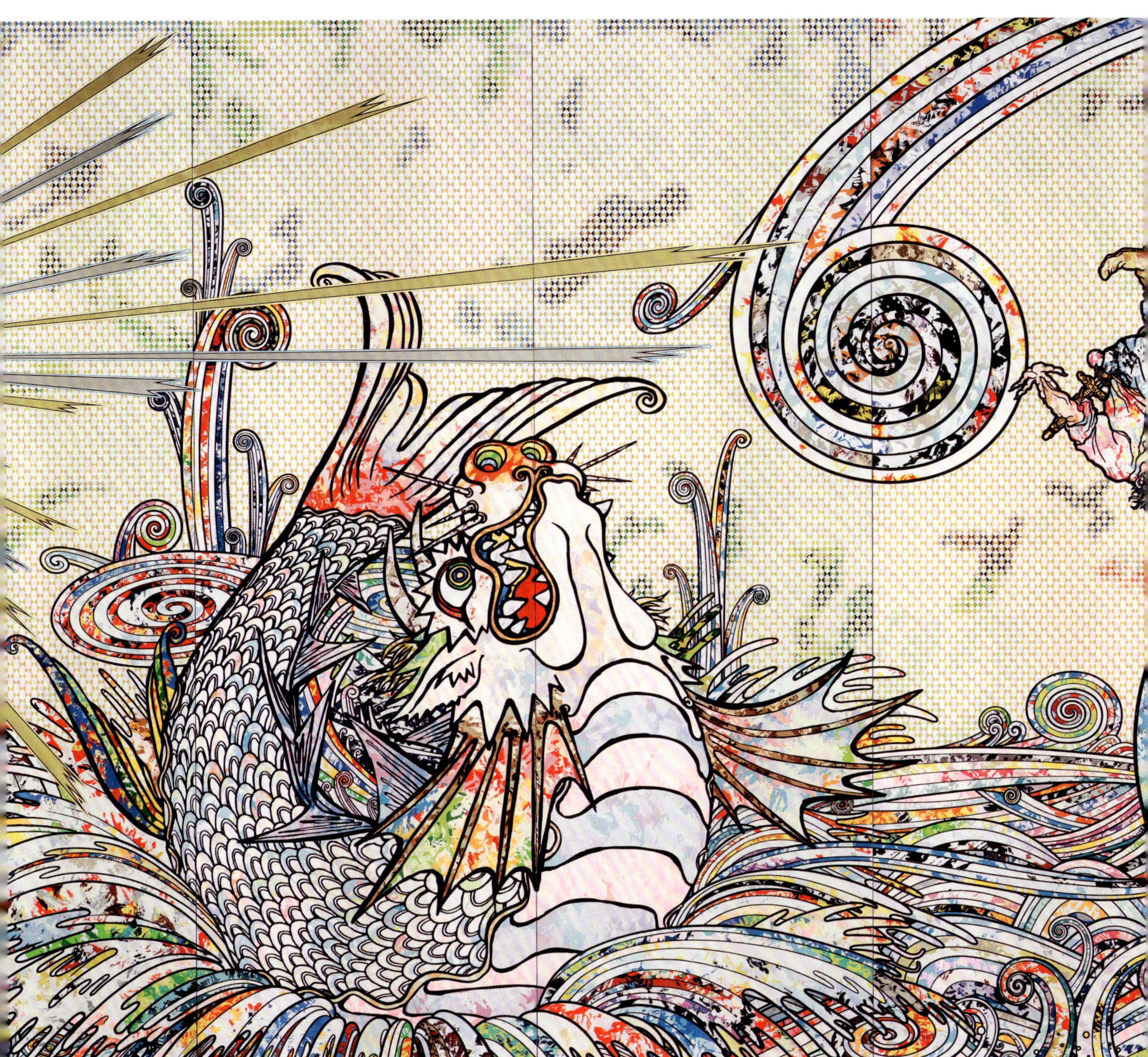

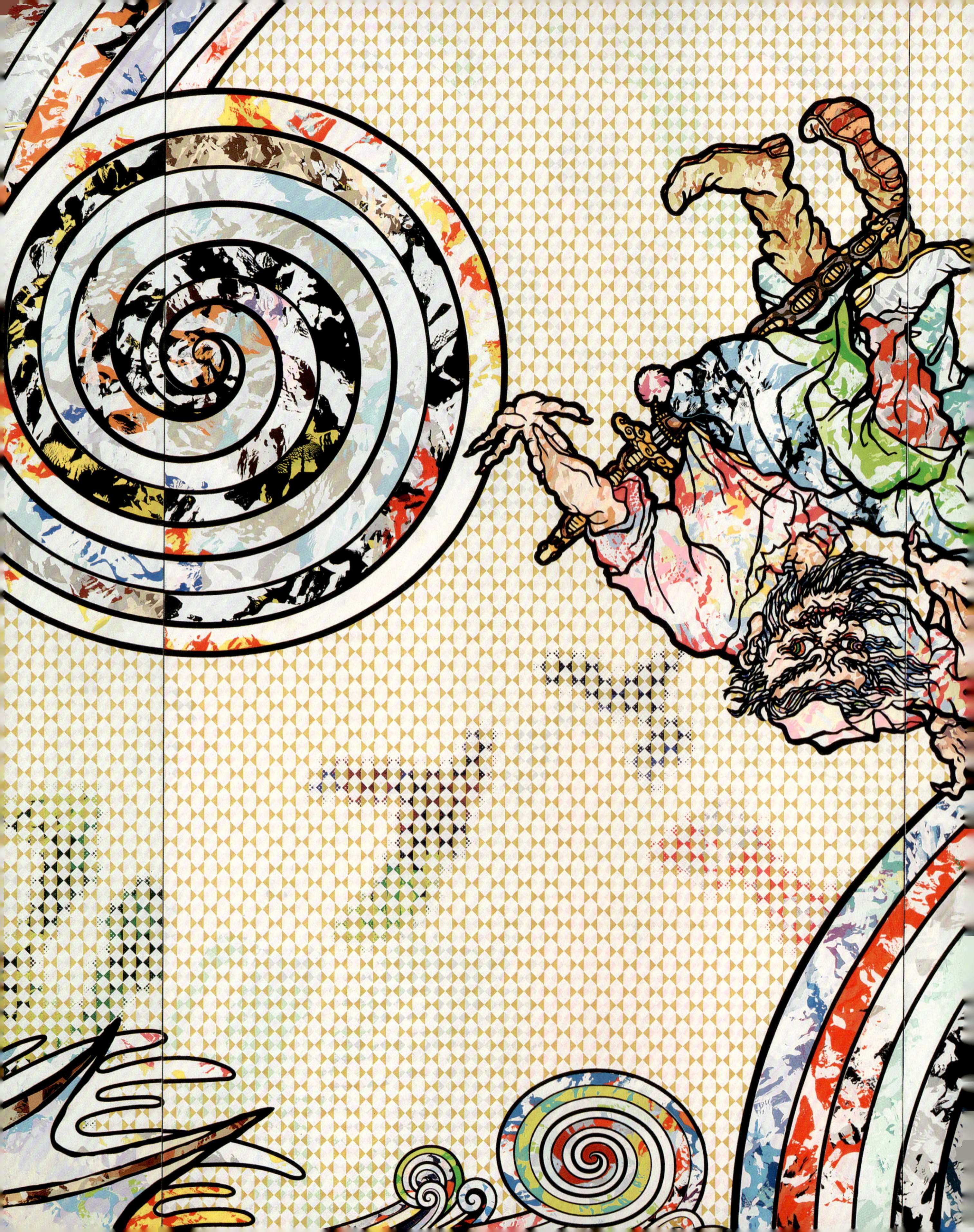

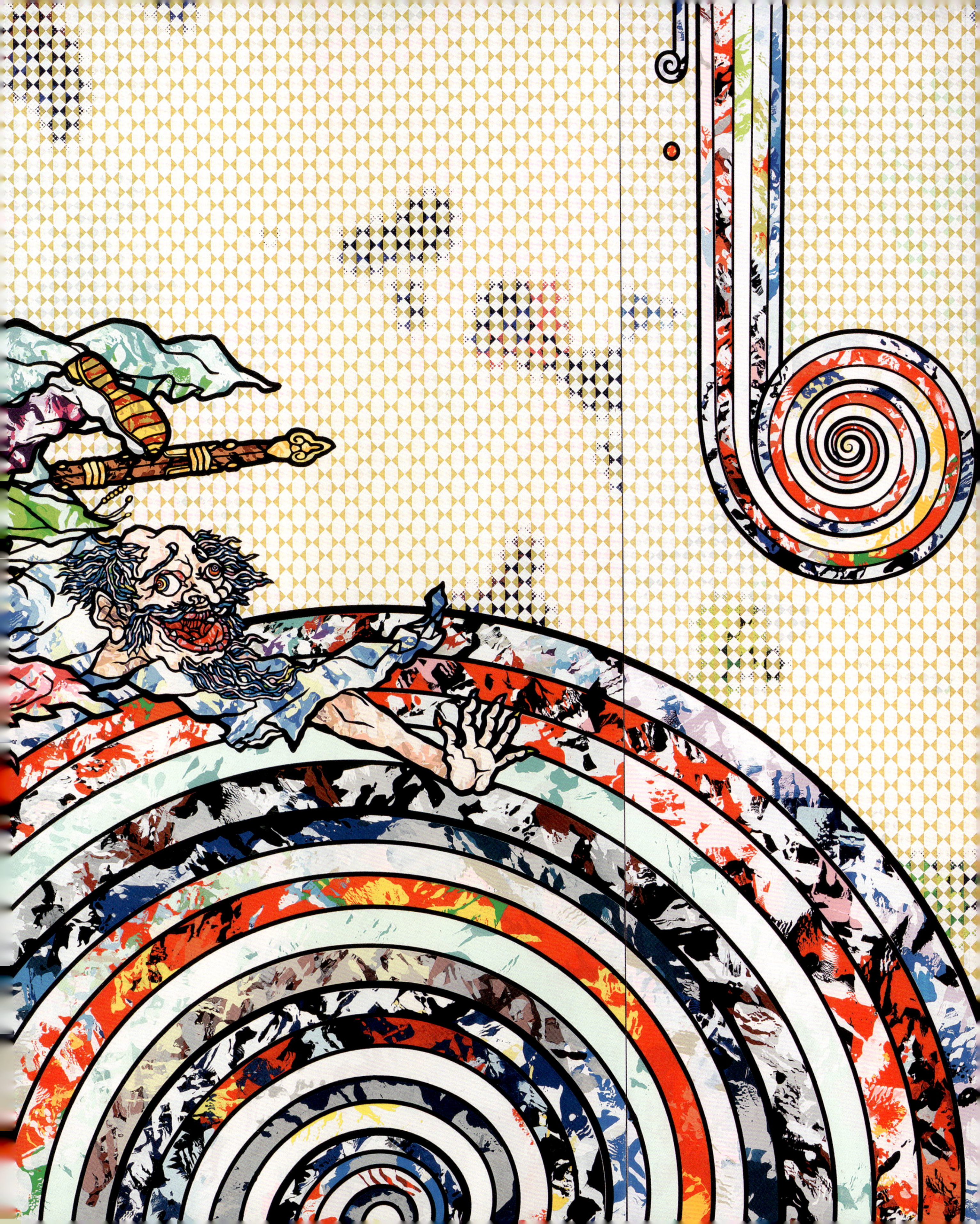

1

SUPER FLAT

In 2000 Takashi Murakami issued his *Superflat Manifesto*, a bold statement about his approach to image making. The term *Superflat* underscored his early embrace of the ideas espoused by Andy Warhol and other Pop artists, in which the distinctions between "high art" and "low art" were completely leveled. However, Superflat also described a method of organizing pictures that lay outside Western art. Critical to the articulation of this visual strategy was Nobuo Tsuji's book *Lineage of Eccentrics*. Tsuji had discussed the careers of little-known artists from the seventeenth through nineteenth centuries who were remarkable for their bizarre images and often unorthodox techniques that frequently relied more upon the two-dimensional picture plane than on the recession into space typically seen in European and American art. He subsequently suggested connections between this avant-garde art and the manga and anime of recent times. Thus, Murakami—who frequently incorporated manga into his imagery—could now point to uniquely Japanese precedents with which he strongly identified.

Superflat may be described as the extreme compression of the space between three-dimensional objects so that the picture plane is particularly emphatic. In his manifesto Murakami acknowledges that rather than relying on words alone, it can be easier to understand these ideas by looking at specific paintings. Thus, this section juxtaposes historical works by some of Tsuji's Eccentrics that demonstrate this intentional flattening of the composition with works from Murakami's early career.

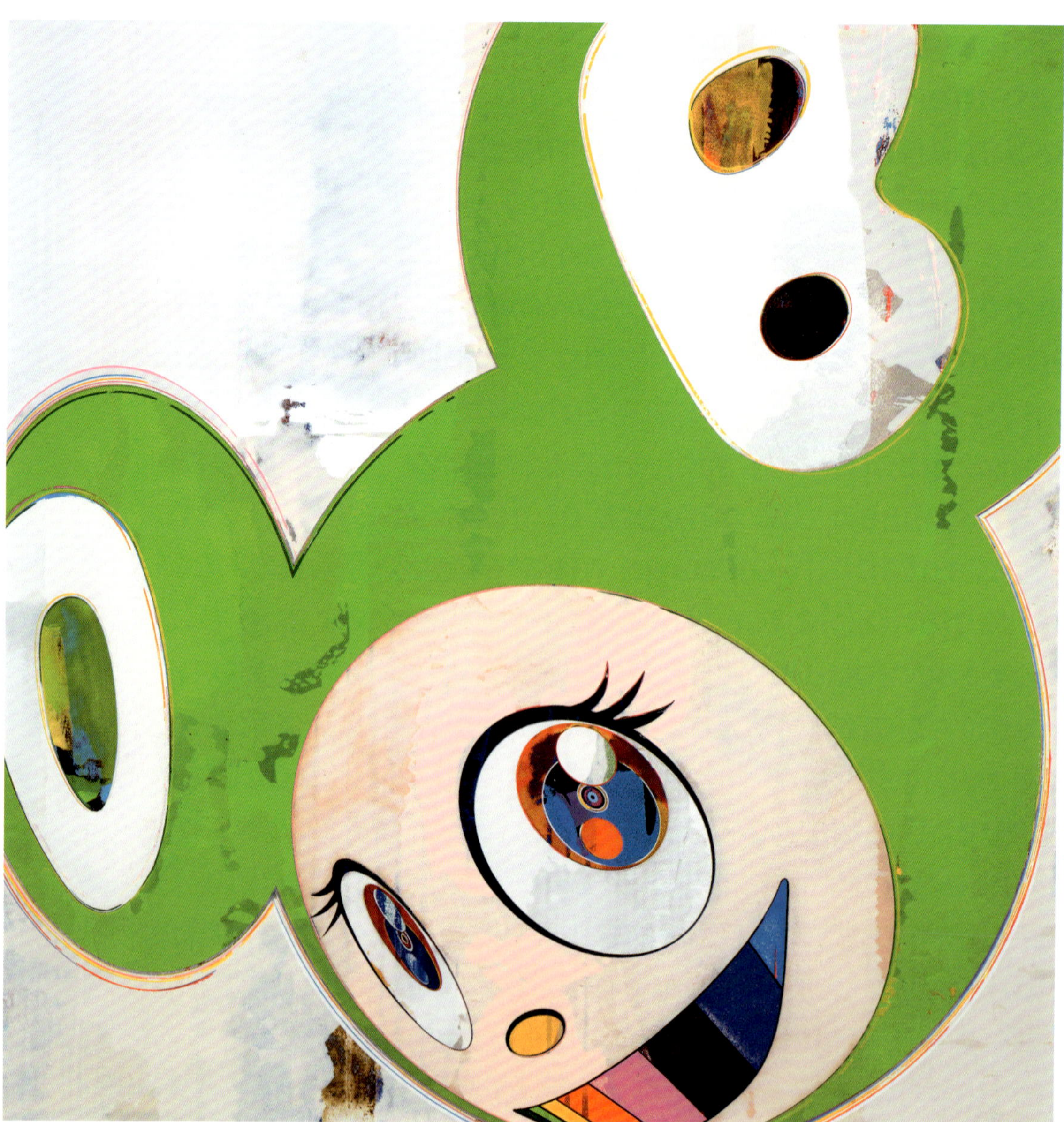

TAKASHI MURAKAMI

And then, and then and then and then and then/Green Truth, Heisei era, 2006
Acrylic on canvas mounted on board, 100 × 100 cm (39 ⅜ × 39 ⅜ in.)
Courtesy of the artist

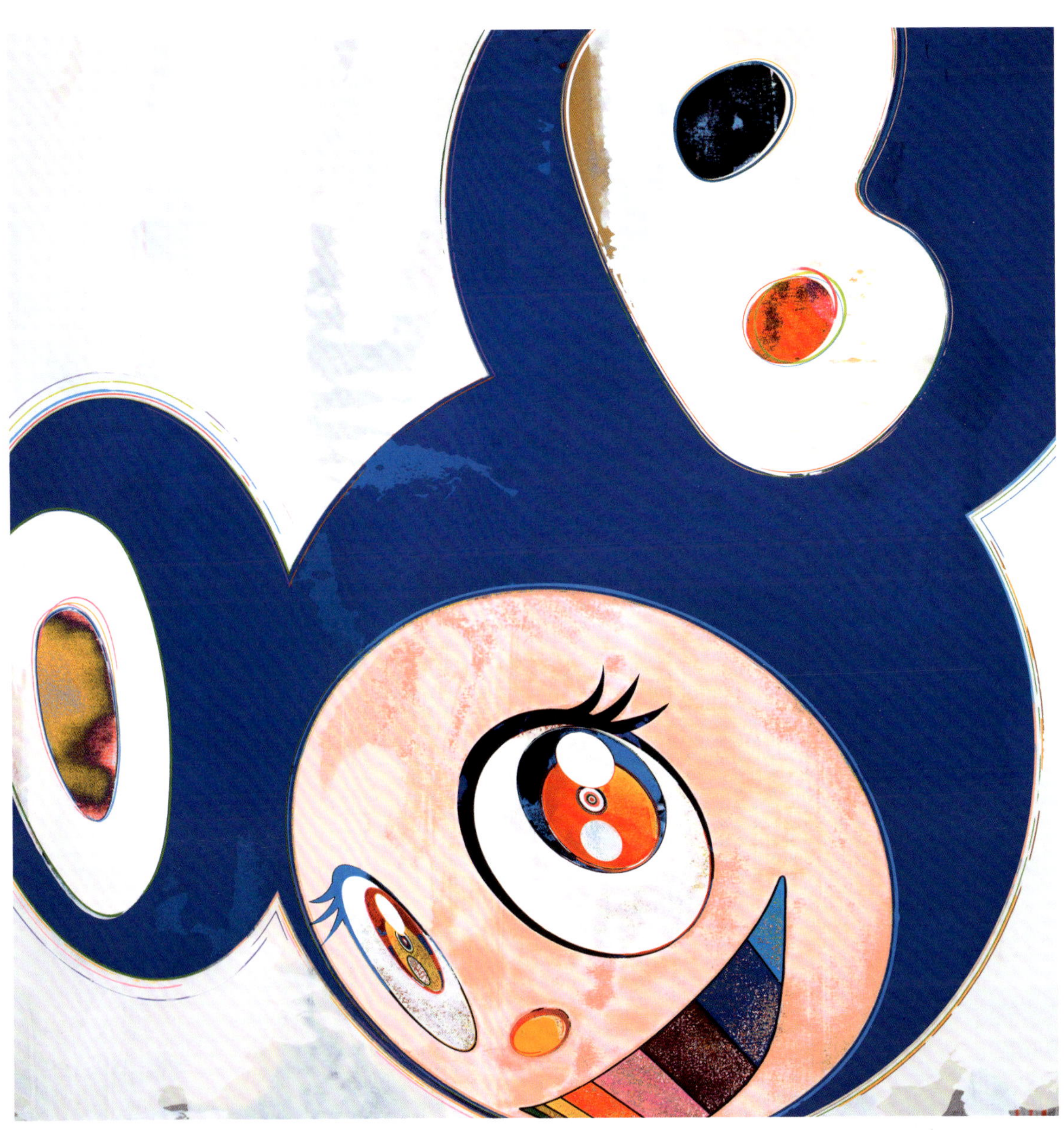

And then, and then and then and then and then/Original Blue, Heisei era, 2006
Acrylic on canvas mounted on board, 100 × 100 cm (39 ⅜ × 39 ⅜ in.)
Courtesy of the artist

MR. DOB, THE MOUSE-LIKE FIGURE with the letters *D* and *B* imprinted on his rounded ears, is the enduring symbol of the conflation of commercial and artistic forces in Murakami's work. Combining the features of two popular Japanese cartoon figures, Doraemon and Sonic the Hedgehog, Mr. DOB was created by Murakami in 1993 to develop an iconography by which he could be immediately identified. The figure's name was derived from a nonsensical phrase (*dobozite dobozite oshamanbe*) meaning "Why? Why" that Murakami devised in a visceral reaction against the blind imitations of the English-language-based art of the Americans Jenny Holzer and Barbara Kruger by his Japanese contemporaries.

Murakami has since described the figure—which can take on many different guises from *kawaii* (cute) to malevolent—as his alter ego. Over the years, Mr. DOB has appeared as the subject of various kinds of works: from monumental paintings to parade floats, to widely available commercial merchandise. In each of these paintings the figure is set off against a mottled surface reminiscent of building walls. When Murakami first began producing the *And then, and then and then and then and then* works in 1994 he was pressed by an exhibition deadline. Needing assistance, he engaged a commercial sign painter, who quickly executed the design in sweeping broad strokes; Murakami then went back and distressed the surface of the canvas. The artist was so pleased by the result that he continued to reproduce these effects, applying the pigments in fractured layers, in later versions of the paintings.

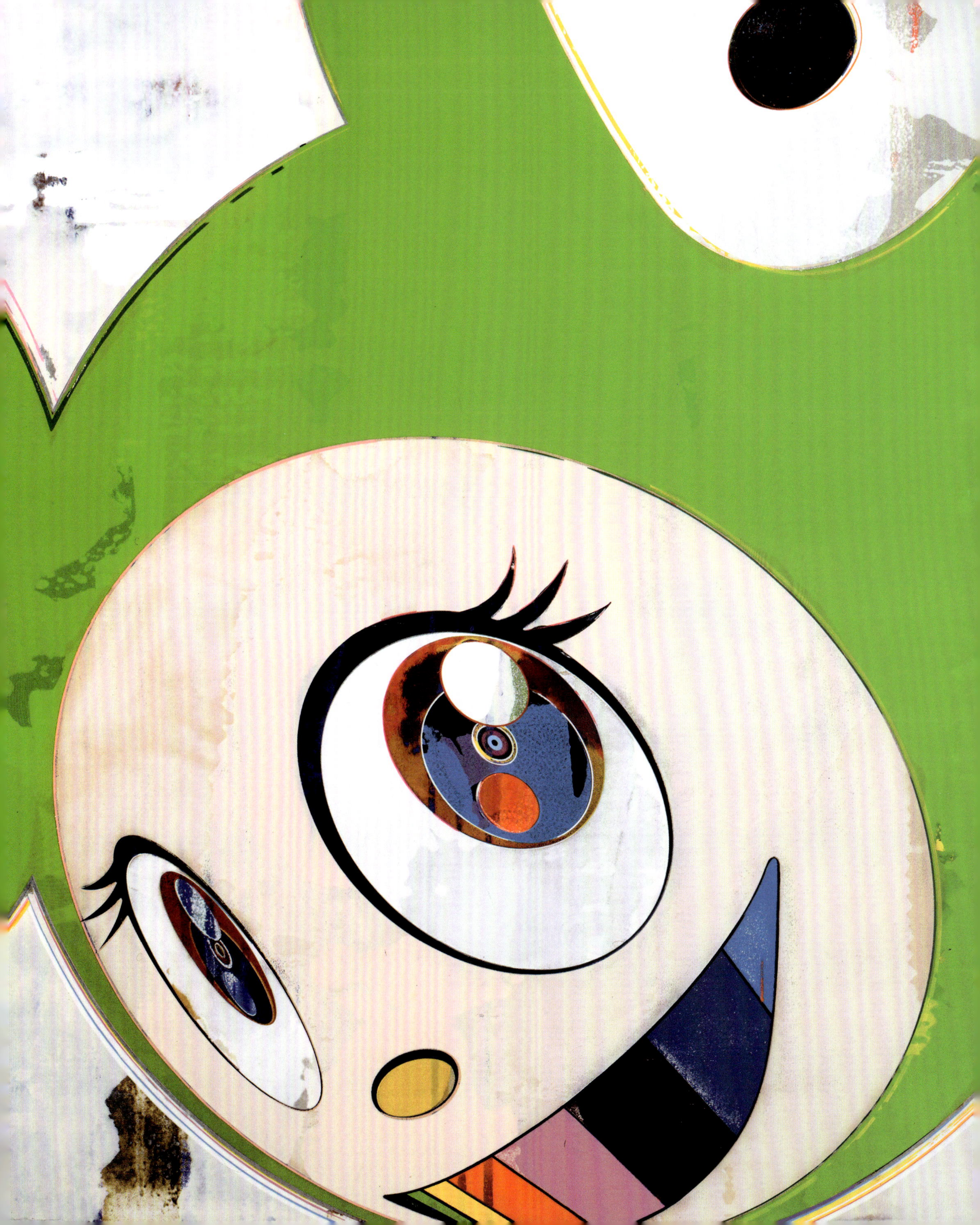

TO REALIZE HIS OWN HIGHLY individual style, the eccentric artist Itō Jakuchū internalized the lessons of both ancient and contemporary eighteenth-century Chinese bird-and-flower paintings. The naturalism of the cockatoo, with its meticulous handling of individual feathers built up in layers of shell white, recalls the avian forms in Qing-dynasty (1644–1911) scrolls that had entered Japan through Nagasaki at that time. In contrast, Jakuchū attacked the silk with broad strokes of ink that yield a two-dimensional, yet energized, setting for the refined bird. The result is a painting that visually shifts back and forth between two and three dimensions, in a manner that can frequently be found in Murakami's works as well.

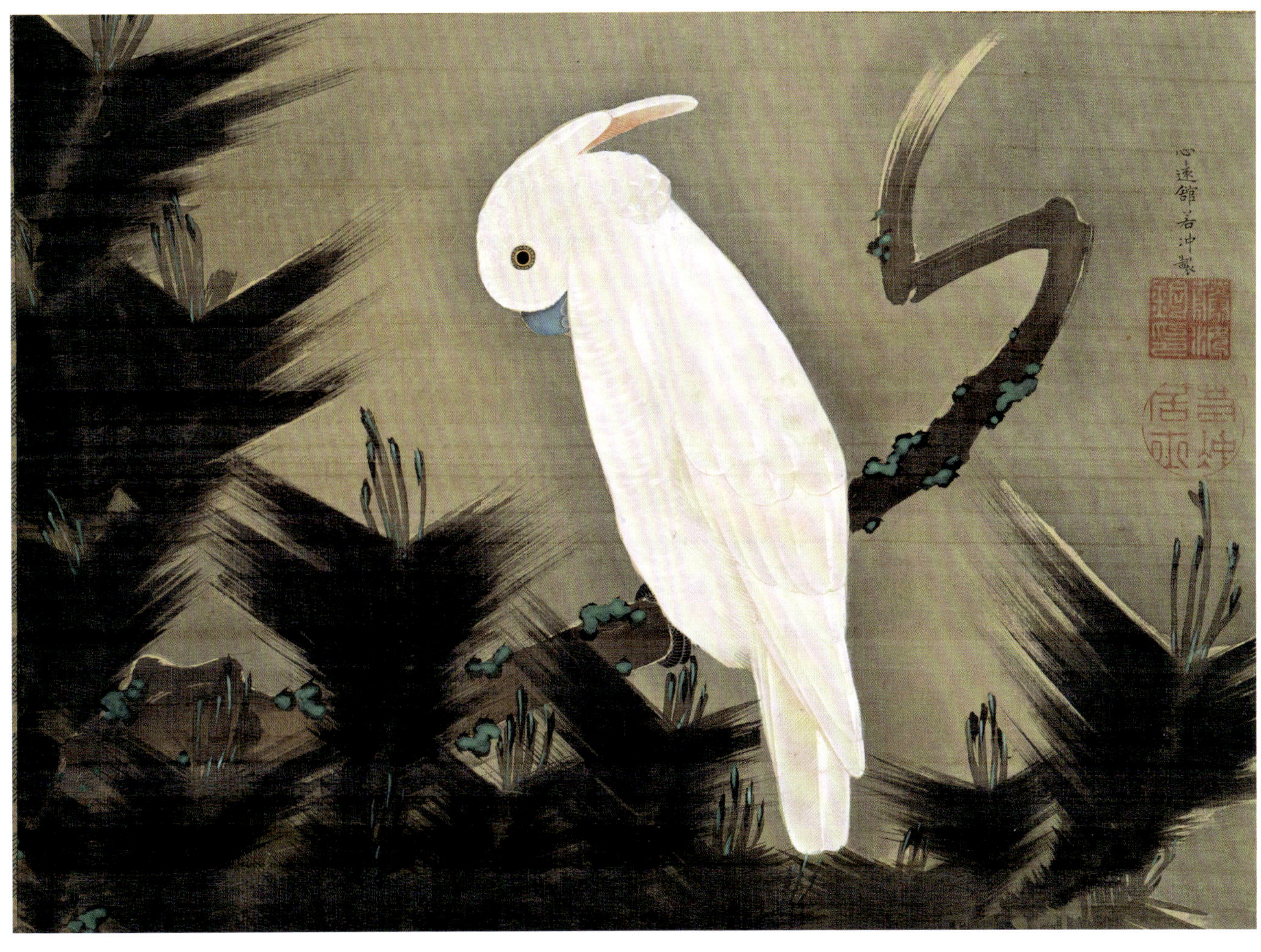

ITŌ JAKUCHŪ
(1716–1800)

White Cockatoo on a Pine Branch, Edo period, late 18th century
Hanging scroll; ink and color on silk, 40.1 × 55.6 cm (15 13/16 × 21 7/8 in.)
Museum of Fine Arts, Boston, Bequest of Charles Bain Hoyt—Charles Bain Hoyt Collection, 1950, 50.1493

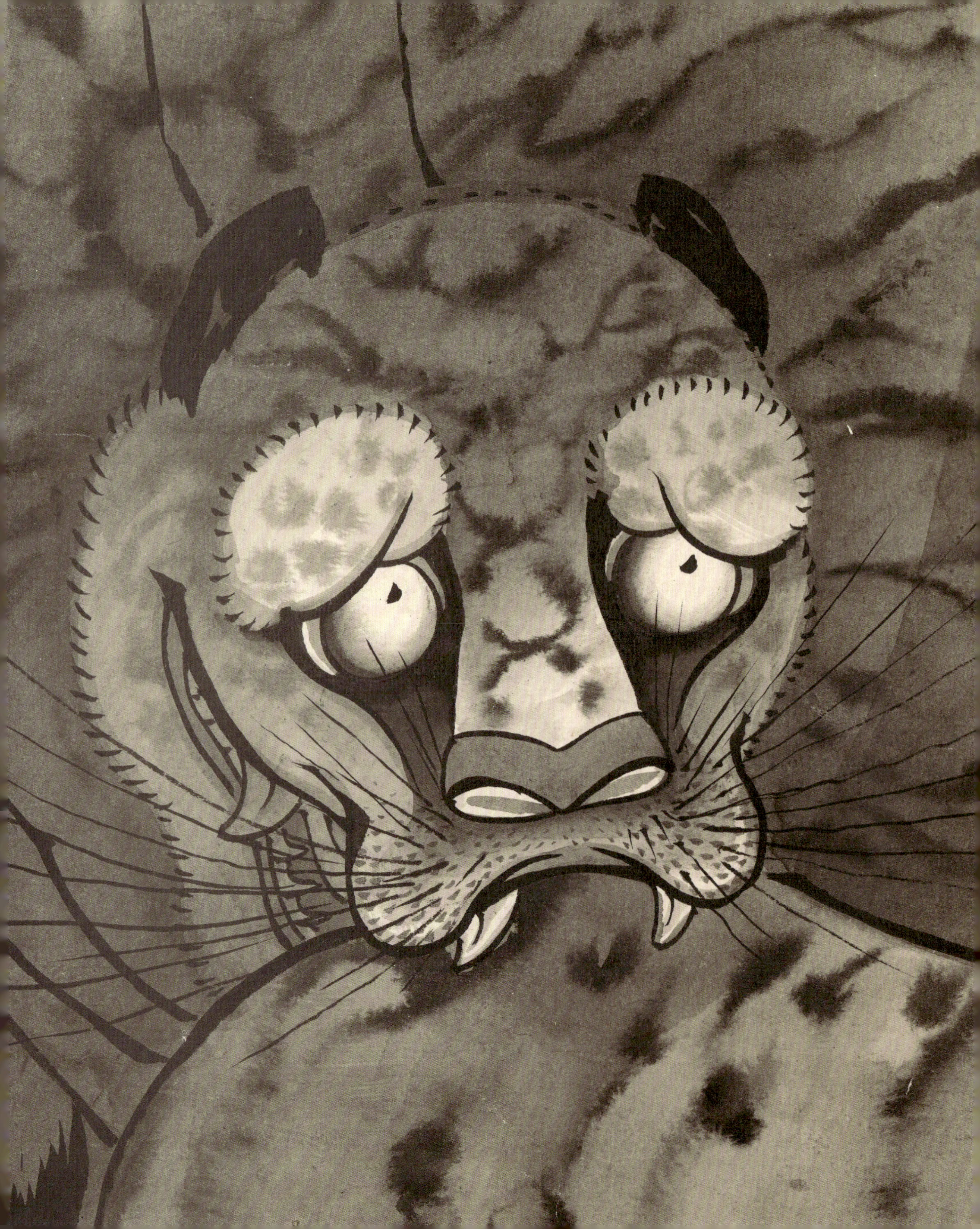

THE DRAGON AND TIGER represent the complementary forces of male and female, East and West. In Japan, a pair of hanging scrolls by the thirteenth-century Chinese artist Muqi, now in the collection of the Kyoto temple Daitokuji, inspired generations of artists. Soga Shōhaku's bizarre interpretation becomes almost a comic-book-like simplification, with the clouds overpowering the dragon and the tiger (right to left) reduced to a cowering, deflated skin. Shōhaku was always concerned with the handling of his brushstrokes—painting in a way that draws attention as much to his application of ink as it does to the forms the strokes describe.

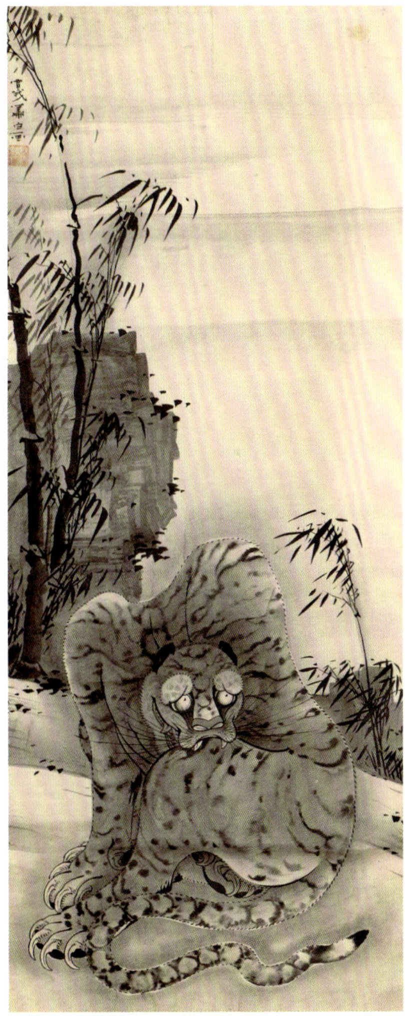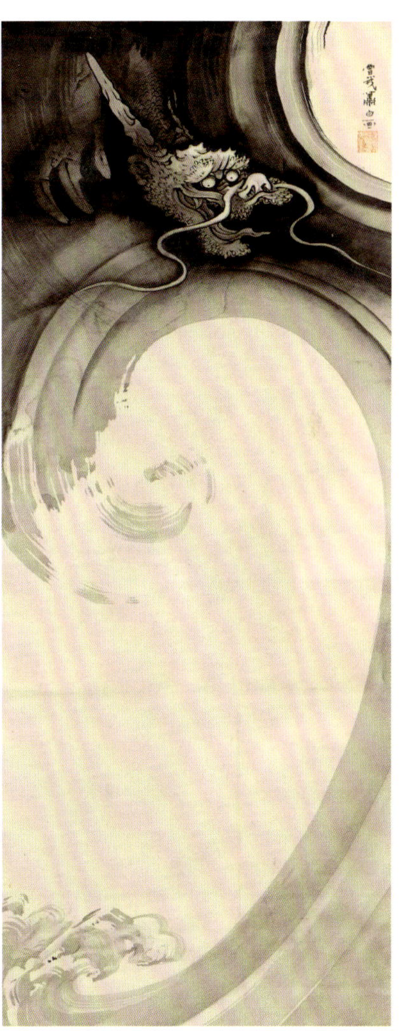

SOGA SHŌHAKU
(1730–1781)

Dragon and Tiger, Edo period, late 1770s
Pair of hanging scrolls; ink on paper, each 133.5 × 53.6 cm (52 9/16 × 21 1/8 in.)
Museum of Fine Arts, Boston, William Sturgis Bigelow Collection, 1911, 11.7051, 11.7052

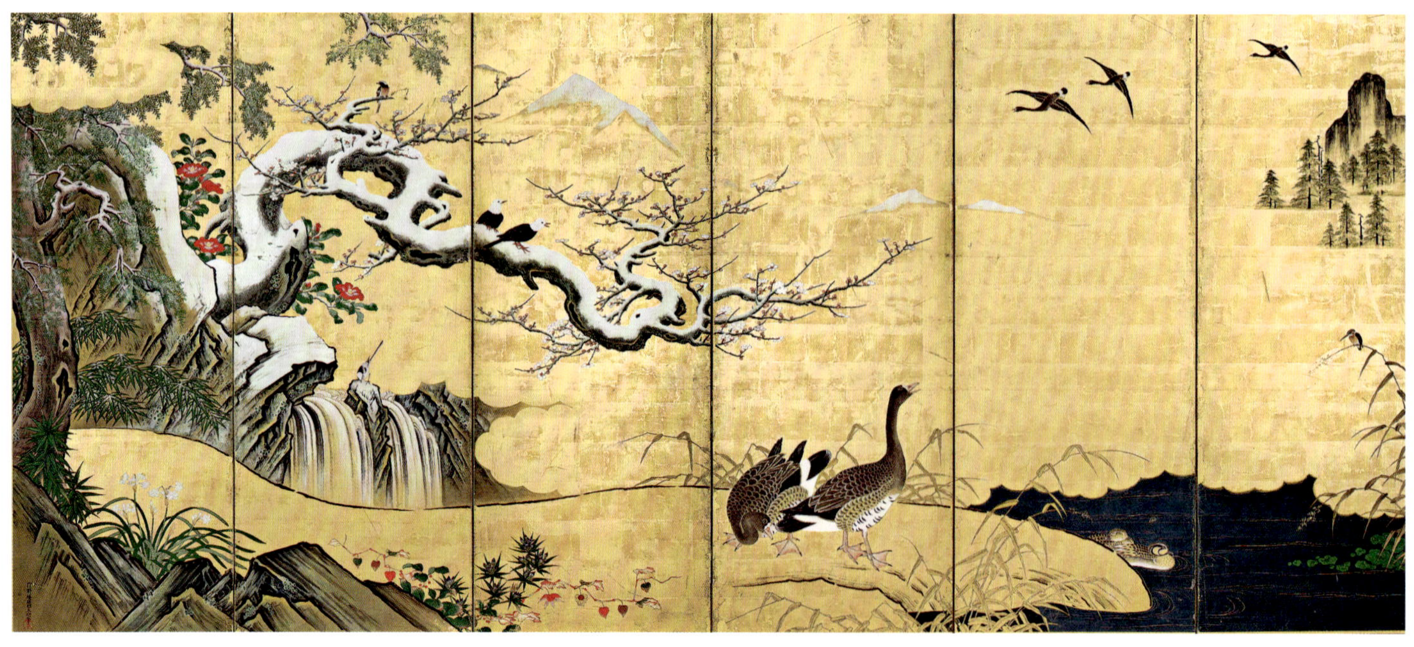

**KANO EINŌ
(1631–1697)**

Birds and Flowers of the Four Seasons, Edo period, latter half of the 17th century
Pair of six-panel folding screens; ink, color, and gold on paper, each about 1.6 × 3.7 m (63 ⅛ in. × 12 ft. 2 in.)
Museum of Fine Arts, Boston, Fenollosa-Weld Collection, 1911, 11.4431, 11.4430

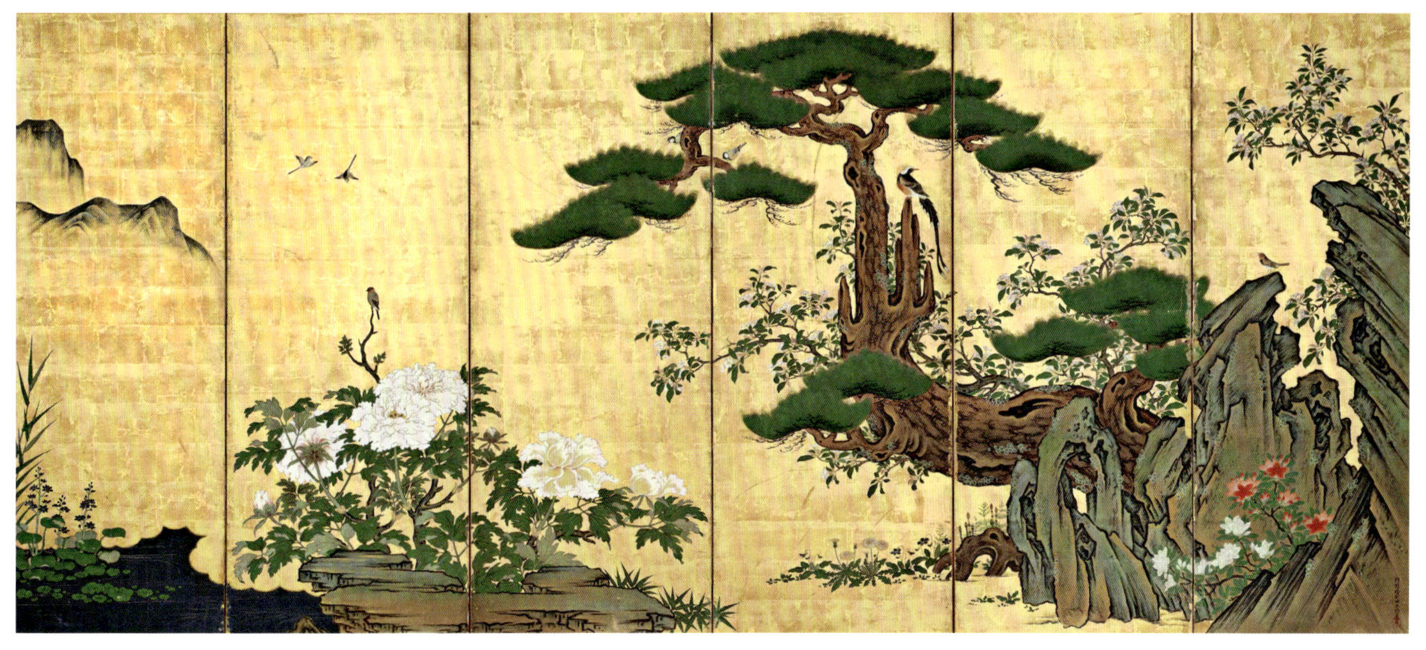

FLORA AND FAUNA of the four seasons progress in a continuous landscape
of foreground wetlands and distant mountains. Such monumental
compositions became part of the established repertoire of the Kano
school, the hereditary painters to the military aristocracy. However, under
Kano Sanraku and his descendants—his son, Sansetsu, and grandson,
Einō, who painted these screens—the foreground rocks and trees assumed
contorted, fantastic forms. Graded ink washes, suggesting recession,
gave way to assertive gold grounds that compress the foreground and
background into a theatrical display of floral decoration. The juxtaposition
of foreground forms extending horizontally across broad compositions and
two-dimensional surfaces is another feature that Murakami has adapted
for his contemporary subject matter.

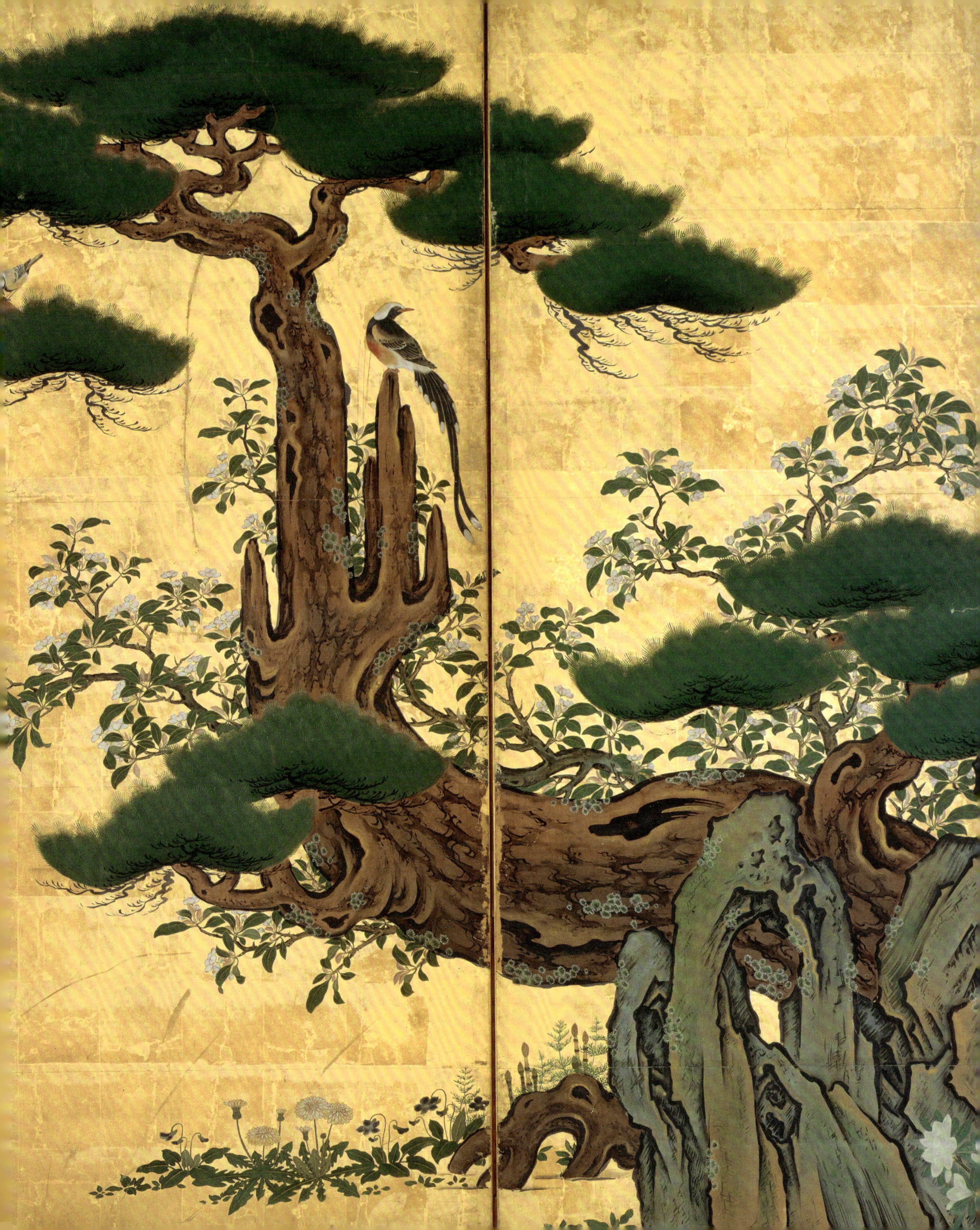

IMPOSSIBLE AIM was produced for Murakami's post-graduate exhibition, *Which Is Tomorrow—Fall in Love*, at SCAI the Bathhouse in Tokyo in 1994. The narrative for the painting was adapted from a twelfth-century story recounted by Nobuo Tsuji in *Lineage of the Eccentrics* about the esoteric practitioner Gisei. Known as a master of *oko*, or amusing drawings, Gisei painted only when he was in the mood. It is said that one day he was presented with a long, blank handscroll and pressured into composing something. Gisei responded by drawing a person shooting an arrow at one end and a target at the other. In between he added a single, continuous line to represent the arrow in flight. Then, to the consternation of the patron, he put his brush down.

TAKASHI MURAKAMI *Impossible Aim*, Heisei era, 1994
Acrylic, silver leaf, and silkscreen on canvas, about 80 cm × 8 m (31 ½ in. × 26 ft. 3 in.)
Courtesy of the artist

In this composition Takashi Murakami positioned a single figure of Mr. DOB, twanging bow in hand, at the left edge; at the other end, he drew Mr. DOB darting from an arrow flying directly at him. Between the two he left a vast expanse of silver leaf, which has traditionally appeared in Japanese screens as a flat, shimmering surface, but here also serves as a critical element of the narrative. Murakami has noted that another inspiration for this composition was a sixty-five-foot horizontal canvas by Gerhard Richter entitled *Yellow Stroke (On Blue)* (1974), in which a powerful, calligraphic gesture in yellow pigment extends across a mottled background of red and blue.

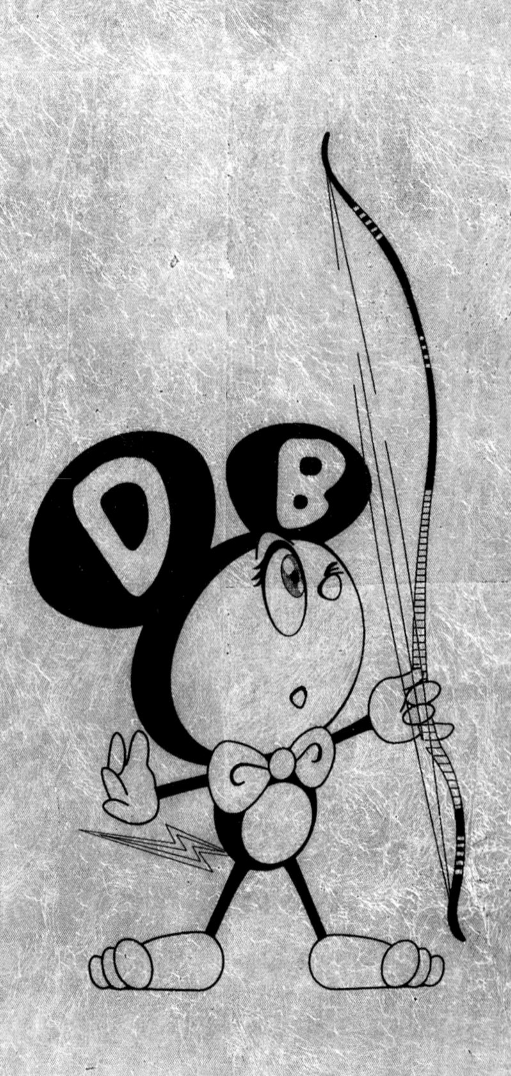

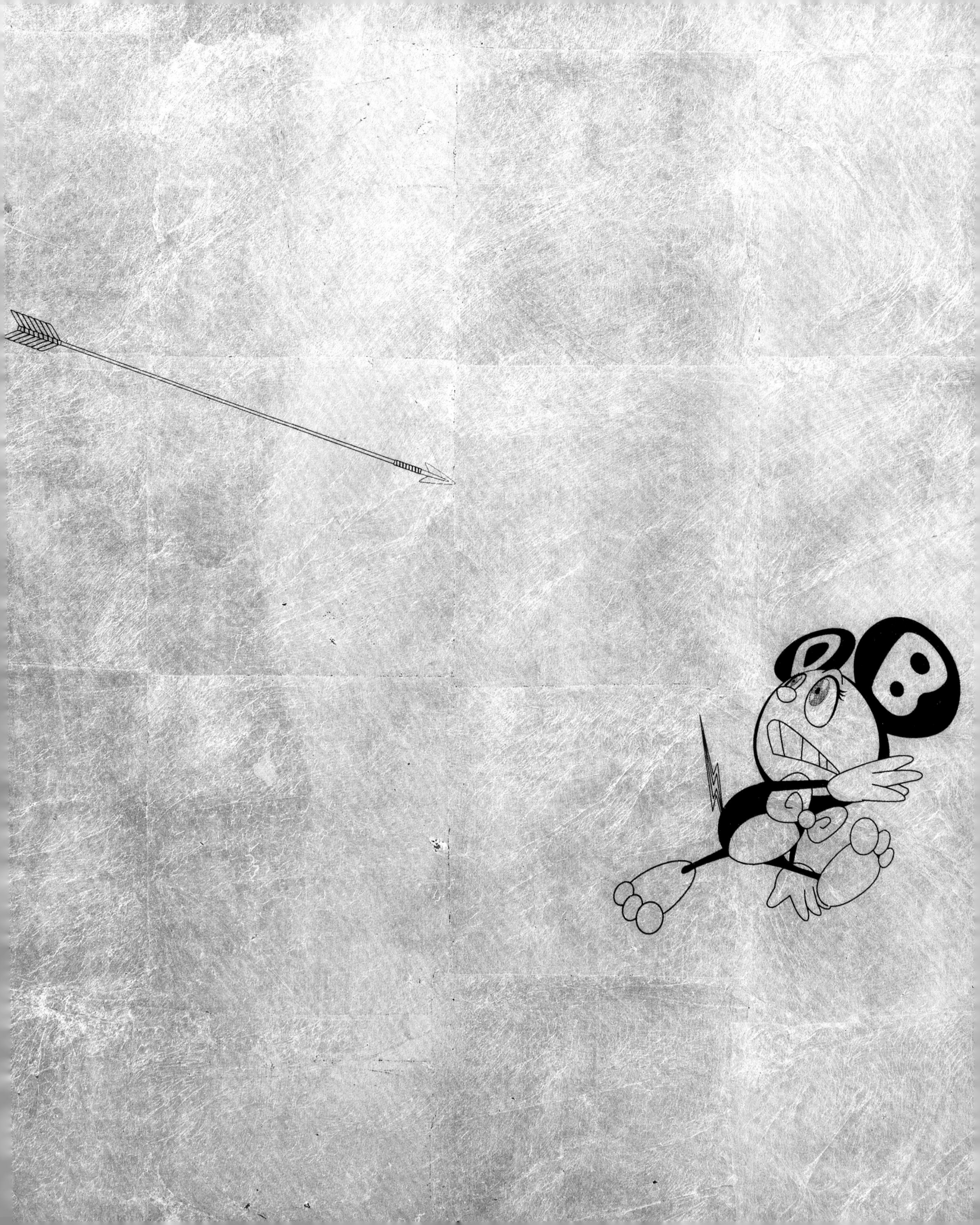

2

ANIMA TION

Murakami argues that his paintings belong to a line of image making that extends from the Edo-period Eccentric artists up through contemporary Japanese anime directors. In animated films, Murakami finds resonant compositional devices that compress the distance between objects, thereby flattening the foreground, middle ground, and background.

Tsuji has long noted that although Japanese anime have been influenced by Western filmmaking, their visual strategies can also be found in twelfth- and thirteenth-century Japanese handscrolls. In these works, the narrative is composed across multiple sheets of joined paper, read from right to left as the scroll is unrolled. The format leads to a sequential presentation of the passage of time and a spatial compression, since the artists are obligated to create their compositions within the borders of the narrow sheets. The narrative unfolds as the viewer unrolls and rolls the scroll, thus privileging a two-dimensional, lateral organization of space and composition. In many of these handscrolls, artists use devices such as the repetition of figures and the whirring of carriage wheels to create a proto-cinematic effect.

These medieval handscrolls were created by groups of artists led by a master, who conceived the original composition. Specialists were tasked with architectural details and the representation of human figures and animals. Similarly, Takashi Murakami directs the production of his large-scale works by providing the initial design, then delegating the execution of the details of the paintings to members of the Kaikai Kiki studio, while carefully supervising the production of the canvases.

FOR HIS LARGE-SCALE PAINTINGS, Murakami works as a master artist in
a tradition that stretches back centuries: developing each work's concept;
making assignments and supervising its execution by members of his
studio; and refining elements of the composition as the painting takes
shape. Throughout the process the Kaikai Kiki studio takes meticulous
care in documenting the developments, noting the dating (down to the
minute) of each alteration. These sketches chronicle the studio's evolving
approach to the eighty-two-foot-long *In the Land of the Dead, Stepping
on the Tail of a Rainbow,* now at The Broad in Los Angeles (see pp. 36–37).

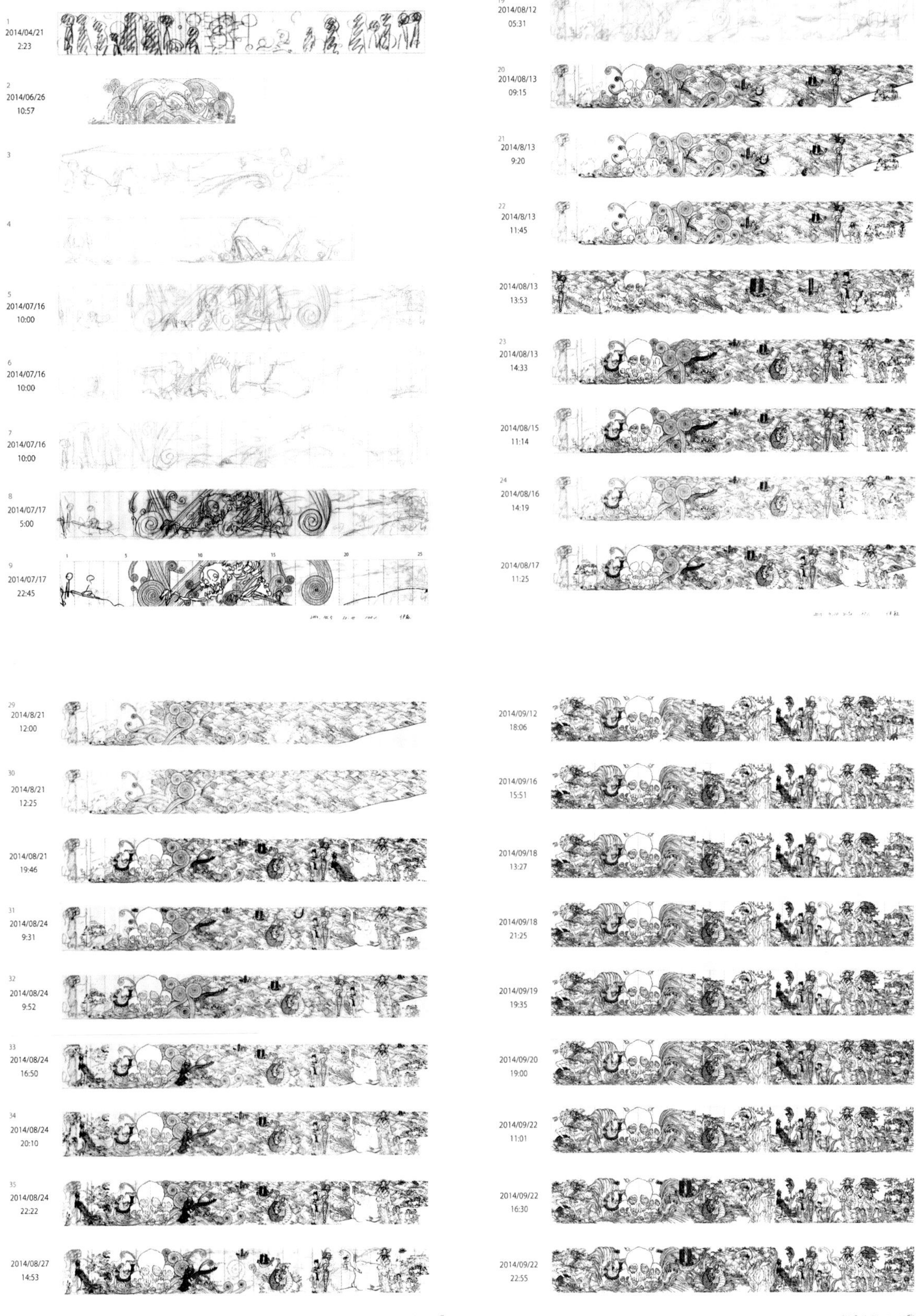

群仙図 全体像アーカイブ（データ）
2015/09/09

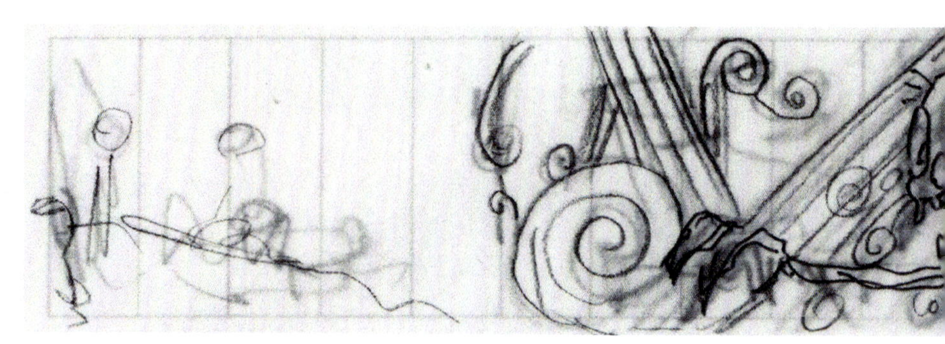

8
2014/07/17
5:00

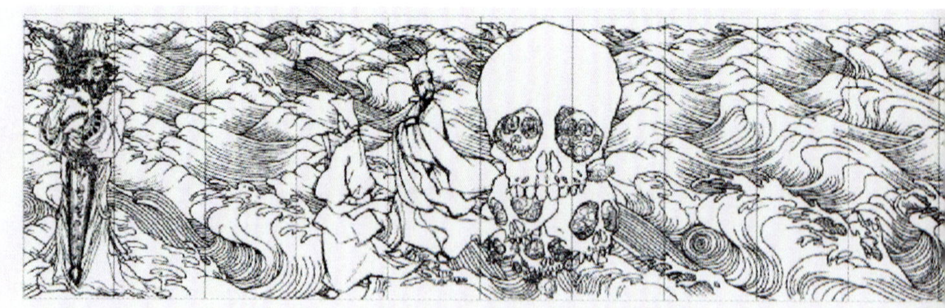

2014/08/13
13:53

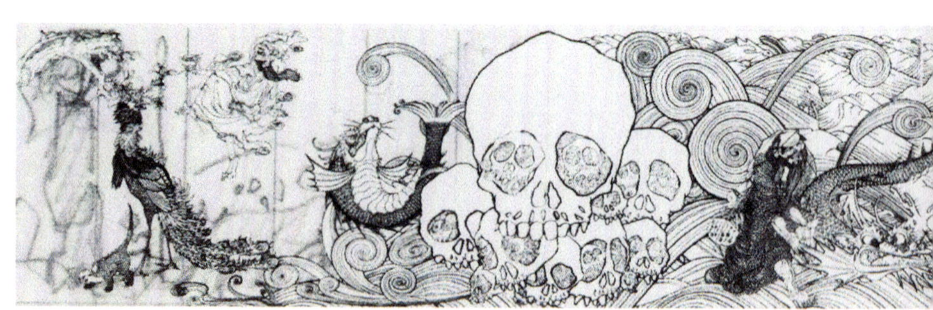

33
2014/08/24
16:50

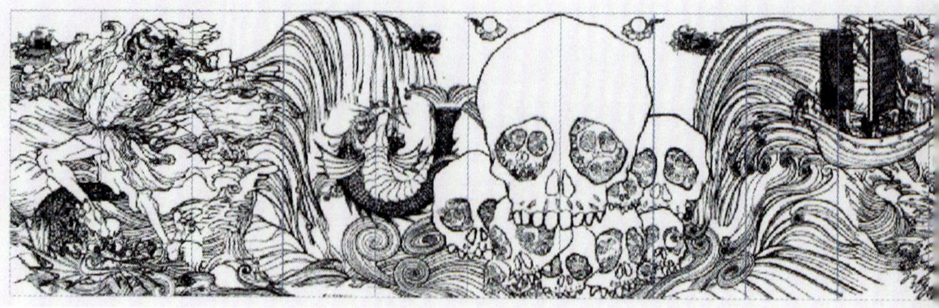

2014/09/22
22:55

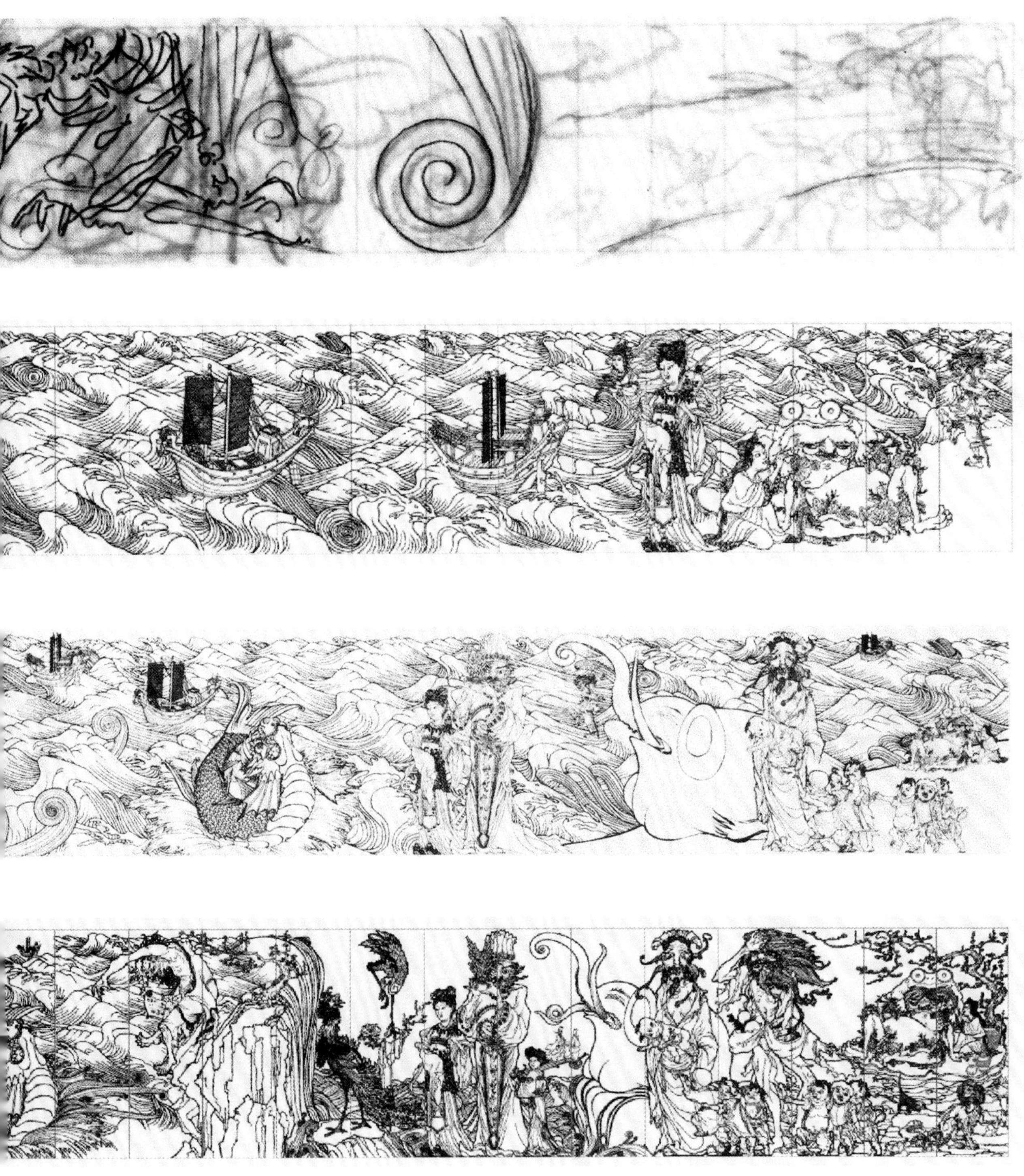

TAKASHI MURAKAMI

In the Land of the Dead, Stepping on the Tail of a Rainbow project documentation, figure at left border, Heisei era, 2014
Laser print collage, with hand-applied black and colored inks and corrective white, overall 43.5 × 41.6 cm (17 ⅛ × 16 ⅜ in.)
Courtesy of the artist

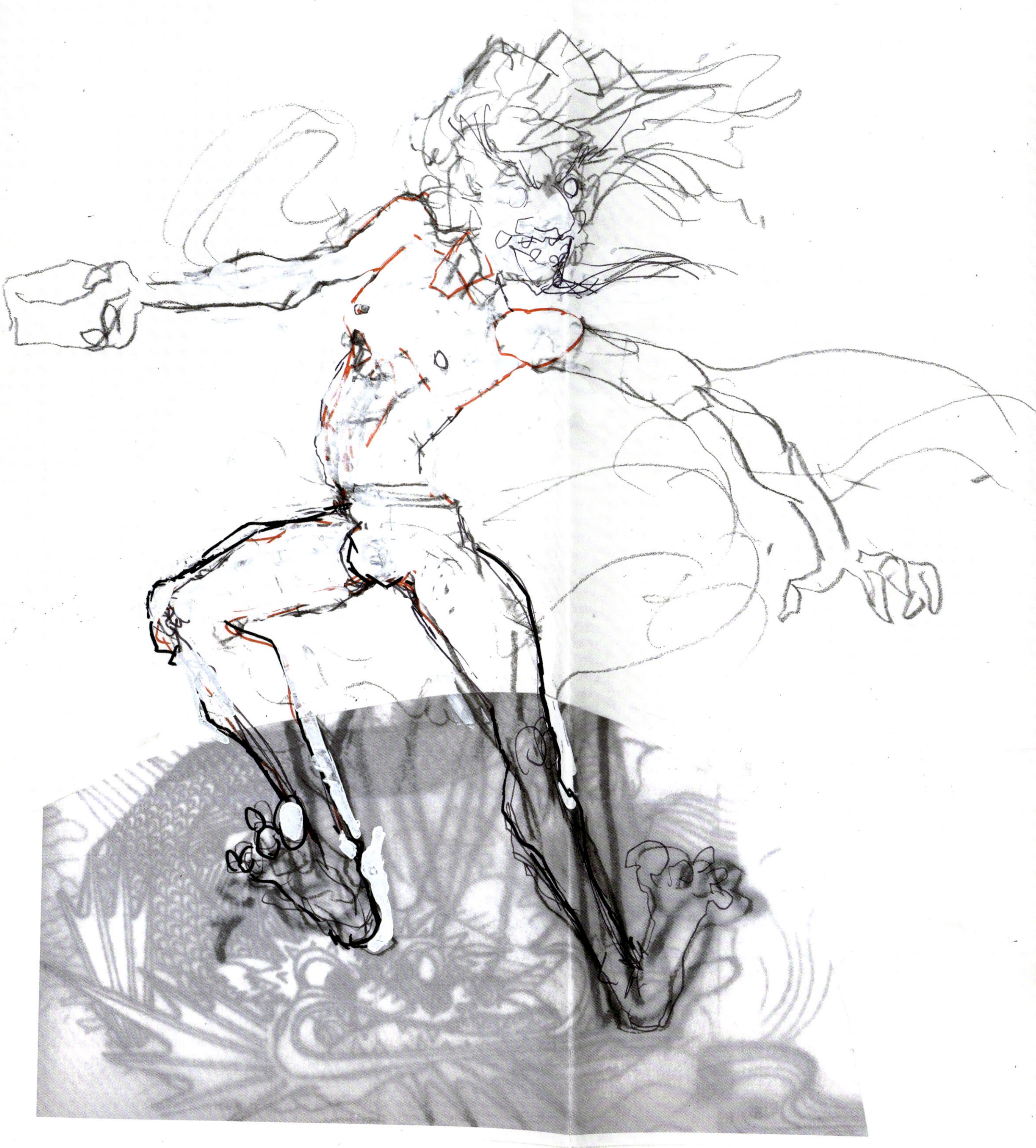

IN THE CENTER OF *In the Land of the Dead*, Murakami has adapted the form of a fish from the thirteenth-century narrative handscroll *Legends of the Kegon Sect (Kegon engi)*; it is a form that he has repeated in *Transcendent Attacking a Whirlwind* (see pp. 40–42). To this, he has added a manga-inspired starburst.

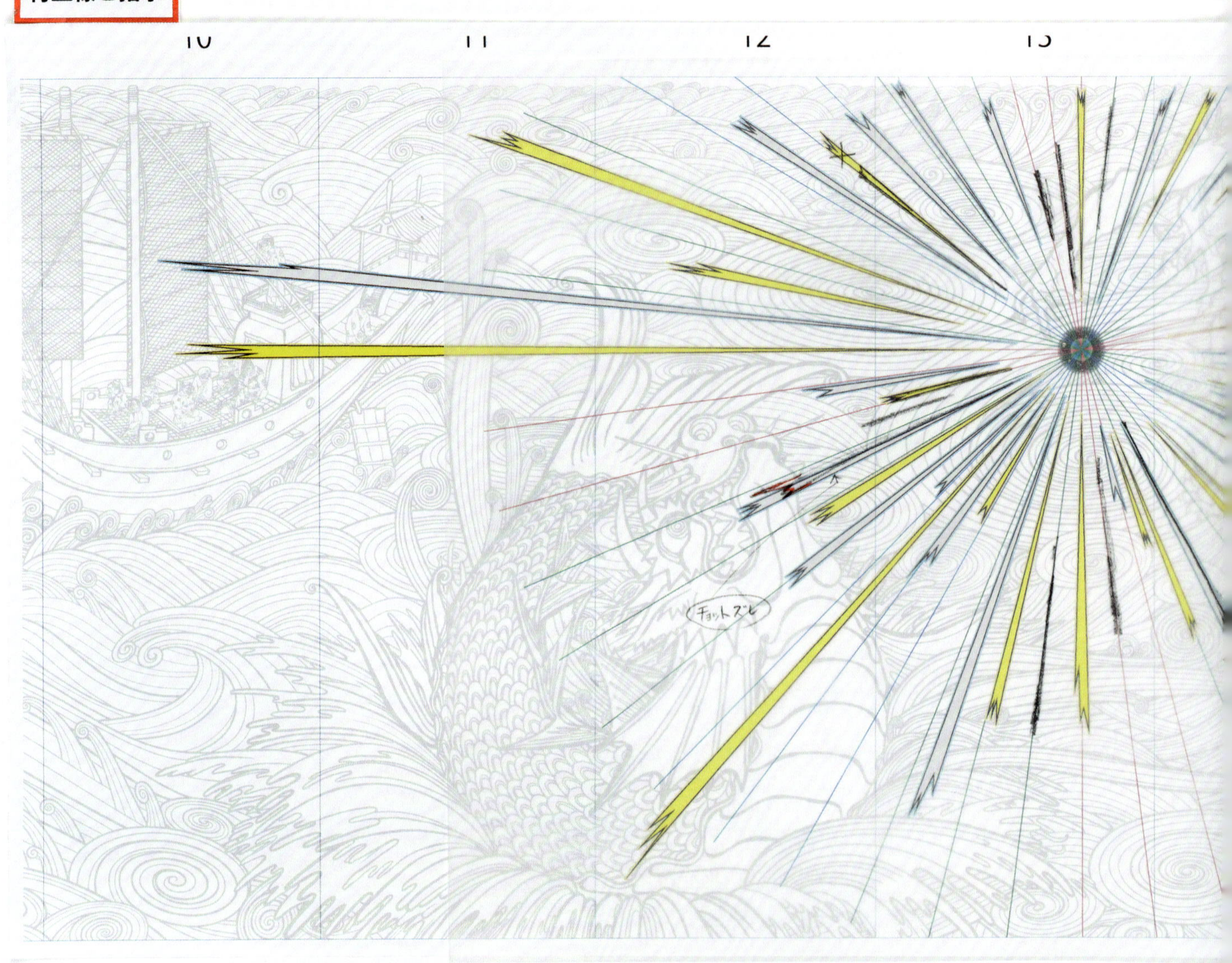

TAKASHI MURAKAMI

In the Land of the Dead, Stepping on the Tail of a Rainbow project documentation, orb 2014: 9-5 9:53
Taped together laser print, tracing paper overlay with graphite and red ink additions, and self-adhesive tab with notation, overall 29.5 × 42.7 cm (11 ⅝ × 16 ¹³⁄₁₆ in.)
Courtesy of the artist

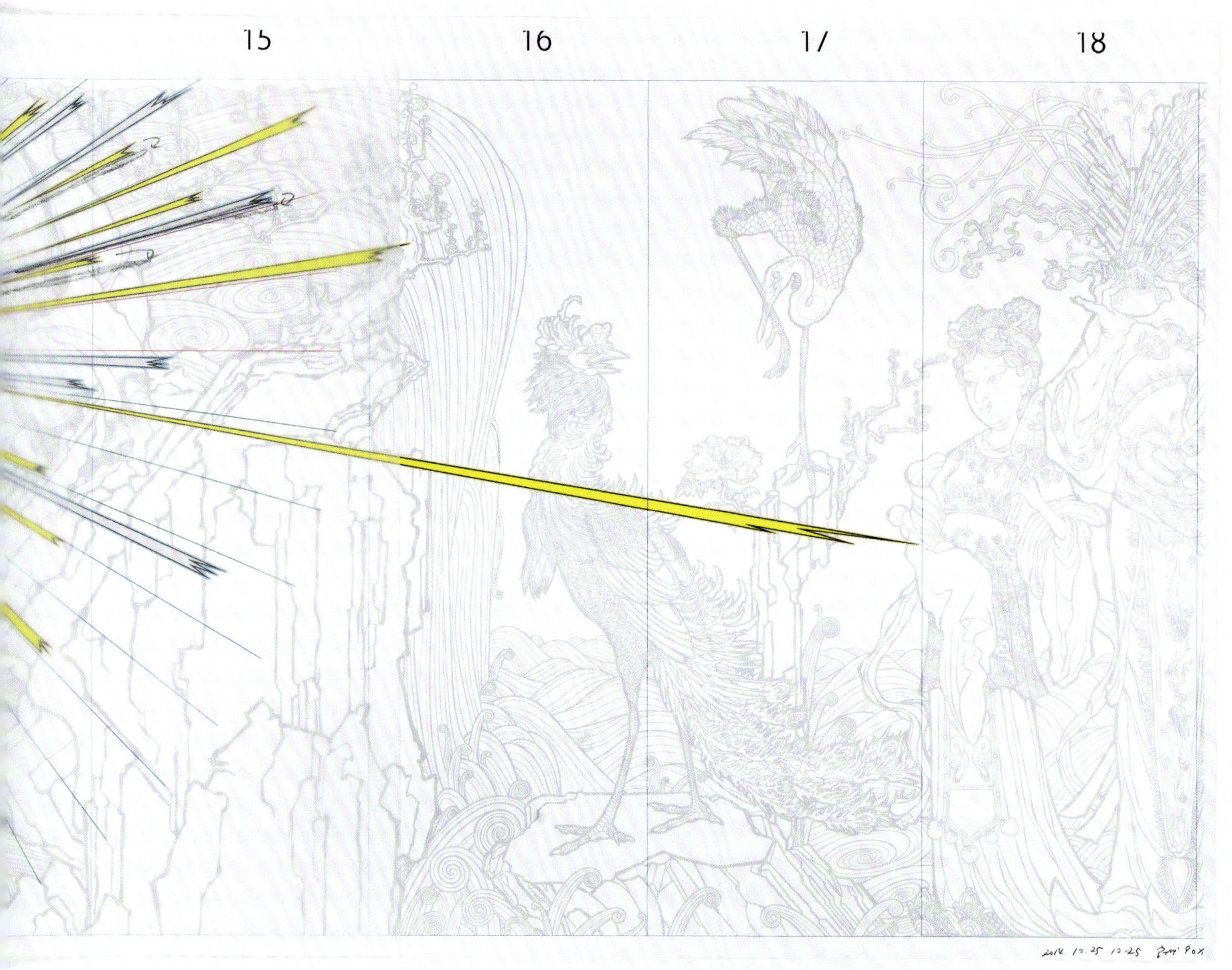

15
16
17
18

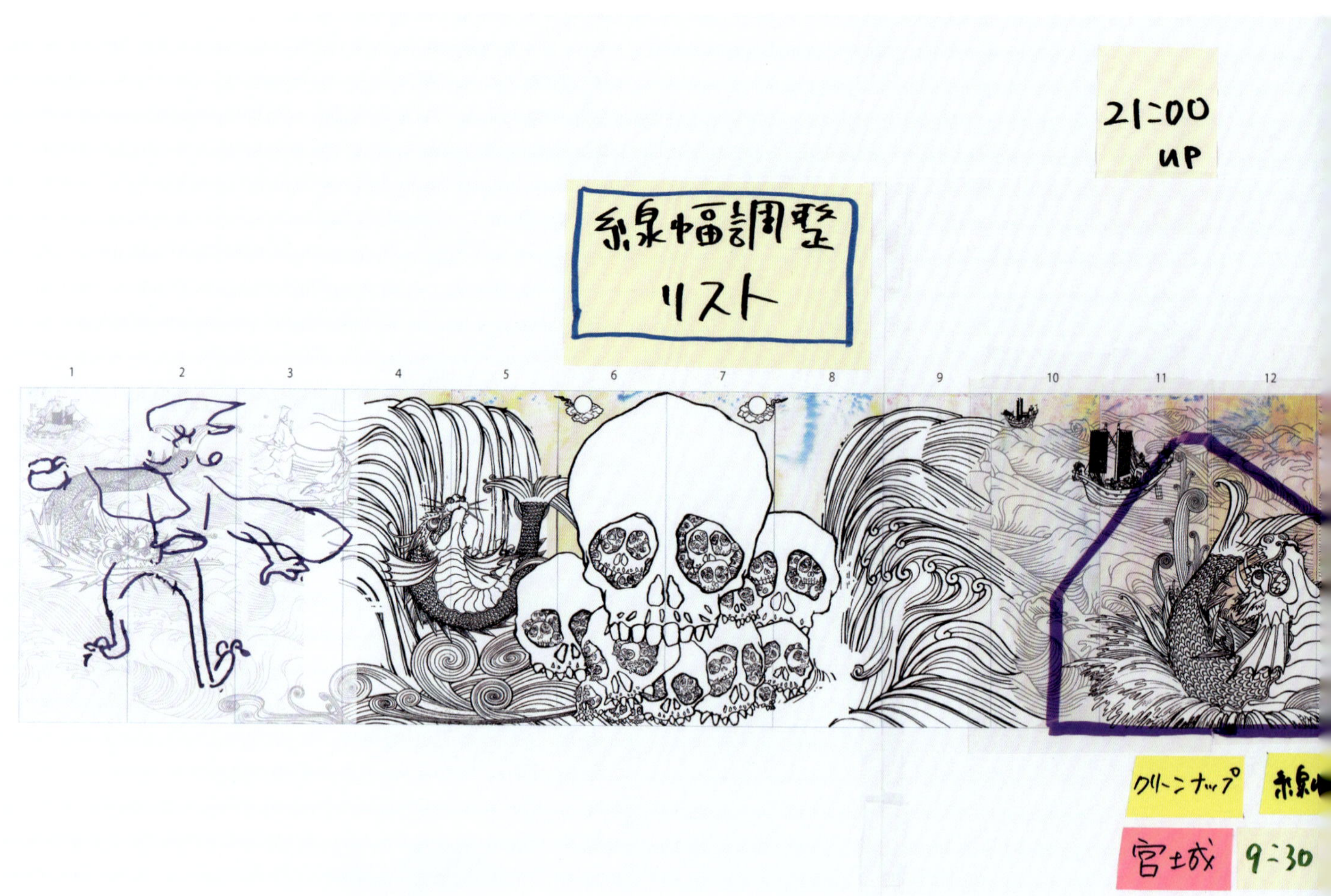

TAKASHI MURAKAMI

In the Land of the Dead, Stepping on the Tail of a Rainbow project documentation, work distribution 2014: 10-25 10:25
Taped together laser print, transparent film overlays with colored ink markings and colored self-adhesive tabs with
notations, overall 29.6 × 115.4 cm (11 ⅝ × 45 ⁷⁄₁₆ in.)
Courtesy of the artist

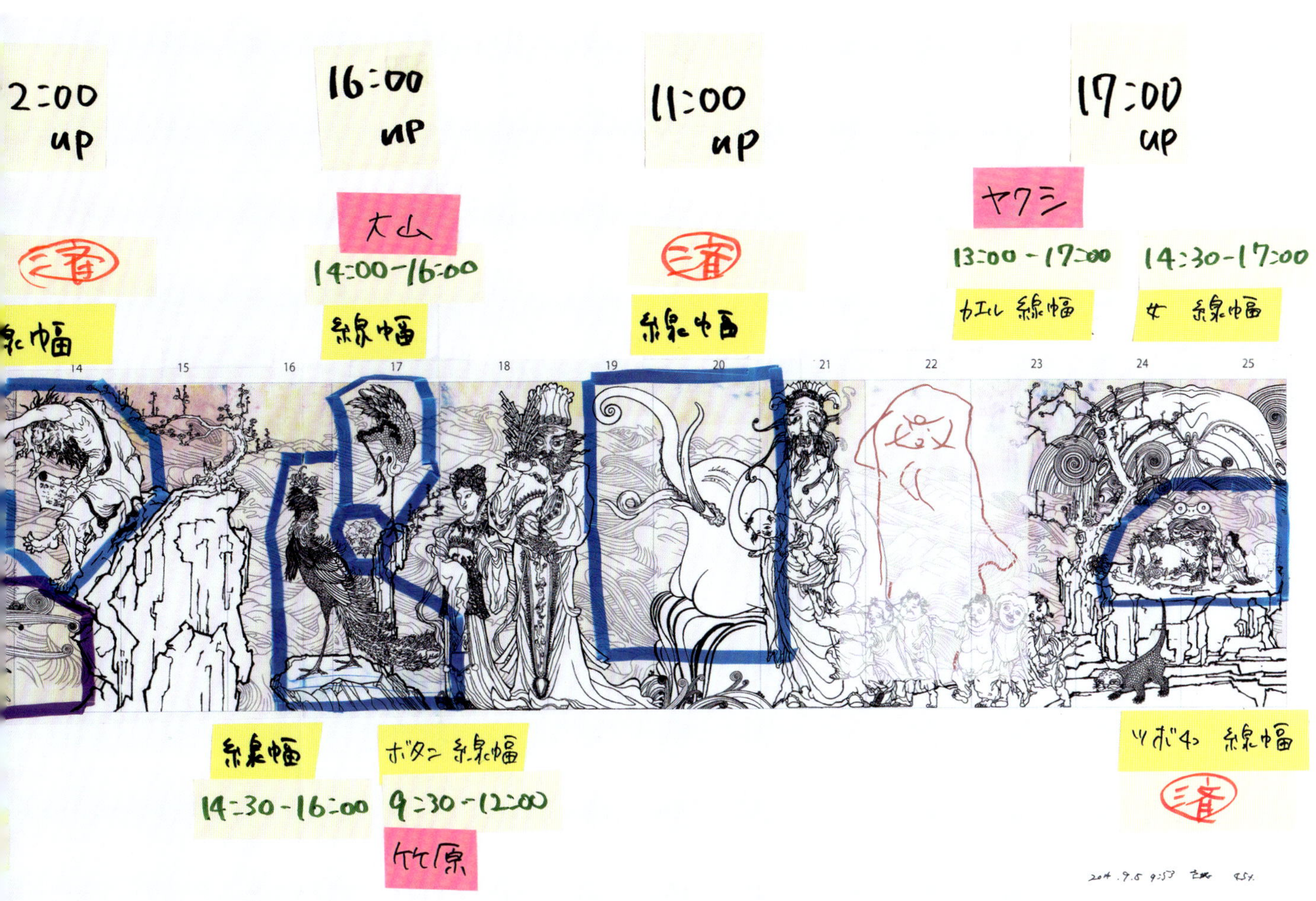

2:00
up

16:00
up

11:00
up

17:00
up

大山
14:00-16:00

ヤクシ
13:00-17:00

14:30-17:00

三済

三済

線幅

線幅

線幅

カエル 線幅

女 線幅

14 15 16 17 18 19 20 21 22 23 24 25

線幅

ボタン 線幅

14:30-16:00

9:30-12:00

竹原

ツボネ 線幅

三済

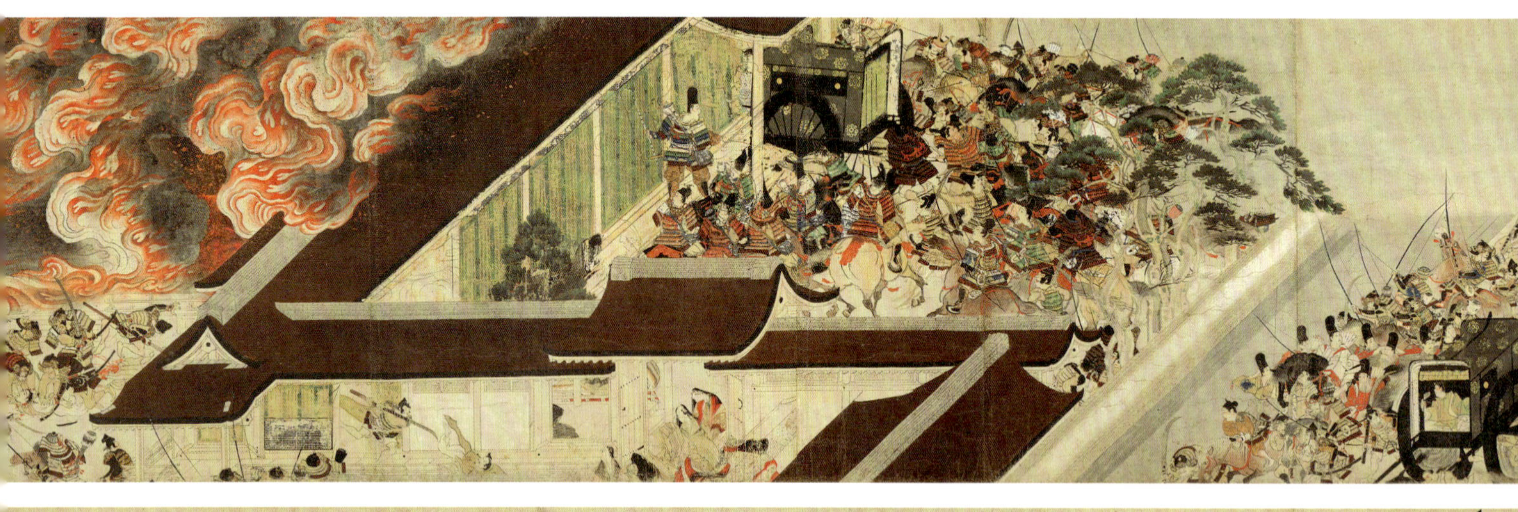
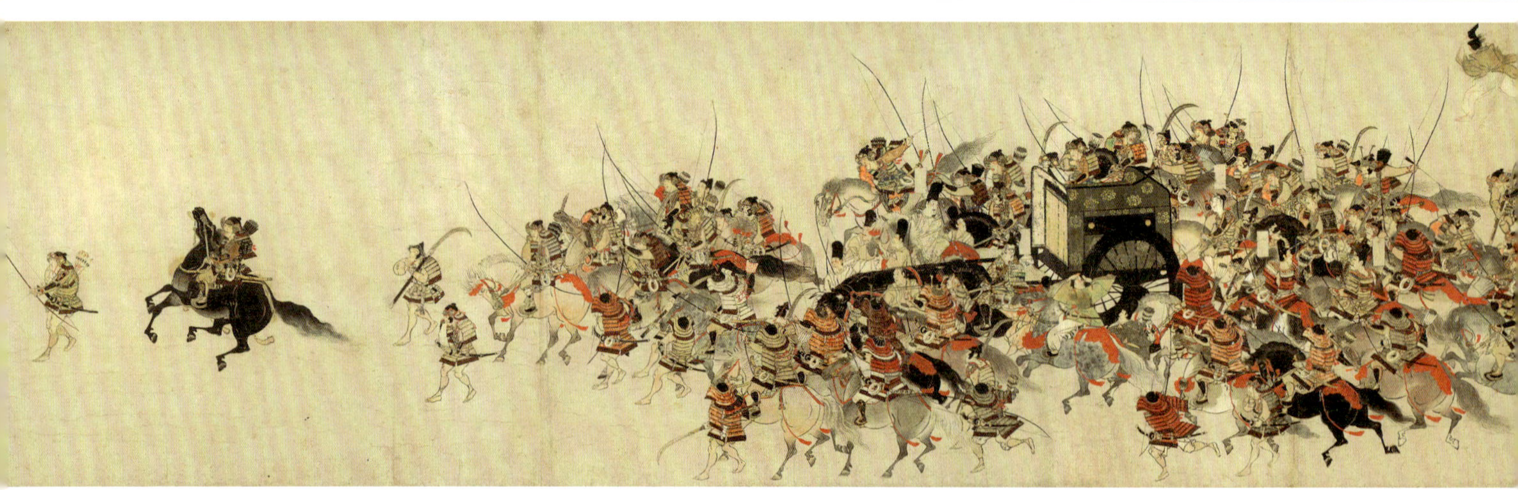

Night Attack on the Sanjō Palace, from the *Illustrated Scrolls of the Events of the Heiji Era* (*Heiji monogatari emaki*), Kamakura period, second half of the 13th century. Handscroll; ink and color on paper, about 41.3 cm × 7 m (16 ¼ in. × 22 ft. 11 in.)

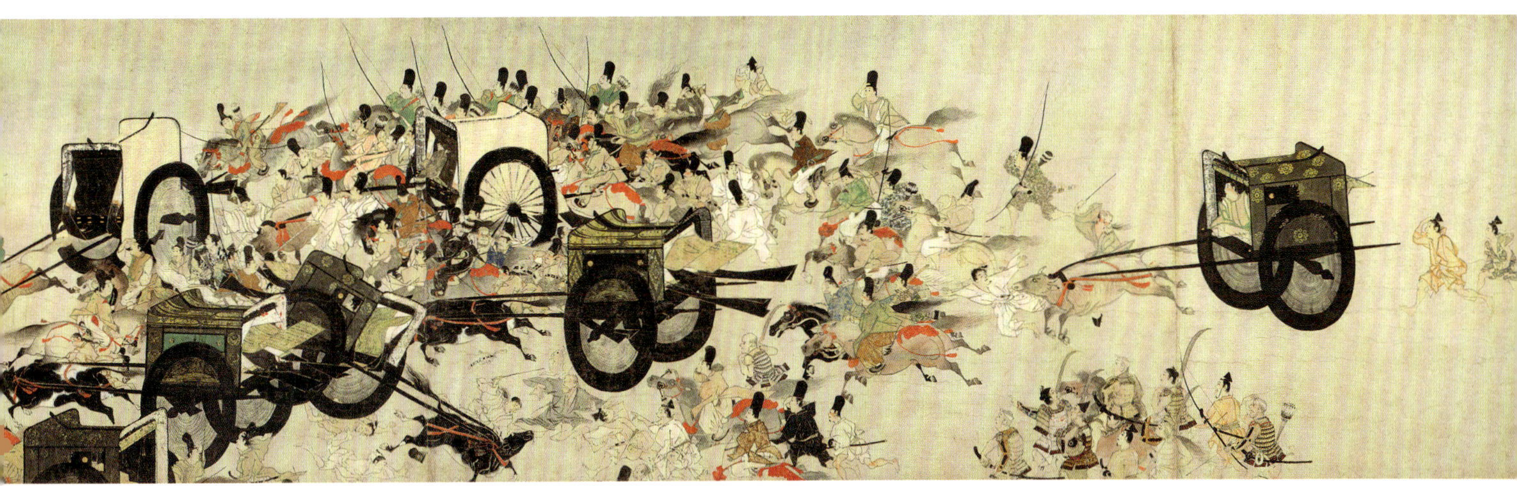

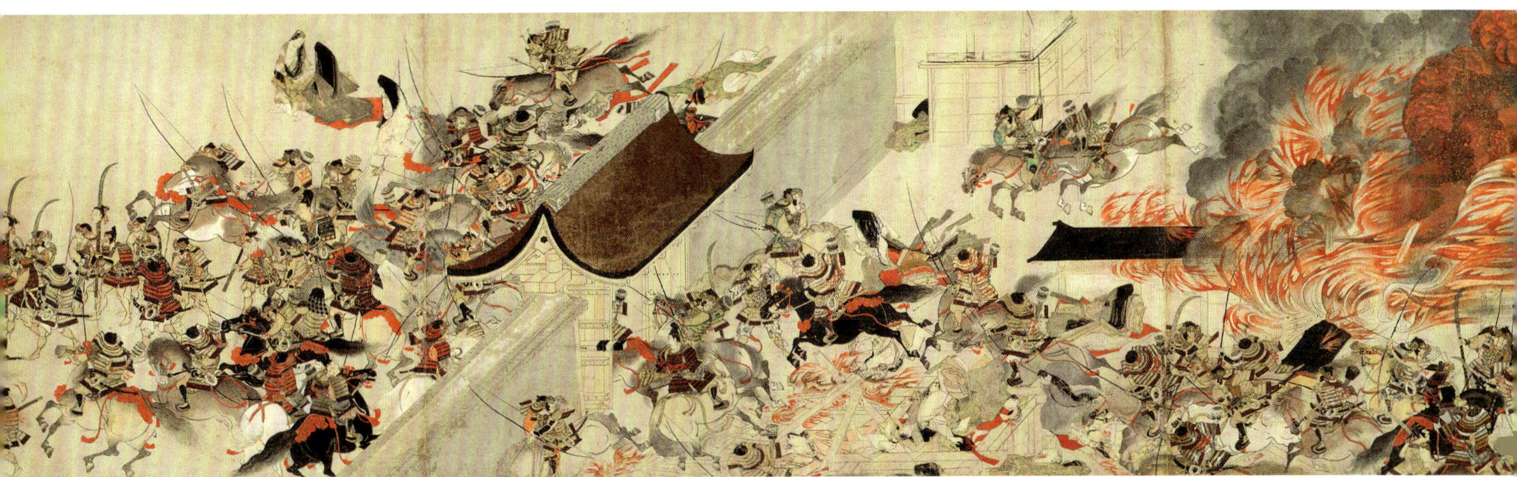

UNIVERSALLY ACCLAIMED AS the most powerful battle scene in all of Japanese art, *Night Attack on the Sanjō Palace* chronicles retired emperor Go-Shirakawa's violent abduction from his residence in 1159. The event took place during the Heiji Rebellion, one of a number of civil wars in the second half of the twelfth century that marked the end of aristocratic rule and the rise of governance by the military. Progressing in time and space, the scroll begins at right with a text describing an early morning attack by several hundred warriors under the leadership of the upstart courtier Fujiwara no Nobuyori and his henchman Minamoto no Yoshitomo.

Like a film director, the master artist has carefully orchestrated the illustration of the sequence of events in a long, continuous narrative that heightens the drama. In the initial sections members of the court race to the Sanjō Palace in their oxen-driven carriages as word spreads about the imminent confrontation. The wheels on their vehicles spin so fast that the artist has indicated the motion with blurred lines, an early attempt at animation. The abduction of Go-Shirakawa and the assault of the members of the court take place within the compressed architectural framework of the palace compound. Clouds of black smoke and forked tongues of flames explode from the structure that has been torched by the attackers. To the left the marauding warriors recongregate around the carriage bearing the retired emperor and move on to their next conflict.

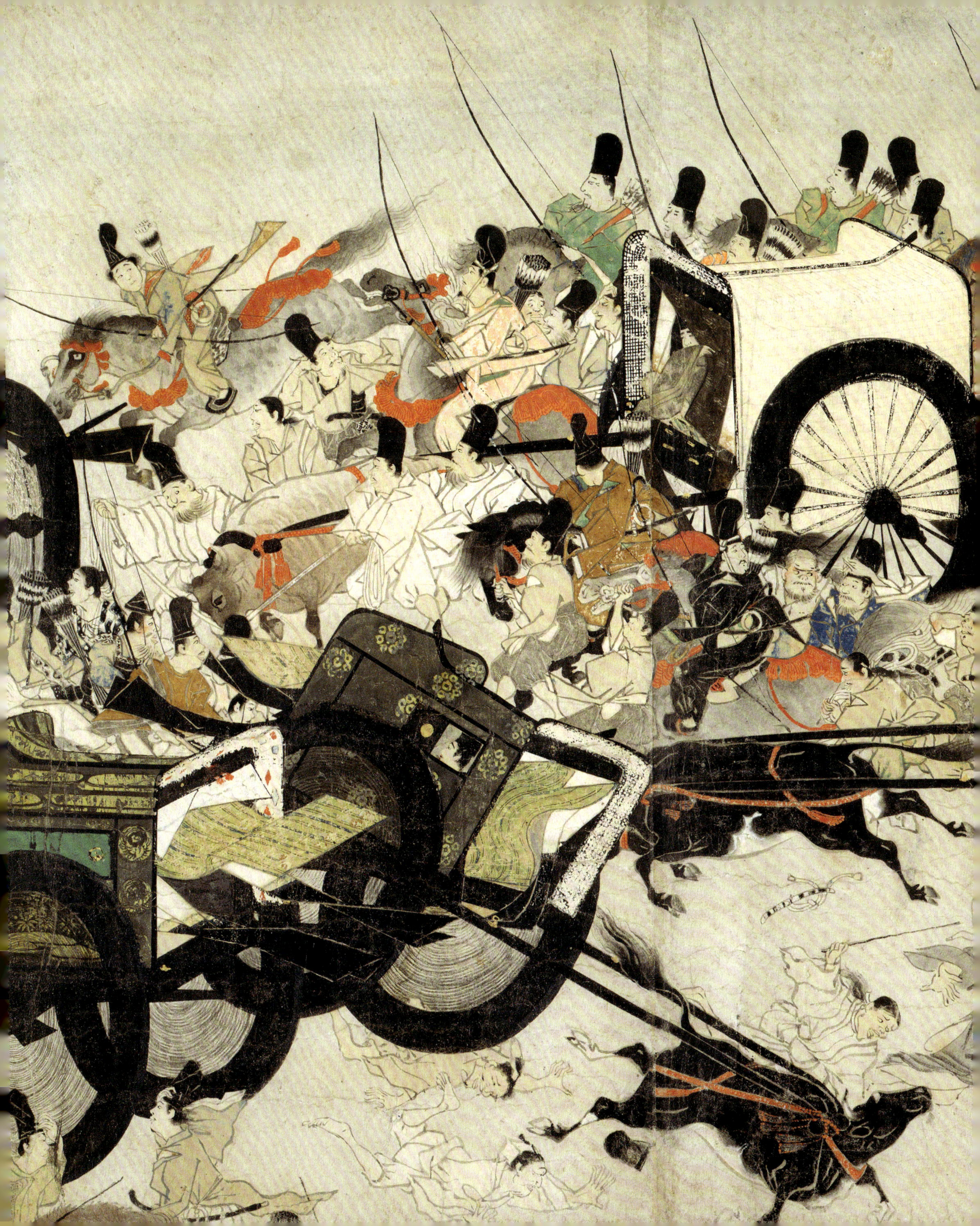

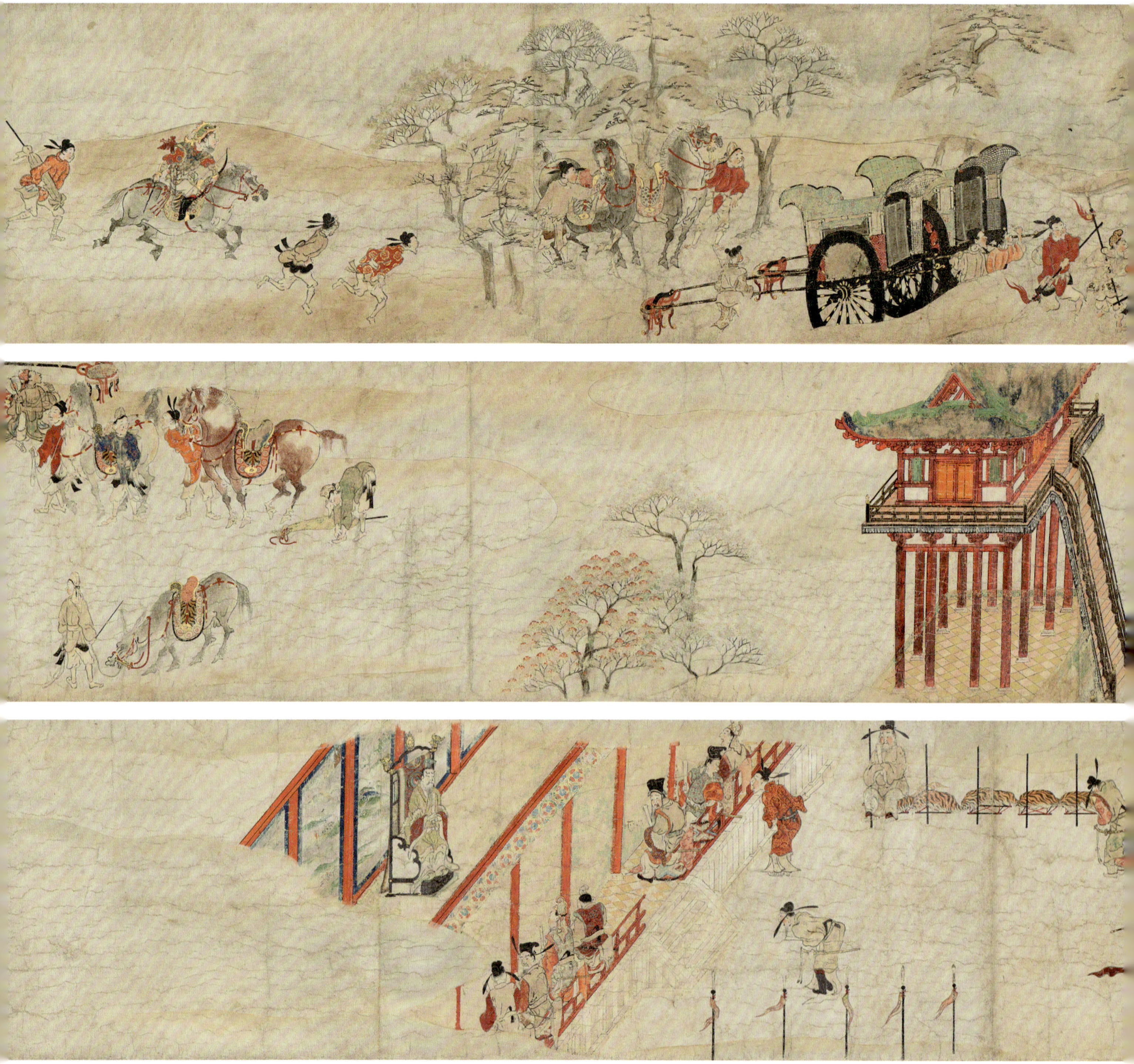

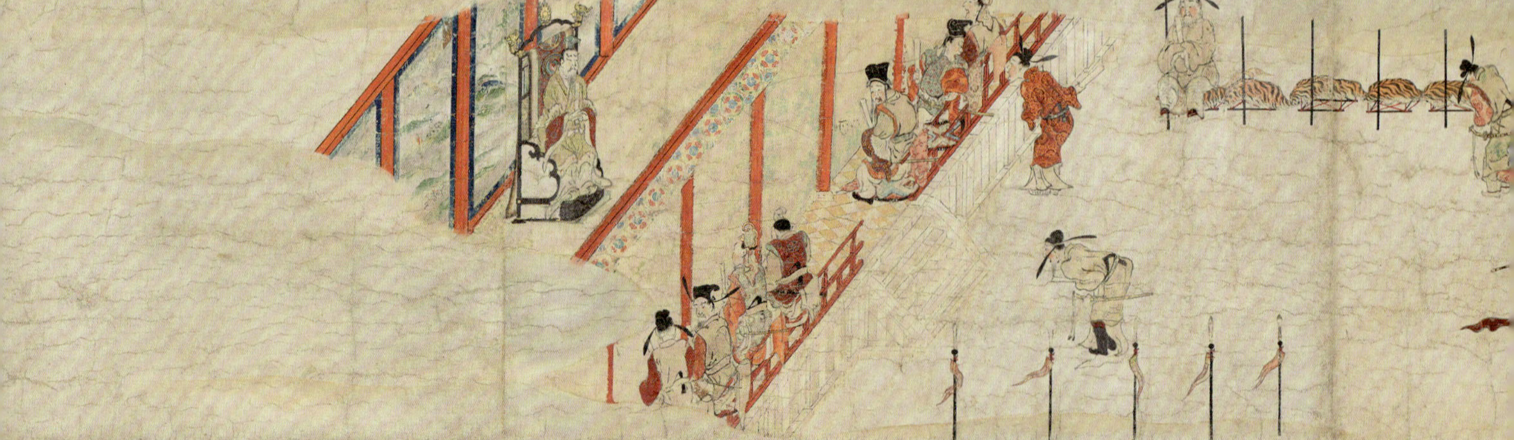

Minister Kibi's Adventures in China (*Kibi daijin nittō emaki*), scroll 1, Heian period, 12th century
One of four handscrolls; ink, color, and gold on paper, about 32 cm × 6.7 m (12 ⅝ in. × 22 ft. 2 in.)
Museum of Fine Arts, Boston, William Sturgis Bigelow Collection by Exchange, 1932, 32.131.1

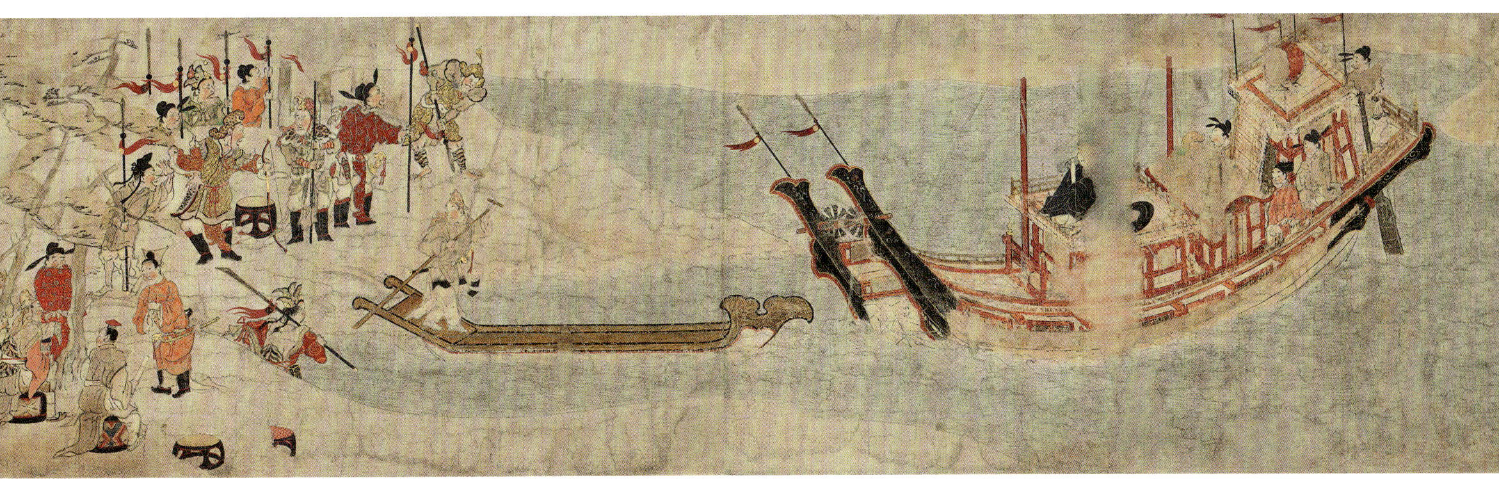

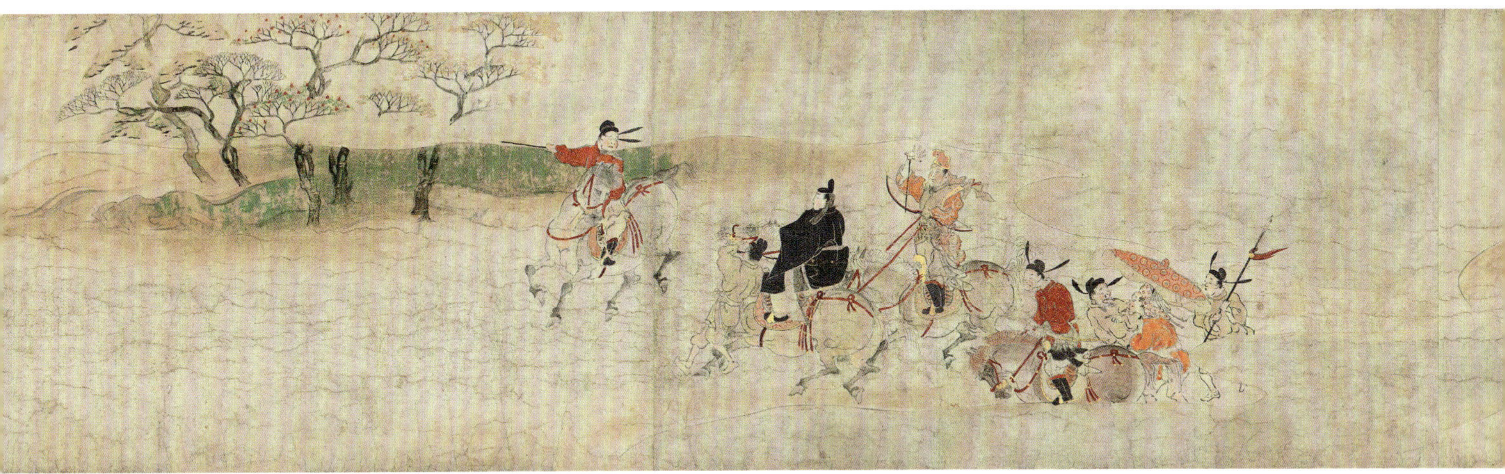

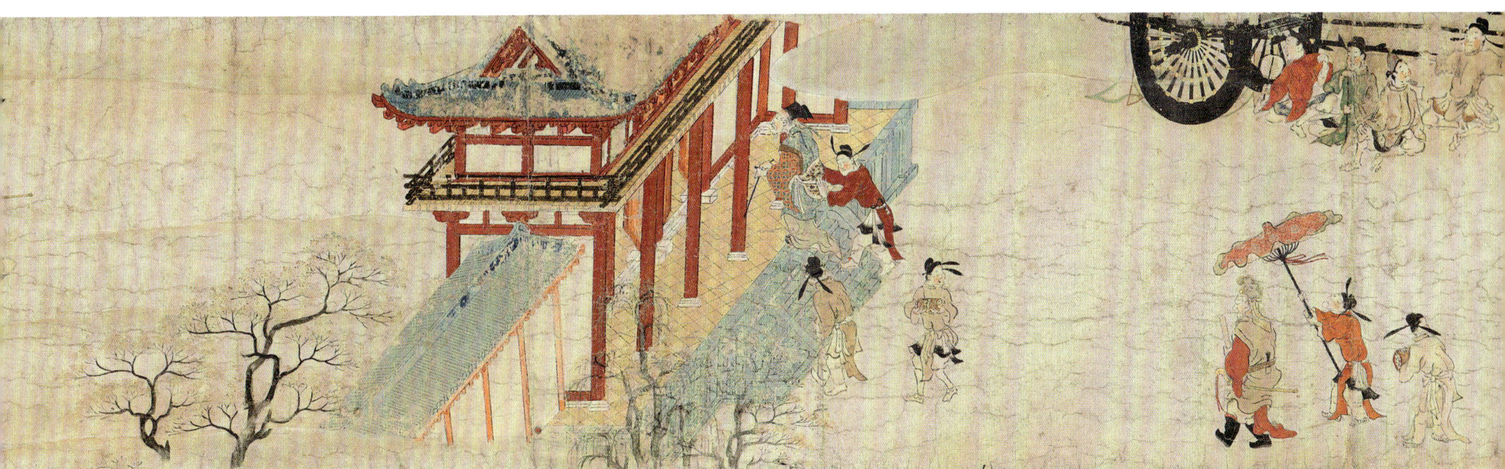

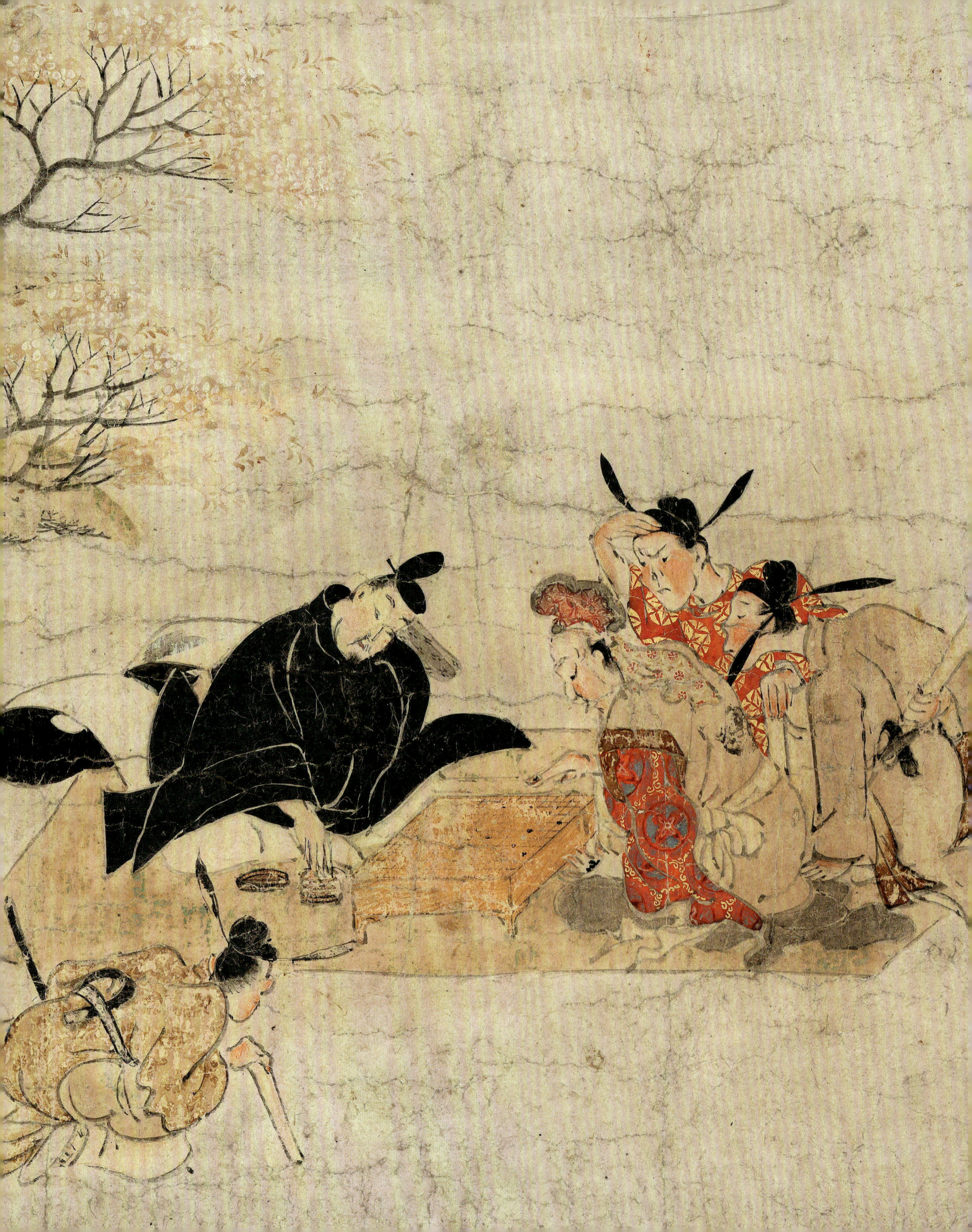

THIS SET OF HANDSCROLLS provides a highly humorous account of the adventures of Kibi no Makibi (695–775), who served as the Japanese ambassador to the Chinese court in the mission of 753. Although based on historical characters, the illustrated story is purely fictional. Aided by the lively ghost of the celebrated poet Abe no Nakamaro (698–770), the ever-resourceful Kibi, who has been imprisoned, successfully passes a series of tests on skills and learning, given as challenges by his incredulous Chinese "hosts," in order to secure his freedom. As seen in the fourth scroll illustrated here, the narrative method in these scrolls is rather straightforward: the landscape and architectural elements repeat from frame to frame to suggest the passage of time. In the first scene Kibi is compelled to engage a famed Chinese master in a game of go. He eventually prevails by swallowing a piece. Although his Chinese captors are suspicious and force him to take a laxative, Kibi is able to retain the piece in his stomach through magical powers.

(scroll 4, right to left)

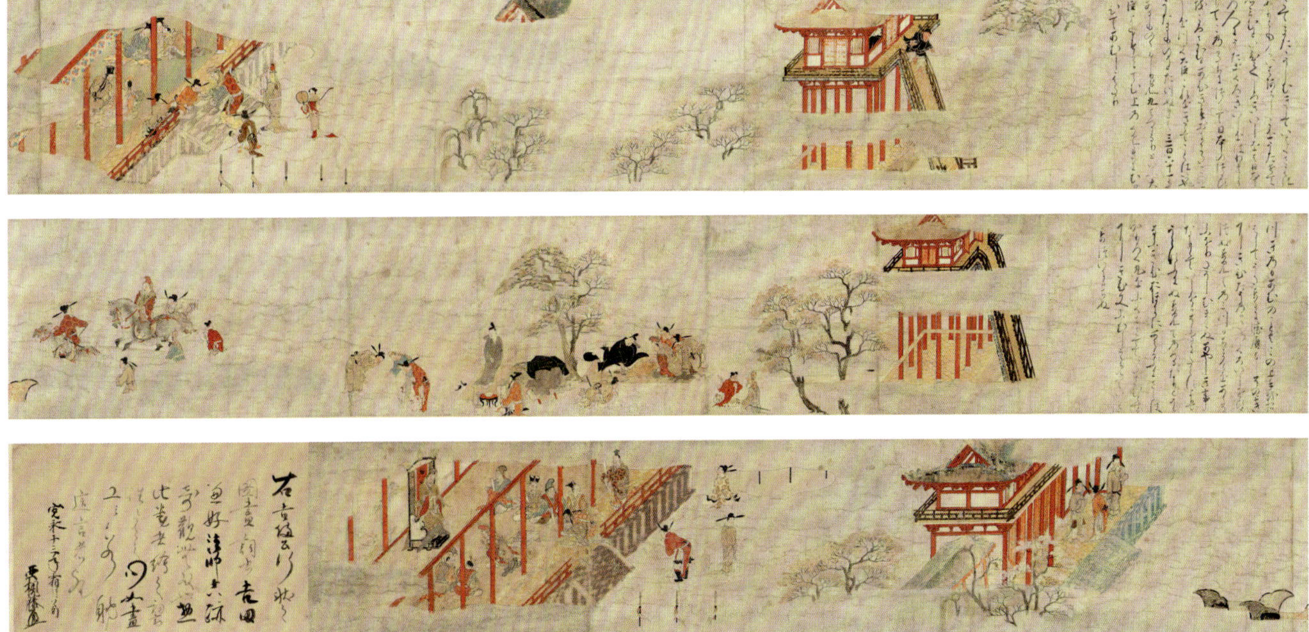

Minister Kibi's Adventures in China (*Kibi daijin nittō emaki*), scroll 4, Heian period, 12th century
One of four handscrolls; ink, color, and gold on paper, about 32 cm × 6 m (12 ⅝ in. × 19 ft. 8 in.)
Museum of Fine Arts, Boston, William Sturgis Bigelow Collection by Exchange, 1932, 32.131.4

3
KAZARI

Tsuji has declared that the decorative can be said to lie at the very core of Japanese art. Unlike in the West, where the "fine arts" (painting and sculpture) are often privileged over the applied arts, in Japan no such distinction is made. Tsuji has introduced to art historical discourse the concept of *kazari,* the Japanese word for the "will to decorate." For him, it involves not just the physical adornment of an object, but also the transformation of an object or space into something extraordinary—something that can put its viewers into contact with the transcendent.

Fantasy and surprise are important parts of the kazari aesthetic, as are asymmetry, exaggeration, stylization, and improvisation. Unlike the Chinese artisans whose traditions were often emulated throughout East Asia, the Japanese have not restricted themselves to a fixed set of authoritative or auspicious motifs such as the dragon and phoenix. Rather, since the eleventh or twelfth century they have drawn upon familiar things close at hand, in particular motifs from the natural world—not only flowers and trees, but also insects and shells. Tsuji believes that decorative imagery of this type has the potential to join the emotions of the viewer with the spirituality of nature.

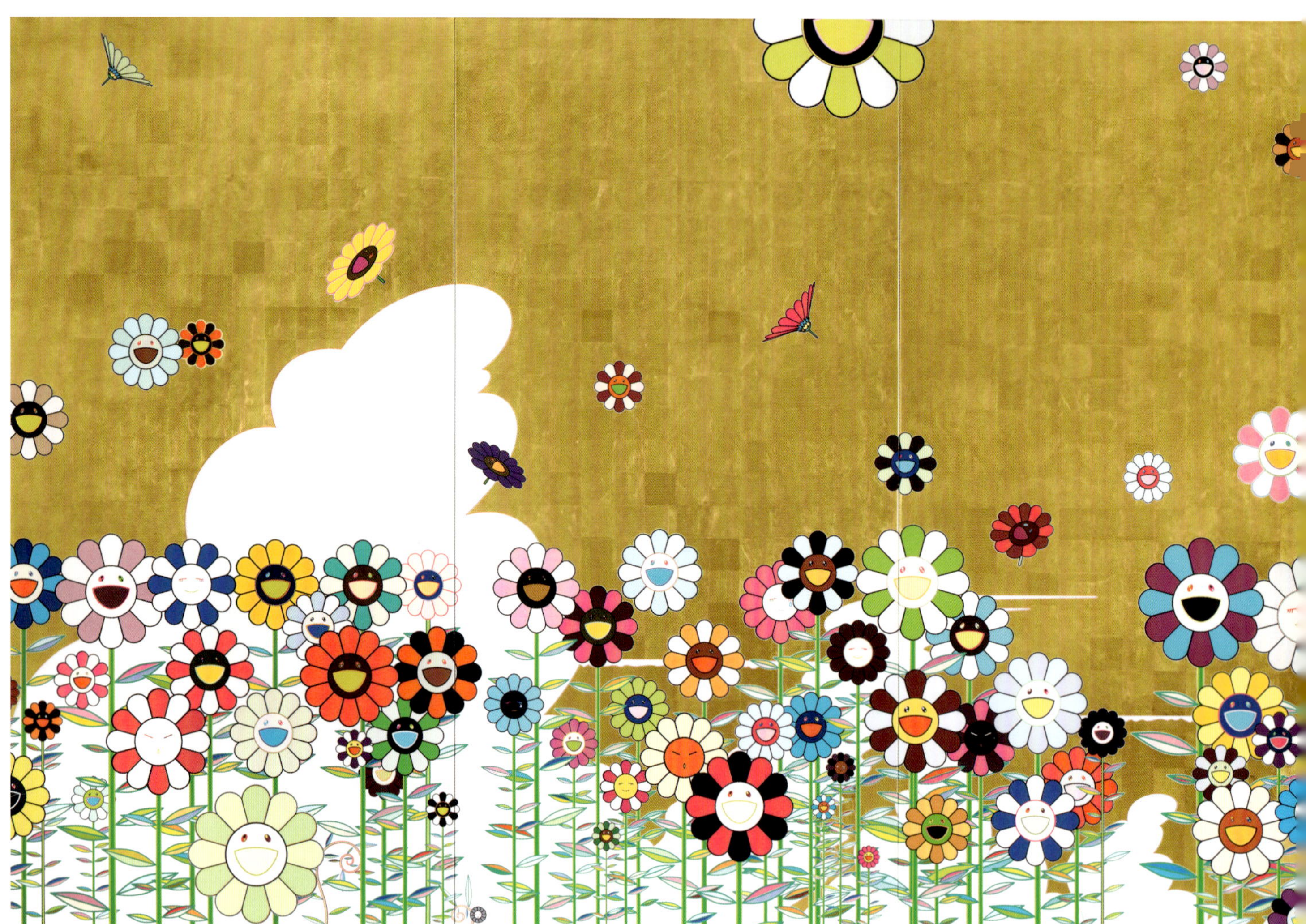

TAKASHI MURAKAMI

Kawaii–Vacances: Summer Vacation in the Kingdom of the Golden, Heisei era, 2008
Acrylic and gold leaf on canvas mounted on aluminum frame, about 3 m × 9 m × 5.8 cm (9 ft. 10 in. × 29 ft. 6 in. × 2 ⅜ in.)
Private Collection

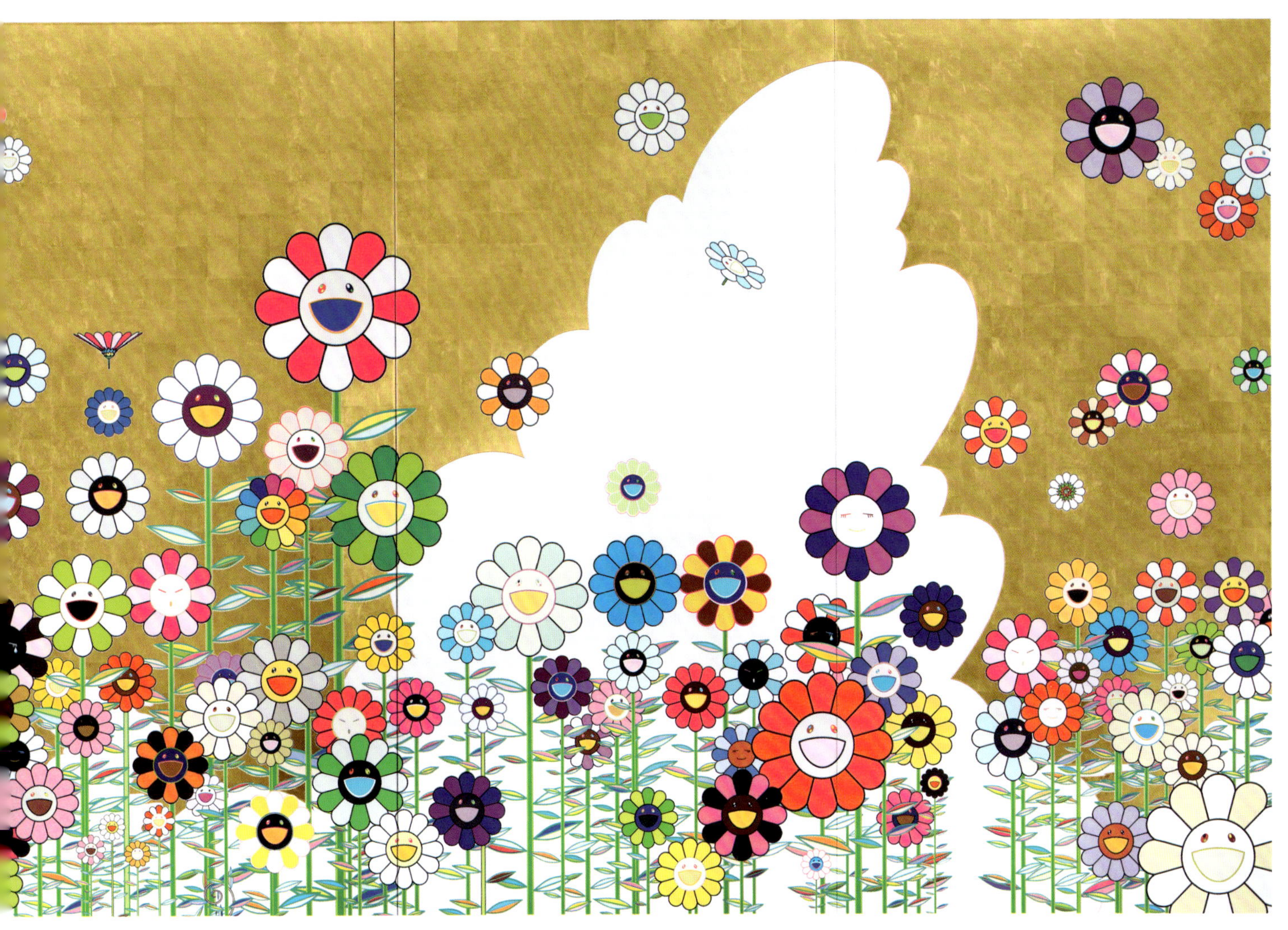

KAZARI MAY BE SEEN as an elevated form of installation art. One of its primary manifestations is the creation of artistic environments—ones that can include paintings as part of a larger program, accompanied by decorative objects. *Kawaii—Vacances* was originally designed by Murakami and produced by members of the Kaikai Kiki studio and other craftsmen in 2010 as part of a display at Versailles, the Baroque palace of French king Louis XIV. The monumental panel painting, with its band of happy-faced flowers set across a background of gold leaf, was illuminated by flowered stained-glass lamps and set off by a similarly patterned floor covering; the ensemble was re-created for the exhibition at the Museum of Fine Arts.

During his graduate school training as a Nihonga artist, Murakami studied many large-scale floral compositions from the sixteenth and seventeenth centuries. And indeed, strong affinities exist between the MFA's *Poppies* screens illustrated in this section. Emphasizing sumptuous visuals over narrative content, both works share a lavish use of gold and highly saturated colors, in compositions that call attention to the surface of the picture plane. Moreover, they frequently repeat motifs, sometimes through the use of stencils.

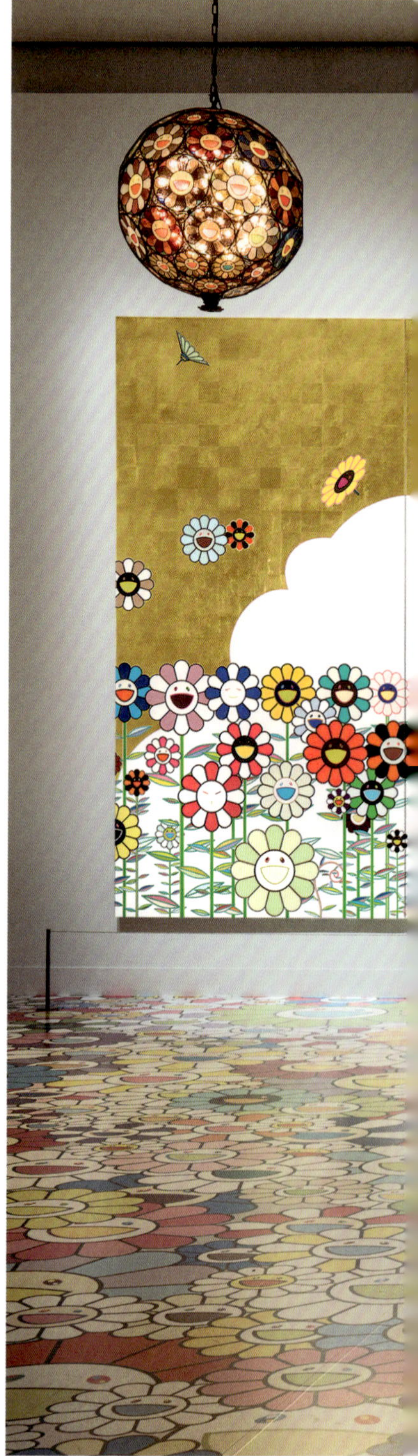

TAKASHI MURAKAMI Flower lamps, Heisei era, 2010, installed with *Kawaii–Vacances: Summer Vacation in the Kingdom of the Golden* at the MFA in 2017. Stained glass, lead, and electrical components, each 72 × 60 × 60 cm (28 ⅜ × 23 ⅝ × 23 ⅝ in.)
Courtesy of the artist

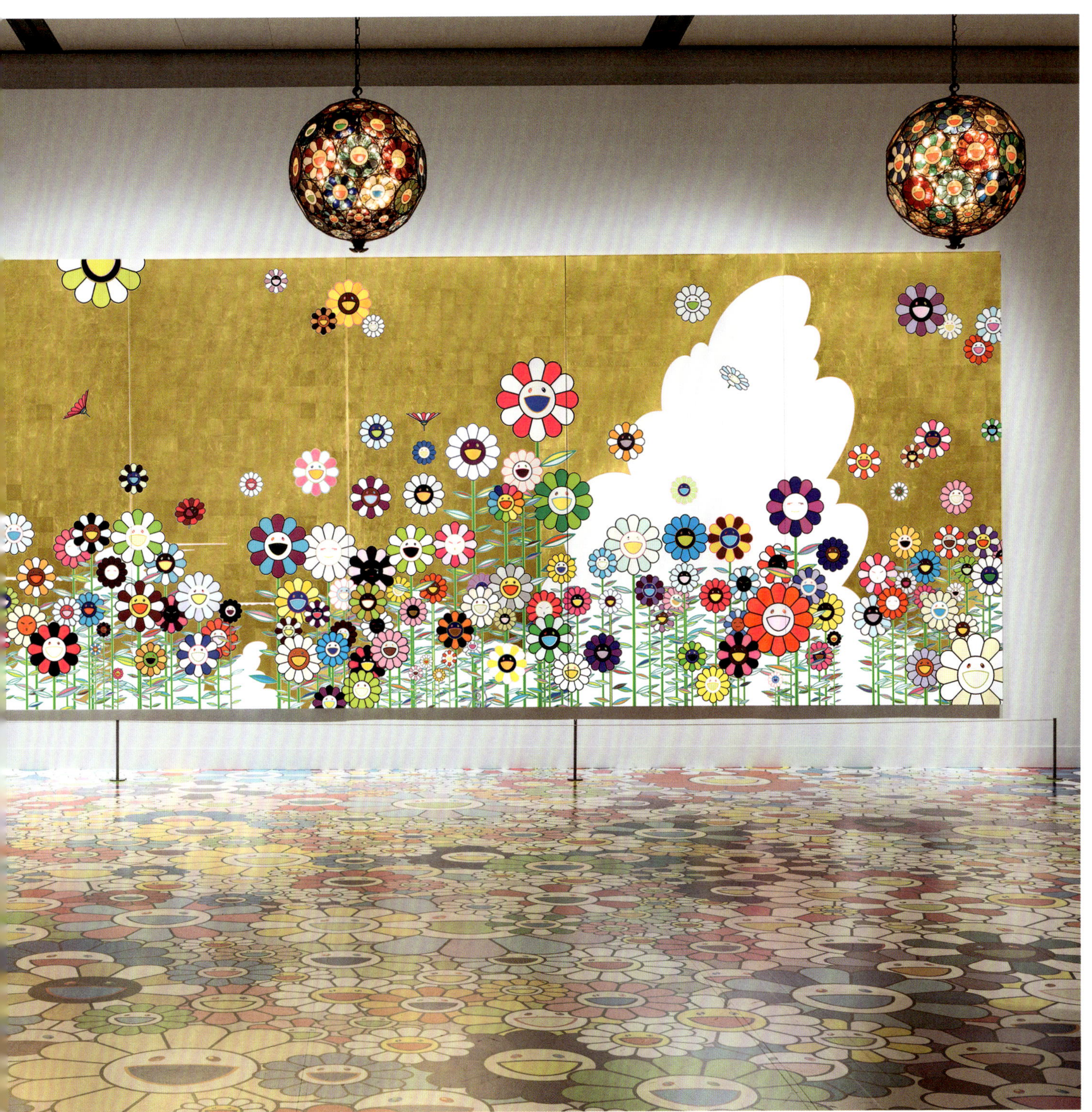

TODAY SCREENS are largely appreciated as paintings, works of "fine art," but traditionally they were used as portable furniture, temporarily dividing interior spaces. In the early seventeenth century, painters in Kyoto created compositions with scenes of poppies amid an early summer landscape, the blossoms scattered among bamboo plants. However, Tawaraya Sōtatsu and members of his school often adopted such traditional themes and reinterpreted them in bold, decorative designs. In this pair of screens the artist has abandoned the idea of a specifically defined ground plane and has positioned the flowers directly against the gold surface.

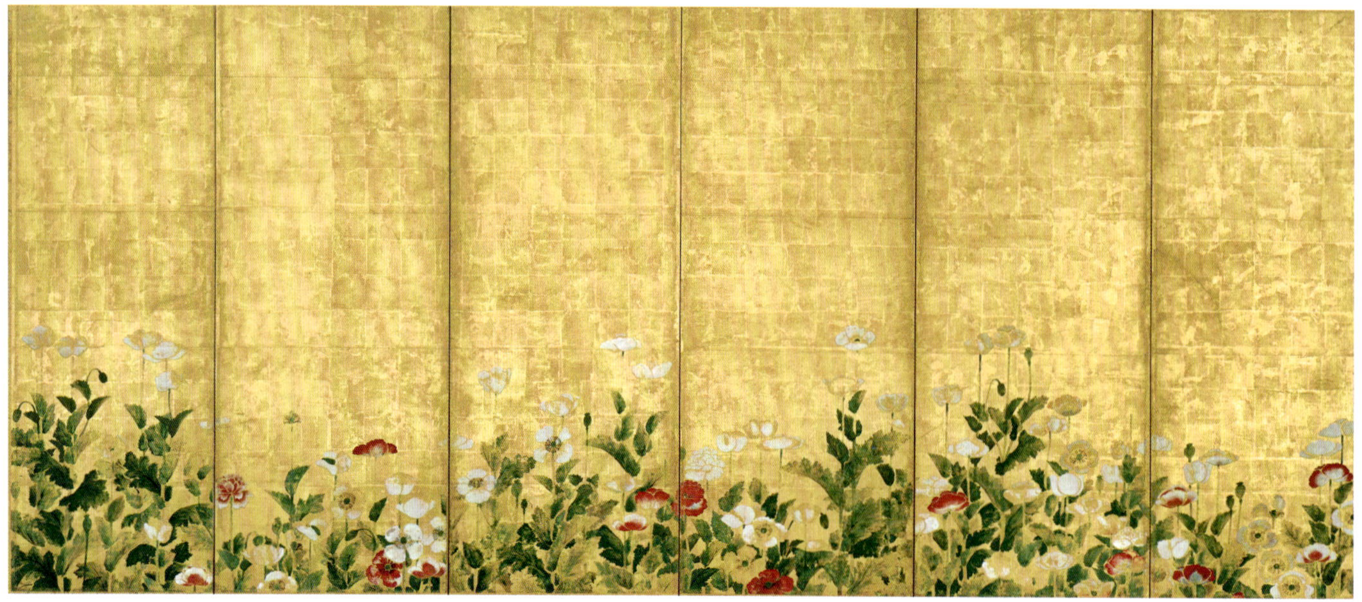

SCHOOL OF TAWARAYA SŌTATSU (DIED ABOUT 1642)

Poppies, Edo period, 17th century. Pair of six-panel folding screens; ink and color on gold-leafed paper, each about 1.5 × 3.5 m (59 ³⁄₁₆ in. × 11 ft. 6 ⅞ in.)
Museum of Fine Arts, Boston, Gift of Mrs. W. Scott Fitz, 1911, 11.1273, 11.1272

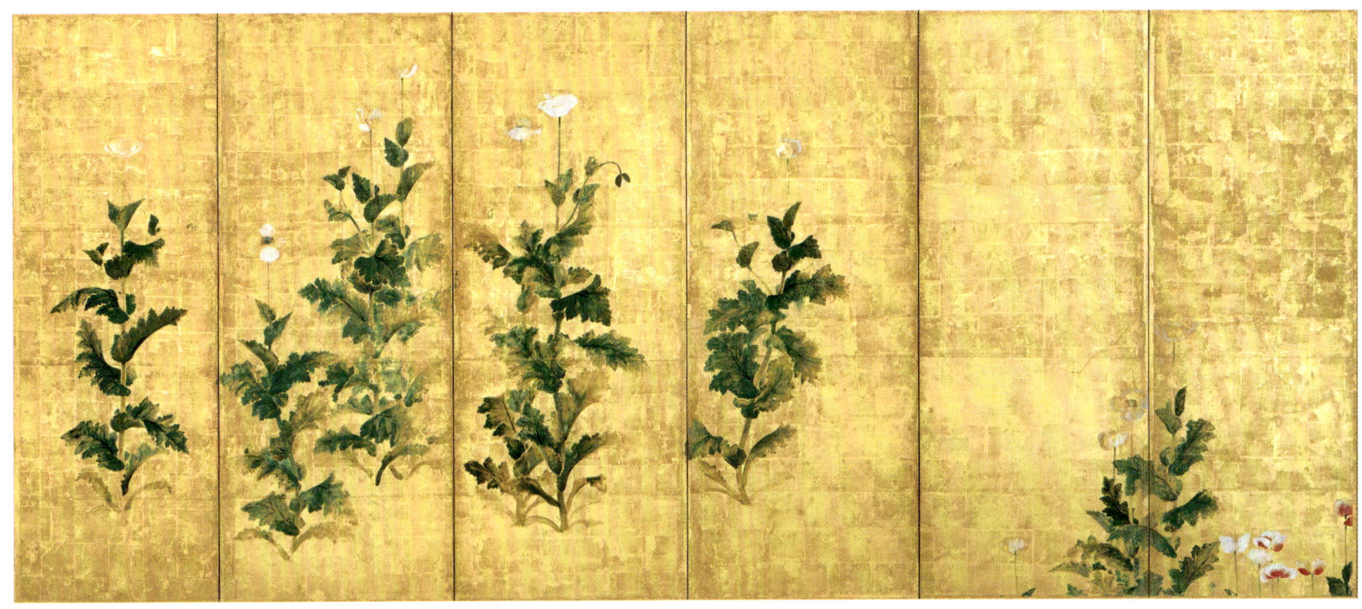

LARGE-WHEELED OX CARTS were the favored transport of Kyoto aristocrats.
Laden with a profusion of flowers, they were frequently used as ornaments
(*tsukurimono*) at festivals to attract the attention of the gods. Textile
designers also adopted them as motifs, emblematic of good fortune. In
this screen, the cart appears isolated against a gold-leaf ground, which
simultaneously suggests the shore of a riverbank as well as a band of clouds.

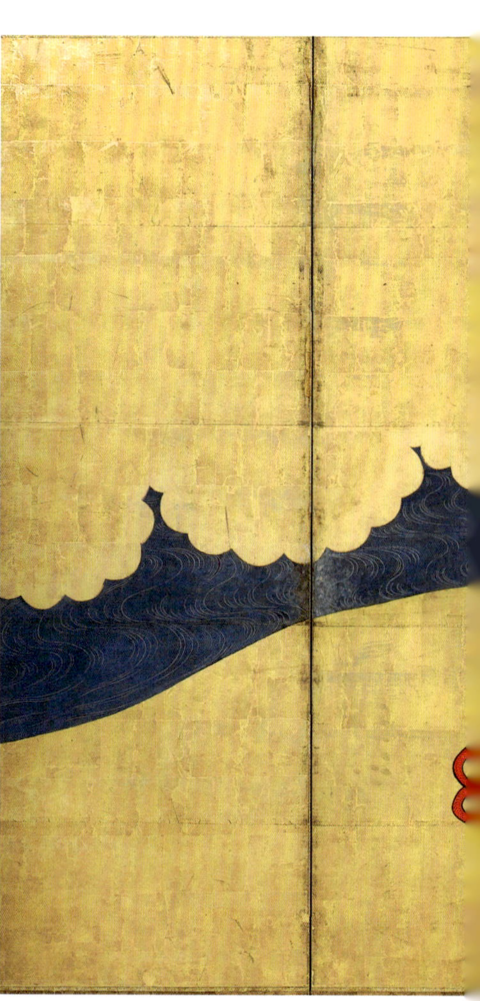

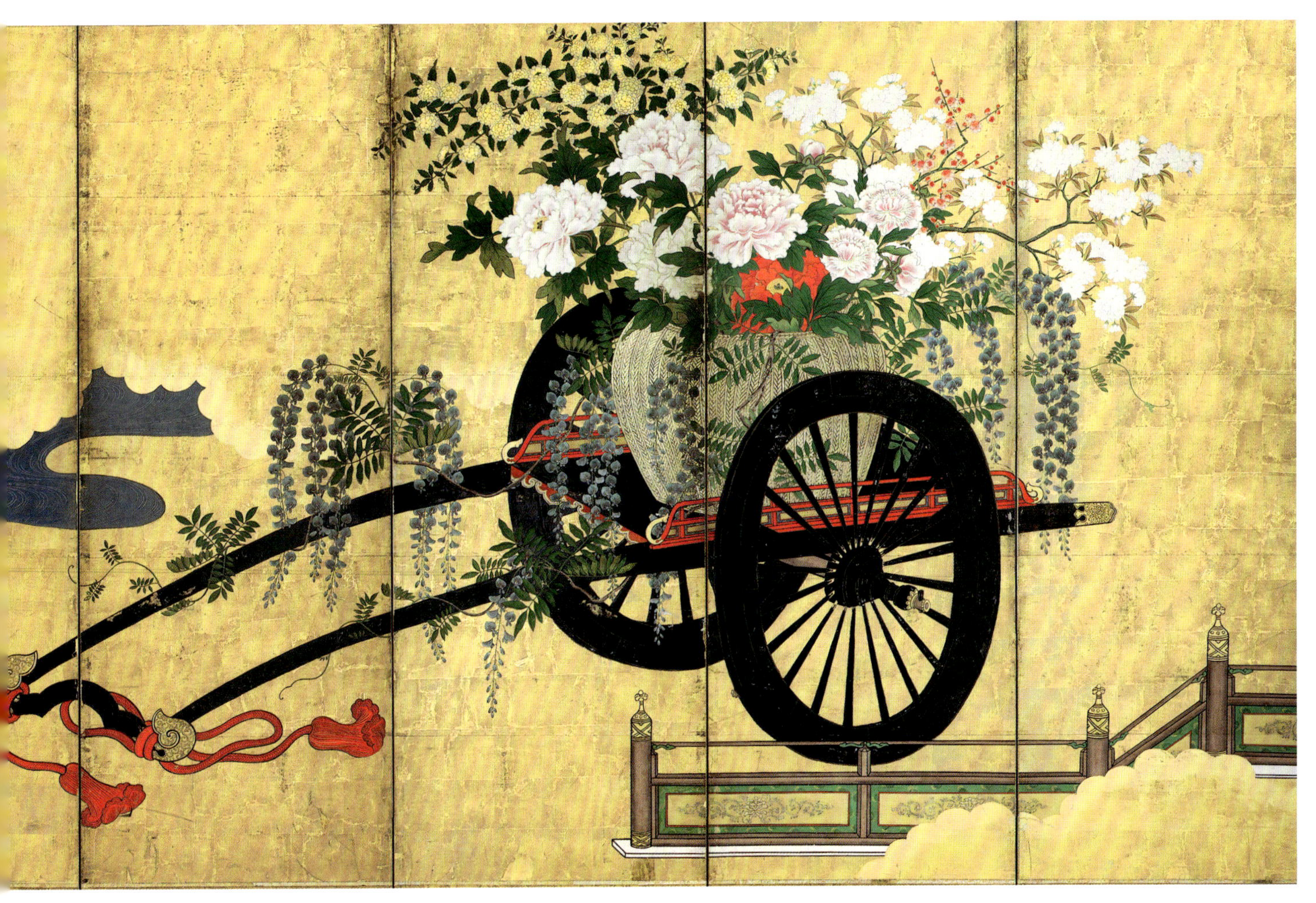

Flower Cart, Edo period, 19th century. One from a pair of six-panel folding screens;
ink and color on gold-leafed paper, about 1.7 × 3.6 m (65 ¹³⁄₁₆ in. × 11 ft. 11 in.)
Museum of Fine Arts, Boston, William Sturgis Bigelow Collection, 1911, 11.6746

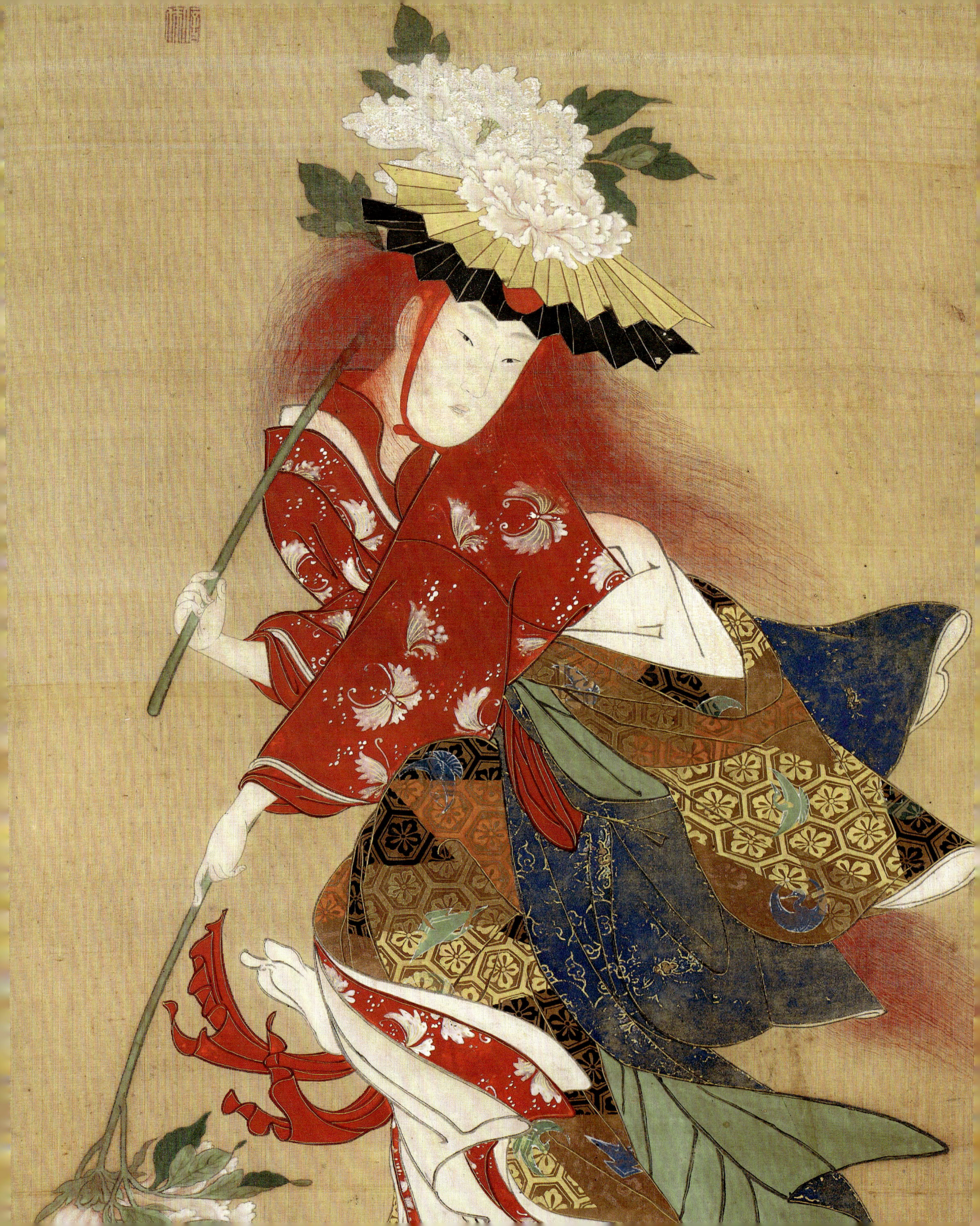

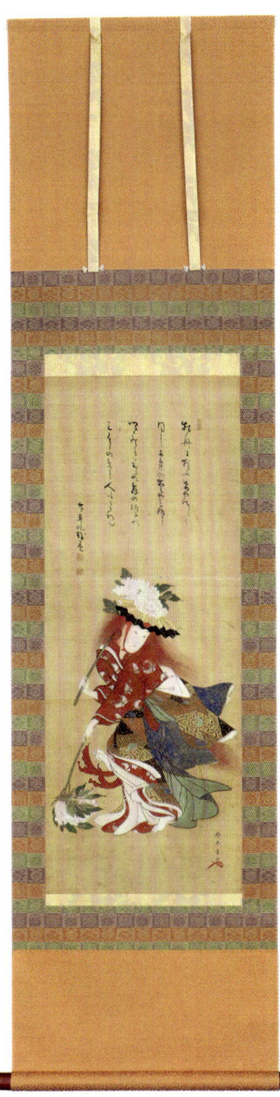

HOLDING LARGE STEMS OF peony blossoms, a swaying figure with delicate, feminine features wears a distinctive, unruly red wig and a peony-adorned headdress. The headdress and floral props indicate that the dance is related to the legend of the Stone Bridge (*Shakkyō*), in which a monk makes a pilgrimage to Mount Tiantai in southeastern China. There, at a celebrated narrow stone bridge, he has a vision of a lion (the mount of Monju, Bodhisattva of Wisdom) frolicking with a peony.

The rich contrasting patterns of the different layers of the figure's robes contribute to the vitality of the dance. Furthermore, the image is complemented by the mounting, composed of several different strips of sumptuous brocade. Japanese paintings are generally remounted about every 150 years, and the selection of the mounting silks is critical to the appreciation of the overall decorative effect of the work of art.

**KATSUKAWA SHUNSHŌ
(1726–1792)**

Shakkyō, the Lion Dance, Edo period, about 1787–88. Hanging scroll; ink, color, and gold on silk, image 82.5 × 32.5 cm (32 ½ × 12 ¹³⁄₁₆ in.), overall 176 × 48.7 cm (69 ⁵⁄₁₆ × 19 ³⁄₁₆ in.)
Museum of Fine Arts, Boston, William Sturgis Bigelow Collection, 1911, 11.7762

4
ASOBI

Asobi—playfulness—has continuously sustained and stimulated Japanese art, according to Tsuji. The concept is even central to the Japanese creation myth, in which the sun goddess Amaterasu, incensed at her impudent brother, sought solace in a cave, thereby plunging the world into darkness. Only the performance of a bawdy dance by another goddess, and the ensuing laughter, distracted her into reemerging and bringing light again into the world.

During times of political suppression, such as under the tight military rule of the Tokugawa shogunate (1615–1868), entertainment districts, as well as the formation of witty poetic circles, cultivated playful artistic outlets for the inhabitants of large urban centers. Images of this Floating World—such as the remarkable folding screen in this section, showing one of Edo's bustling kabuki theaters—reveal a highly sophisticated sense of humor. With the introduction of Western art in Japan in the nineteenth century, seriousness became more dominant in the arts. Yet the popularity of manga today testifies to the vitality of the Japanese playful tradition, which in turn has provided Murakami with inspiration.

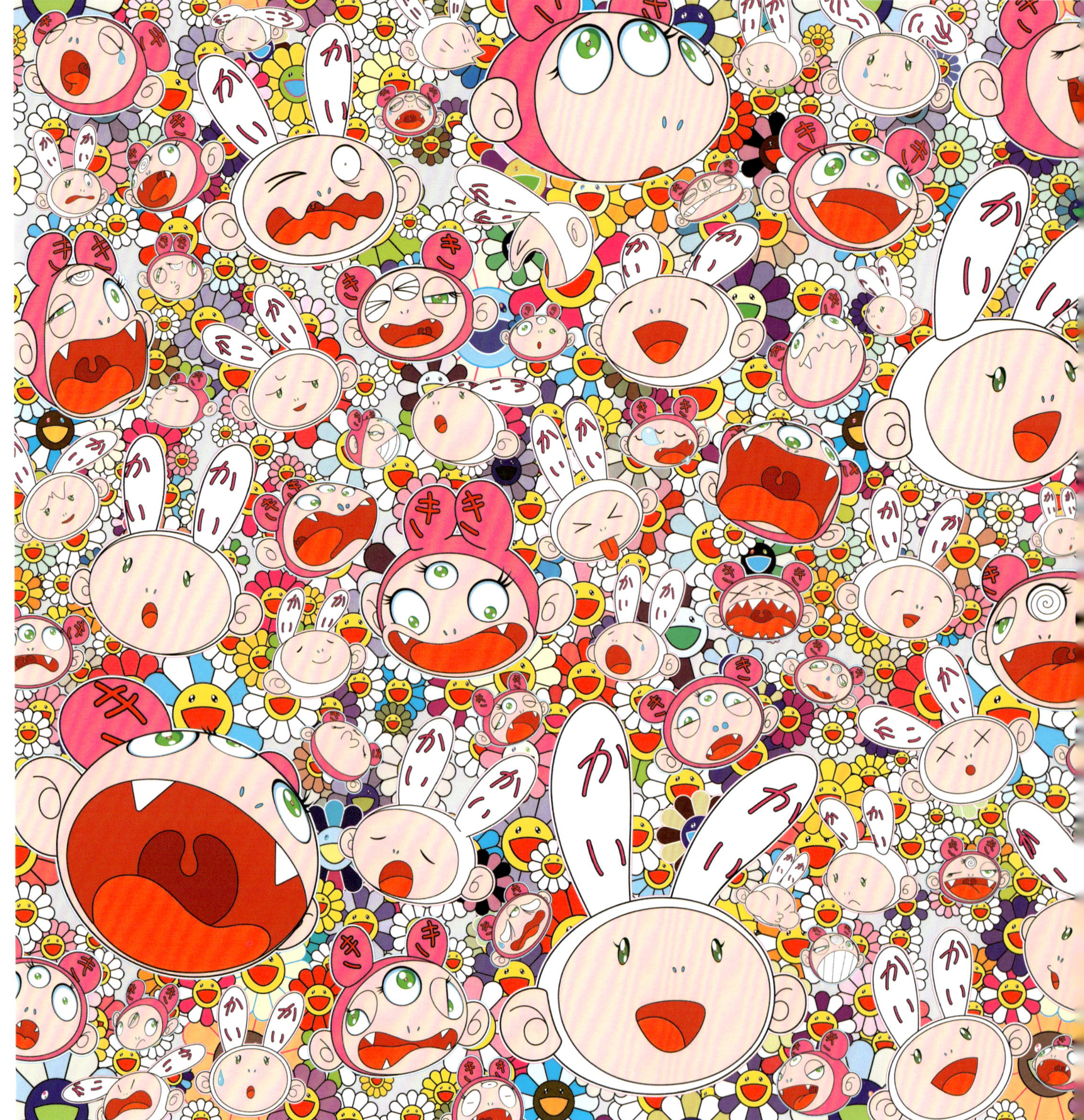

TAKASHI MURAKAMI

Lots, Lots of Kaikai and Kiki, Heisei era, 2009
Acrylic and platinum leaf on canvas mounted on aluminum frame, about 3 m × 6.1 m × 5.1 cm (9 ft. 10 in. × 19 ft. 11 in. × 2 in.)
Private collection

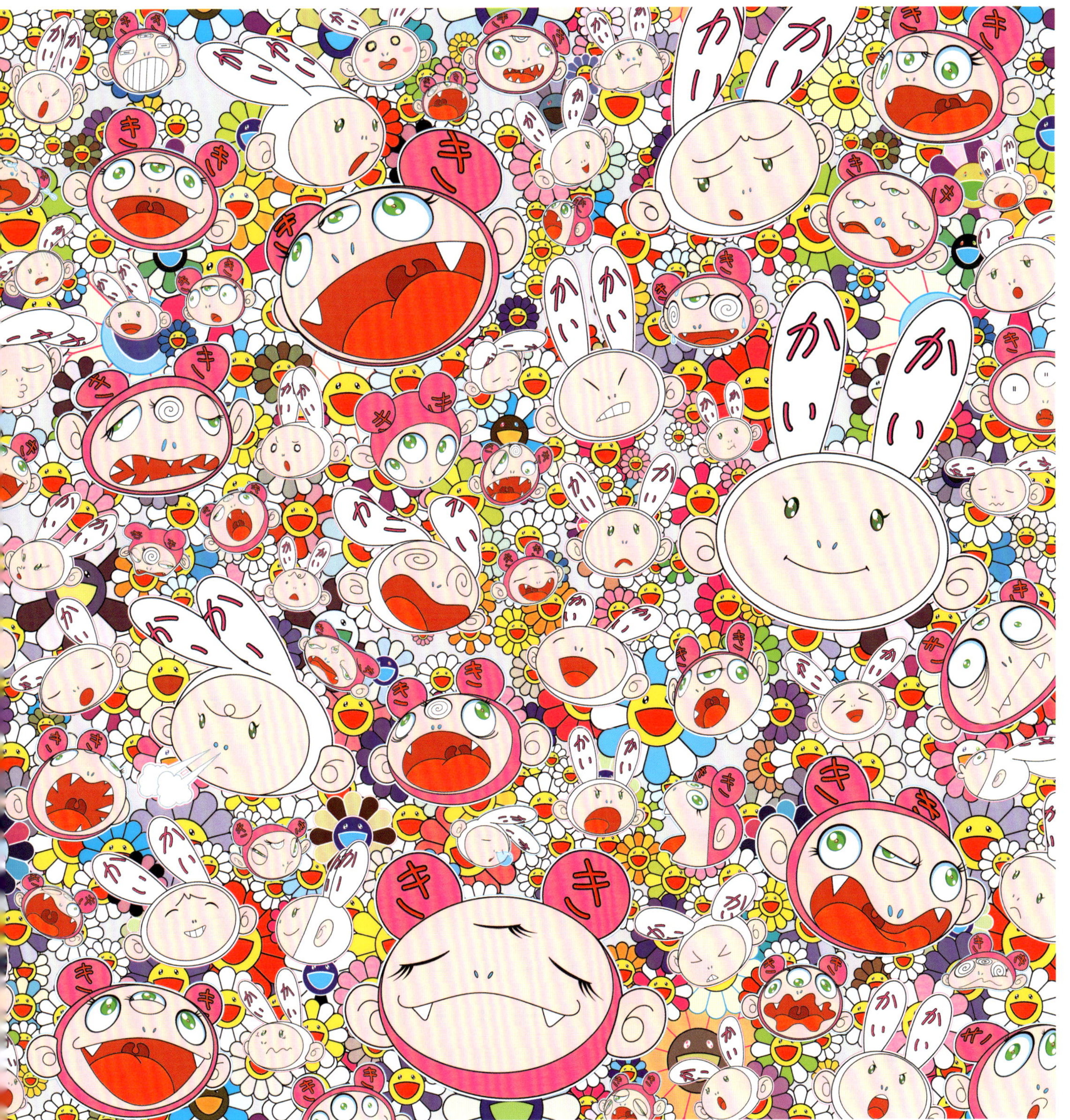

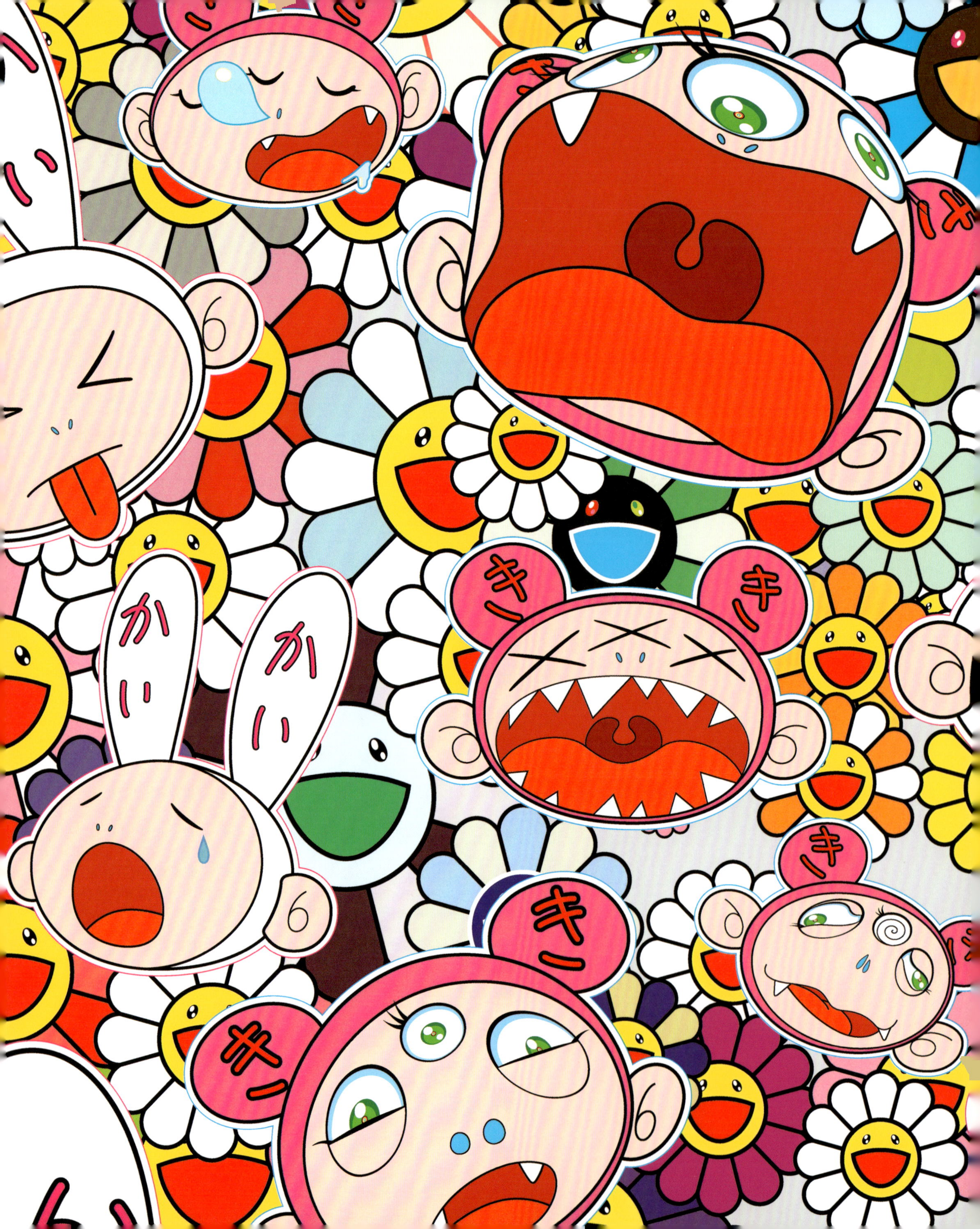
い
い
かい
かい
キー
キー
キー
キー
キー

ALTHOUGH MURAKAMI HAS LONG BEEN fascinated by dark and grotesque sci-fi images, *Lots, Lots of Kaikai and Kiki* abounds with multiple images of his humorous signature monsters, set against a background of smiling flowers. The characters have been part of the artist's iconography since 2000, beginning with just Kiki (with mouse ears and a Cyclopean third eye), born out of Murakami's interaction with a child with cognitive disabilities. Kaikai (with rabbit ears) was later created as the former's companion. The embodiments of children's pure, unconstrained desires, Kaikai and Kiki have been made into animations and merchandise, as well as appearing on a T-shirt for a well-known Japanese TV charity program and as enormous Macy's Thanksgiving Day Parade balloons. In a sense, they are Murakami's artistic ambassadors.

Murakami adopted the names of the characters from the expression *kaikaikiki*, meaning "dangerous yet appealing," used in the *Honchō gashi* (A History of Painting in Japan, 1691) to describe the style of the sixteenth-century master Kano Eitoku. However, when the syllables are transposed they describe a supernatural atmosphere inhabited by ghosts and other phenomena. Thus, Murakami found that the term suggested an image in concert with his own art and adopted it for the name of his company in 2001.

THE NAKAMURA THEATER—one of the four leading kabuki stages in
the city of Edo (modern Tokyo)—dominates this screen. In the lower
left corner, the artist depicts the bustle of activity at its entrance, where
a barker encourages passersby to attend the day's performances.
At right, a procession of male actors (some in female costume) makes its
way along a wooden stage; while, at center, a pickpocket takes advantage
of the hustle and bustle to relieve an unsuspecting samurai of his purse.

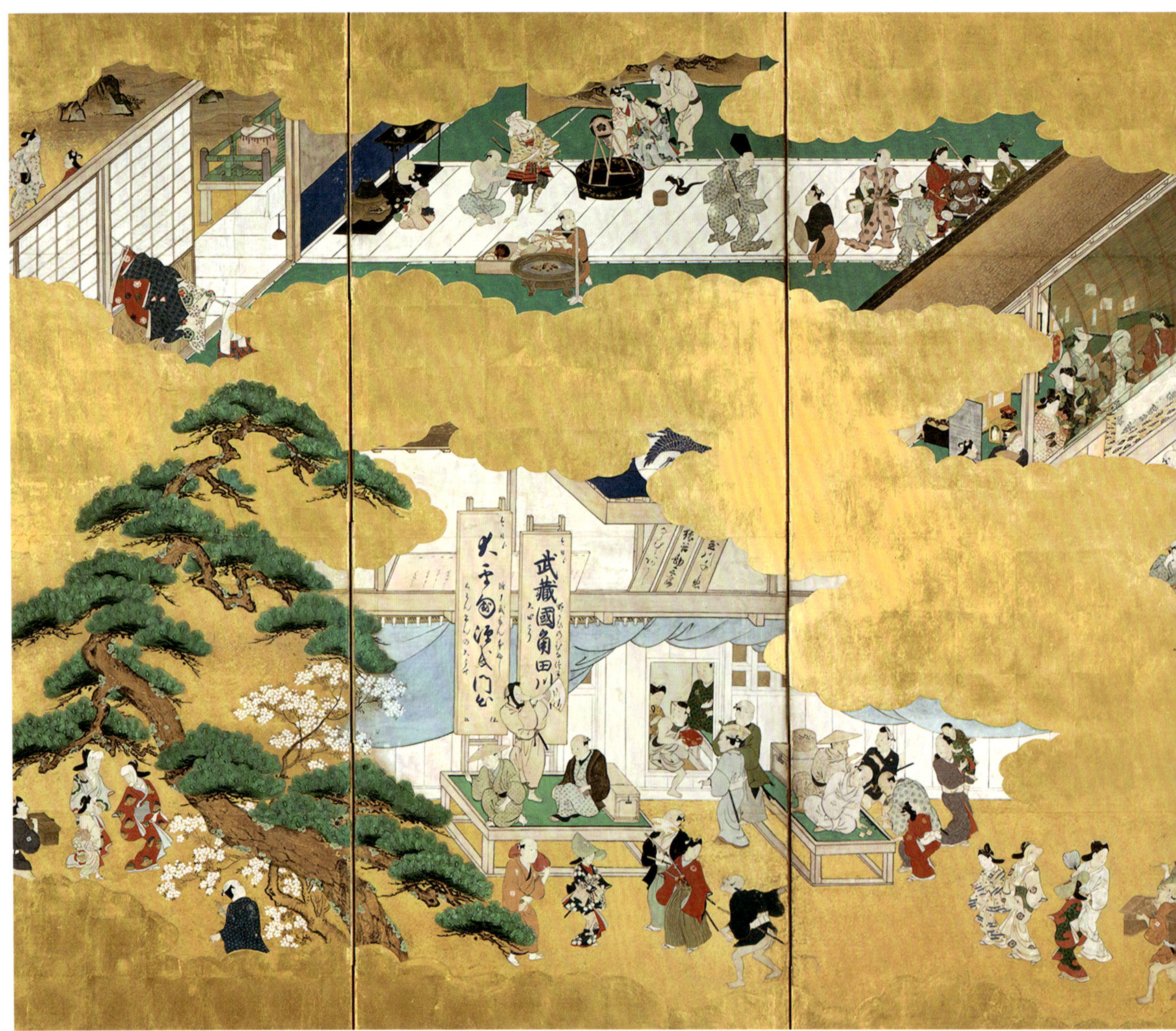

Scenes from the Nakamura Kabuki Theater, Edo period, 1684–1704. One from a pair of six-panel folding screens;
ink and color on gold-leafed paper, about 1.4 × 3.6 m (55 1/16 in. × 11 ft. 8 in.)
Museum of Fine Arts, Boston, Gift of Oliver W. Peabody, 1879, 79.468

Despite the efforts of the Tokugawa shogunate to exert control over the city, lively popular subcultures arose within Edo's two *akusho*, or "bad places": the brothels of the Yoshiwara pleasure quarters, and the kabuki theater district. Hishikawa Moronobu was among the first artists to capture the fashionable preoccupations of the urban trendsetters who frequented these sites.

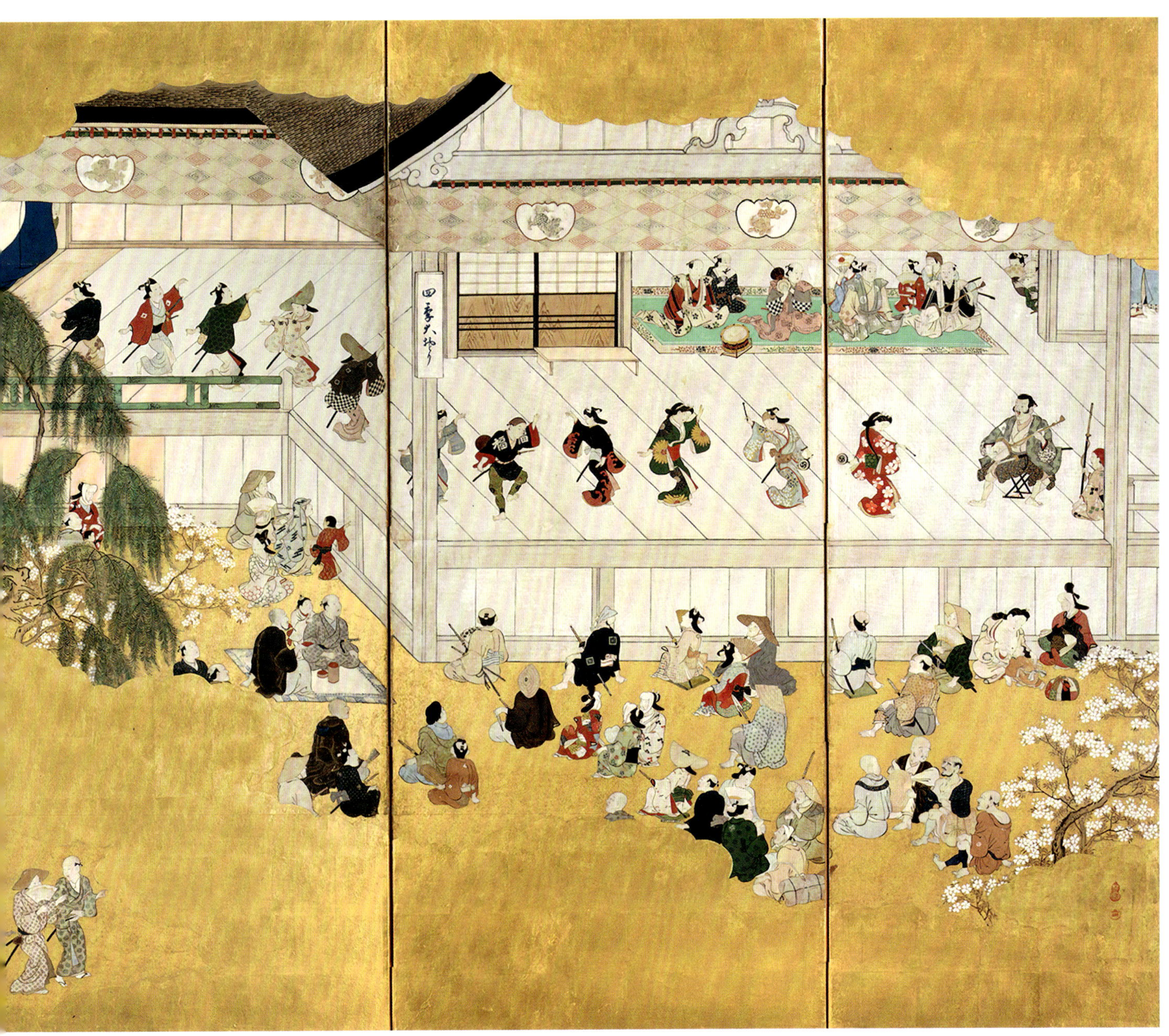

STORIES ABOUT GHOSTS, DEMONS, AND MONSTERS have always been extremely popular in Japan. Supernatural beings can assume many guises; not all are sinister, and some can even be rather amusing. This narrative handscroll recounts the story of the harassment of a samurai household by a group of foxes, which took on the form of ogres, only to be repelled eventually by a brave warrior. Paintings by Hishikawa Moronobu, the so-called father of *ukiyo-e* (pictures of the Floating World), are extremely rare. This scroll is one of the earliest examples of a ghost painting by an ukiyo-e artist.

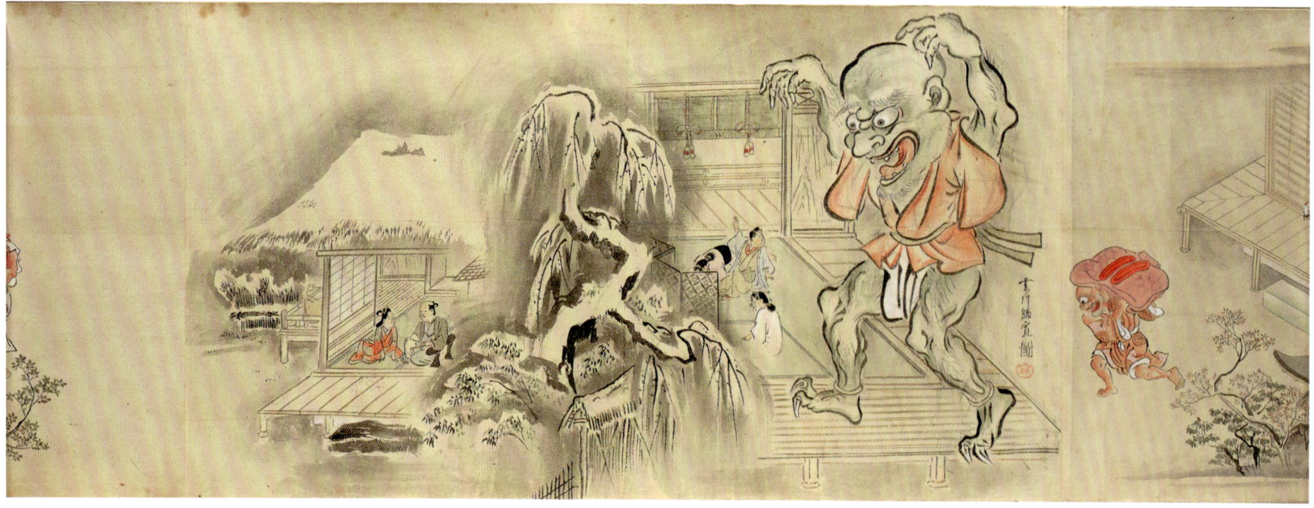

HISHIKAWA MORONOBU (DIED IN 1694)

Fantastical Scenes, Edo period, 1685. One from a pair of handscrolls; ink and light color on paper, about 45.6 cm × 13.7 m (18 in. × 45 ft.)
Museum of Fine Arts, Boston, William Sturgis Bigelow Collection, 1921, 21.262

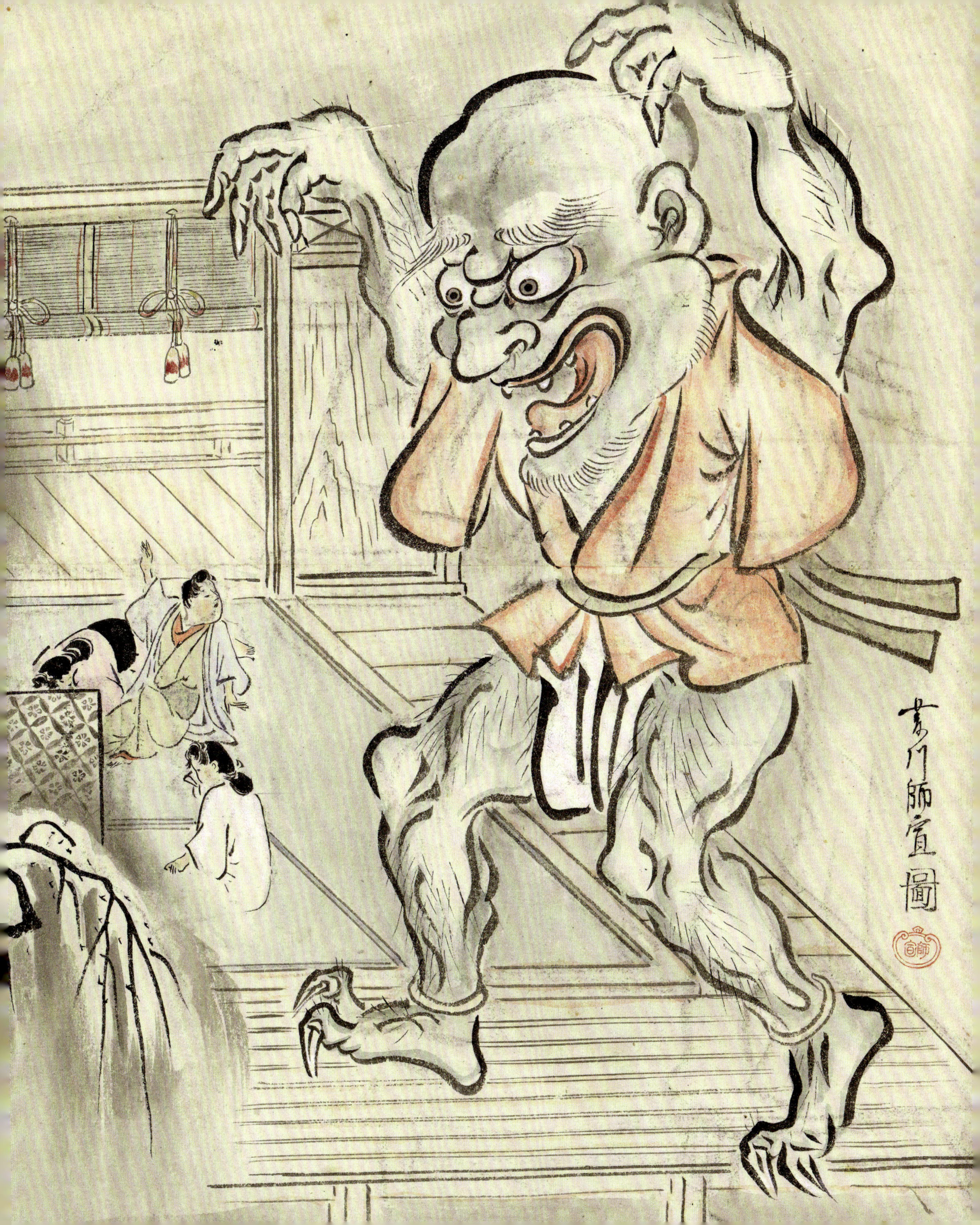

菱川師宣圖

 with a demon, the legendary thirteenth-century strongman Asahina is shown with eyes bulging. With the red blush of his skin, his clenched hands, and his outstretched muscular legs, Shōhaku emphasizes Asahina's exertion. However, the ogre has tried to tip the results by anchoring himself down with a rock tied around his waist, and even using his hands.

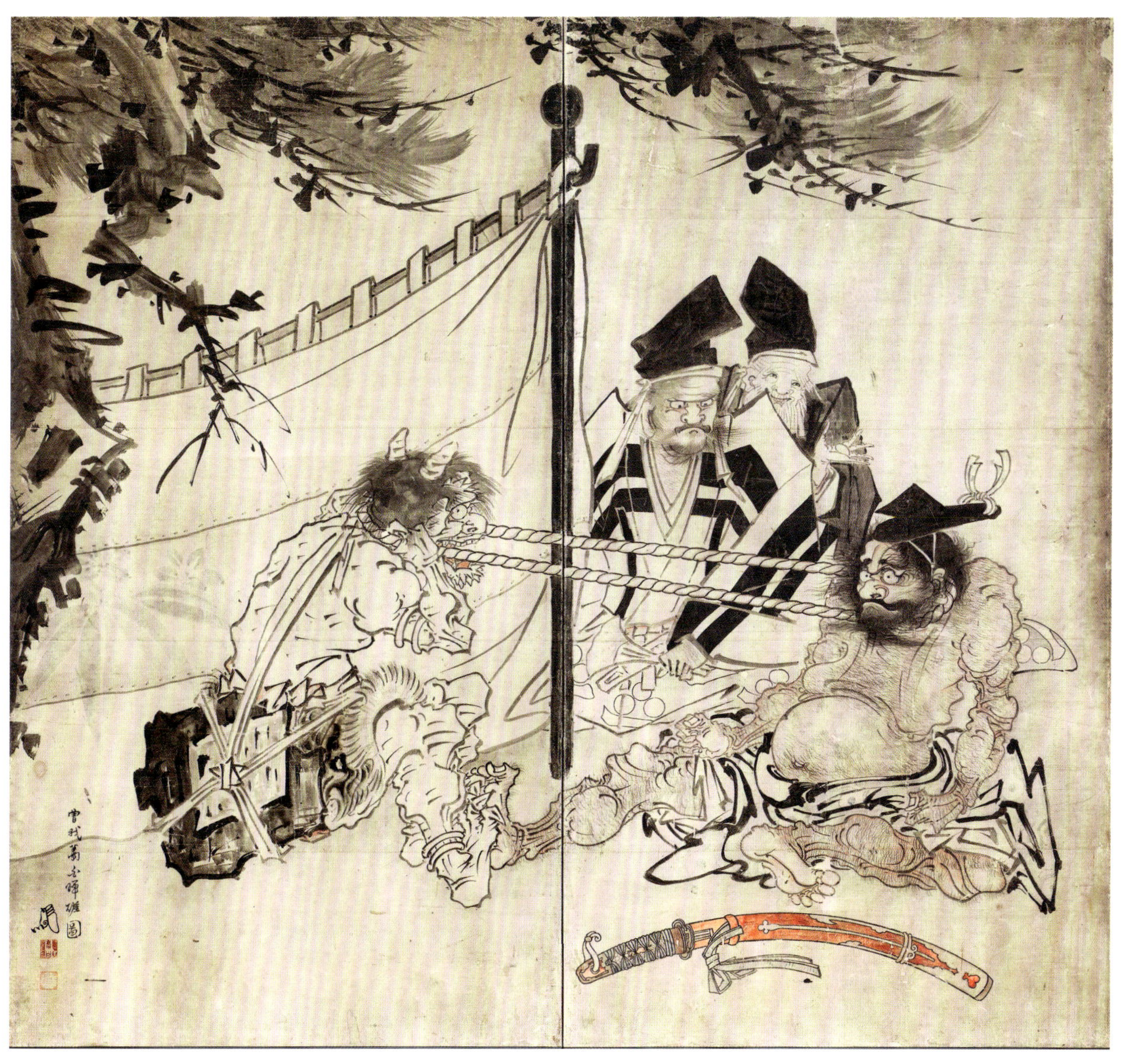

SOGA SHŌHAKU
(1730–1781)

Asahina in a Tug-of-War with a Demon, Edo period, around 1763–64
Two-panel folding screen; ink and color on paper, 165.4 × 180.8 cm (65 ⅛ × 71 ¼ in.)
Museum of Fine Arts, Boston, Fenollosa-Weld Collection, 1911, 11.4516

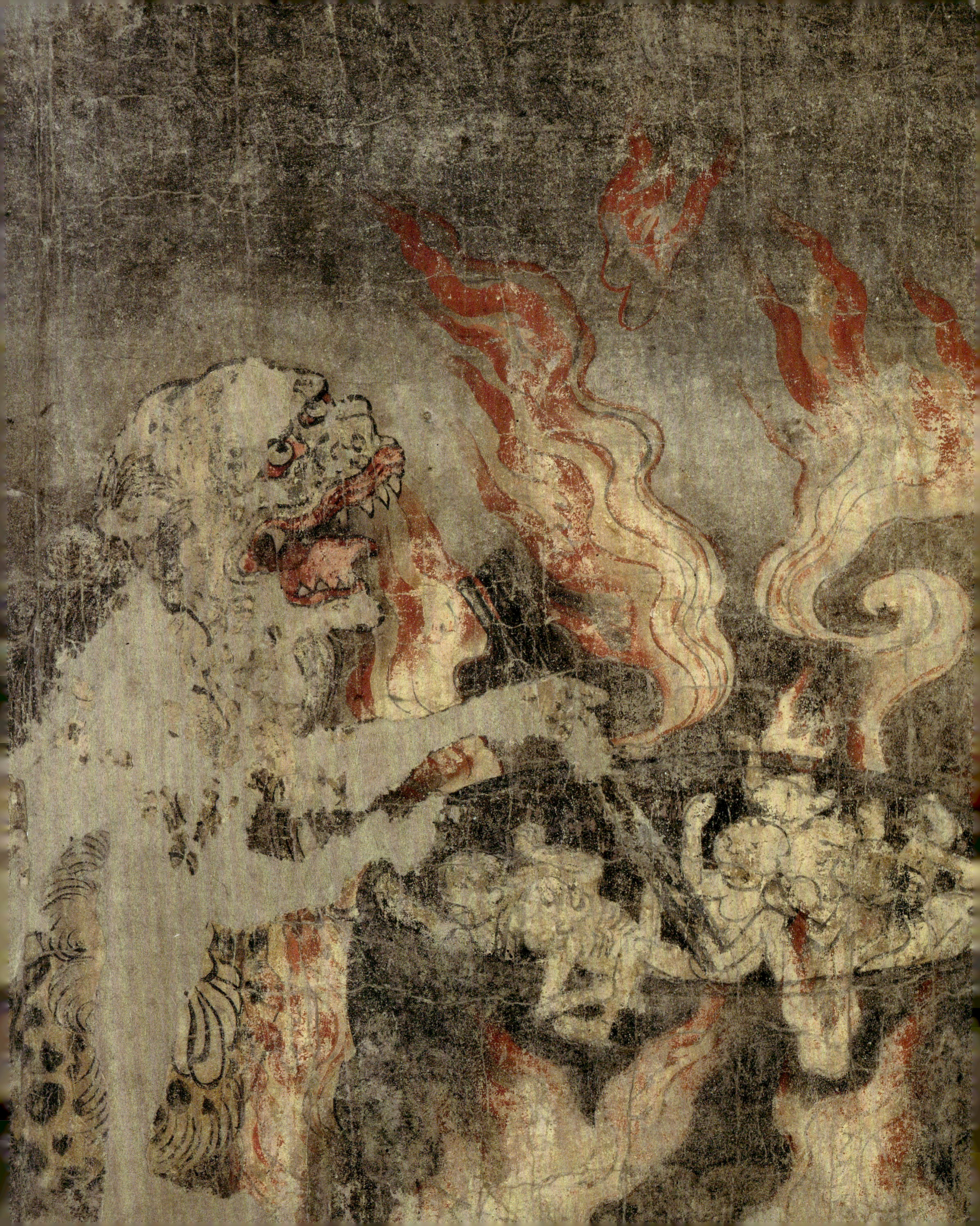

ORIGINALLY PART OF a longer composition now in the Nara National Museum, this segment of the *Hell Scrolls* describes the horrible tortures awaiting those who transgress against the Buddhist law. The calligraphic text relates that those who torment human beings or animals will be consigned to the Hell of the Copper Cauldron. Almost as an expression of black humor, this cartoon-like illustration shows anguished sinners left to boil under the supervision of a threatening demon, who prevents their escape with a pair of metal chopsticks.

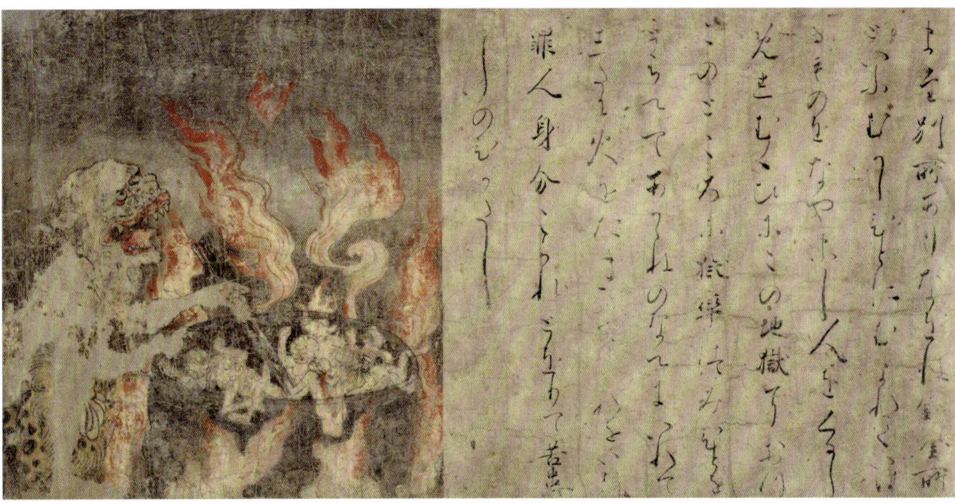

The Burning Cauldron, a section from the *Hell Scrolls* (*Jigoku zōshi*), Heian period, 12th century
Section from a handscroll; ink and color on paper, 25.6 × 52 cm (10 ¹/₁₆ × 20 ½ in.)
Museum of Fine Arts, Boston, William Sturgis Bigelow Collection, 1911, 11.6254

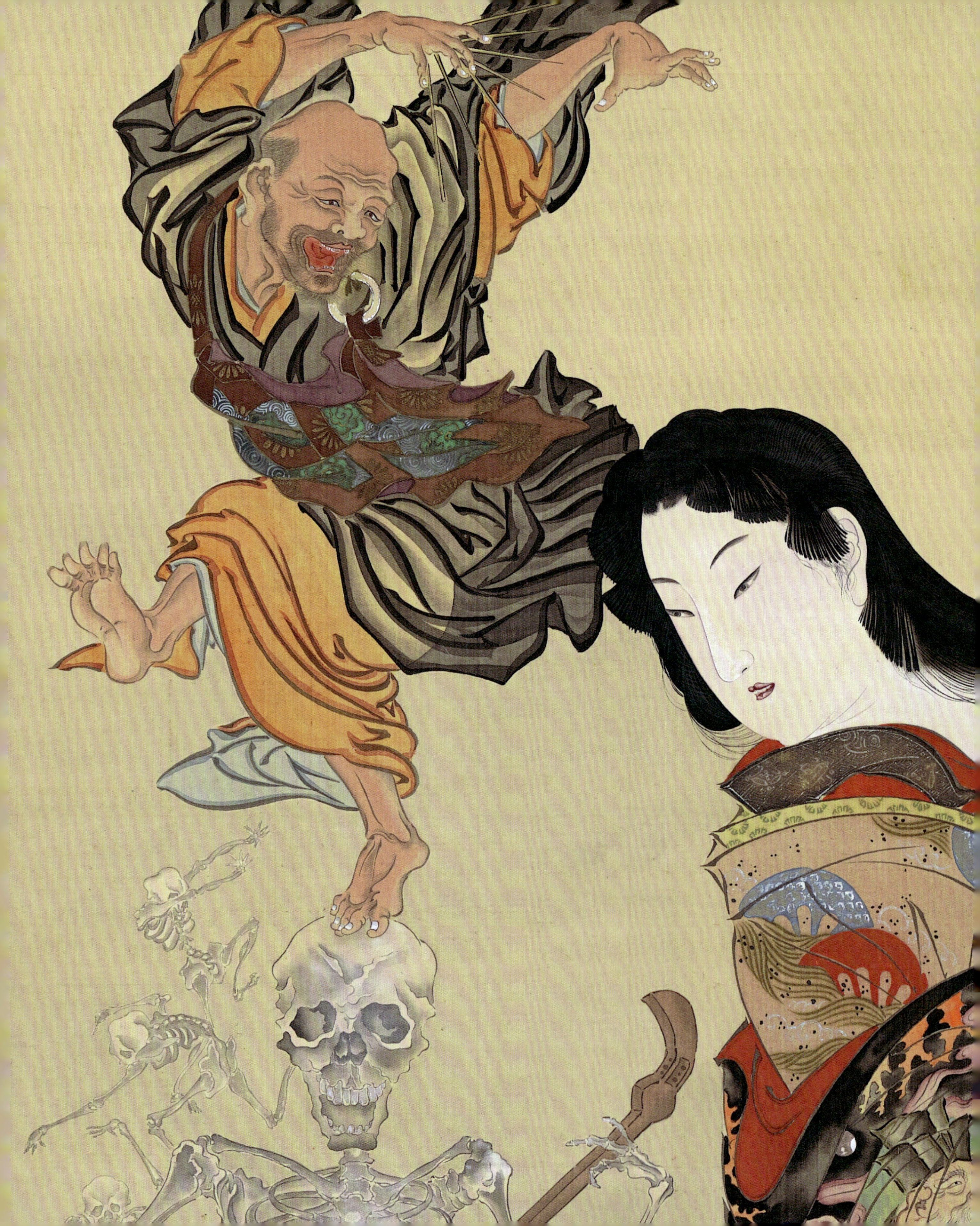

ECCENTRICITY AND HUMOR are often indicative of an individual's enlightened being, as shown in this hanging scroll by Kawanabe Kyōsai. According to legend, a famed fifteenth-century courtesan doubted the religious sincerity of the unconventional Zen monk Ikkyū, who rejected the usual vegetarian diet and drank sake with pleasure. She spied on him from behind a screen and saw the prelate engaged in a lively dance with a retinue of merry-making skeletons. The woman immediately recognized Ikkyū's elevated spiritual state and became one of his followers.

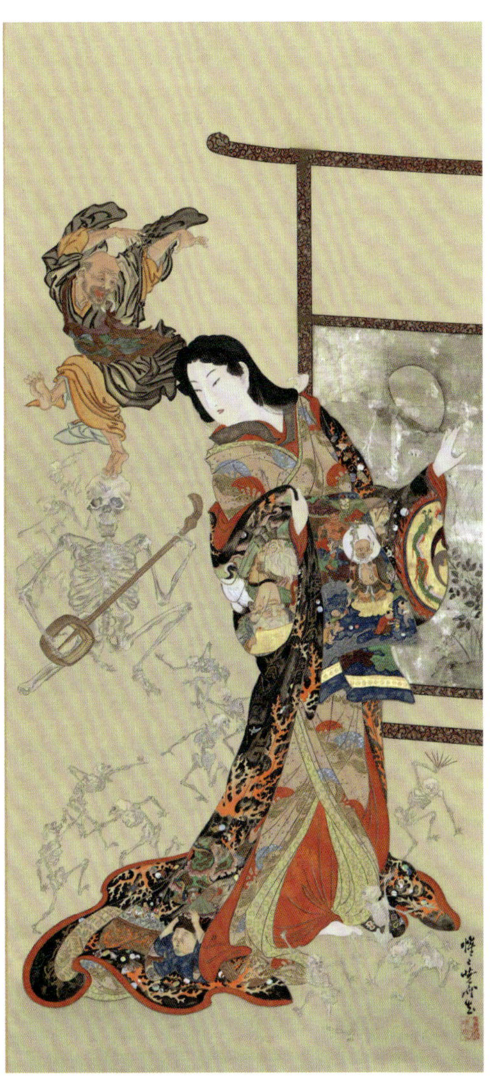

**KAWANABE KYŌSAI
(1831–1889)**

Hell Courtesan, Meiji era, about 1870s–80s
Hanging scroll; ink, color, gold, and silver on silk, 149 × 70.1 cm (58 ¾ × 27 ⅝ in.)
Museum of Fine Arts, Boston, Charles Bain Hoyt Fund and funds donated by John C. Weber, 2010, 2010.373

NETSUKE, MINIATURE CARVINGS that were threaded onto a cord, were used as toggles to secure tobacco pouches and small medicine containers onto the sashes (obis) of fashionable Japanese men. The selection of these accessories allowed the wearers to display their wit. Subject matter included real and imaginary animals, ghosts, demons, monsters, as well as elements of natural life. During the nineteenth century, when traditional dress was largely abandoned for Western attire, netsuke were no longer necessary. Many carvers turned their energies to producing nonfunctional works (*okimono*), both for the domestic and international markets.

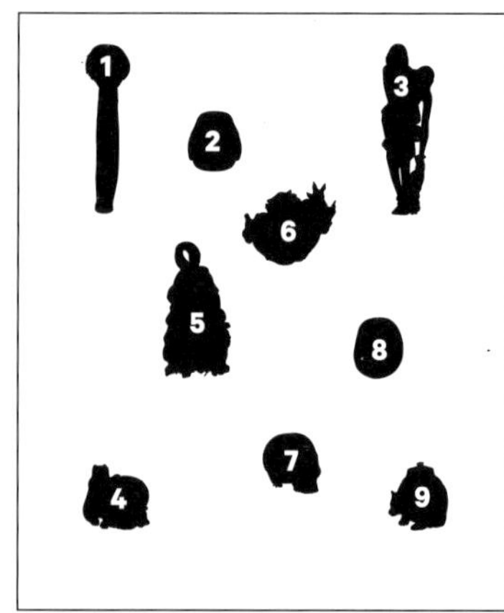

1 KOKUSAI
(DIED IN 1894)

Netsuke in the shape of a *kappa* with movable tongue, Edo period–Meiji era, 19th century
Stained stag antler and fur, 12.9 × 3.3 × 3.3 cm (5 ⅟₁₆ × 1 ⁵⁄₁₆ × 1 ⁵⁄₁₆ in.)
Museum of Fine Arts, Boston, William Sturgis Bigelow Collection, 1911, 11.23722

2 DŌYŪ
(DATES UNKNOWN)

Netsuke in the shape of Bodhidharma (Daruma) making a face, Edo period, 19th century
Ivory, 3.4 × 3.5 × 2.9 cm (1 ⁵⁄₁₆ × 1 ⅜ × 1 ⅛ in.)
Museum of Fine Arts, Boston, William Sturgis Bigelow Collection, 1911, 11.23163

3 KIKUGAWA MASAMITSU
(DATES UNKNOWN)

Netsuke in the shape of Tenaga with his long arms, carried by Ashinaga with his long legs, Edo period, mid-19th century
Stained ivory, gilding, coral, silver, and *shakudō* alloy, 11.6 × 4 × 3.6 cm (4 ⁹⁄₁₆ × 1 ⁹⁄₁₆ × 1 ⁷⁄₁₆ in.)
Museum of Fine Arts, Boston, William Sturgis Bigelow Collection, 1911, 11.23342

4 SHŪGETSU II
(DATES UNKNOWN)

Netsuke in the shape of a badger with distended scrotum crushing a hunter, Edo period, 19th century
Ivory, 3.6 × 5 × 3.5 cm (1 ⁷⁄₁₆ × 1 ¹⁵⁄₁₆ × 1 ⅜ in.)
Museum of Fine Arts, Boston, William Sturgis Bigelow Collection, 1911, 11.23543

5 ATTRIBUTED TO ASAHI
GYOKUZAN (1843–1923)

Okimono in the shape of a skull, snake, frog, and severed heads, Meiji era, about 1900
Stained ivory, horn, and pigment, 10.3 × 7 × 4 cm (4 ⅟₁₆ × 2 ¾ × 1 ⁹⁄₁₆ in.)
Museum of Fine Arts, Boston, William Sturgis Bigelow Collection, 1911, 11.23727

6 SŌZAN
(DATES UNKNOWN)

Okimono in the shape of a demon stung by a bee, Edo period, 19th century
Ivory and tortoise shell, 4.8 × 8.4 × 5.5 cm (1 ⅞ × 3 ⁵⁄₁₆ × 2 ³⁄₁₆ in.)
Museum of Fine Arts, Boston, William Sturgis Bigelow Collection, 1911, 11.23558

7 GYOKUZAN
(DATES UNKNOWN)

Netsuke in the shape of a skull with snakes, lizards, and frogs, Meiji era, late 19th century
Stained ivory, 2.9 × 3 × 3.8 cm (1 ⅛ × 1 ³⁄₁₆ × 1 ½ in.)
Museum of Fine Arts, Boston, Collection of Dr. Ernest G. Stillman, 1947, 47.414

8 HIDEMASA
(DATES UNKNOWN)

Netsuke in the shape of Bodhidharma (Daruma) with his whisk as a beard, Edo period, early to mid-19th century
Ivory and dark horn, 4.2 × 4 × 2.4 cm (1 ⅝ × 1 ⁹⁄₁₆ × 1 ⁵⁄₁₆ in.)
Museum of Fine Arts, Boston, William Sturgis Bigelow Collection, 1911, 11.23209

9 POSSIBLY BY MASANAO IV
(DATES UNKNOWN)

Netsuke in the shape of a badger kettle, Edo period–Meiji era, 19th century
Stained boxwood, 4.2 × 3.8 × 4.5 cm (1 ⅝ × 1 ½ × 1 ¾ in.)
Museum of Fine Arts, Boston, Collection of Dr. Ernest G. Stillman, 1947, 47.635

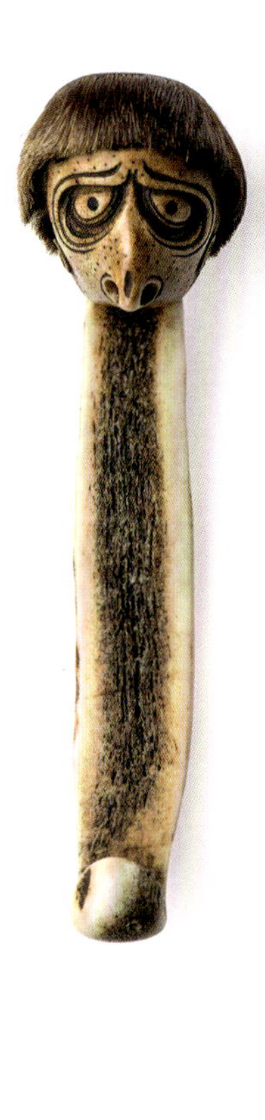
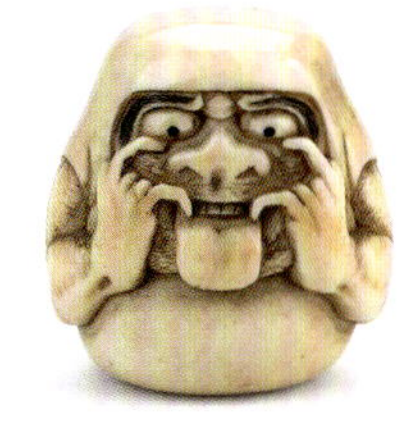
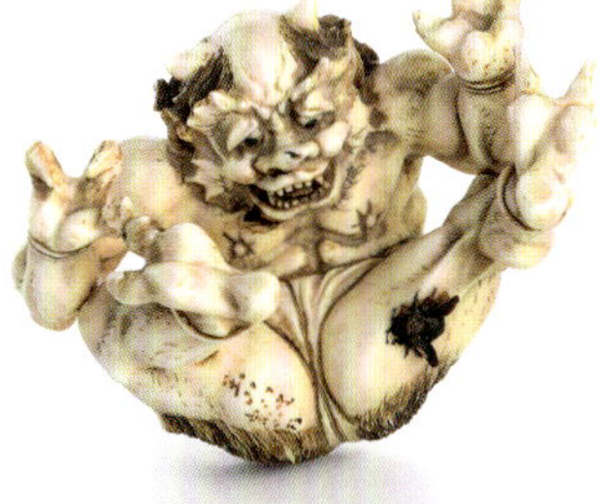
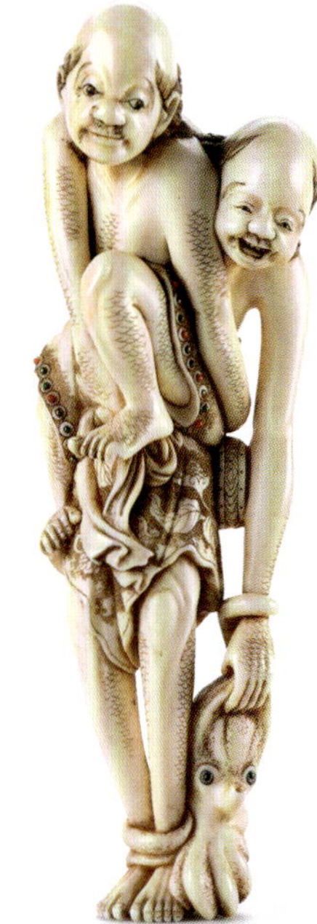
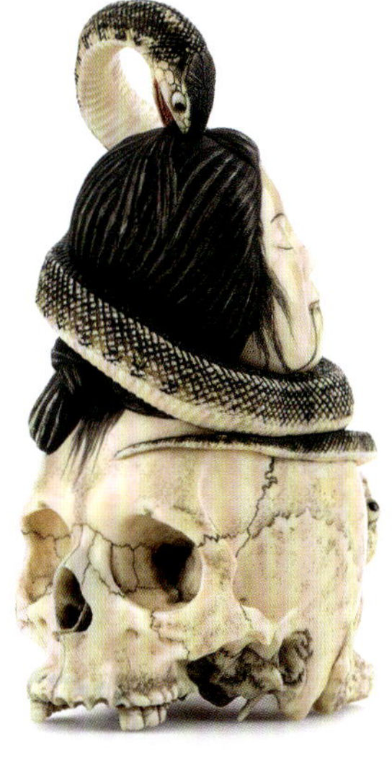
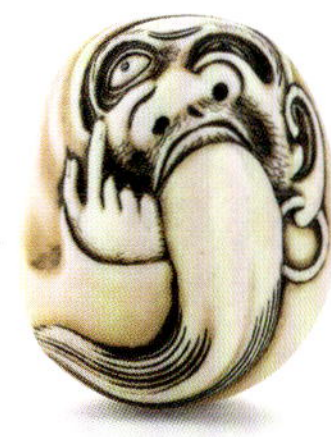
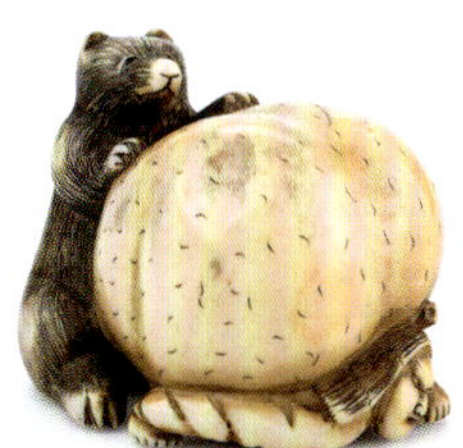
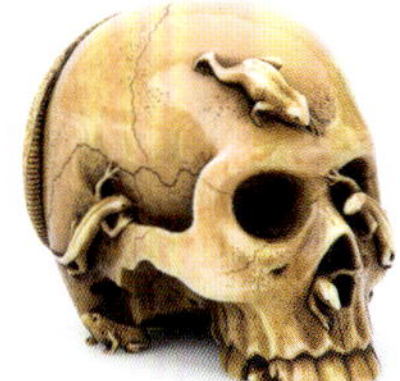
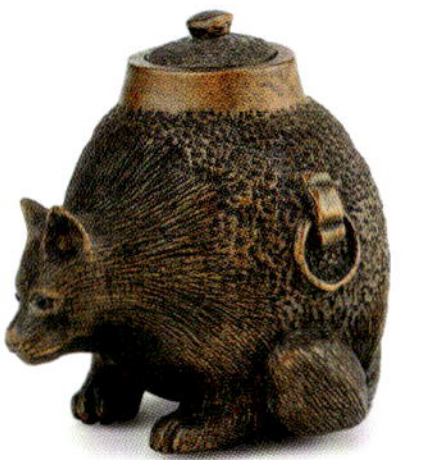

5

RELIGIOSITY

The earliest Japanese worshipped spirits that they found in mountains, rivers, trees, rocks, and other natural forms. According to Tsuji, such animistic beliefs—which came to be known as Shinto—constitute the core of the Japanese religious experience. Buddhism, the highly complex philosophical religion developed in India based upon the teachings of the Historical Buddha Śākyamuni (about 560–480 BCE) and which spread across Asia, arrived in Japan in the sixth century. Over time it absorbed a number of indigenous animistic practices. For example, the idea that grasses, trees, the earth, and other things that do not have human-like emotions could all become Buddhas, or enlightened beings, reflects the Japanese transformation of the religion.

The Japanese were frequently as impressed by the visual manifestations of the Buddhist religion as they were by its doctrines. Early in its history, the aristocratic faith's rituals and physical manifestations, including images and their adornment, were of vital importance; but in later centuries, spiritual discipline as advocated by the Zen sect became not just a religious but also a cultural force.

Particularly since the disasters of March 11, 2011—the earthquake, tsunami, and nuclear meltdown—that afflicted Japan, Murakami has explored the idea of impermanence, the transience of life, central to both Shinto and Buddhist ideas. Through these works he has offered his "non-denominational prayers."

THROUGHOUT ASIA IMAGES of the Buddha historically have preserved
a standard iconography that underscores the transcendent nature of the
deity. However, for Murakami religions must dramatically change in order
to remain relevant to new generations and therefore the forms of the
deities must also mutate.

Citing Lilith, the Second Angel, with its multiple appendages
emerging from its torso in the anime series *Neon Genesis Evangelion*
(1994–95), as one of his inspirations, Murakami introduced his own
Buddha form. The Buddha is double faced. One side with lowered eyes and
a vacant expression sports appendages erupting from its cheeks and
a goatee on its chin. The other on the reverse has a wide-open mouth with
leering fangs, reminiscent of some of Murakami's Mr. DOB figures. Unlike the
perfect proportions of traditional Buddhas, Murakami's deity has an oversize
head and a small frog-like body with a distended stomach. The emphasis on
the head originates from an earlier project in which Murakami was asked by
Naoki Takizawa of Issey Miyake Men's line to create his own version of the
egg-like character Humpty-Dumpty celebrated in English nursery rhymes.
He titled this figure "Oval." Murakami has also pointed out resonances in
the proportions of his Buddha with kawaii mascots or mascot characters
(*yuru chara*) now ubiquitous in Japan.

Oval Buddha is seated on a lotus pedestal on which historic images
of the Buddha and his attendants are typically enthroned. The upper section
of the pedestals of all of Murakami's deities has been directly inspired by
that of the tenth-century statue of Shaka, the Historical Buddha, in the
Museum of Fine Arts, Boston. In 2001, when Murakami visited the Museum's
collection, he was immediately impressed by the highly geometric form
of the base. Although he later misplaced his original sketches, the artist
produced the lotus form from memory. After being told that the distinctive
shape of the Boston pedestal was the result of the loss of the original lotus
petals, Murakami has subsequently contended that the present form is
better and has continued to appropriate it. For this statue he has added
a bottom tier of an elephant-like form reminiscent of the demonic figures
used to support some traditional Buddhist deities.

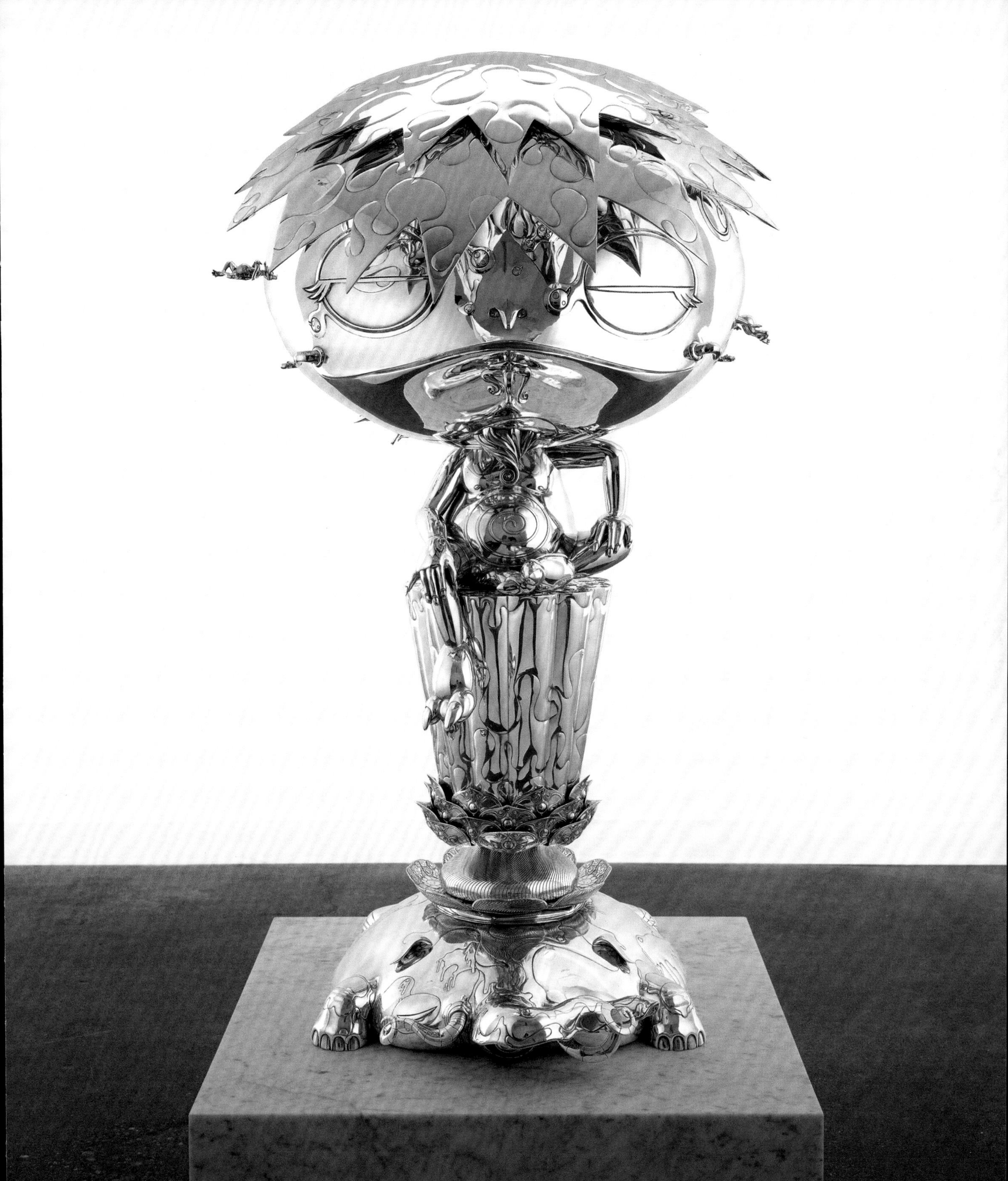

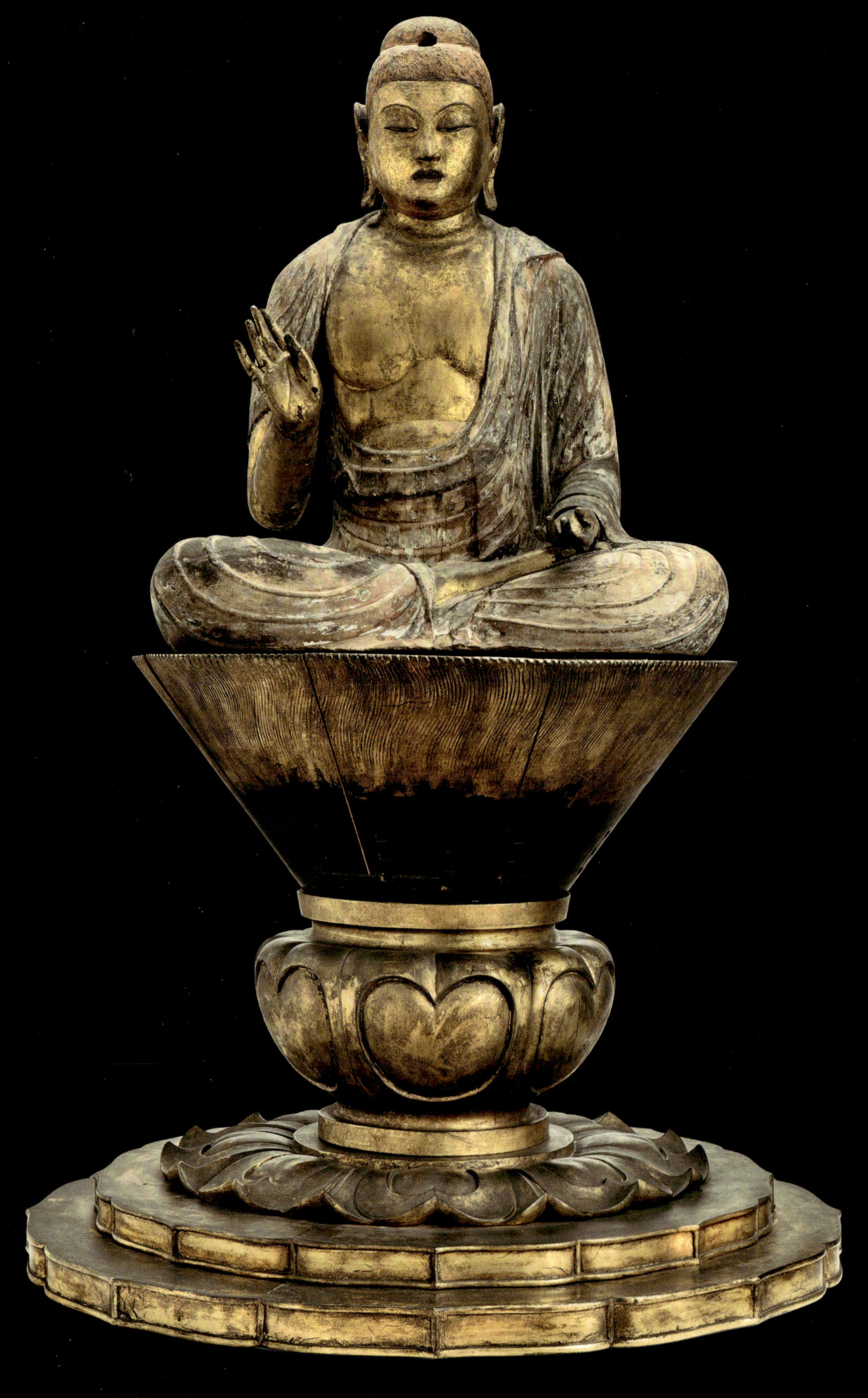

ŚĀKYAMUNI (CALLED SHAKA IN JAPAN) was the founder of the Buddhist faith. Although emulated simply as a superior human being after his death, he later became deified. This statue reflects the standard iconography for traditional sculptures: the Buddha sits in a posture of meditation, with his right hand held in the gesture of reassurance. A protuberance at his head symbolizes his knowledge (it once would have held a crystal); elongated ears bespeak his renunciation of a princely life; and a golden complexion testifies to the perfection of his being. Originally, this image would have had characteristic spiral-shaped curls.

The Buddha customarily sits on a lotus pedestal, symbolizing his purity in the mundane world. Here, however, the petals have not been preserved. The pedestal's uncharacteristic geometry, however, led Murakami to adopt the form for his *Oval Buddha*.

Shaka, the Historical Buddha, Heian period, late 10th–early 11th centuries. Single woodblock construction from Japanese cypress, polychromed and gilded, 140.3 × 77.5 × 77.5 cm (55 ¼ × 30 ½ × 30 ½ in.), including pedestal
Museum of Fine Arts, Boston, Denman Waldo Ross Collection, 1909, 09.72a-b

 While the explanations can be complex, for Tsuji, the answer is simple: it is the art of *shōgon*, ritual adornment. The representations of garments and jewelry worn by the Buddhas, bodhisattvas, and celestial beings; the palaces, garden ponds, and grounds where they reside; and the plants and trees that grow there are all transformed by gold, silver, and richly colored jewels—and thus into adornment itself.

Portrayed with his three heads (each with three eyes and fanged teeth), eight arms, and intense red skin, Batō is worshipped as one of the six forms of Kannon, the Bodhisattva of Compassion. Identified by the horse head in his crown and by his distinctive hand gesture with palms pressed together, Batō is believed to preside over the fate of beings reborn in the form of animals because of their misdeeds.

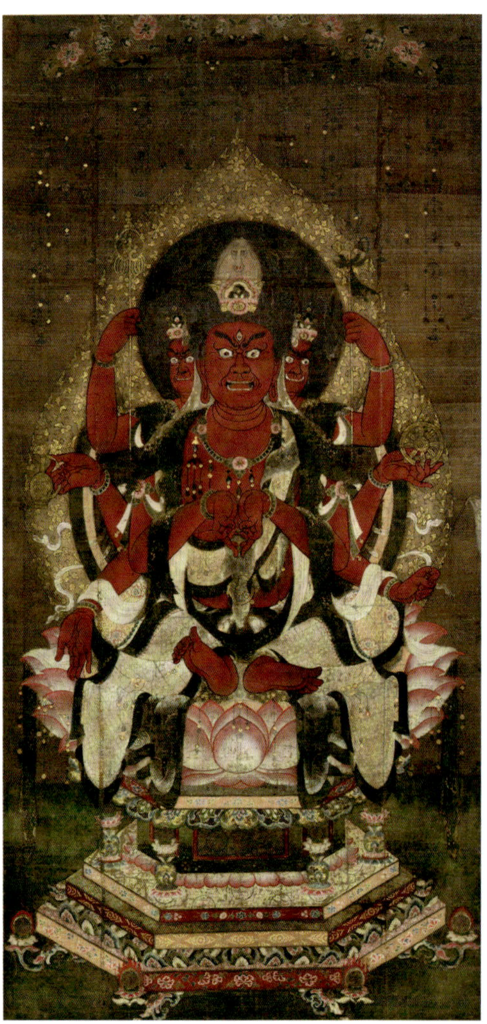

Batō Kannon, the Horse-Headed Bodhisattva of Compassion, Heian period, 12th century
Panel; ink, color, gold, and silver on silk, 166.1 × 82.7 cm (65 ⅜ × 32 ⁹⁄₁₆ in.)
Museum of Fine Arts, Boston, Fenollosa-Weld Collection, 1911, 11.4035

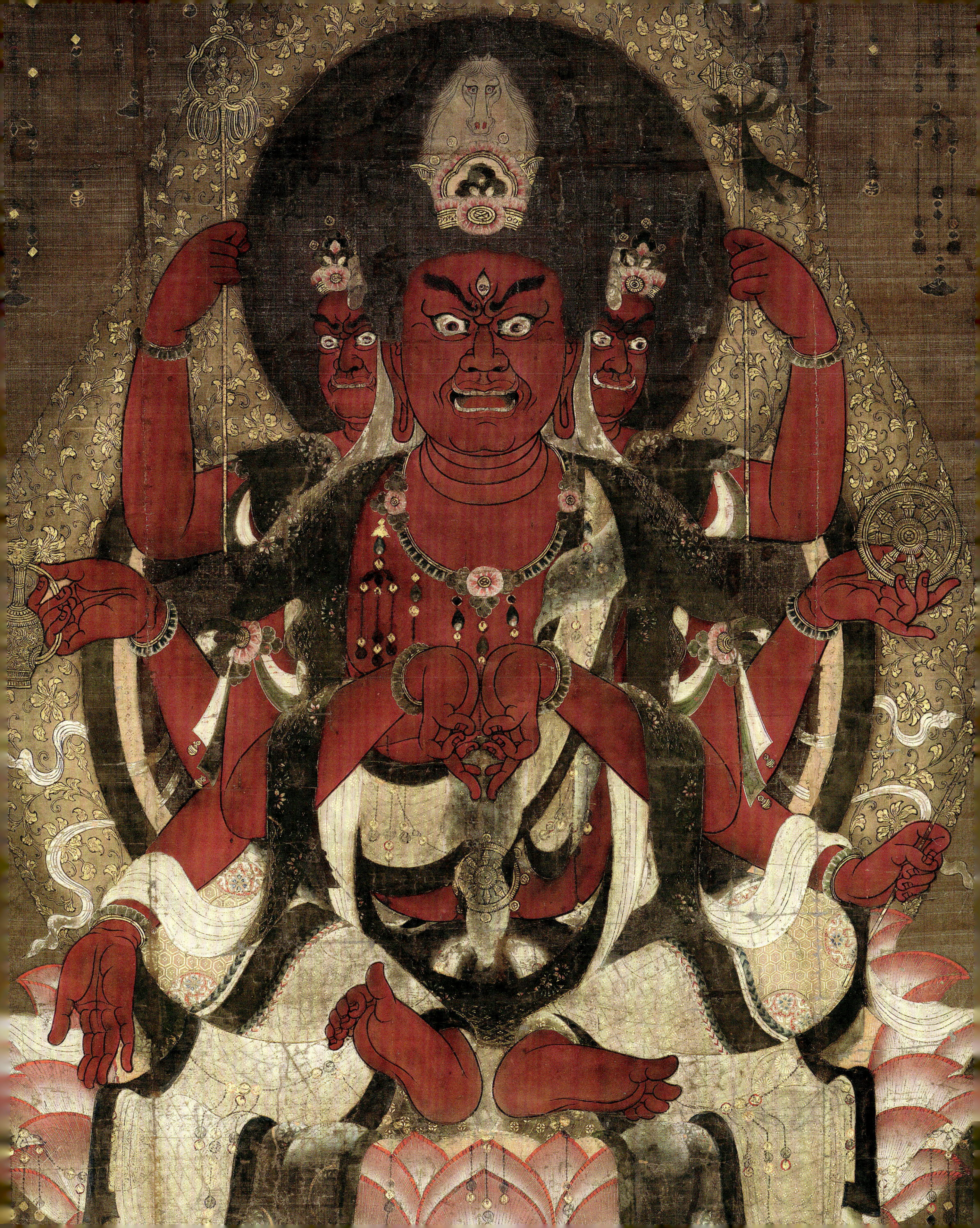

DAIITOKU MYŌŌ REPRESENTS the ability of the enlightened believer
to triumph over death. Devotees direct rituals to him for the protection
of the state, and also for personal needs. Omniscient, stronger than
any human, Daiitoku possesses six heads, six arms, and six legs.
The staff, sword, club, bow, and arrow are his weapons, used to help
a believer remove obstacles to enlightenment. He rides a water buffalo,
symbolizing his ability to domesticate the animal that is usually
associated with the King of Death.

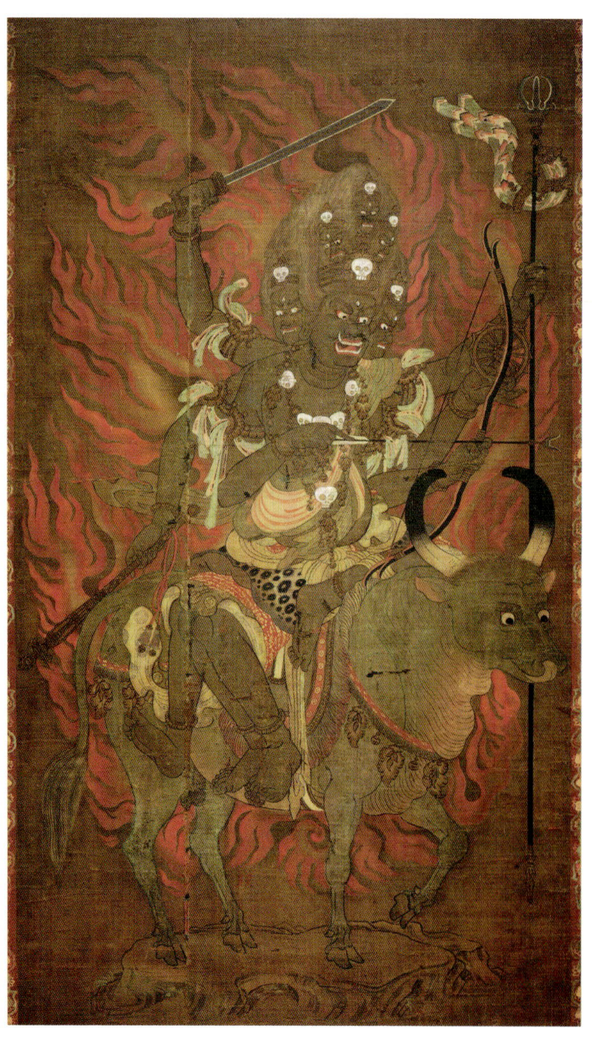

Daiitoku myōō, the Wisdom King of Great Awe-Inspiring Power, Kamakura period, first half of the 13th century
Panel; ink, color, and gold on silk, 113.3 × 65.2 cm (44 ⅝ × 25 ¹¹⁄₁₆ in.)
Museum of Fine Arts, Boston, Fenollosa-Weld Collection, 1911, 11.4037

THE ZEN SECT (CALLED CHAN IN CHINA) traces its legendary beginnings to the arrival in China of the sixth-century Indian monk Bodhidharma, shown here with a bushy beard and gold earrings. Bodhidharma allegedly tried to convince China's ruler, Emperor Wu, of the superiority of meditation over traditional devotional practices. But the emperor was confounded by the responses that Bodhidharma gave to his questions—all phrases that defied conventional logic. Discouraged by this apparent lack of understanding, Bodhidharma departed and miraculously rode a broken reed across the Yangzi River into northern China.

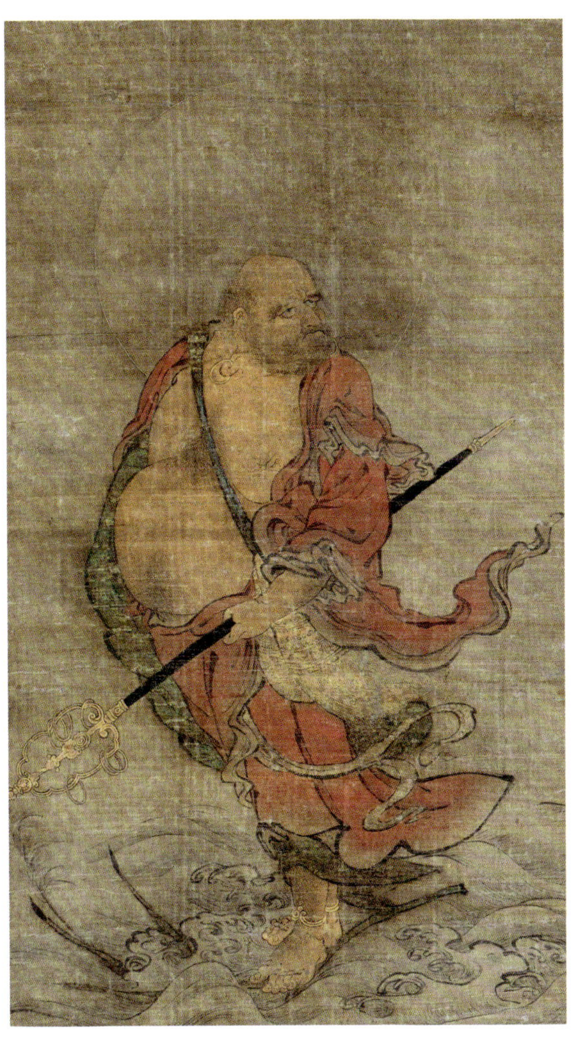

Bodhidharma (Daruma) on a Reed, Nanbokuchō period, 14th century
Hanging scroll; ink, color, and gold on silk, 69 × 40.6 cm (27 ³⁄₁₆ × 16 in.)
Museum of Fine Arts, Boston, William Sturgis Bigelow Collection, 1911, 11.6312

ALTHOUGH THE ZEN SECT has eschewed devotional paintings, portraits of its legendary patriarch Bodhidharma and other revered teachers have long provided aspiring practitioners with exemplars in their paths to enlightenment. Bodhidharma (Daruma in Japanese) traveled from India to China in the sixth century, arriving at the Shaolin monastery there. For nine years he stood before a rock cave, so deep in meditation that his legs and arms atrophied. Finding himself distracted by sleep, he cut off his eyelids.

In Japan during the Nanbokuchō (1333–1392) and Muromachi (1392–1568) periods, Zen had been the sect favored by the warrior class, which found resonance in its meditational practices with their insistence on self-reliance. Normally, artists have portrayed the figure with spare calligraphic strokes on paper. Murakami has reinterpreted the subject with highly saturated colors and a luxurious platinum leaf ground. He turned to this Zen Buddhist theme for a series of paintings exhibited in New York in 2007, six years after the terrorist attacks on the World Trade Center, and with the United States embroiled in the war in Iraq. For Murakami, war has also taken an economic form, with American investors forever engaged in fierce financial battles. Thus, the series is his critique of the current political and social order.

TAKASHI MURAKAMI

"I open wide my eyes but see no scenery, I fix my gaze upon my heart," Heisei era, 2007
Acrylic and platinum leaf on canvas mounted on board, about 2.4 × 2.8 m (7 ft. 11 in. × 9 ft. 3 in.)
From the collection of Gerald and Sandra Fineberg

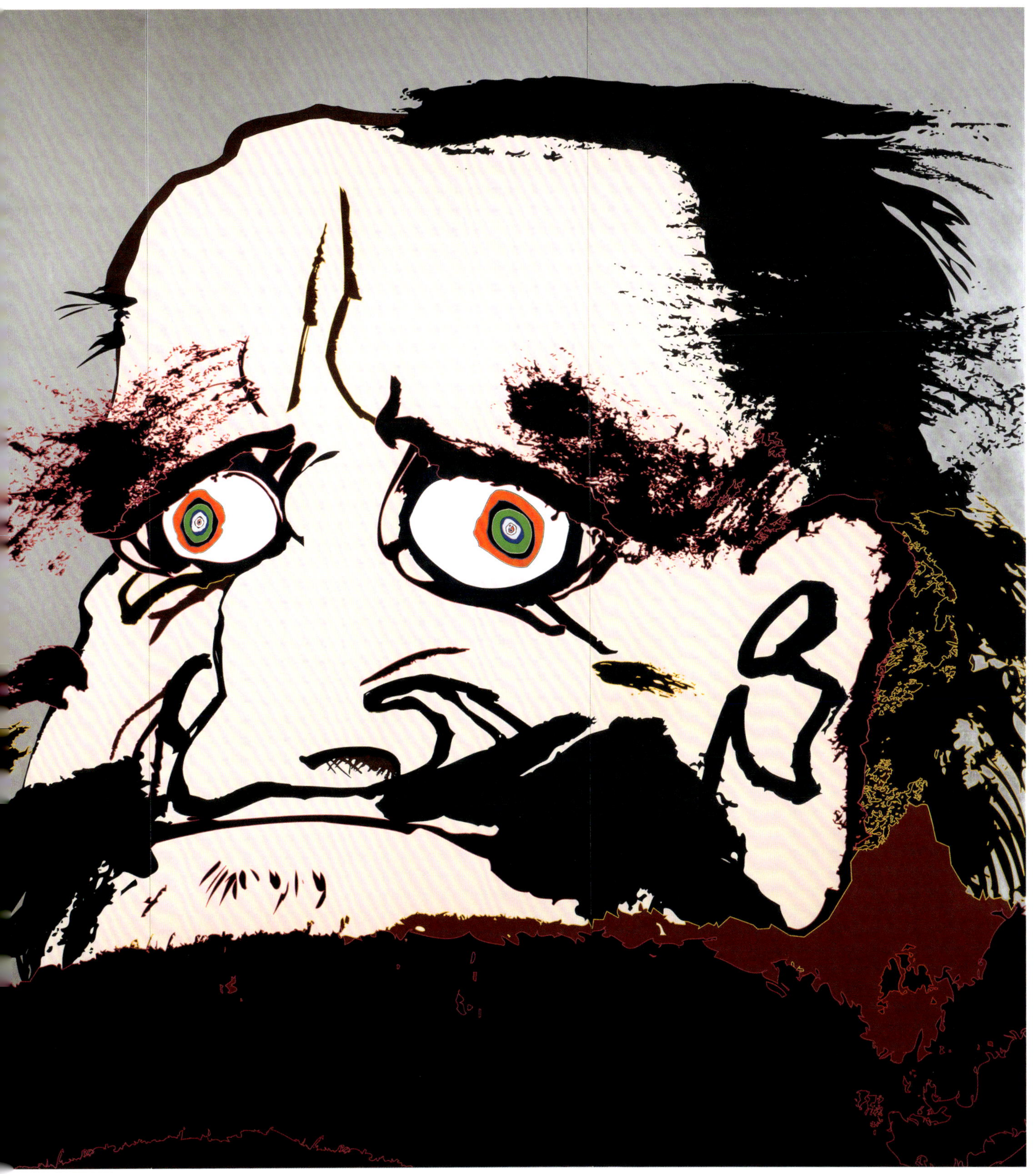

For all Buddhists, the ultimate goal is to achieve enlightenment, often associated with emptiness—a state free from the cycles of birth and rebirth. For practitioners of Zen Buddhism the circle, or *ensō*, executed with a powerful sweep of the calligraphic brush, is the perfect symbol of emptiness. Murakami has juxtaposed his version against a white-on-white background of skulls. However, rather than producing the circle with a brush, he has captured the spontaneity of the stroke through the use of his favored techniques of computer-generated graphics and silk-screen. According to traditional Zen imagery, skulls serve as *memento mori*, reminders of death. For Murakami, they are motifs that, on one hand, recall the horrors of nuclear war, but can also appeal to audiences brought up on *Pirates of the Caribbean.*

Tsuji and Murakami have expressed their admiration for the Zen priest, calligrapher, and painter Hakuin Ekaku (1685–1768). Hakuin produced a small number of ensō, noted for their unselfconscious simplicity. The title of this work, *Ensō: Hachiman*, makes reference to the indigenous Shinto deity who was the first to support Buddhism and became revered as the god of war. When Hakuin attempted to bring Zen teachings to the populace, he adopted Shinto gods as well as traditional Japanese folk deities as painting subjects.

TAKASHI MURAKAMI *Ensō: Hachiman—Black Circle on White,* Heisei era, 2017
Acrylic on canvas mounted on aluminum frame, 120 × 120 × 51 cm (47 ¼ × 47 ¼ × 20 in.)
Courtesy of the artist

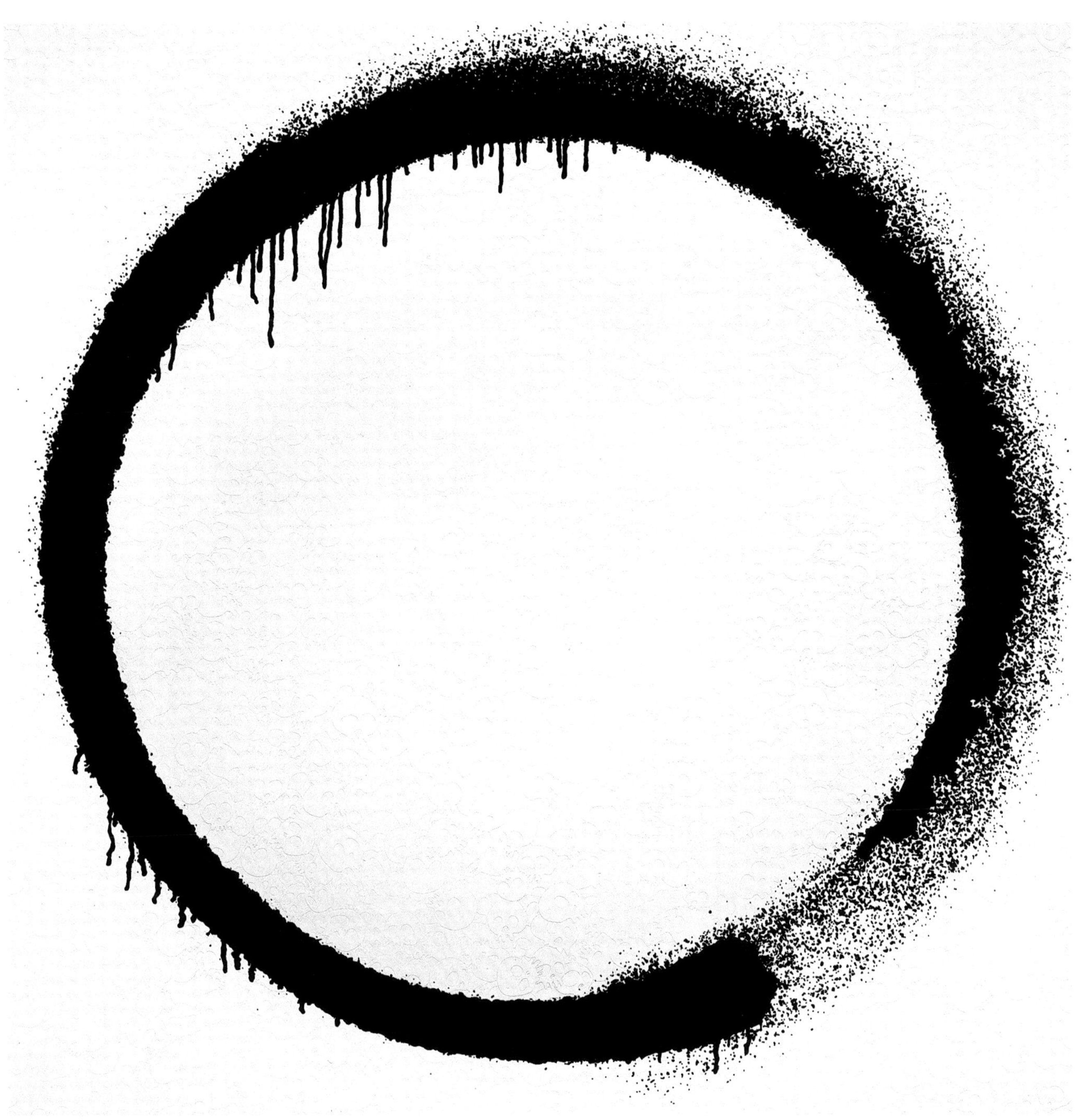

ALTHOUGH A ZEN BUDDHIST HIMSELF, the priest, painter, and calligrapher Hakuin frequently proclaimed that both the native and imported faiths—Shinto and Buddhism—provided effective teachings. He inscribed this scroll, the focus of worship, with the names of three indigenous Japanese deities: Tenshō kōtaijingū (Amaterasu), the sun goddess and progenitor of the imperial family (center); Hachiman daibosatsu, god of war and protector of warriors (at right); and, at left, Kasuga daimyōjin, the tutelary god of the powerful Fujiwara family. These three were also associated with important shrines—Ise, Iwashimizu Hachiman, and Kasuga—and represent a synthesis of Shinto and Buddhist beliefs.

**HAKUIN EKAKU
(1685–1768)**

Three Deities, Edo period, 18th century
Hanging scroll; ink on paper, 96.5 × 28.9 cm (38 × 11 ⅜ in.)
Museum of Fine Arts, Boston, Gift of the Gitter-Yelen Collection, 2008, 2008.655

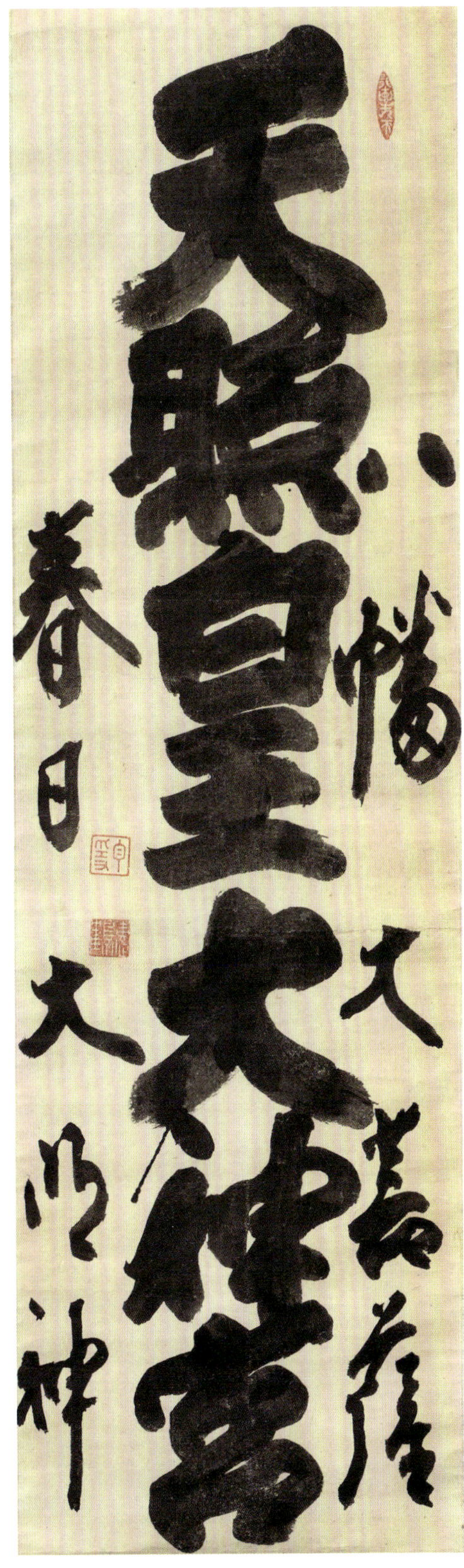

6

ECCENTRICITY

Eccentricity has long been valued as a positive characteristic in Japanese art. Particularly in response to the imposition of strict codes of social behavior by the Tokugawa military government in the seventeenth century, artists began to express their individuality by flouting the conventions of the academic schools favored by the establishment. Traditional themes became sources for parody; time-honored brushwork was abandoned for more unconventional painting modes.

In his groundbreaking book *Lineage of Eccentrics*, Tsuji identified six little-studied artists from the Edo period, distinguished for their expressionistic bent and eccentric manner of painting. Through his efforts they have become some of the most celebrated artists today. Two—Soga Shōhaku and Itō Jakuchū—are represented here. Although these artists did not participate in master-to-disciple relationships, they form their own art historical grouping in their unorthodox approaches to painting.

Tsuji's book has had a profound impact on Murakami. In reading the accounts of these earlier artists' careers (particularly that of Soga Shōhaku), he has found irreverent approaches to image making that resonate with his own. With Tsuji's encouragement, Murakami has been able to effectively channel Shōhaku's energy and presented his own bold and unconventional compositions, establishing a claim to be the most recent member of this lineage of eccentrics.

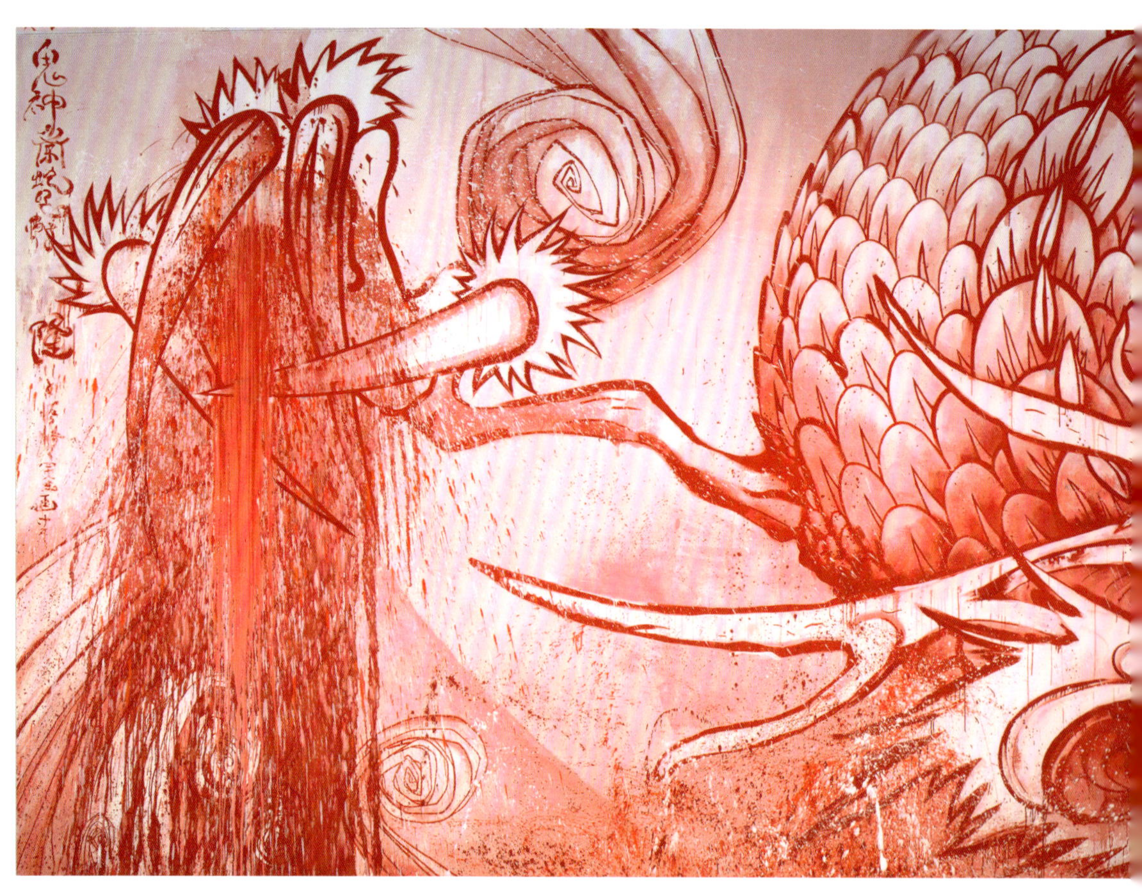

TAKASHI MURAKAMI *Dragon in Clouds—Red Mutation: The version I painted myself in annoyance after Professor Tsuji told me, "Why don't you paint something yourself for once?"* Heisei era, 2010. Acrylic on canvas, about 3.7 × 18 m (12 × 59 ft.)
Courtesy of the artist

DRAGON AND CLOUDS (1763) by the eccentric painter Soga Shōhaku has long loomed large in Murakami's artistic imagination. Early in his career Murakami had seized upon Tsuji's *Lineage of Eccentrics* as the foundation for the conceptualization of his own oeuvre, and a reproduction of Shōhaku's monumental painting had been emblazoned on the cover. Many years later when Murakami and Tsuji embarked upon a spirited repartee of art production and criticism in the series of twenty-one articles commissioned by the magazine *Geijutsu shinchō* from 2009 to 2011, Tsuji offered up the MFA's Shōhaku dragon as the focus of the sixth contest. Noting that Murakami almost always engages the members of the Kaikai Kiki studio in the production of his works of art, Tsuji pointedly challenged Murakami to paint something on his own.

As the full title of Murakami's painting reflects, Murakami found himself "backed into a corner, [his] hands and heart paralyzed with fear of exploring the first pangs of love between [them]." While he struggled, he ruminated on a watercolor by the English artist and poet William Blake, *The Great Red Dragon and the Woman Clothed with the Sun* (about 1803–5). The picture had figured in Thomas Harris's *Red Dragon* (1981), part of a series of books that included, *The Silence of the Lambs*; a serial killer, obsessed with the watercolor, machinates to devour a copy. Murakami also looked to virtuosic works such as the fifty-five-foot curtain with sketches of monsters for the Shintomi Theater by Kawanabe Kyōsai (1831–1889), which the artist painted in four hours while drunk, and the banner of Shōki, the Demon Queller, which Katsushika Hokusai (1760–1849) composed completely in vermillion. Contemporary works including the album jacket for the British rock group King Crimson's 1969 *In the Court of the Crimson King* were part of his studies, too.

Then Murakami took on the challenge and within a twenty-four-hour period completed his interpretation of Shōhaku's thirty-foot masterpiece. The result was a sweeping composition, all in red, that spans nearly sixty feet, with explosions of pigment flying at the canvas—a true investment of Murakami's being. Since that time Murakami has credited the encounter with Shōhaku's *Dragon and Clouds* and Tsuji's challenge with giving him the confidence to orchestrate massive scale paintings. The dragon itself has been produced in two other editions, one in red and one in blue, and featured as a motif in his landmark 2012 painting *500 Arhats*.

In 2013 Murakami came face to face with Shōhaku's *Dragon and Clouds* for the first time at an exhibition of masterpieces of Japanese art from the collection of the MFA at the Tokyo National Museum. He remembers feeling an immediate communication with Shōhaku, as one artist to another, through the painting. For Murakami it was like "meeting my father for the first time. Oh, this is my DNA!"

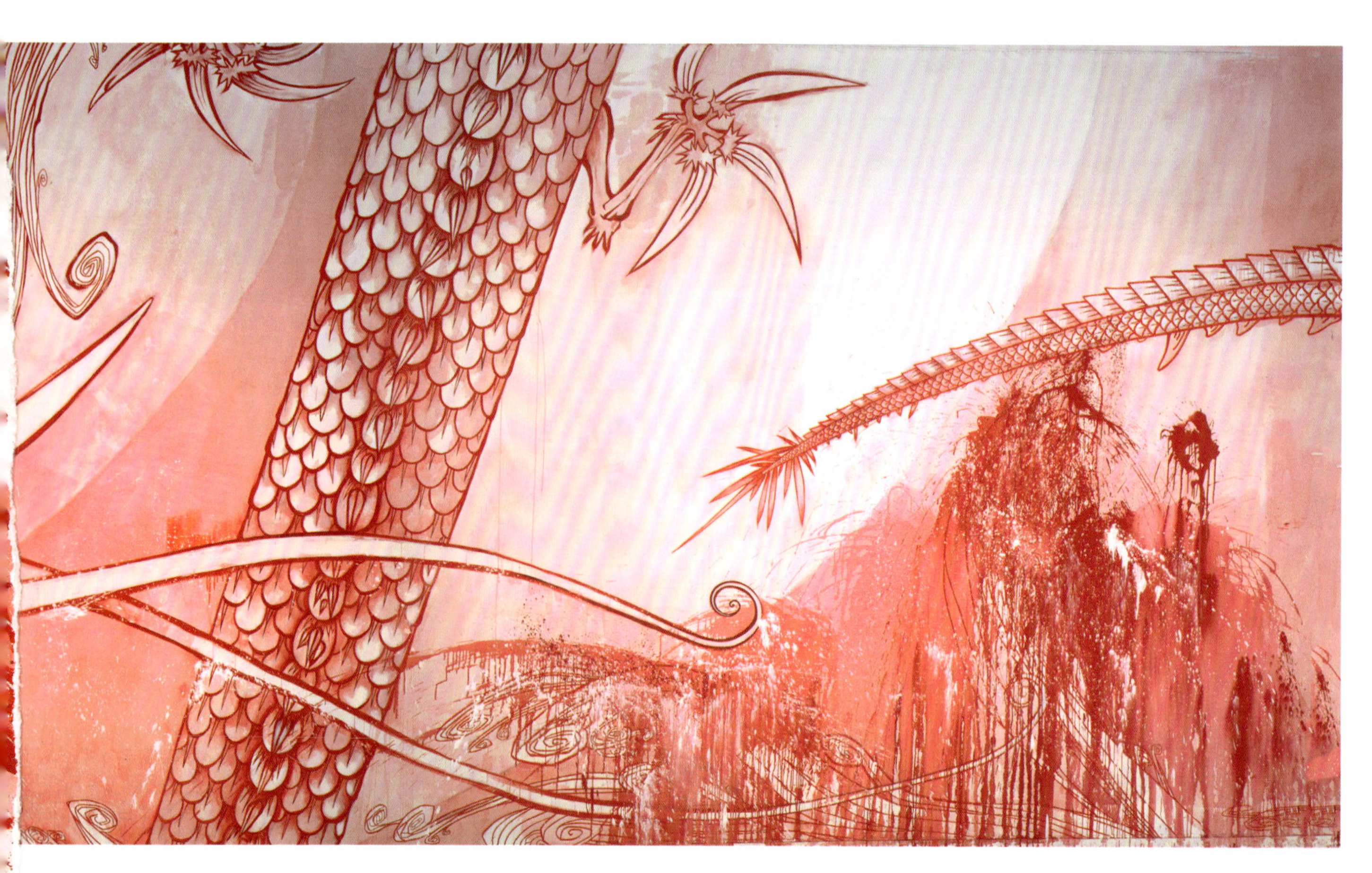

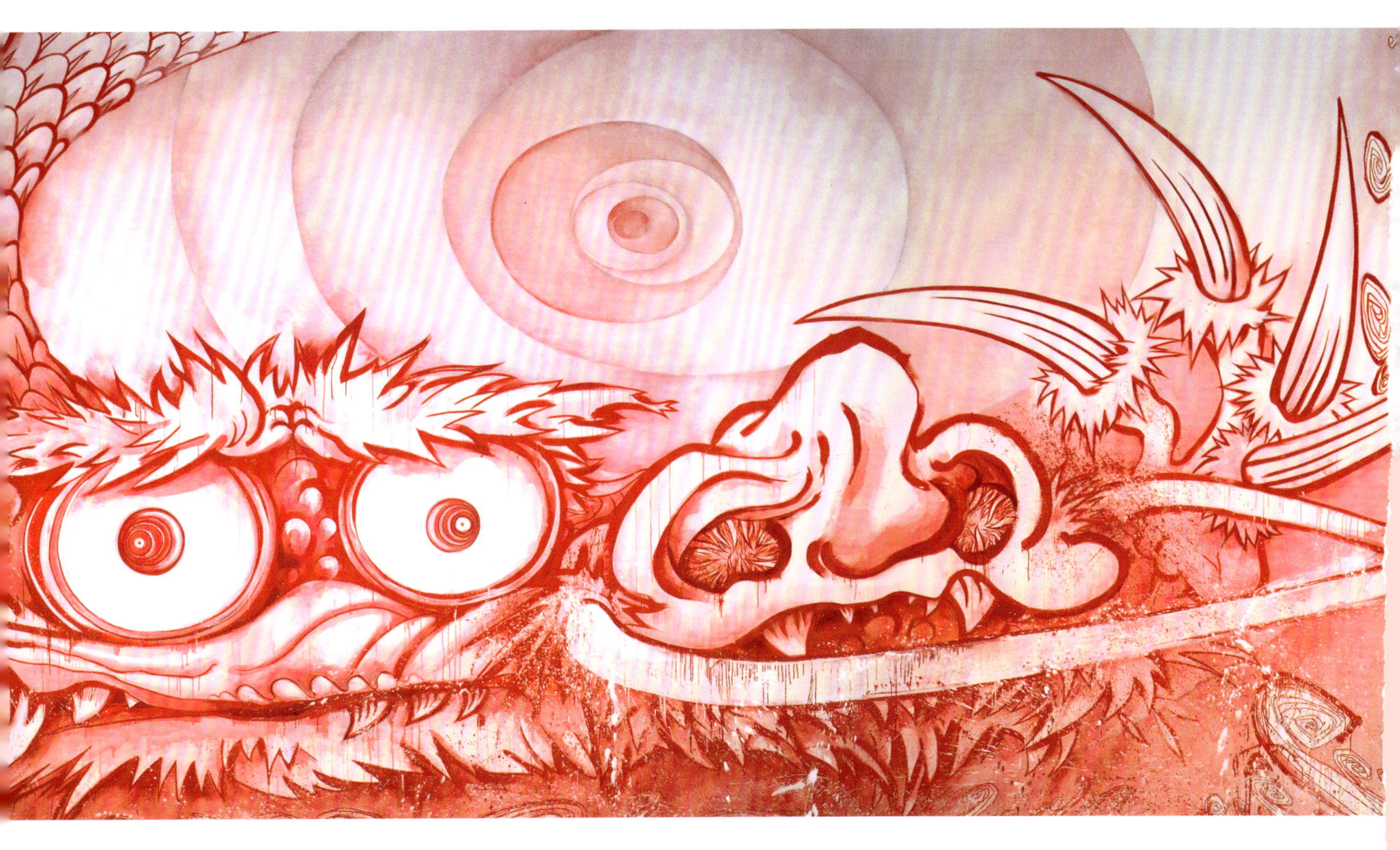

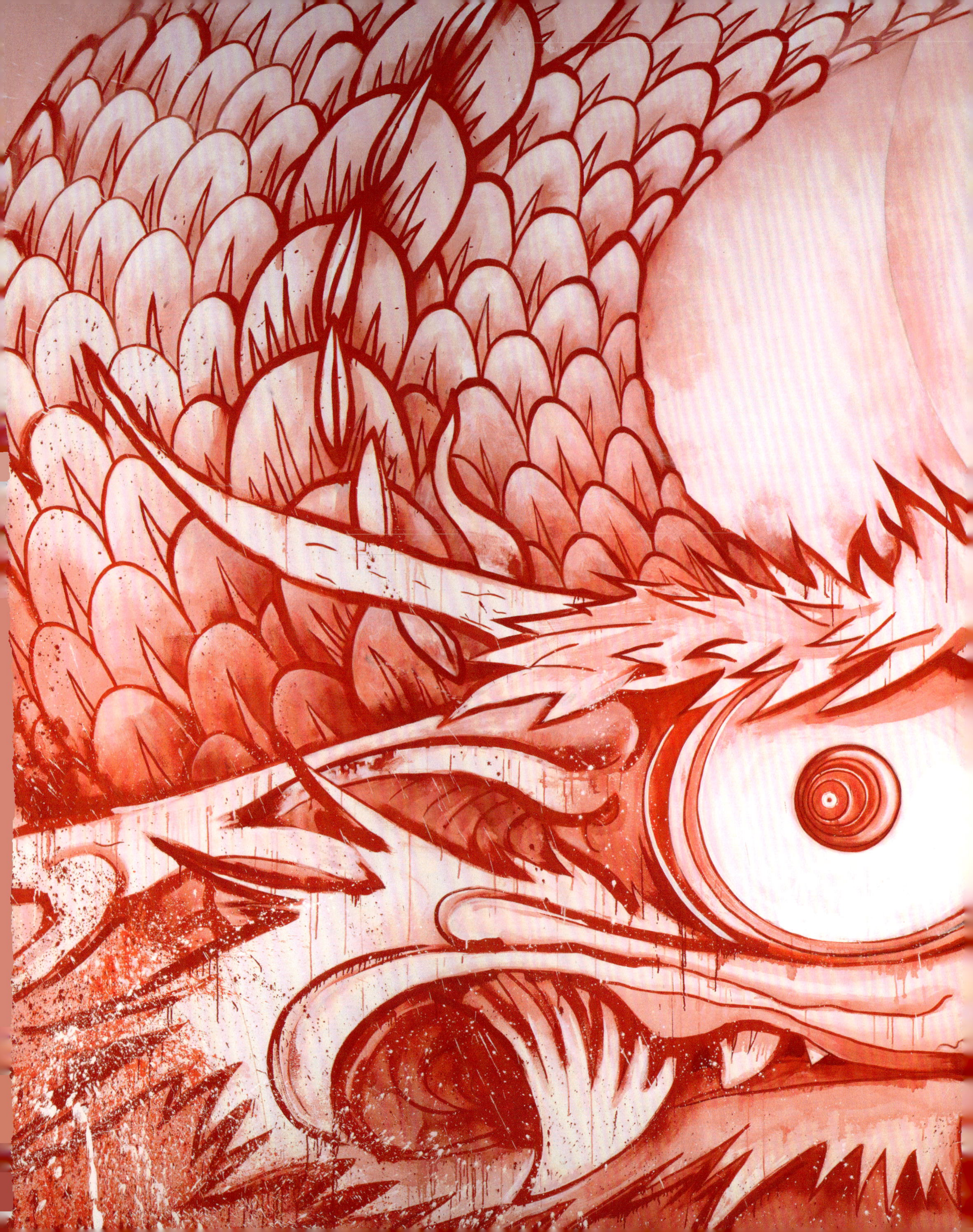

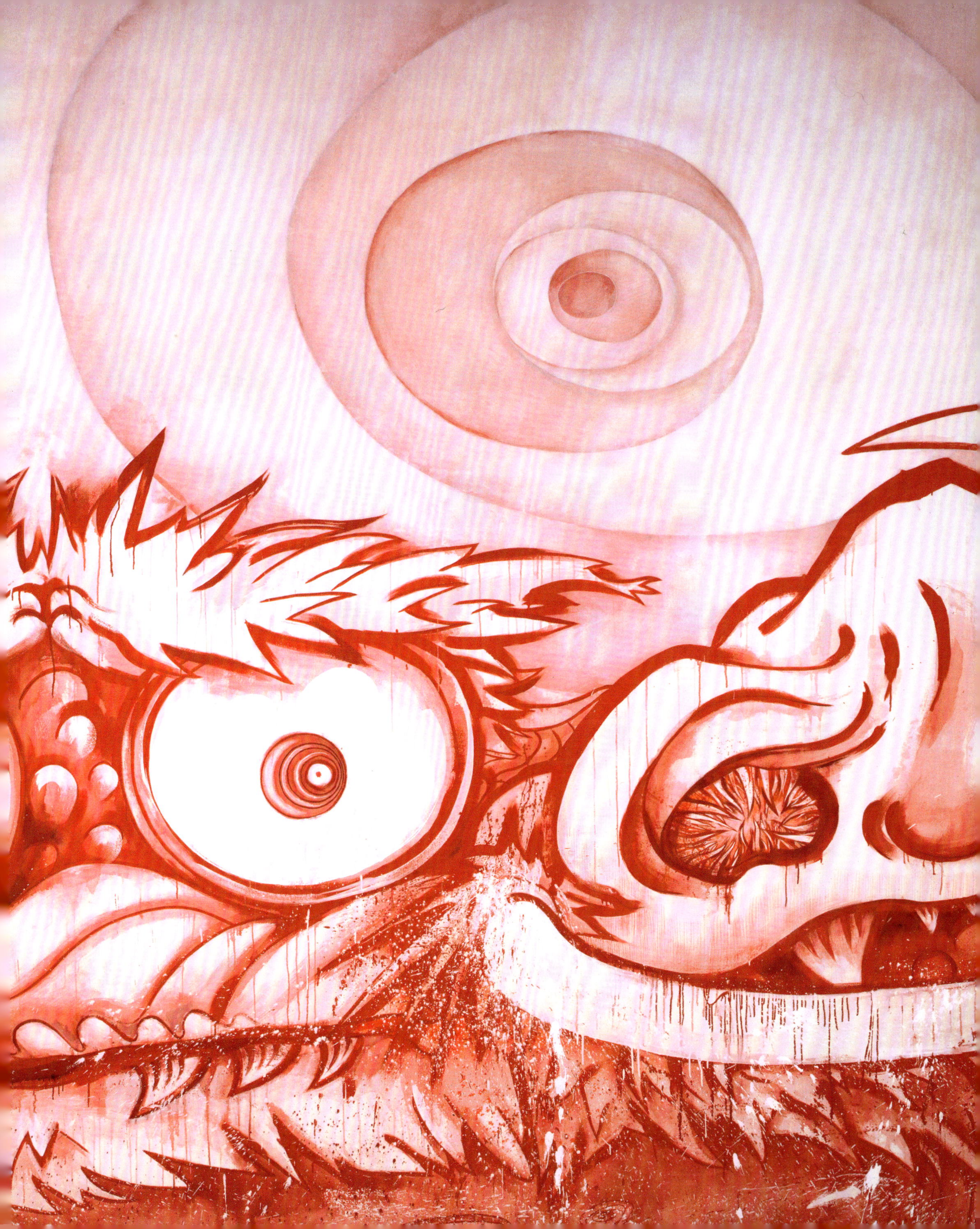

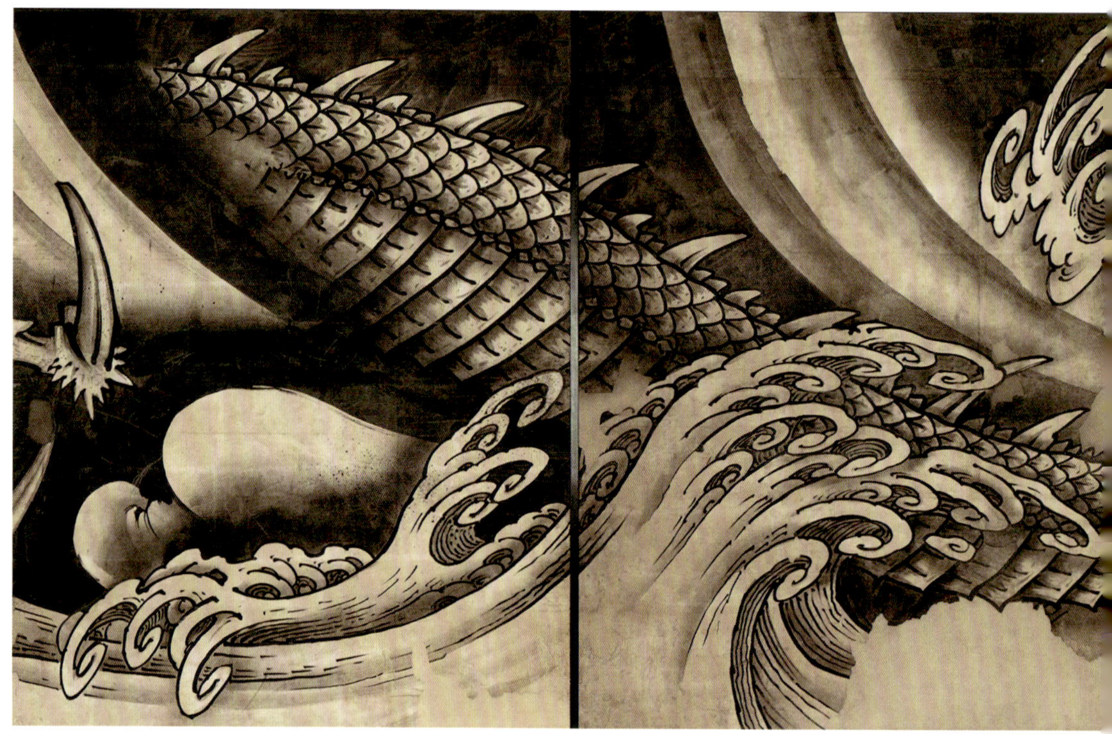

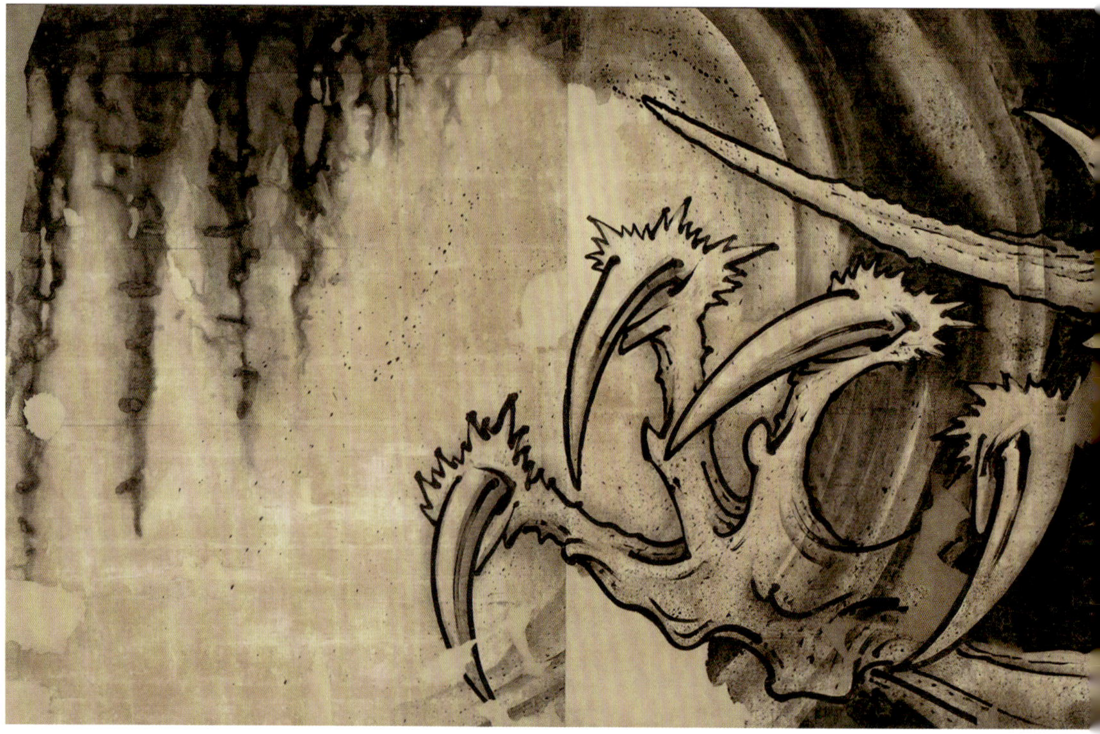

SOGA SHŌHAKU
(1730–1781)

Dragon and Clouds, Edo period, 1763
Originally mounted as fusuma, now remounted as eight panels; ink on paper, each 165.6 × 135 cm (65 ³⁄₁₆ × 53 ⅛ in.)
Museum of Fine Arts, Boston, William Sturgis Bigelow Collection, 1911, 11.7040–11.7043.1-2

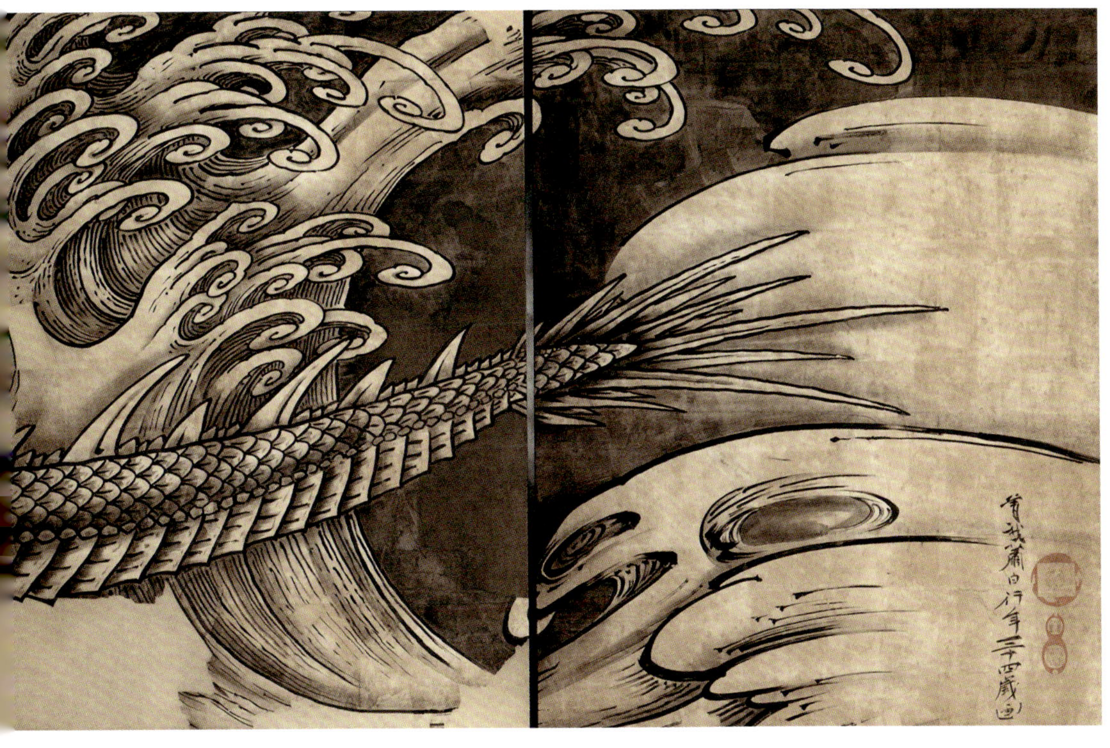

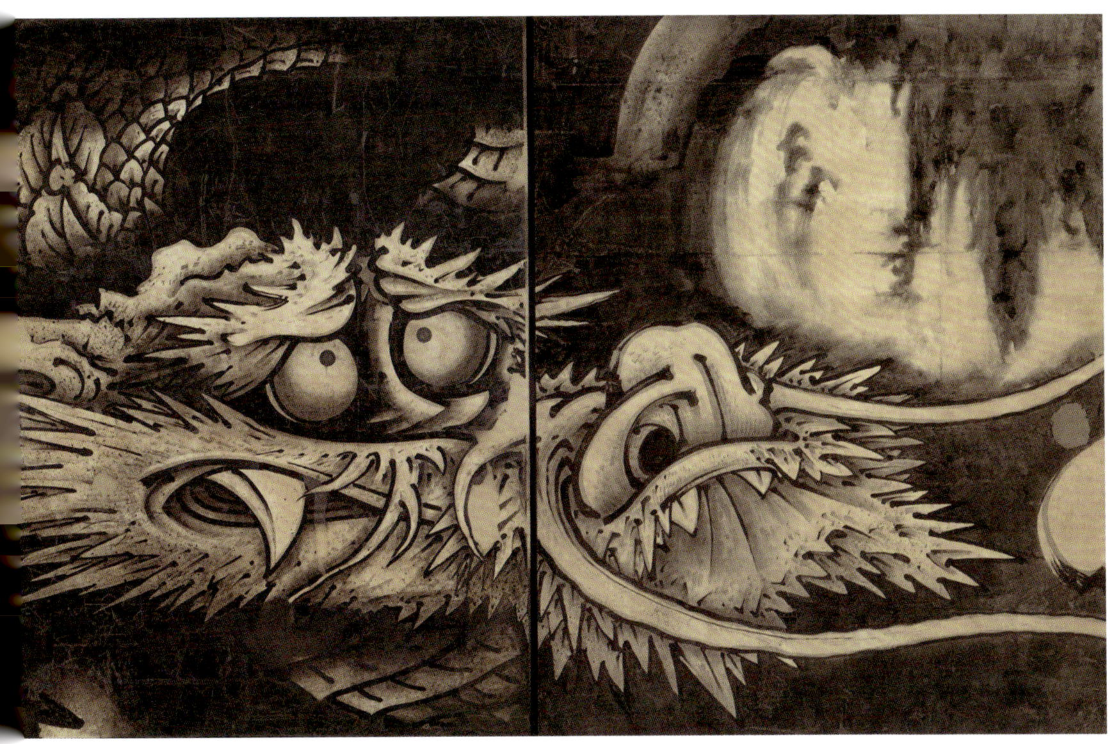

SHŌHAKU'S DRAGON SWOOPS DOWN through whirls of clouds and mist and lashes its scaly tail through roiling waves in a rhythmic symphony of rich shades of ink extending across the monumental composition. Tsuji recently determined that the tail section would have lined one interior wall of a temple structure; the head would have ornamented the opposite wall. Four additional fusuma, or sliding panels, of a smaller size (now missing), with the rest of the body of the dragon, would have flanked a central altar. While it is certain that the paintings were once installed in a Buddhist temple, unfortunately the provenance of the paintings is not known.

Shōhaku greatly admired the style of the thirteenth-century Chinese painter Chen Rong. Indeed the energy of the mercurial, mythical beast found on these fusuma has parallels to the images found in Chen Rong's *Nine Dragons* scroll dated 1244 (and in the MFA's collection). However, Shōhaku brought his own dynamism to the execution of this work in the forceful gestural brushstrokes that sweep across the vast surface of the painting. It is these qualities that Murakami has captured in his reinterpretation of the work.

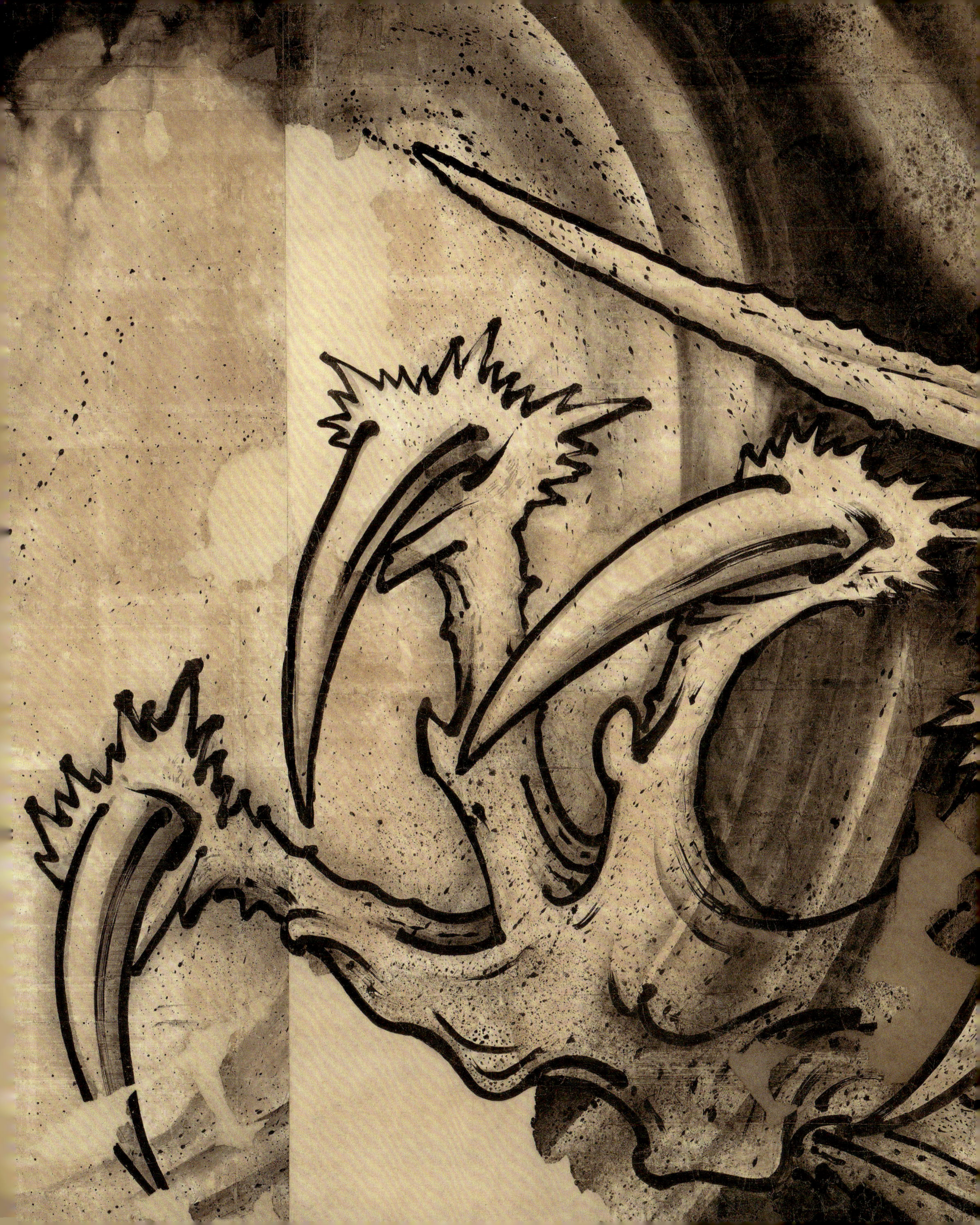

THE FACT THAT BIRDS OF PREY were one of Shōhaku's favorite subjects might have been related to his self-identification with the Soga school, which favored the hawk as a motif. However, compared to works on this theme by the earlier Soga artists, Shōhaku's hawks show a close attention to minute detail and an ambition to depict each bird as a unique individual. This particular hawk is undoubtedly Shōhaku's most monumental work among his birds of prey.

This painting is almost identical in size to *Dragon and Clouds* by Shōhaku. Conservators in the MFA's Asian Conservation Studio recently discovered that in-fills they removed from the dragon fusuma appear to have been taken from other sections of this hawk composition that are no longer extant. Thus, these two works must have been produced and displayed at the same temple.

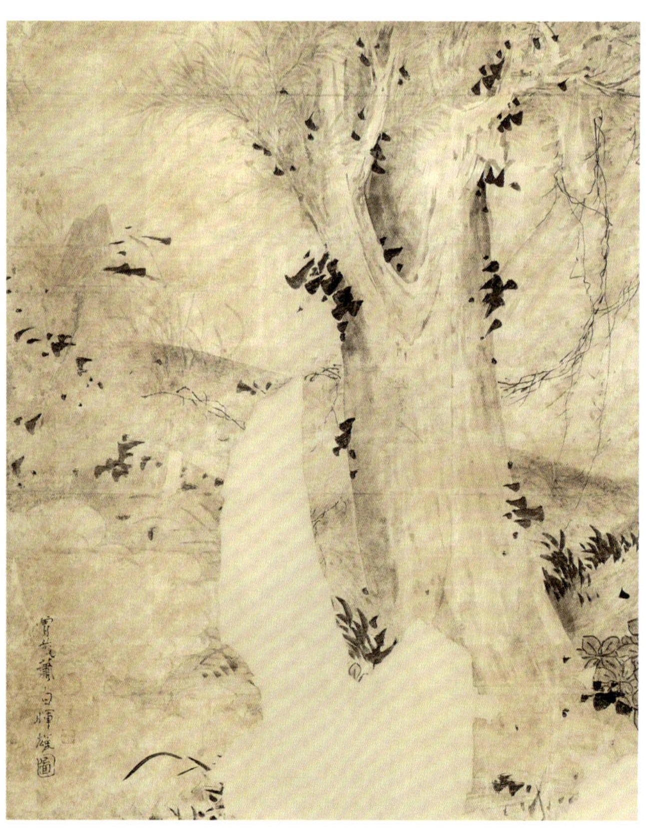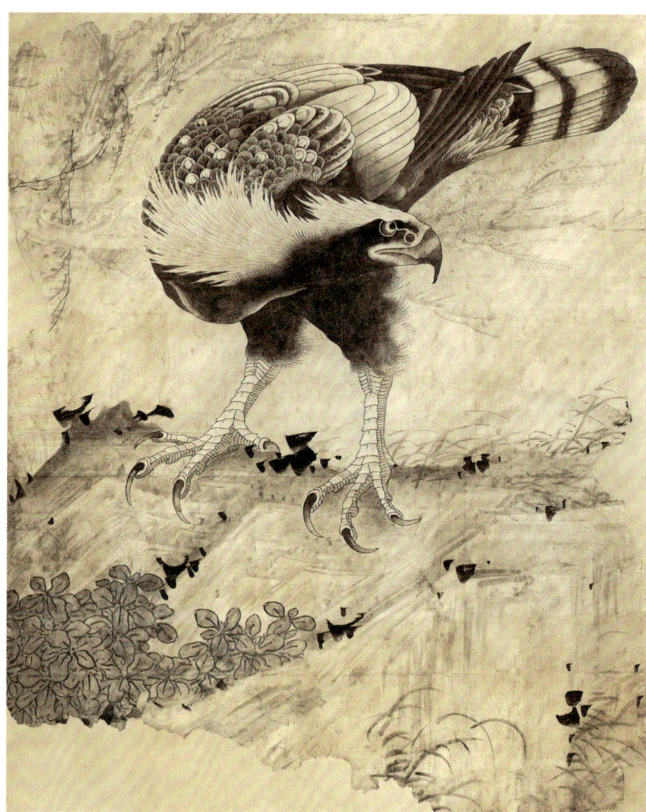

SOGA SHŌHAKU
(1730–1781)

Hawk, Edo period, possibly 1763
Originally mounted as fusuma, now remounted on two panels; ink on paper, each 165.8 × 135.3 cm (65 ¼ × 53 ¼ in.)
Museum of Fine Arts, Boston, William Sturgis Bigelow Collection, 1911, 11.7049.1-2

IN THESE SCROLLS ITŌ JAKUCHŪ has copied "archaic and wild" Chinese images of *rakan* (Chinese, *lohan*)—the enlightened beings who will protect Buddhist law until the arrival of Miroku, the Buddha of the Future. Jakuchū's works are now widely admired in the United States and Japan, partially due to Tsuji's enthusiastic praise of their technique and unconventional compositions. But in fact the MFA founding collectors of Japanese art—Ernest Fenollosa and William Sturgis Bigelow—were the first Westerners to acquire and display his paintings. Since the earthquake, tsunami, and nuclear disaster of March 11, 2011, rakan, as beings who can provide hope to those who survive, have become some of Murakami's favored subjects.

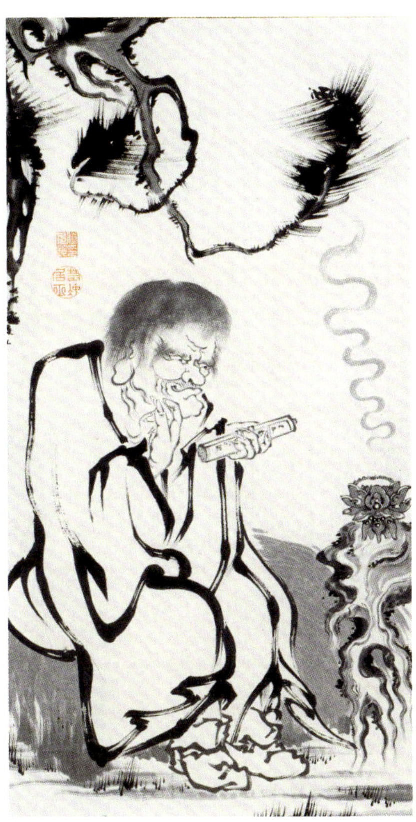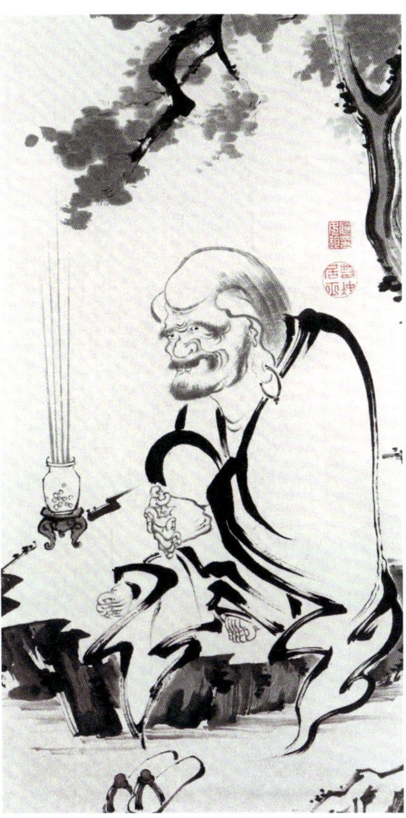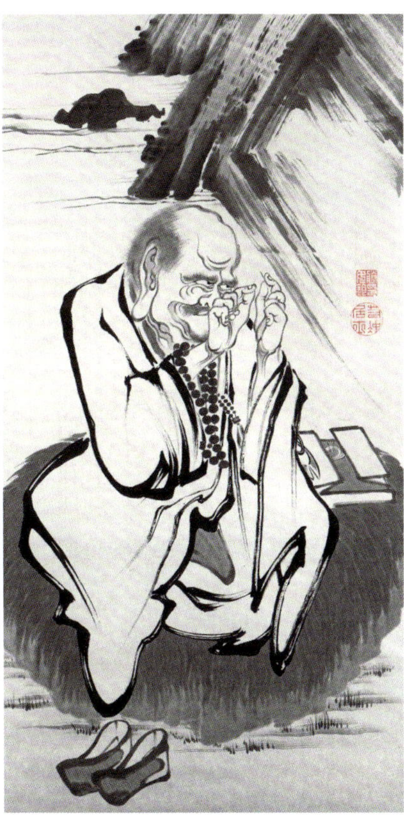

ITŌ JAKUCHŪ
(1716–1800)

Rakan, Edo period, second half of the 18th century
Three from a set of sixteen hanging scrolls; ink on paper, each 113.7 × 59 cm (44 ¾ × 23 ¼ in.)
Museum of Fine Arts, Boston, William Sturgis Bigelow Collection, 1911, 11.6919, 11.6926, 11.6922

SHŌHAKU OFTEN DREW FIGURES from Chinese legends and classical
literature. The subject of this painting, the eighth-century lay Buddhist
Pang Jushi, is said to have achieved enlightenment and retreated with
his family (including his daughter Ling Zhaonu) to the countryside, where
he produced bamboo baskets. However, the iconography of Shōhaku's
paintings is not so straightforward: it also seems to make reference to
the Daoist immortal Jiumei, who was transformed into a mortal when he
became attracted by the bare legs of a woman washing her clothes by
a riverbank.

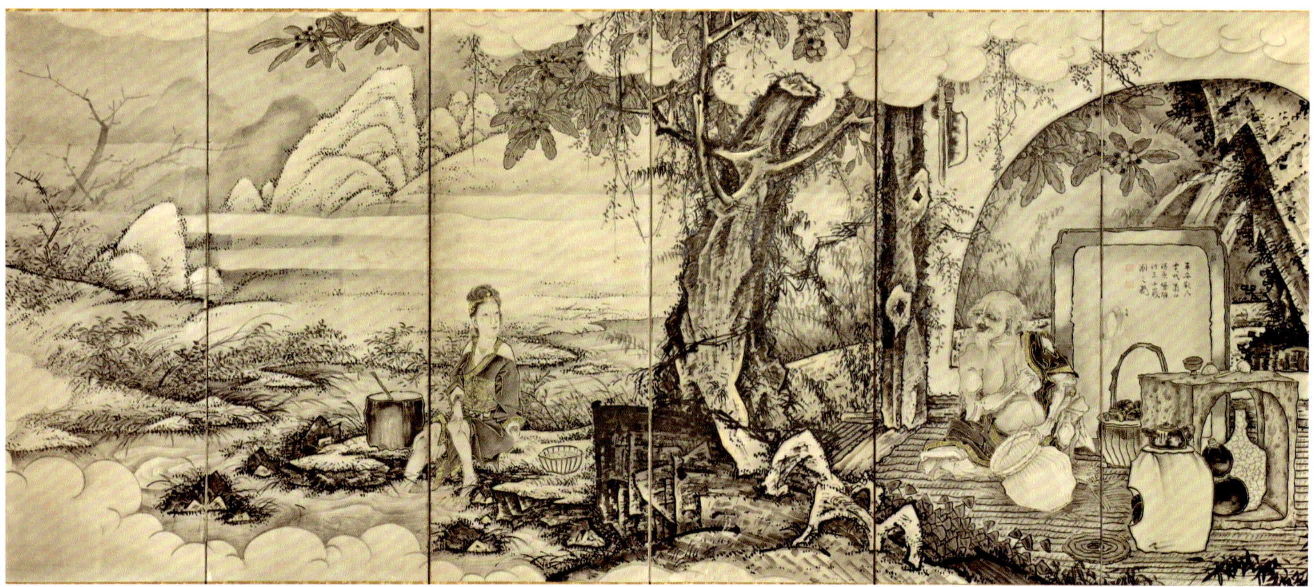

SOGA SHŌHAKU
(1730–1781)

Pang Jushi (Hōkoji) and Ling Zhaonu (Reishōjo): Parody of Jiumei (Kume) the Transcendent, Edo period, 1759
Six-panel folding screen; ink, color, and gold on paper, 156.1 × 363.8 cm (61 ⁷⁄₁₆ × 143 ¼ in.)
Museum of Fine Arts, Boston, William Sturgis Bigelow Collection, 1911, 11.7028

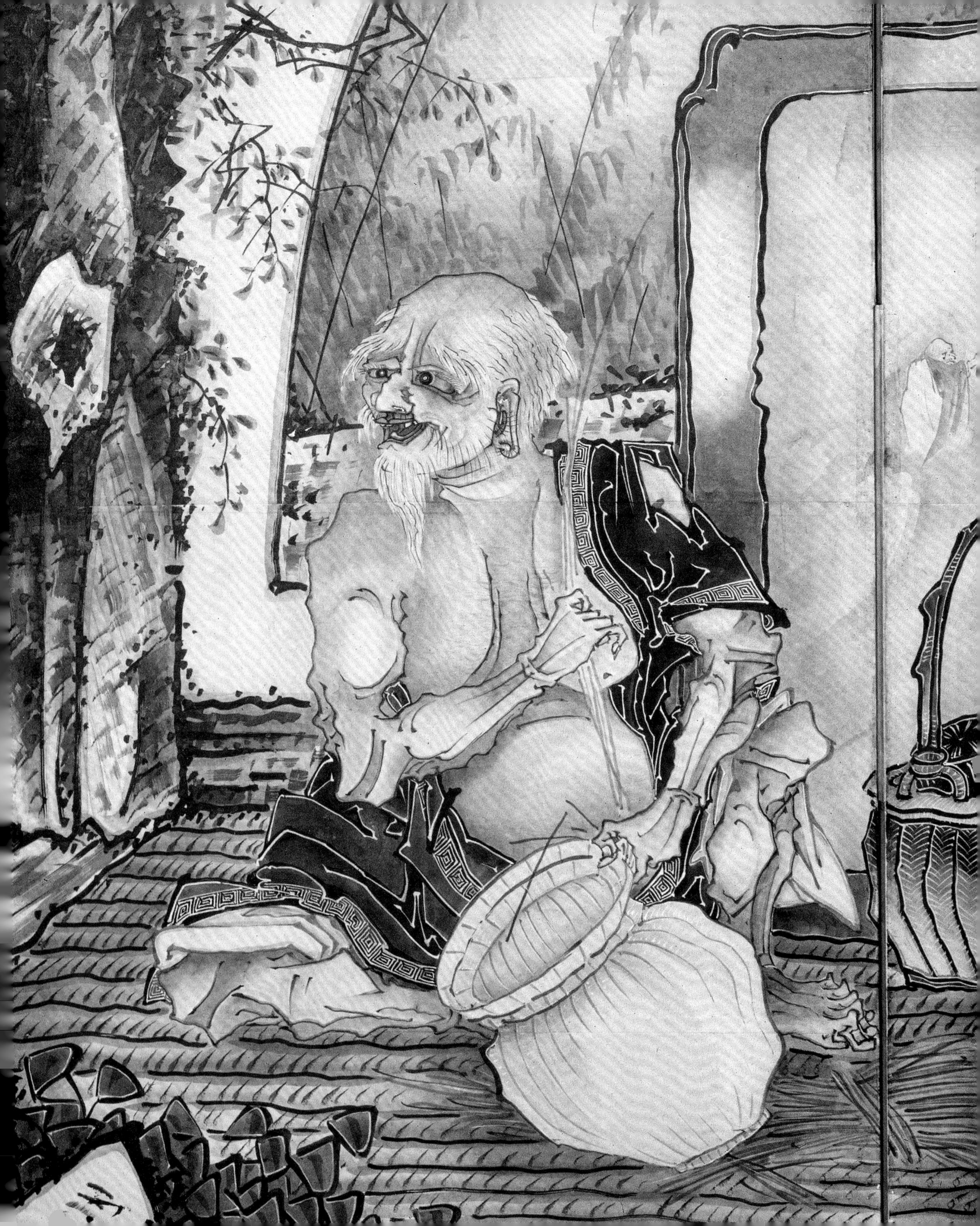

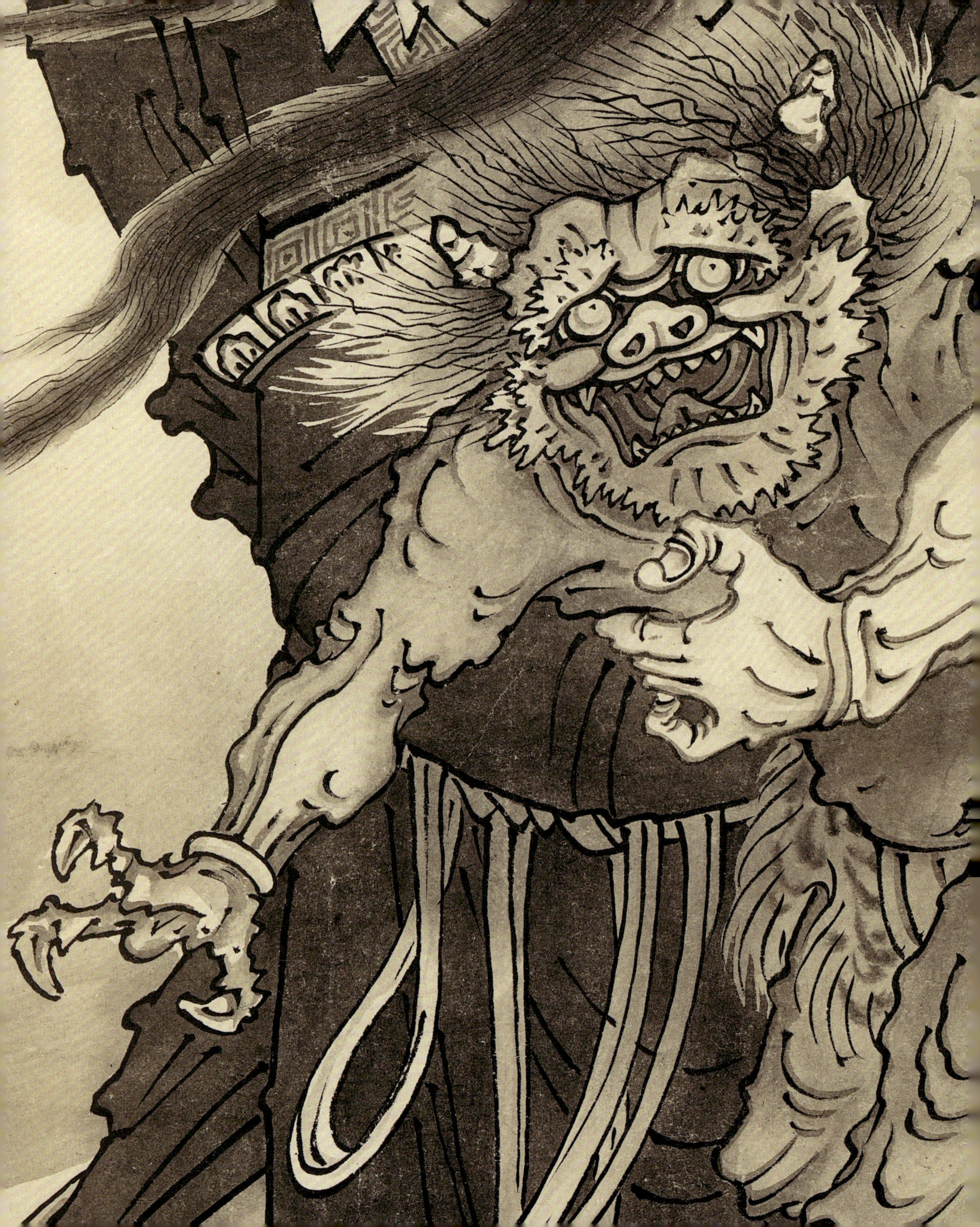

THE LEGENDARY Chinese figure Zhong Kui is easily identified by his bulging eyes, sharpened sword, and heavy boots. He is said to have been unfairly passed over during the career-determining civil service exams. In response, he committed suicide, but his honor was eventually restored by the emperor. Zhong Kui (Shōki in Japan) later appeared as an apparition and declared that, in gratitude for this posthumous recognition, he would protect the nation from demons and disease. In Shōhaku's humorous interpretation, Zhong Kui holds a demon as if it were a recalcitrant child. Bats, a Chinese symbol of good fortune, fly above.

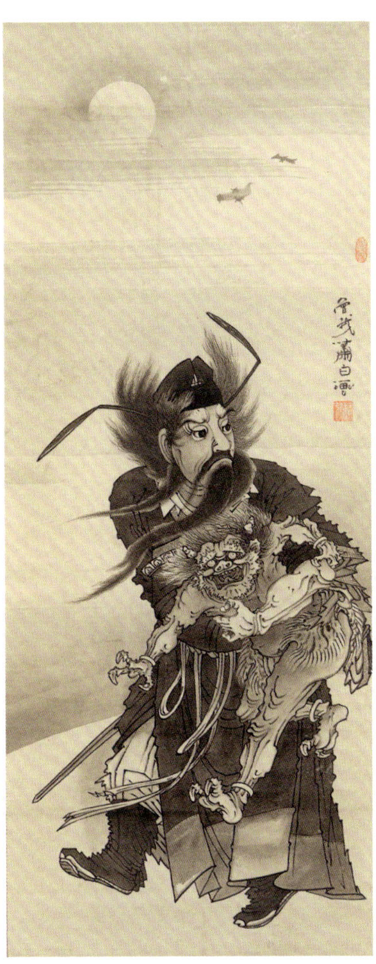

**SOGA SHŌHAKU
(1730–1781)**

Zhong Kui (Shōki), the Demon Queller, Edo period, 1770s
Hanging scroll; ink on paper, 130.8 × 53.2 cm (51 ½ × 20 ¹⁵⁄₁₆ in.)
Museum of Fine Arts, Boston, William Sturgis Bigelow Collection, 1911, 11.7014

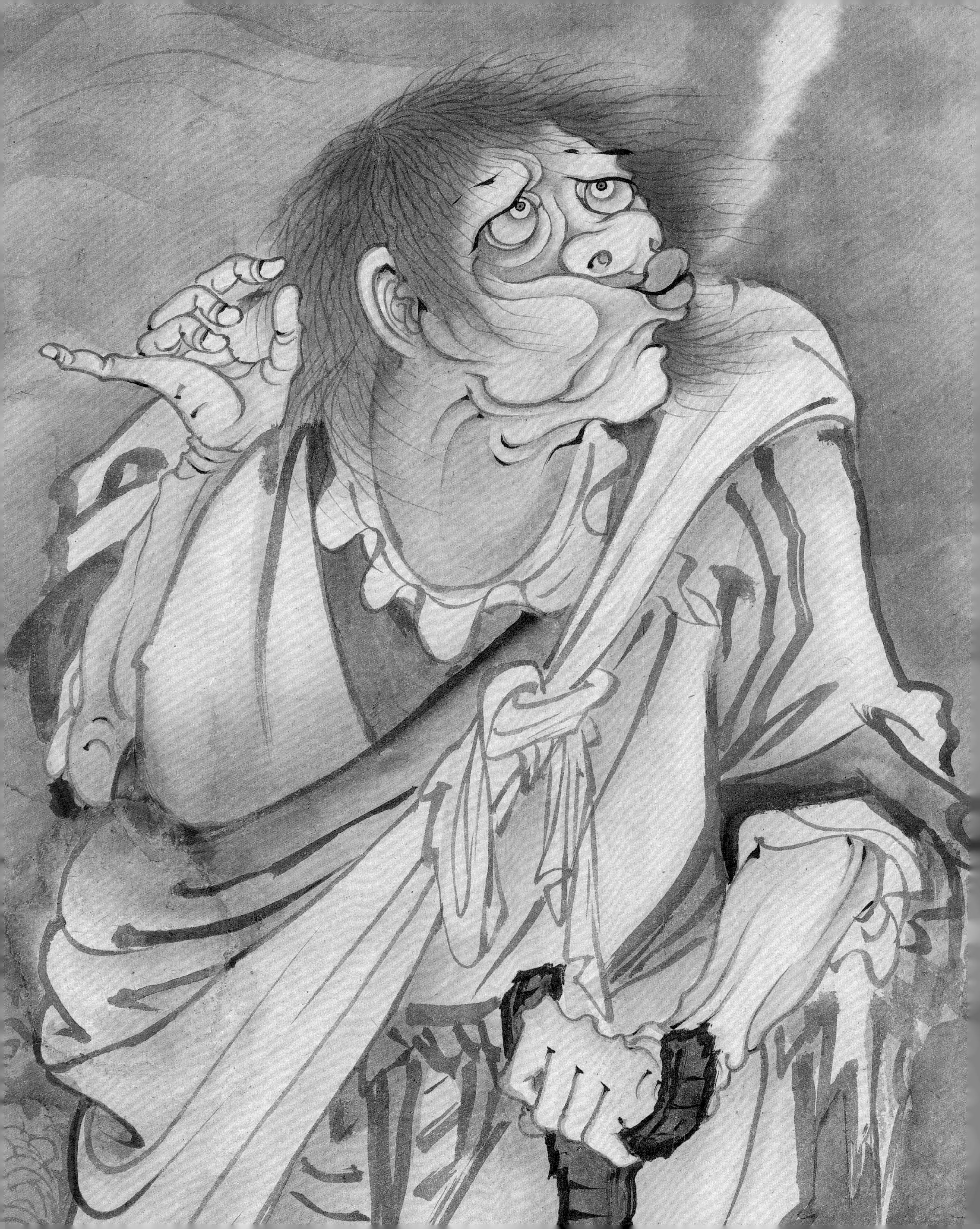

LIU HAICHAN AND LI TIEGUAI are two of the Eight Daoist Immortals, who
are said to have attained their state through the practice of magical
arts. Artists generally depict Li Tieguai as a beggar with an iron crutch.
According to legend, he had the ability to leave his body and one day
instructed his disciple to cremate his body if he did not return within
a given period. On one occasion, due to unforeseen circumstances,
Li was detained and could not get back in time, and so his disciple made
good on his promise. Thus, Li was subsequently forced to inhabit the
body of a recently deceased beggar. The Immortal Liu Haichan appears
with his constant companion—a three-legged toad—and the peaches
of immortality. Shōhaku's figures often have distorted features, which
are of great interest to Murakami. Recently, as evidenced in his painting
Transcendent Attacking a Whirlwind, he has explored the contorted forms
of seemingly double-jointed men with extended arms in the manner of
Shōhaku's originals (see pp. 39–42).

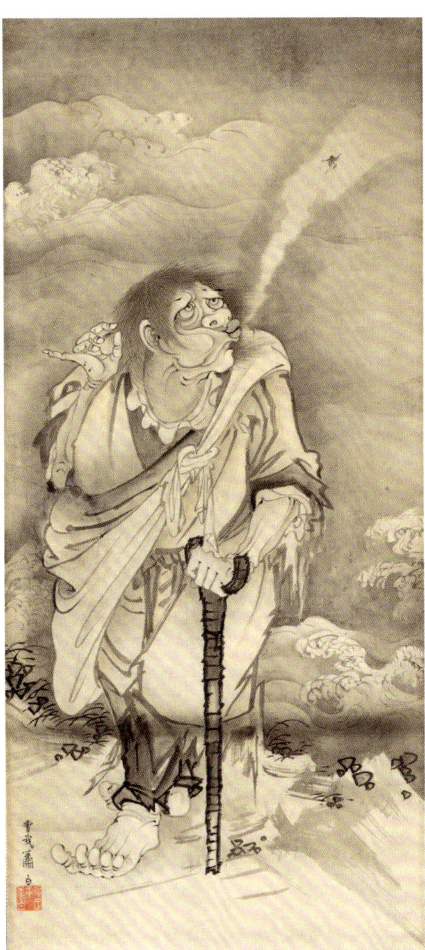
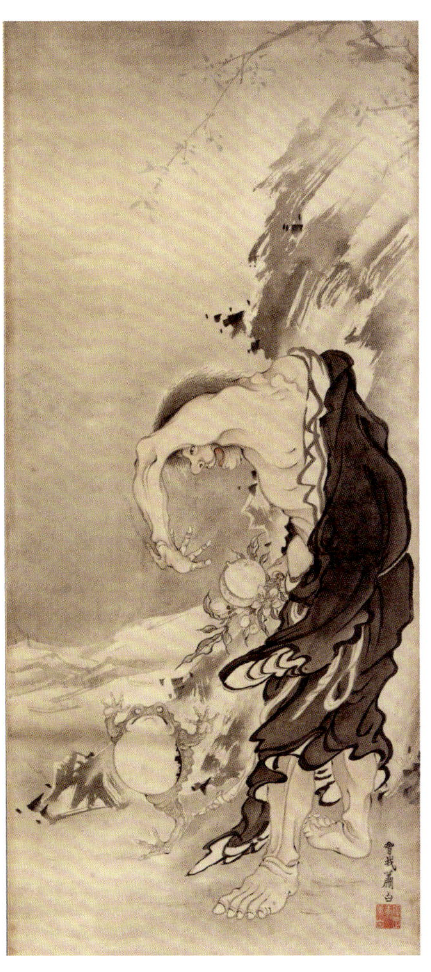

**SOGA SHŌHAKU
(1730–1781)**

The Daoist Immortal Liu Haichan (Xia Ma, Gama) and *The Daoist Immortal Li Tieguai (Tekkai)*, Edo period, around 1770
Pair of hanging scrolls; ink and light color on paper, 125.2 × 56.9 cm (49 ⁵⁄₁₆ × 22 ⅜ in.) and 124.9 × 57 cm (49 ³⁄₁₆ × 22 ⁷⁄₁₆ in.)
Museum of Fine Arts, Boston, William Sturgis Bigelow Collection, 1911, 11.7031a-b

THE FOUR SAGES are said to have retreated to Mount Shang to escape from the tyranny of Emperor Qin (259–210 BCE; r. 246–210 BCE) in order to maintain their moral rectitude. They were the subject of numerous paintings both in China and Japan as emblems of conviction of character in the face of bad government. While the iconography of Shōhaku's painting is traditional, his treatment of the subjects is far from conventional. His forms, poised on the edge of complete abstraction, revel in the explosive expressionism of his brushwork. However, details, such as the reins of the donkey or the needles of the pine tree, provide clues for deciphering the composition.

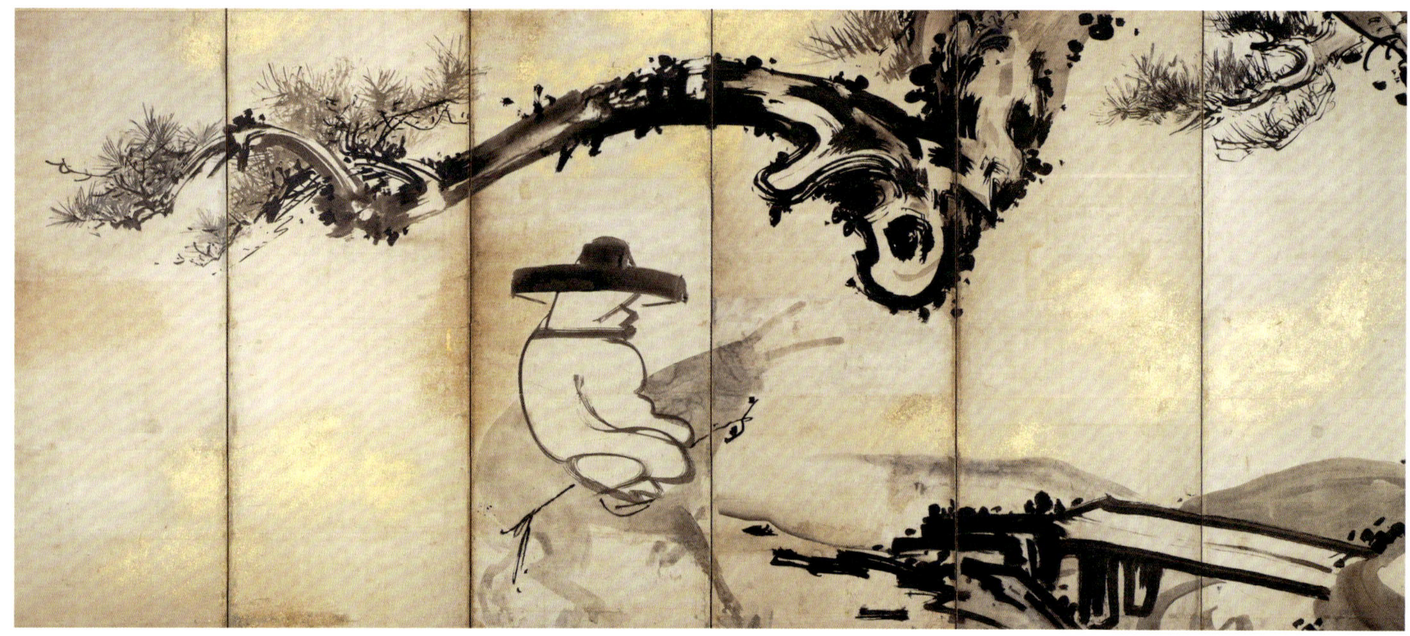

**SOGA SHŌHAKU
(1730–1781)**

The Four Sages of Mount Shang, Edo period, around 1768. Pair of six-panel folding screens; ink and gold on paper, each about 1.5 × 3.6 m (60 ¹³⁄₁₆ in. × 11 ft. 10 in.)
Museum of Fine Arts, Boston, Fenollosa-Weld Collection, 1911, 11.4514, 11.4513

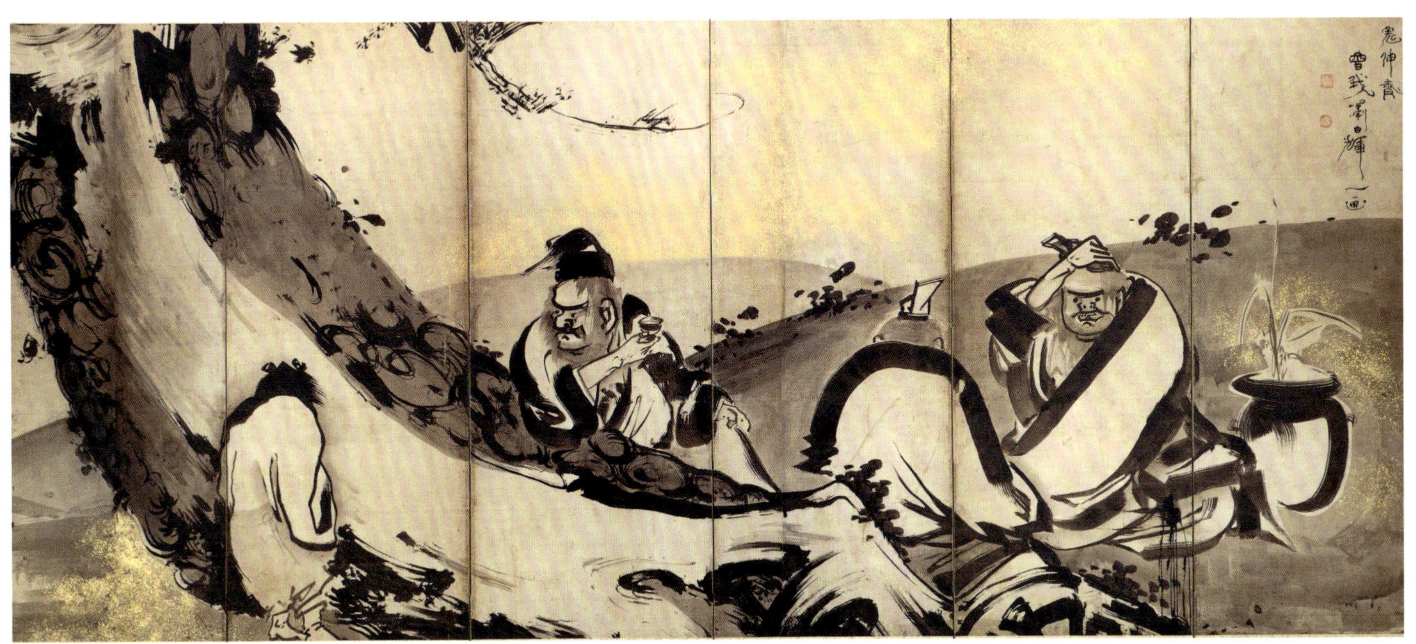

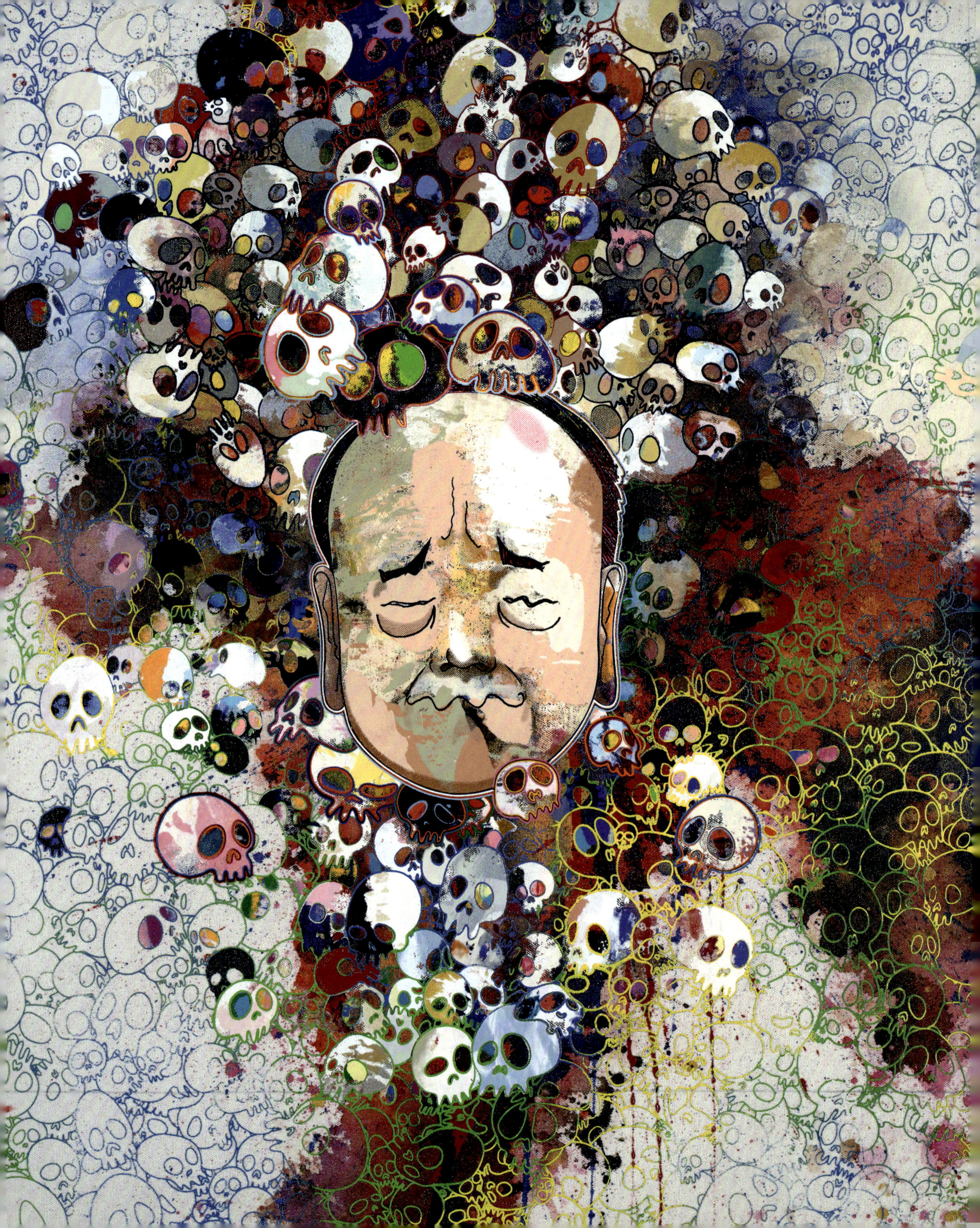

LOOKING AT JAPANESE ART

NOBUO TSUJI

Nobuo Tsuji, who has taught at Tōhoku University and the University of Tokyo and led premier cultural institutions such as the International Research Center for Japanese Studies (Nichibunken), Tama Art University, and the Miho Museum, is perhaps the most authoritative voice for Japanese art in Japan. With the publication of his book *Kisō no keifu* (*Lineage of Eccentrics*) in 1970, Tsuji presented new approaches to the study of Japanese art, introducing a narrative that was distinct from the standard chronological discussions of traditional schools. Throughout the following decades, Tsuji has continued to examine Japanese art through the lens of different aesthetic principles, such as kazari, asobi, and animism, which he argues predate the establishment of an art history discipline informed by European and American scholars.

The selection of Tsuji's writings included here highlights a few of the contributions he has made in formulating these thought-provoking narratives of Japanese art history. They represent only a small fraction of his publications. We have worked closely with Tsuji in choosing essays that can identify ways of looking at Japanese art that are relevant not only to historical works but also to those of contemporary times, particularly of Takashi Murakami.

These writings have been drawn from a number of sources; some are in Japanese and others have already been translated into English. In the notes, a full bibliography of the original publications is provided. For this volume, Tsuji has included new comments as well. — ANM

ANIMATION

The Russian film director Sergei Eisenstein, in his 1949 essay "The Cinematographic Principle and the Ideogram," pointed out certain affinities between traditional Japanese modes of imagery and the modern European cinematic medium. Eisenstein also commented on the current state of Japanese filmmaking. Because Japanese ways of reading and viewing pictures have been conditioned by an ideographic writing system in which the components of characters must be viewed simultaneously, Eisenstein argued, "The principle of montage can be identified as the basic element of Japanese representational culture."[1] Tahei Imamura, in an essay published in 1941, suggested a more explicit connection to premodern Japanese pictorial arts and focused on characteristics shared by early medieval illustrated handscrolls (emaki) and animated films, which were just starting to acquire commercial viability.[2] Imamura specifically emphasized similarities in techniques used to connote a sense of motion and the progression of time.

More recently, the noted film director and producer Isao Takahata has published a stimulating study examining various levels of visual correspondence between early medieval pictorial arts and the contemporary medium of popular animated films known as anime.[3] In 1999 the Chiba City Museum of Art, with Takahata's participation, organized an exhibition about the origins of anime, which brought together various examples of early medieval handscrolls. Both Takahata's recent publication and the Chiba exhibition were confined to exploring coincidences of pictorial conventions in early hand scrolls and in the cinematographic techniques of anime. A central tenet in Takahata's work is that the contemporary enthusiasm for anime among the Japanese can be traced to modes of viewing images established as far back as the twelfth century, when artists experimented with sophisticated pictorial techniques to express movement and the passage of time in narrative picture scrolls. I should like to extend the discussion to include manga (especially considering how many popular manga have been made into anime, such as Katsuhiro Ōtomo's *Akira*).

The intimate format of emaki provided a personalized experience for the viewer and was well suited to depicting narratives. Originally based on Chinese prototypes, emaki soon developed into a dynamic art form that surpassed its Chinese counterparts and reached the height of expression during the twelfth to sixteenth centuries. All varieties of subjects were grist for the artist's attention, but tales with a large appeal to basic human emotions—whether tragedy or comedy—could be translated most effectively into pictures of this sort. Images of nature or landscape scenes for the most part serve no more than as intermezzos or backdrops to vignettes of human or supernatural activities.

The illustrated handscrolls *Miraculous Tales of Mount Shigi* (*Shigisan engi emaki*) and *The Tale of the Major Counsellor Ban* (*Ban dainagon ekotoba*), both created in the twelfth century, are among the oldest surviving examples of the genre (figs. 14 and 15). Emaki were still in an early stage of development in the twelfth century, yet these two handscrolls are highly regarded examples of the medium. Their recognition

14

Detail from *Miraculous Tales of Mount Shigi* (*Shigisan engi emaki*), scroll 1, Heian period, 12th century

The story of a miraculous golden alms bowl that conveyed a wealthy squire's granary to a monk's mountain retreat is told in a continuous visual narrative. In the opening scene startled bystanders watch the storehouse start to lift off.

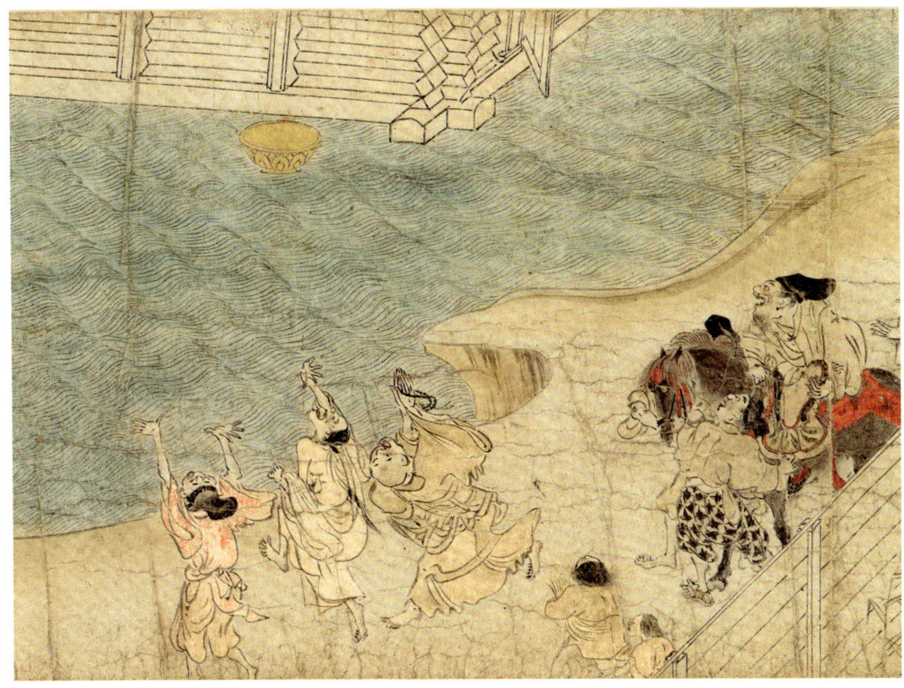

15

Detail from *The Tales of the Major Counselor Ban* (*Ban dainagon ekotoba*), scroll 2, Heian period, 12th century

In a cinematic sequence children are shown arguing in the street. The figures of the scrappy boys and the enraged man who intervenes are repeated, indicating the progression of time.

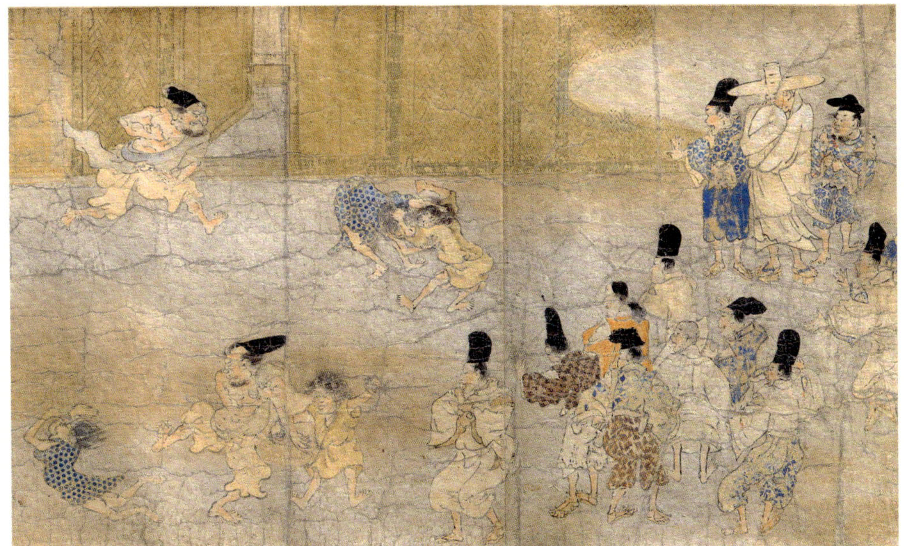

as masterworks—both have been officially designated as national treasures in Japan—owes much to the way in which the artists experiment with the stylistic and functional possibilities of the format by suggesting the passage of time, dynamic movement, and mise-en-scène. The long handscroll format was developed in northeast Asia to accommodate continuous scenes of narrative painting and related texts by pasting together separate sheets of paper horizontally. The scroll is held in both hands and slowly unrolled, exposing a section of approximately twenty inches at a time. The pace of viewing, and therefore the unfolding of narrative time, is entirely in the viewer's control. The section rolled in by the right hand becomes the hidden past while the section unfurled by the left hand holds the unseen future. The image before the viewer, expressing imaginary time, intersects with the passage of real time in the physical handling of the scroll.

In recent years Japanese animation and comic books have attracted a great deal of scholarly interest in Europe and North America. One appeal is the inherent international aspect of these film and book formats, which allows reflection on how cultural forms are altered as they move across national boundaries. The earliest Japanese animated films, produced from around 1916 onward, were based on French examples. In the 1930s filmmakers like Kenzō Masaoka (1898–1988) were the pioneers of a commercially viable animated film industry in Japan. In 1943 Masaoka's protégé Michiyo Seo (1911–2010) produced the first feature-length animated film titled *Momotarō no umiwashi* (*Momotarō and His Eagles of the Seas*) using cell-animation techniques. Even the term *anime* suggests the complex intellectual appeal of the medium: originally a Japanese abbreviation of "animation," the term has been reimported into Western languages and has gained wide currency.

There is a recent tendency to downplay or disregard issues of national identity in discussions of contemporary Japanese culture. However, certain characteristics might be linked to traditional cultural practices. A special 1993 issue of the journal *Iris* was devoted to image culture in contemporary Japan. The editors' introduction broached issues of national identity in light of a perception of a modern transnational culture—issues that perhaps are relevant to ones raised in this essay:

> The old hypodermic model, of one set of images "influencing" another
> when injected into a culture, should perhaps give way to a more
> dynamic model wherein signs of the foreign are deployed within host
> cultures less for their immanent significance than for local, broadly
> political ends. Thus, Japanese nationalism need not be thought to
> dissolve into a global image culture, but may in fact reinforce itself
> with a rapid reworking and recontextualising of images that flow to
> and through its territory from abroad.[4]

If I interpret this argument correctly, it is encouraging scholars to consider the possibility that Western-inspired visual media as they function in Japan may still be affected by indigenous modes of viewing images. By being open to such an approach, we may find validity in the arguments of the art historian Toyomune Minamoto, who has written that historically the Japanese did not appear to perceive space in three-dimensional depth, but interpreted it more in relation to the progression of time. "Japanese paintings are often described as flat, lacking in three-dimensional depth, but this quality is irrelevant to technical ability," he observed. "Japanese artists consciously opted for an elimination [*hatsumu*] of the appearance of depth."[5] Minamoto's use of the word *hatsumu*, usually restricted to Buddhist texts, is most revealing. For instance, in the early thirteenth-century Zen classic *Shōbō genzō* (The Eye Treasury of the True Dharma) by Priest Dōgen (1200–1253), the term has the connotation of fundamentally not believing a particular premise. Minamoto continues, "In the Japanese pictorial arts, the passage of time was captured in horizontal, two-dimensional movements that resulted in a flattening of space, and this led to the unique development of the treatment of time in illustrated handscrolls."[6]

The Japanese word *manga*, originally used in the late Edo period to suggest random sketches, was appropriated during the Meiji era as a translation for "comic strip" or "cartoon," but has now returned to the West to designate cartoonlike art created in Japan or rendered in a Japanese style. Manga, which treats a wide array of subject matter—not only the ubiquitous soft porn and violent fantasy tales its critics castigate—should be thought of as a visual medium (like film or emaki), and not a genre of illustrated narrative defined by content. Manga in Japan appeals to readers of all ages, and is not solely aimed at a youthful readership, as comic books in the West largely are (or a least were before the influx of manga). Animated film and cartoon art, which are generally seen to have emerged in Europe and North America, are now exported back to the West from Japan in the form of anime and manga. Clearly, there are many shared social and economic factors behind the surge in popularity of anime and manga on both sides of the globe, but still it seems reasonable to suppose that some culturally specific factors explain why the anime and manga boom first took off in modern Japan and how the two genres won such a wide audience.

Among scholars in Japan and the West who have taken up the study of Japanese popular culture, especially anime and manga, many have rightly pointed out the immediate socioeconomic context of postwar Japan in which these genres arose. In her recent study on manga, Sharon Kinsella observed, "Like the democratic political systems of the post-war period in which they flourished, pop cultures like manga represent a highly specific form of culture based on the institution of political opposition and open social organization."[7] Kinsella focuses on the reasons behind the rise of modern adult manga in Japan from a sociological perspective. She also notes that to stave off criticism of the popular art by conservative elements, certain professional manga critics and supporters of the industry have promoted views that manga belongs to a long and distinguished history of illustrated narratives in Japan. The purpose of this essay is not somehow to impart legitimacy to manga by attempting to place it in a more venerable tradition. Still, there is merit in looking at it from a broader art historical perspective to examine transhistorical resonances when they can be discovered: we should look at anime not simply as a direct import from the West that evolved in Japan according to postwar consumer tastes.

KAZARI

The decorative can be said to be at the very core of Japanese art. The term most frequently used in Japan to designate decoration is an indigenous one—*kazari,* which is derived from *kazasu,* "to insert in [to adorn] the hair." Variants of the word appear in a few early poems, including one in the eighth-century anthology *Man'yōshū* (Collection of Myriad Leaves).

Ume no hana	Blossoms of the plum
Ima sakari nari	Now are out in full flower;
omou dochi	Boon companions all
Kazashi ni shite na	Let us deck our brows with bloom—
Ima sakari nari	Now is the full of the flower![8]

Apparently a sprig of plum or a branch of pine placed in one's hair served as a type of charm, and it was traditional for people to go out on an early spring day and pray for their mutual health, placing plum or peach flowers in each other's hair. *Kazashi* also became the root of *kanzashi,* the name given to the decorative hairpins worn with kimonos.

Another, more formal word for decoration is *sōshoku,* from the Chinese *zhuangshi.* Although long used in China and introduced to Japan with the influx of continental words and ideas in the eighth century, it was rarely utilized, until the beginning of the Meiji era, when it resurfaced as a somewhat artificial translation of words adopted from Western languages, such as *decoration* and *ornament.*

Until the mid-nineteenth century there was no division in Japanese art between painting and the applied arts as there had been in the West. Japan's decorative style, when examined in the context of painting, has been characterized by pronounced craftsmanship. But when examined in the context of the applied arts, the style shows a definite painterly quality. It is that duality that makes Japanese art distinctive, and thus the term *kazari* is a more appropriate term for decoration, since it frees us from the distinctions that have characterized pure art and applied art in the Western context.

Furthermore, *kazari* is the more familiar word in Japan, whether used for art or for decoration in the broad, practical context of daily life. It has been intimately woven into people's lives for well over a millennium, and is an integral part of the Japanese language and aesthetics. By examining Japanese art through the lens of kazari, one can encounter many interesting objects that would otherwise be overlooked using conventional art historical approaches.

The French critic Ernest Chesneau wrote of the works that were shown at the 1867 Paris Exposition, "The charm of Japanese art lies in its sense of fantasy and an element of surprise which is always present in its decoration."[9] Certainly fantasy and surprise are part of the kazari aesthetic. Other aspects of Japanese decoration are asymmetry, exaggeration, stylization, and improvisation. Unlike Chinese artisans, the Japanese have not restricted themselves to a fixed set of authoritative or auspicious motifs such as the dragon and the phoenix, but since the eleventh or twelfth century they have drawn upon familiar objects and creatures close at hand. Artists have shown a penchant for anything and everything, including dragonflies, cicadas, and grasshoppers. The eminent early twentieth-century art historian Yukio Yashiro declared in 1965 that "the decoratively transformed image of natural things" was indeed one of the important characteristics of Japanese art.[10] As he explains, for example, flowers are seen as linked to huge, brightly shining stars. Ignoring all natural proportions, Japanese artists depict them as motifs that face the viewer. Although at first glance this type of imagery may seem a clumsy handling of revered nature, the decorative quality integrates the spirits of individuals with the spirit of nature.[11]

Other aspects of kazari include the linked concepts of the ordinary (*ke*) and the extraordinary (*hare*). Daily life was traditionally divided into the largely mundane and the special or ceremonial events that punctuate routine. Kazari has of course been important in all art, but perhaps the arena in which it has flourished most is *matsuri*, the festivals that have taken place on *hare* days to celebrate the gods. In Japan festivals involve inviting the gods to temporarily inhabit floats, portable shrines, or even paper ornaments, and then enjoying the feeling of being together with the divine. Kazari can function as a device for transforming the utilitarian and practical drabness of ordinary, workaday life into the special site and excitement of a festival. Thus eccentric and impromptu designs amuse the deities and delight and rejuvenate the celebrants.

The story of kazari in Japan can be traced back to the mid-eighth century, particularly the Tenpyō era (729–749), when there was a huge influx of decorative arts from Tang China. Tang-dynasty culture was richly international, suffused with diverse arts brought on the Silk Road from the west and also filtered in from India, as well as from other areas to the south. One persistent theme in Tang art that had originated in India was *alamkāra* (*shōgon* in Japanese), which means "to ornament" or "decorate" in Sanskrit. The term is most commonly used to refer to manifestations of sacred realms in the everyday world, for instance, re-creating in pictorial art, temple architecture, or gardens images of the western paradise of the Buddha Amitabha as described in Buddhist sutras.

We cannot think of Japanese art separately from color. Japanese art tends to feature a wide range of hues and to use gold and silver to enhance decorative effects. Luminous gold and silver are employed to express the transcendental light of the sublime Pure Land. Gold and silver make earthly scenes as resplendent as paradise, as well as represent natural light or atmospheric brightness. Gold does not dominate the other colors but serves to enhance them. Under the guidance of naturalized continental craftsmen, Japanese artisans of the seventh and eighth centuries acquired a high level of skill and created impressive works of their own. The Shōsōin collection of treasures on the grounds of the temple Tōdaiji in Nara preserves some examples of Tang works brought to Japan, showing us that they were truly embodiments of color and decoration (fig. 16).

The decline of the Tang Empire in the late ninth century brought official relations between Japan and China to a standstill until the twelfth century. As a result, the arts of Japan from the ninth century onward gradually began to take on less of a continental character. Patrons of the arts were the nobility who resided in Kyoto, the capital. During the Heian period (794–1185), the court culture of decoration had greatly advanced in painting, sculpture, and craftwork. The word *furyū,* meaning "elegance,"

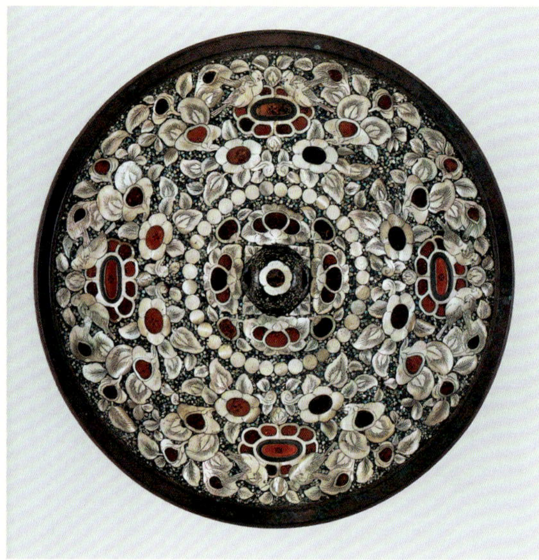

came to symbolize the intimate relationship between the daily lives of the elite and the use of decoration. The very act of decorating a space and objects is inherent in the word *furyū,* another manifestation of kazari. It is furyū that imbues the special decorations with exquisite renderings of various objects (*tsukurimono*) made for banquets or contests.

Descriptions of these gatherings and decorated spaces survive only in written records. However, the elegant lifestyle of the Heian nobility is evident in the twelfth-century transcription of the poetry anthology *Sanjūrokunin-shū* (Collection of Thirty-Six Poets), mostly preserved in the collection of the temple Nishi Honganji, Kyoto, with one fragment at the Museum of Fine Arts, Boston (fig. 17). Poems in this anthology are written in flowing script over groupings of collaged Chinese-style Japanese papers placed in asymmetrical patterns and decorated with various designs. The refined craftsmanship and juxtaposition of word and decoration on textured papers testify to the sophisticated sensibilities of the Heian elite.

At about the same time, in Song-period China (960–1279), a significantly different artistic movement emerged. A scholarly elite of intellectuals and artists strove to capture the essence of truth (Chinese: *zhen*; Japanese: *shin*) in their works. This trend had a profound effect on decoration in the arts. As painting and calligraphy came to be considered the appropriate means of expressing inner character, decoration was demoted. This approach was combined with a heightened class consciousness, which marginalized artisan workmanship. Included in the *Xuanhe huapu* (Compendium of the Xuanhe Era) of 1120 is a catalogue of paintings in the collection of the Chinese emperor Huizong (1082–1135), which contains the following comments on Japanese screen painting:

> There are painters in Japan, but we do not know their names. Their works portray natural objects, landscapes, and intimate scenes of their own country. The pigments are laid on very thick, and they make use of gold and jade color. Study shows that they are not necessarily truthful, that they are meant [to be] brilliant display[s] by their bright colors and to win admiration for their beauty.[12]

16
Round mirror with animals and flowers, Chinese, Tang dynasty, 8th century

In memory of her husband, Emperor Shōmu, Empress Kōmyō dedicated items from the imperial household to the Great Buddha at Tōdaiji; these were kept in storehouses known as the Shōsōin. Among the treasures is this sumptuous mirror inlaid with mother-of-pearl and amber.

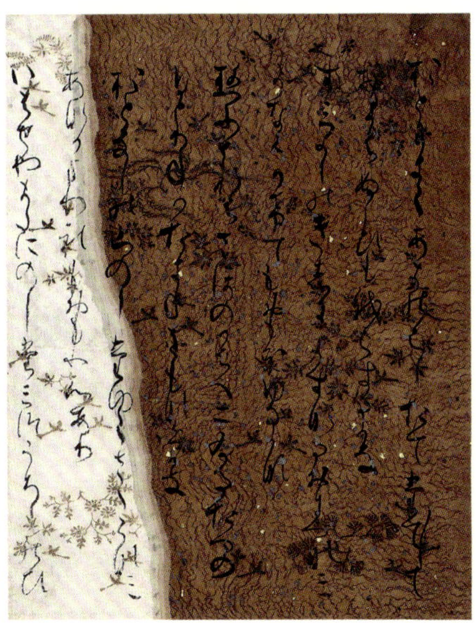

Various Japanese warrior clans, dominated by the Ashikaga family, resumed trade with China in the later fourteenth century. Ink paintings, ceramics, metalwork, and lacquerware of the Song, Yuan (1279–1368), and Ming (1368–1644) periods, collectively labeled *karamono*, or "things Chinese," were imported into Japan with increasing frequency. The Japanese elite emulated and replicated these Chinese objects. With the exception of ink paintings, however, the Japanese copies were not as successful as the Chinese originals.

In the fifteenth century, the Ashikaga shoguns began to exhibit their Chinese art treasures in "reception room decoration" (*zashiki kazari*). Reception room decoration referred to the display of Chinese objects in rooms where the shogun might receive the emperor or other important guests, or hold banquets. These rooms were decorated to give the impression that they were replicas of the Buddhist Pure Land paradise in the west, calling to mind similar earlier instances but now in a more secular context.

The conventional taste for elegance, or furyū, among aristocrats continued to play an important role. The reception room decoration in aristocratic mansions might juxtapose Chinese hanging scrolls in ink with Japanese screens in Yamato-e style (paintings with native themes and bright coloration). This elegant counterpoint created a Japan–China dialectic within a single space. Such manifestations of elegance expanded from temporary, static interior displays to include performances with dancers.

The second half of the sixteenth century was a golden age of kazari. The short Momoyama period (1568–1615) was dominated by the warlord Oda Nobunaga (1534–1582) and his successor, Toyotomi Hideyoshi (1536–1598). Castles built from the mid-sixteenth century onward are perhaps the most potent visual symbol of that war-torn era. The formal reception hall in such castles dazzled visitors with sliding doors, folding screens, and furniture made with gold and silver and painted with vivid colors.

Another form of decoration based on ideals of simplicity and sobriety was also adopted at the same time, occasionally within the same architectural setting. This was the aesthetic of restraint (*wabi*) promulgated by the tea master and tastemaker Sen no Rikyū (1522–1591), who was patronized by Hideyoshi. The Toyotomi clan was defeated

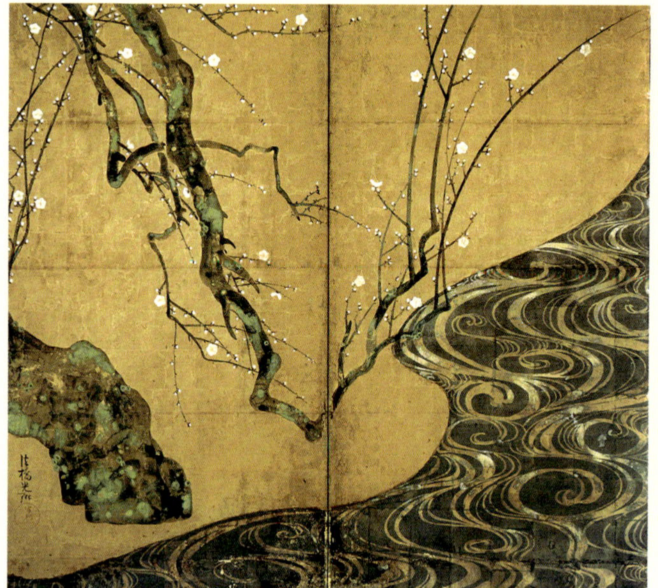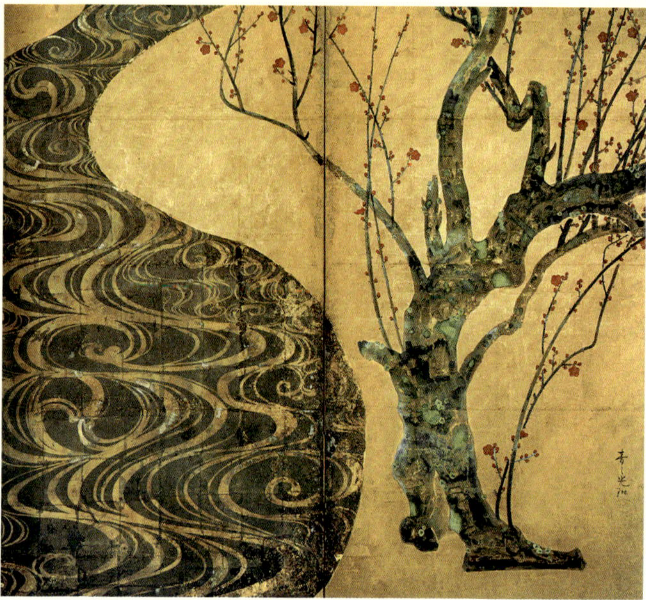

at the Siege of Osaka Castle in 1615. The victorious Tokugawa quickly established their regime of shogunal government in the newly regenerated city of Edo (modern-day Tokyo). The peace of the next two and a half centuries fostered a cultural flowering in Edo, Kyoto, and Osaka, led principally by the merchants of those cities. Kabuki, the licensed brothel quarters, ukiyo-e paintings and prints, festivals and pleasures of all the senses, were integrally linked with kazari. Decoration in the metropolis spread to smaller cities, as well as to farming and fishing communities, and gradually penetrated the entire archipelago.

In the second half of the nineteenth century, Japanese decoration was introduced to the West via international expositions organized to highlight the technological and cultural achievements of various countries. Europeans and Americans were surprised by the eccentric and fresh style of the Japanese arts that were on display in these fairs, which took place in Vienna, London, Paris, and Philadelphia. In contrast to contemporary French decorative arts, which rigidly followed rules of symmetry, the asymmetrical and inventive Japanese objects, whether luxurious or inexpensive, held their own unique fascination.

The scholar Ernst Gombrich, in his book *The Sense of Order* (1979), wrote about the psychology of the decorative arts, noting that unexpected breaks in the rules of continuity that govern vision engage our attention.[13] Japan's artists intuitively understand and boldly exploit this effect. In other words, they do not ignore symmetry, but rather they break it down, thereby giving vivid movement and interest to designs (fig. 18).

Europe's encounter with Japanese kazari led to the development of Japonisme. It also led to an admiration for the artist Ogata Kōrin (1658–1716), previously not well known in the West, as the greatest decorative artist. Siegfried Bing, the Parisian dealer who coined the term *Art Nouveau*, promoted him as a genius who spanned the realms of both the applied arts and painting. Laurence Binyon, the keeper at the British Museum and an early Western authority on Japanese art, also praised Kōrin in his *Painting in the*

Far East (1908): "'Decorative' is a term that carries with it to our ears associations of what is abstract, systematized, restful in art; it does not suggest the stimulating qualities, the energy and daring of Kōrin."[14]

Despite the nineteenth- and early twentieth-century fascination with Japanese decoration in the West, art history studies on Japanese art in the Meiji era privileged what were considered the fine arts, mainly painting and sculpture. The decorative or applied arts were considered lesser or inferior. Okakura Kakuzō (Tenshin), author of *The Book of Tea* (1906) and Curator of Japanese and Chinese Art at the Museum of Fine Arts, Boston, was a student of the Bostonian Ernest Francisco Fenollosa at Tokyo Imperial University. The attitudes of Fenollosa, Okakura, and their cohorts were in part influenced by the previously described Chinese literati painting theories of the Song period, which propounded that calligraphy and paintings created in ink were the highest art form, for they reflected a person's character. They belittled jewelry and applied arts as the work of vulgar crafts-people. Fenollosa and Okakura also subscribed to Western concepts of pure art that had prevailed since the Renaissance, in which applied arts were considered one rank lower than the pure arts. Splendid paintings and sculpture were seen as the visual form of the human spirit, God's creation. Conversely, decorative arts were the workings of anonymous craftspeople and were differentiated from the fine arts as objects created for practical use. Thus, these nineteenth-century historians of Japanese art gave little credence to the tradition of the applied or decorative arts, considered a treasure chest of kazari.

The late professor Seiichi Taki, who taught Japanese and Asian art at Tokyo Imperial University, said the following in a 1941 lecture:

> When I met Fenollosa in Tokyo near the end of his life, he told me that Japanese art was abstract and decorative, and should be most highly appreciated as applied arts. However, we Japanese think this view is not correct. The special character of Japanese art is spirituality; therefore it is abstract. Even the famous Kōrin folding screen painting of irises is indeed an object of abstract beauty and must be recognized as possessing a surprising strength that is more than mere decoration.[15]

Professor Taki took issue with the Western notion of the inferior status of decorative or applied arts and argued against it by bringing up the concept of spirituality. It is not necessary now to ask to what extent this decorative intention possesses cognitive meaning; it suffices to state that the act of decorating expresses a universal human delight through its purely visual richness and ingenuity.

Renaissance art theory holds that decoration is an adjunct to something more essential and is not of itself independent. If we examine Japanese culture, however, we see that kazari is an essential aspect of human life, one that transforms everyday objects into extraordinary ones. More than offering mere amusement, the act of decoration is a spiritual operation that consecrates that which it touches; it releases the heart of humankind from bondage to ordinary life and offers to every class and status the experience of animated joy.

ASOBI

Playfulness has performed the vital role of continually sustaining and stimulating Japanese art. By itself, it is not the essence of Japanese art, for there are, of course, threads of seriousness, lofty and spirited in character, noble and religious in feeling, and solemn and majestic in shape. However, the spirit of playfulness is present as an essential component to the same extent as seriousness, and perhaps even more so. These two extremes, seriousness and playfulness, do not necessarily contradict each other. Even in works of the utmost seriousness the spirit of playfulness can creep in, preventing the work from looking too stiff, giving it a warm-hearted feeling.

In Japanese the expression *asobi* corresponds to the English term *play*, but the Japanese language does not have an adjective that is the equivalent of *playful*. In English *playful* contains no negative connotations. In contemporary Japanese, however, *asobi* and its verb form, *asobu,* frequently carry a morally critical tone. To say that children are playing is acceptable, but to say that adults are playing is not; this represents the general way of thinking in Japan. The expression *asobinin*, literally "one who plays," means a gambler. This may be linked to the fact that following the Meiji era, the Japanese placed much emphasis on seriousness and sobriety as virtues.

In 1868 the rule of the Tokugawa shogunate ended and the Meiji era started. Japan, released from its exclusive "closed-door" policy, now for the first time squarely faced the modern West. Surprised by the vastness and profundity of Western civilization, the Japanese hastily and single-mindedly tried to learn from it. An excessive seriousness was revealed in the attitude of studying Western art, and the spirit of playfulness, which had continued within the tradition of Japanese art, could not find an outlet.

The Dutch cultural theoretician Johan Huizinga, in his seminal book *Homo Ludens* (1938), wrote about the important role of play in the development of societies. He described play as a "well-defined quality of action which is different from ordinary life."[16] He went on to say, "It is a stepping out of 'real life' into a temporary sphere of activity with a disposition all of its own, being not serious, but at the same time absorbing the player intensely and utterly."[17] Noting that except for Japanese culture, there were few cases where style and fashion, hence art and play, have blended so intimately as in the Rococo, Huizinga suggested that despite the facade of Japanese seriousness, there was still a playful heart underneath.[18]

From the sixth century on, when Buddhism with its attendant arts was introduced to Japan from the Asian continent, until the mid-nineteenth century, when Western art became the new form to follow, Chinese art was admired as a model to learn from. The world of playfulness is found, of course, in Chinese art also. To cite an excellent example, there is the untrammeled (*yipin*) mode of painting. The pioneers of this singular artistic mode were the eighth-century landscape painters Wang Mo and Zhang Zhihe. Their works no longer exist, but according to literary documents, their manner of producing works was quite extraordinary and eccentric. While onlookers watched, these artists would drink wine and, when the mood was right, would spread out large pieces of silk and paint. Shapes seemed to appear quite accidentally on the silk, instantly becoming mountains, rocks, clouds, and water. It is also recorded that people would sit on top of splashed ink and be pulled about—at one time there was an extravagant demonstration of this feat in front of a hundred musicians.

The outlawlike, apparently self-indulgent methods these "untrammeled" artists used in this large-scale playful performance were based on a philosophical system. This was the Daoist philosophy of Laozi (604–531 BCE) and his follower, Zhuangzi (370–287 BCE), in which it is said that if one can act within a realm of freedom that approaches Zao Hua—the divine force that created the universe—then the landscape that has been produced will also approach the miraculous achievements of the creative process of the divine.

In contrast, a passage in the thirteenth-century anthology *Kokon chomonjū* (A Collection of Notable Tales Old and New), compiled by the low-level courtier Tachibana Narisue, indicates that the Japanese had a slightly different attitude toward playfulness. Narisue noted that "pictures use the five colors of the palette to present the forms of all creation without artifice. There are things worth viewing in that which is depicted, and there are rules for their actions."[19] While this is nothing more than a sensible concept derived from ancient Chinese views of painting, Narisue continued with a phrase that I find noteworthy: "The paintings give rise to flights of the imagination."[20] The sense of freedom in untrammeled Chinese paintings seems playful, yet it derives from philosophical underpinnings. For Narisue, paintings allow the individual to respond with a playful mind. They have no other purpose than to delight.

Narisue defines paintings as "toys" for "leisure time." The word *gan* he uses means "amusement" in English; however, as the Japanese use the Chinese word *seigan*, *gan* also becomes part of its meaning, denoting a way to appreciate art in Chinese painting theory. Although saying "amusements in one's spare time" in English suggests an undervaluation of painting, in this case the phrase does not have that connotation. Rather, it shows how Japanese noblemen appreciated paintings. In contrast to (or against) the Chinese theory of *jigo*, which means "amusement by artists for themselves," Narisue seemed to say as a viewer, "Paintings are amusements for both artists and viewers." Toys (*gangu*) were requisites for children, and paintings seemed toylike for noblemen in the earlier Heian period.

During that period, the Japanese imperial court still maintained its cultural interchange with Tang China. But the collapse of Tang rule meant that the great flow of continental art to Japan was nearly halted for more than two hundred years, and it has been held that a purely Japanese art form emerged at this time. The Fujiwara aristocrats frequently used the word *aware* to convey the sense of the mutability of things, and this is reflected in the art of the time. Simultaneously they also sought out lighthearted things to enliven their spirits, which they would describe as *okashi* (funny or amusing). The early twelfth-century anthology *Konjaku monogatari shū* (Tales of Times Now Past) recounts the story of Gisei Ajari, a monk on Mount Hiei, who was a master of *oko* drawings—*oko* meaning "funny" in a commendable sense. If he was not in the mood, he would not draw. Once, when he was pressed to draw something on a long scroll, he drew at one end a person shooting an arrow and at the other a target, with a single long line between them representing the arrow in flight. The person who made the request became angry and said, "In doing that you've made it impossible to paint anything else!"[21] The *Tales of Times Now Past* states that Gisei gave a look of unconcern.

The twentieth-century scholar of Japanese folklore Kunio Yanagita examined the tales included in the twenty-eighth volume of *Tales of Times Now Past* and stated

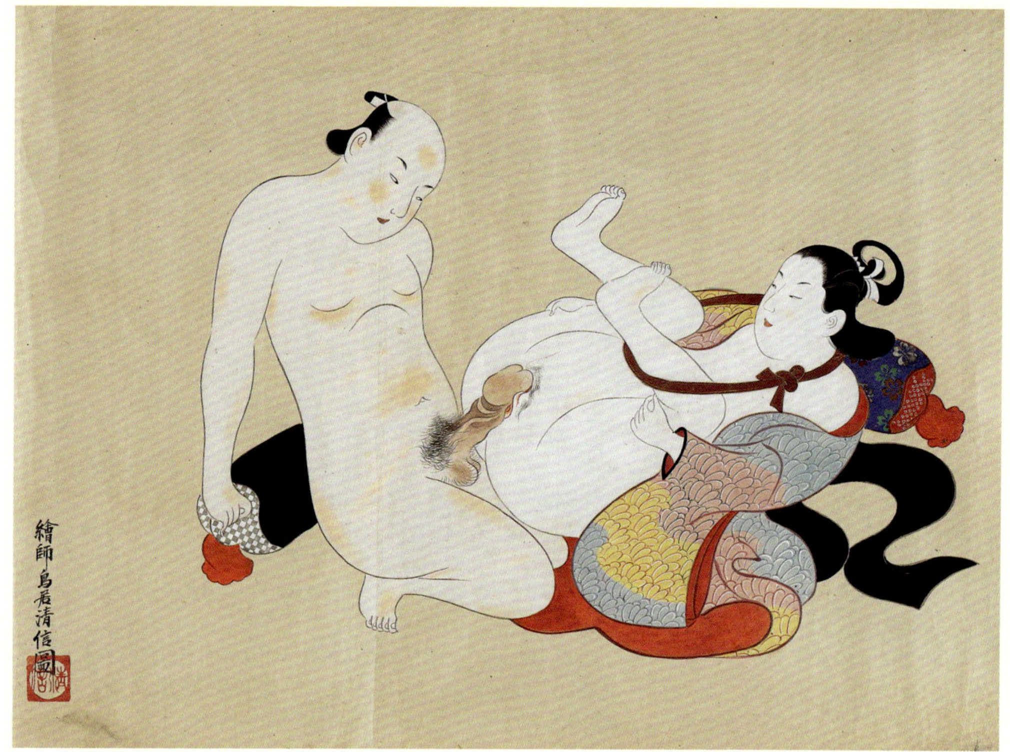

that it was oko people who made others think that something was okashi. As Yanagita explained, *oko* derives from an ancient Chinese word that means "thoughtless acts of folly."[22] In no way does it mean the foolishness of people lacking discretion or sense, however. Rather, it is the opposite; it refers to those who are a bit more acutely attuned than ordinary, who can be discerned both in oko situations and in artificially staged ones. Although these acts of oko are not "play," they amuse and prompt laughter. Oko people like Gisei perform the role of the fool on purpose to appall people and make them laugh. Yanagita claimed that oko became an art through the exercise of one's imagination rather than from the mere practice of everyday life. The concepts of oko and asobi are closely linked.

For the Japanese, sexual behavior could be oko, or laughter provoking. Although I cannot speak at length on Japanese ideas about sex, if I were to characterize them in one word, it would be "naturalness." Buddhism and Confucianism, as well as the feudal mores of the Middle Ages and the early modern period, regulated sexuality. The Christian concept of sex as sinful is foreign to the Japanese. Particularly in ancient Japanese society, sexuality was accepted as something quite natural. In the *Tales of Times Now Past* there are numerous frank descriptions of erotic behavior, and erotic paintings (*osokuzu no-e*) with exaggerated depictions of genitalia continued to be produced by members of the imperial court during the Middle Ages. This tradition gave rise to the well-known spring pictures (*shunga*) that were popular among the plebeian merchant class from the seventeenth century onward. These erotic paintings were also called *warai-e,* or "laughing pictures" (fig. 19).

19
Torii Kiyonobu I (1664–1729)
Detail from *Erotic Contest of Flowers,* Edo period, Hōei era (1704–11)

Almost every genre of Edo-period art had some involvement with play and amusement; the most outstanding of these is the so-called *shimin geijutsu*, or "art of the city dwellers." The arts that the court-affiliated aristocracy, the warrior class, and other privileged classes had cultivated since the eighth century were introduced into the lives of the politically powerless townspeople of the major urban centers of Edo, Kyoto, and Osaka in the Edo period. Under the severe oppression of the class system established by the Tokugawa shogunate, the fine arts, along with the performing arts of kabuki and puppet shows (*ningyō-jōruri*) and "light" literature (*gesaku*), were imaginary genres that could emancipate people regardless of differences in social classes. The tradition of the pursuit of play in the arts of the Heian and Kamakura aristocrats was succeeded and revived in various forms by Edo art.

The culture of the Edo period was strongly colored by features brought on by the "closed-door" policy of the Tokugawa shogunate, and can be considered the second flourishing of national culture after the Heian period. *Nanshūga* (Chinese: *nanzonghua*), a popular Chinese mode of painting practiced in Suzhou and Wuxi in Jiangsu Province, and in Henan and Anhui Provinces during the late Ming and early Qing dynasties, was imported into Japan and became literati painting (*nanga*). Ike Taiga (1723–1776), Yosa Buson (1716–1783), and Okada Beisanjin (1744–1820) used their native Japanese sensibilities to adapt the concepts and expression of *you* (play) and *qi* (strangeness), which were traditional in Chinese literati painting. Itō Jakuchū (1716–1800), Soga Shōhaku (1730–1781), and Nagasawa Rosetsu (1754–1799), eccentric artists who were active in the mid- to late eighteenth century, also reflect in their art the style and manner of Chinese eccentric painters of the late Ming and early Qing eras; further, they present resourceful and witty interpretations of their models through parody and unusual changes in scale.

Miniature works of art (*saikumono*), much treasured by city dwellers in the latter half of the Edo period, such as the sculptural toggles (netsuke) that were used to secure tobacco pouches and medicine containers to men's kimono sashes, are deeply indebted to techniques of the unusually elaborate Ming and Qing handicrafts. When they are compared with their continental prototypes, however, the touch of humor newly added to the designs gives the strong impression of being a Japanese characteristic. In the book *Smaller Is Better: Japan's Mastery of the Miniature* (1984), the Korean critic O-Young Lee pointed out the inclination of the Japanese to appreciate things that are small and, if possible, to reduce in size familiar objects.[23] When applied to trends in art such as netsuke, Lee's views become powerfully persuasive. Netsuke, which are miniaturized almost beyond belief, reflect this notion of play among the citizenry of Edo. In another respect, netsuke complement the extraordinary magnificence of forms. In other words, what the townspeople of the Edo period sought from their artists and artisans was a wizard-like ability to freely alter the size of objects from micro to macro and vice versa, from macro to micro.

Despite the excessive seriousness that accompanied the introduction of Western art, the hearts of the Japanese, which seek the excitement of the fabulous, endure. The popularity of manga suggests this. More than one billion manga are printed every year—not only for children, but also for university students and adults over thirty, who are avid readers of it. This is lamented by critics, who claim there has been a decline in the intellectual maturity of the younger generation. However, I do not necessarily deplore this phenomenon. As seen earlier, for more than a thousand years the Japanese have loved comic art and have been successful in frequently joining comic expression to the highest forms of art.

RELIGIOSITY

Animism is the foundation of religiosity in Japan. In an eloquent essay entitled "Rethinking Animism," the preeminent Japanese philosopher and cultural historian Takeshi Umehara described the concept as a belief in the existence of a spirit in inanimate objects, such as water and stones, as well as in plants, animals, and other living beings.[24] According to Umehara, animism includes the belief that all phenomena of the natural world are guided by the power of spirits. When an animal dies, its spirit separates from its body, returns to its abode in the heavens, and takes a new form; it subsequently returns to this world. The same is true for plant life. Thus, according to animism all living beings are reincarnations.

The indigenous religion of Japan, today known as Shinto, has animism at its core. Throughout history, many of its tenets and rituals have been period. Umehara surmises that Shinto's original form during the Jōmon period (about 14,000–300 BCE) must have been similar to the religion of the Ainu people, which centers on a belief in the spiritual power of animals. It is certainly true that in Shinto the worship of animals is widespread, and at many shrines foxes, monkeys, deer, and snakes are exalted as the attendants of the gods.

Objects dating from Japan's Kofun period (about 300–538), an era when horse-riding clans from the Asian continent consolidated power and constructed elaborate keyhole-shaped burial mounds in the greater Yamato region, attest to the early importation of sophisticated works of art from China and the Korean Peninsula. Continental mirrors, horse tack, weapons, armor, jewelry, and musical instruments and their Japanese copies were all given as diplomatic gifts. They were also used as burial goods adorning the tumulus graves of various kings and as ceremonial offerings. What were the underlying principles of the beliefs that resulted in these types of burials? What did people of the time think about the deceased royals' spirits as they performed their burial rites? The extant objects and artworks do not provide many answers to these questions, but the representations of animals (such as deer and monkeys) in the terracotta figurines placed around the burial mounds can be seen as the representations of the spirits that transported the deceased to the place from which they came (fig. 20). However, the joyful expression of the animals seems to be unconnected with the dark mystery that must have surrounded the incantations recited on behalf of the departed.

We can surmise that the indigenous animistic beliefs that first appeared in the Jōmon period, the Daoist philosophy newly imported from the Asian continent in the Kofun era, and shamanism were all integrated in some fashion; likewise, continental art forms were not adopted in any systematic way. The twelfth-century *Fusō ryakuki* (Abbreviated Chronicles of Japan), which provides a chronicle of early Japan, relates that in 522, Tang-dynasty Chinese émigrés built a grass hut in the province of Yamato in which they enshrined a Buddhist image. The official transmission of Buddhist images to Japan took place in 538 when King Seong-myeong of Baekje presented Buddhist sculptures and sutra commentaries to Emperor Kinmei (one theory is that this occurred

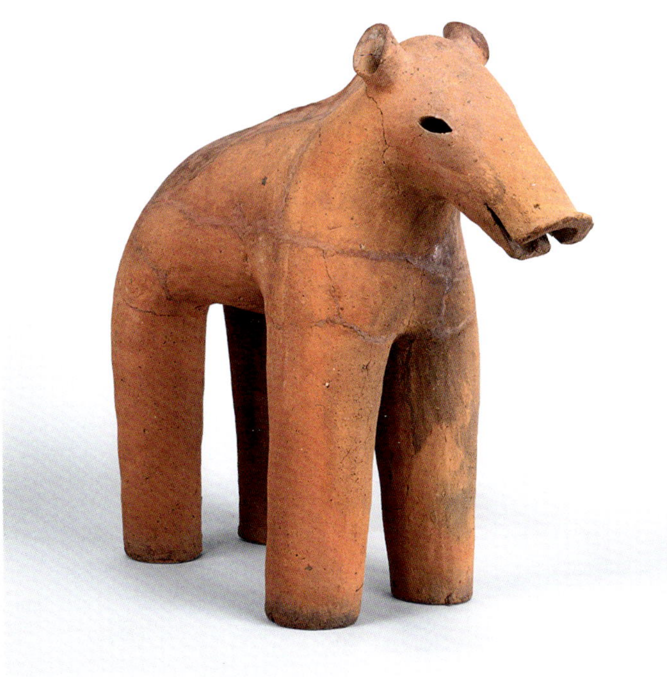

in 552). However, over time Japanese Buddhism was influenced by animism. The idea that grasses, trees, the earth, and other things that do not have human emotions could all become Buddhas did not exist in India. The doctrines encapsulated by the idea that grass, trees, and the earth can all attain Buddhahood gained currency in China through the intermingling of Tientai and Daoist beliefs, although there it was widely debated. In Japan, however, the ideas were readily accepted and became central to Japanese Buddhist thought.

Although scholars often focus on Buddhist teachings, rituals, and iconography, when the question "What is Buddhist art?" is posed, the answer is simple. It is the art of ritual adornment, or *shōgon,* from a Sanskrit term meaning "decorate beautifully." The appearance of Buddhist paradises as described in the Buddhist sutras is shōgon. The bodies of the Buddhist deities glow golden. The garments and jewelry worn by the Buddhas, bodhisattvas, and celestial beings; the palaces, garden ponds, and the grounds; and the plants and trees that grow there are all transformed by gold, silver, and richly colored jewels into adornments. Thus, all of the architectural structures, sculptures, paintings, and decorative arts created to realize such scenes in the real world are lavishly ornamented—a unified art of kazari, indeed, a visually dazzling kaleidoscope of color (fig. 21). That is the true nature of Buddhist art. And yet, today the gilding has worn off of many Buddhist sculptures, and the pigments coloring the canopies, ceilings, and pillars of halls have faded away. Often all that is left is the physical form of the Buddhist images.

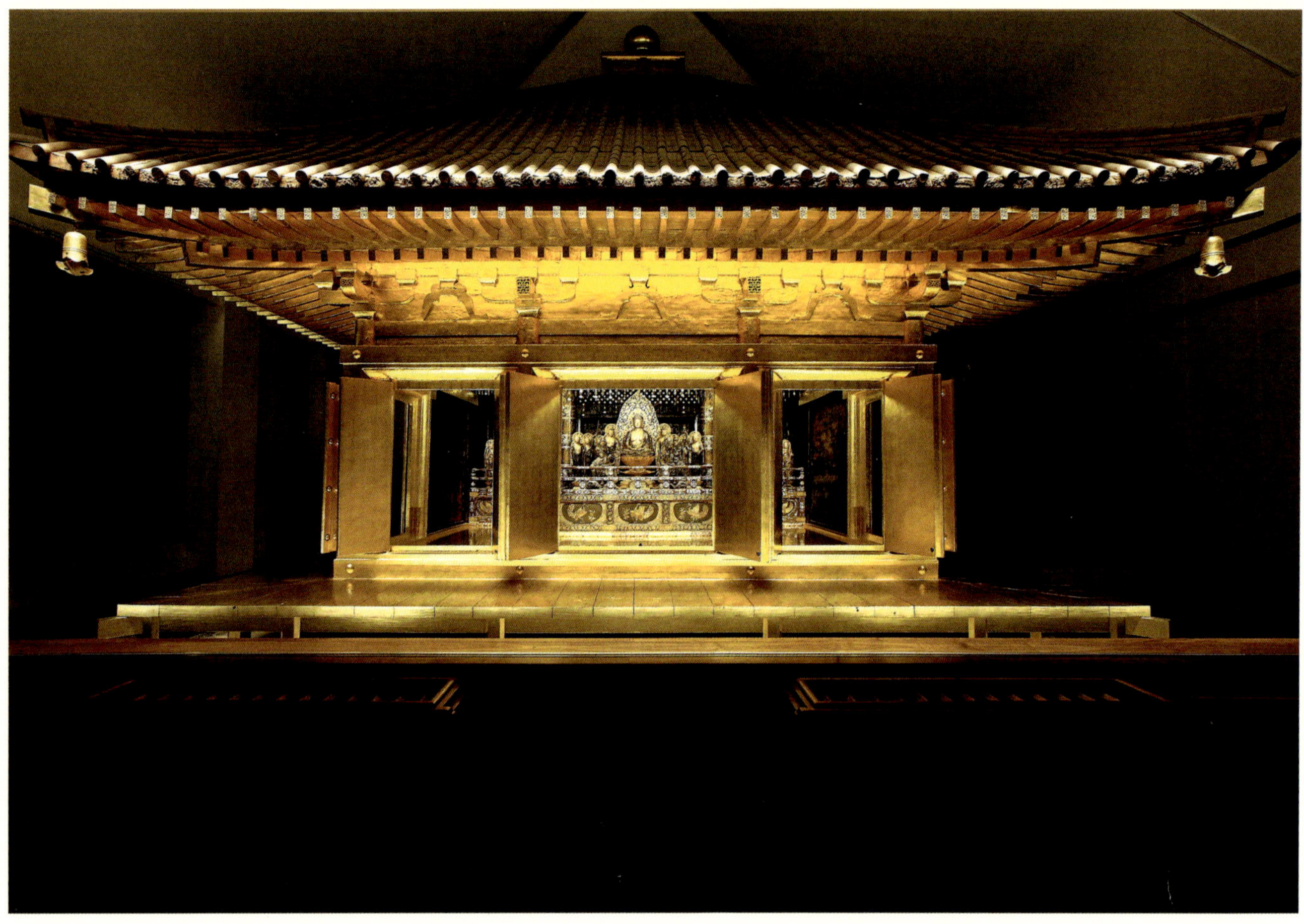

Until recently research on the history of Japanese sculpture and painting
was based on Western art methodologies such as detailed analyses of style and
form. Treating Buddhist images simply as sculptures and paintings has resulted in
important determinations about the dates of production. However, what we can hope
for in the future is a newfound focus on the re-creation of the original image, which will
bring greater attention to the notion of Buddhist art as the art of shōgon adornment.
According to the scholar Takeo Izumi, the Buddhist sculptures and paintings used in
Heian-period rituals were recorded simply as *butsu,* or Buddhas. When it was necessary
to indicate that an image was a painting, not a sculpture, in many instances the work
was recorded as an "e-butsu," "ga-butsu," or "butsu no ezō," variant ways of designating
paintings of Buddhas.[25] Unlike our current method of differentiating the media by using
separate terms for Buddhist paintings and sculptures, it seems that at that time they did
not explicitly distinguish between the function of the two, which was to present an image
of the Buddha. Thus, Buddhist art, sculpture and painting, is often inextricably linked
with rituals and shōgon.

Certain paintings did play another important role in Buddhist temples. On high
holy days or special days when there were image viewings, the priests would narrate the

21

Main altar in the Golden Hall,
Chūsonji, Hiraizumi, Iwate
Prefecture, constructed in
the Heian period, 1124

This jewel-like structure is the
only twelfth-century temple
hall that retains its original
appearance with its gold-leafed
interior, mother-of-pearl inlaid
pillars, and intricate openwork
metal fittings.

pictorial biographies of the Historical Buddha and patriarchs or illustrations of Buddhist hell. From the Heian period onward they would exhort the crowds with oratory rivaling that of the finest movie actors, describing the various states of hell as well as Buddhist paradises. From the medieval to the premodern era, these pictures and performers became all the more specialized and theatrical, aiming at an even broader cross section of the social classes of the day. Images of hell that had been described by the tenth-century priest Genshin had to be transformed into something easily understood and familiar, in line with the everyday sensibilities of the populace. At the same time, because the paintings were supposed to scare these people into reforming, they had to make a strong impression on their viewers. These new requirements sometimes led to the adoption of exaggerated, vulgar elements straight out of the theater—a trend that became even more pronounced in the Edo period, particularly during the nineteenth century.

There was a tendency in the Edo period and later, as compared with antiquity and the medieval period, for people to seek worldly gain more than rebirth in paradise. The renowned religious historian of the prewar era Zennosuke Tsuji presented various explanations for the apparent decline of premodern Buddhism. One centered on the lack of spiritual qualifications of those who entered the priesthood. As an illustration, Tsuji cited a passage in the seventeenth-century novelist Ihara Saikaku's *Honchō nijūfukō* (Twenty Cases of Unfilial Children): "There is nothing stranger than the quality of the people entering the priesthood today."[26] Those who were raised in military-class families and had knowledge and talent, but who were either deficient in the martial arts or physically weak, along with those in the merchant class who were bad at accounting and record keeping, were forced to shave their heads and become priests. Some became the unsavory *tako bōzu*, or octopus priests—so called because of their round bald heads— who took advantage of the unsuspecting.

The second reason for the decline of Buddhism in the premodern era, as cited by Tsuji, was the religious regulations issued by the Edo shogunal government. These aimed to place all Buddhist temples throughout the country under their control. Furthermore, all citizens had to be affiliated with a Buddhist sect and a parish temple. The head priest of each temple was entrusted with controlling the movement of the masses; it was his prerogative to issue the necessary documentation for permission to travel or to marry. Resentment often arose because the people were forced to donate money to their temples.

Although the decline of the priesthood and the shogunal regulation of temples is said to have made Edo-period religion—with its two pillars of Buddhism and Shinto— powerless, vulgar, and lacking in creativity, this view is extremely one-sided. Religion in the Edo period, through its explicit outreach to the masses, lost the lofty sacredness that characterized it when it was directed toward the aristocrats. However, dismissing this as simply secularization or vulgarization overlooks the fact that Edo-period religion was overwhelmingly filled with diversity and vitality.

Ordinary people of the day were stimulated by images produced by painters such as Itō Jakuchū and Katsushika Hokusai (1760–1849), who had their own unique beliefs. It is almost without question that Jakuchū's thirty-scroll *Colorful Realm of Living Beings* (now in the collection of the Imperial Household) is not simply a set of bird-and-flower paintings; the set can be considered Buddhist paintings that reflect the belief that all the grass, trees, and earth have become Buddhas. The ukiyo-e artist Hokusai became absorbed in the subjects of the *Lotus Sutra* and is said to have walked the streets reciting it.

There were also exceptional priests in various regions who garnered the respect of the people and were effective in their efforts to educate and proselytize the populace. Temples affiliated with two Zen monasteries that were then out of favor, namely those in the lineages of the Daitokuji and Myōshinji, produced exceptional priests such as Hakuin Ekaku (1686–1768) and Sengai Gibon (1750–1837). These two men transformed the nature of ink paintings from the lofty works that had been created during the thirteenth through sixteenth centuries by Zen priests for their own enjoyment into something filled with bright humor for the masses. The pictures of Bodhidharma, the first patriarch of the Zen sect, as well as those of high-ranking priests that Hakuin produced and gave to his disciples, testify to Hakuin's powerful spiritual nature, which had been honed by years of difficult Zen training and practices. His massive images of Bodhidharma, painted with unrefined, twisting lines, are so authoritative that they blow away the paintings by professional artists with their displays of specialized techniques (fig. 22).

Hakuin also created playful images of deities that appealed to the populace— deities that could prevent catastrophes and bring them happiness, such as the Seven Gods of Good Fortune. Within Buddhism, Kannon, the Bodhisattva of Compassion, and Jizō, the Bodhisattva of the Earth Matrix, were seen as protective deities who granted children to couples and watched over them as they were reared. Yakushi, the Buddha of Medicine, provided immunity from disease, while Fudō myōō, one of the Five Wisdom Kings, known as the Immovable One, protected against fire and disaster. Inari, the Shinto deity who took the form of a fox, was widely revered as the patron saint of agriculture. Each of these Shinto and Buddhist deities was identified as having particular powers and became suddenly popular, only to be forgotten to such a degree that they were called *hayari gami*, "trendy gods."

As the realities of life, old age, sickness, and death do not change, the hearts of people even today turn to religion. However, if today's religions do not suit people's needs, then they might consider the religions of the Edo period, which were quite something with their many deities given form by exemplary artists.

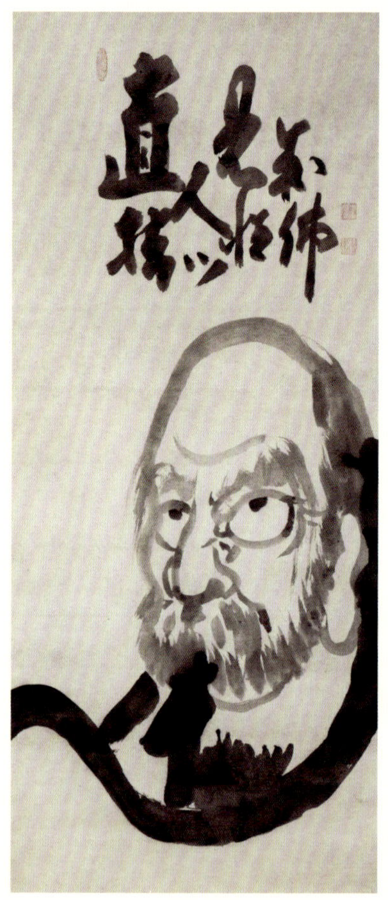

22
Hakuin Ekaku (1685–1768)
Giant Bodhidarma, Edo period,
18th century

ECCENTRICITY

The word *kisō* (eccentricity) is not an art term. It derives from the Japanese phrase *kisō tengai yori kitaru*, which can be translated as "strange thoughts come from outside heaven"; today that phrase has taken on the colloquial meaning of "having a wacky idea."[27] In his groundbreaking exhibition at the Asia Society in New York and the accompanying book, *Fantastics and Eccentrics in Chinese Paintings* (1967), the eminent art historian James Cahill identified a group of individualistic painters in China, whom he described as "eccentrics."[28] These artists—Dong Qichang, Wu Bin, Gong Xian, Cheng Hengshou, and Bada Sharen—were active during the political and social tumult of the seventeenth century, as the Ming dynasty gave way to the Qing. Cahill discussed their bizarre painting styles in terms of twentieth-century Western art—primarily Expressionism and Surrealism. At around the same time, I published a series of articles about five Edo-period artists who had been little studied—Iwasa Matabei, Kano Sansetsu, Itō Jakuchū, Soga Shōhaku, and Utagawa Kuniyoshi—which, together with an essay about Nagasawa Rosetsu, were reissued as a book entitled *Kisō no keifu* (*Lineage of Eccentrics*). As the title of the book suggests, I argued that these artists formed their own lineage—not a conventional master-to–disciple-lineage, but one marked by a certain expressionistic bent. These artists were distinguished by their bizarre and fantastic image making.

Of course, there are important differences between Chinese eccentrics and Japanese eccentrics. Somewhere in the background of the pictures created by the Chinese eccentrics lies Daoism, tying their idiosyncratic and imaginative expression to a realm of Daoist eccentricity. But what are we to make of that expressed by eccentric painters in Edo-period Japan? Even if their eccentricity is derived from Daoist thought, their purpose differs. The kisō painters' eccentricity is an offer of amusement meant to satisfy the curiosity of townsfolk, and it infuses the artists' expression with what appears to the viewer as innocent laughter and at times frightening black humor. One could argue, however, that the uninhibited freedom and diversity of expression nurtured by Japanese eccentrics are characteristics not shared with their Chinese counterparts.

During the Edo period in Japan, paintings were produced by various schools or artistic groups that were patronized by the burgeoning commoner class. Asserting their respective characteristic methods of expression, they competed among themselves, and effectively displaced the hereditary Kano and Tosa schools that the military elite and the court nobility had supported. In standard introductory histories of Japanese art, beginning with *Kōhon Nihon teikoku bijutsu ryakushi* (The History of the Art of the Empire of Japan), which was compiled on the occasion of the Exposition Universelle in Paris in 1900, these different schools are accorded individual chapters that introduce their characteristics and development and provide discussion of the biographies and oeuvre of the affiliated painters.[29] This narrative model, which brings together the histories of the schools, including Rinpa, ukiyo-e, literati painting,

Maruyama-Shijō, Western-style painting, and Yamato-e Revival painting, is in keeping with the organization of these schools in the household (*iemoto*) system. Thus, it provides an easy means of organizing and categorizing the many known painters who were active over the course of the Edo period and of the overwhelmingly large number of their extant works. However, by emphasizing a vertical history through almost two and a half centuries of artistic production, there remained the danger that we would lose sight of the overall organic development of the history of painting in the Edo period. The actual development correlates to subtle shifts and influences that occur between individual painters and the schools themselves, and to sensitive responses to movements within society.

More than anything else, what was needed for future Edo-period art history studies was the liberation of painters from the spell of a doctrinaire view engendered by the emphasis on these schools, and the reevaluation of artworks through the lens of contemporary aesthetics and values. Such an approach makes it possible to discern important, previously unnoticed characteristics and the fascinating points of resemblance or connection between artists or artworks that had previously been considered unrelated or opposites. It would be possible to hypothesize about a new "school that does not become a school" as an experiment in creating a single genealogy. Such is my lineage of eccentrics. I also believed this would be an effective way to fill in the blank spots of the existing static school-based arrangement by family lineage or method.

Of the artists that I included in *Lineage of Eccentrics*, two are featured prominently in the collection of the Museum of Fine Arts, Boston—Itō Jakuchū and Soga Shōhaku. Jakuchū, the eldest son of a greengrocer in Kyoto, was born in 1716 some ten plus years before Shōhaku. Naturally, he was in line to inherit the family business, but he was not interested in commerce. While he was reported to be an uncouth, strange person who did not like social interaction, his one deep interest was in painting. It appears that he became enlightened to the fact that art was his true calling.

Jakuchū was an extremely devout Buddhist who shaved his head in the manner of a lay Buddhist, did not eat meat, and remained a lifelong celibate. His decision to not marry may not have been because he had entered the Buddhist priesthood or felt there were reasons he had to be alone. Jakuchū was befriended by Daiten (1719–1801), the erudite head abbot of Shōkokuji, the Zen monastic complex in Kyoto, and a member of the cultured elite. The monk was moved by Jakuchū's actions. In a poetic anthology, Daiten related an episode about when Jakuchū, distressed to hear that sparrows were being caught and killed for *yakitori* meat, went out and bought several dozen of the birds and released them in his own garden.

According to the inscription that Daiten had carved onto Jakuchū's gravestone at Sekihōji in Kyoto, the artist followed the usual path of aspiring painters, seeking admission to a Kano school studio. But not content with its offerings, he enthusiastically copied the Song and Yuan paintings in Kyoto's many temples. He also raised chickens in his own yard so that he could observe them, and through his naturalistic images of birds, beasts, plants, trees, insects, and fish, he established himself as a painter.

Jakuchū produced the thirty hanging scrolls of his celebrated *Colorful Realm of Living Beings* (now in the Imperial Household Collection) between 1758 and 1766 and presented the set, along with a triptych of the Historical Buddha and his attendants, to Shōkokuji. These paintings in full color on silk can be considered his greatest masterpieces. The subjects of these scrolls are traditional to Chinese art, and technically the set could be classified within the genre of bird-and-flower paintings. Daiten wrote in his epitaph that many of these works derive from Song and Yuan dynasty compositions, though the inspirations were mainly those of the Ming dynasty. Thus, Jakuchū's paintings were also influenced by the detailed bird-and-flower works brought to Nagasaki by the Qing painter Shen Nanping (born in 1682)—which had European-style naturalistic elements—and the tradition of animal and plant sketching from life, as seen in the studies by the academic painter Kano Tan'yū (1602–1674) and the Rinpa artist Ogata Kōrin. And yet, neither influence is enough to explain fully the true nature of the *Colorful Realm of Living Beings*. In these works he established a strikingly vivid world of imagery that was not borrowed from anywhere else and that can be credited only to Jakuchū's own originality (fig. 23). The sheer diversity of motifs he presents makes them almost an illustrated natural history, and in them we can see the results of Jakuchū's thorough observation of "things." The *Colorful Realm of Living Beings* was produced at a time when naturalist studies, as well as artists' renditions of the natural world, were the craze.[30]

While our views of art today have been shaped by Surrealism, thus making us more cognizant of the super-realism of the cinematic realm created by Jakuchū, it is unknown how much the people of his day were able to perceive this innovation. And yet, surely Jakuchū's powers of concentration embedded in the detailed painting of the natural world overwhelmed everyone.

Jakuchū also incorporated ink-painting methods introduced by the newly arrived Ōbaku Zen sect to create innovative forms. For example, in 1759 he produced a set of *fusuma* paintings for Rokuonji, the temple complex that houses Kinkakuji, one of the best-known sites in Kyoto. These works are the primary examples of this style. In them, he displayed a broad stylistic range, from the *Grapes* with their masterly handling of ink, to the almost Disney-like humor of his *Bamboo Grove*. Perhaps the best-known painting of his late period is his *Vegetable Nirvana* (Kyoto National Museum, fig. 24), where it is possible to also find similar impromptu strokes. In a work like this we are able to sense that Jakuchū's true personality as an artful humorist has fully developed. As can be seen in his polychrome works and the ink paintings of his very last years, the aged Jakuchū, who in his long career had achieved stylistic freedom by creating images on his own terms, became, more than ever, the essence of painting.

The member of the lineage of eccentrics who is best represented in the collection of the MFA is Soga Shōhaku. The Boston collection, which includes over twenty-seven works that can be attributed to the artist, is the largest anywhere. Shōhaku is believed to have been born into a merchant family but studied painting under the Kano school artist Takada Keihō (1674–1755). However, by the time he was in his twenties, he boldly declared himself the tenth-generation successor to the fifteenth-century ink painter Soga Jasoku, and sought to revive the Soga school traditions, which by that time had become essentially defunct.

New styles with European perspectival methods and Chinese Southern-Song painting ideals were emerging in Kyoto at the time. However, Shōhaku appropriated the legacy of works from a previous generation, which fit into a more monumental tradition with roots in early Song China. His motive for doing so is not clear, but if we focus on the works themselves, it becomes apparent that in the rough and eccentric mode of expression espoused by the nonconformist sixteenth to early seventeenth-century artist Soga Chokuan, he found a rough, eccentric expressiveness that was probably influenced by Korean painting. Furthermore, from a young age Shōhaku also took on the methods of two other schools—the Unkoku and Ami—as part of his tool chest in the establishment of his own novel mode. Thus, Shōhaku deftly wielded great technical

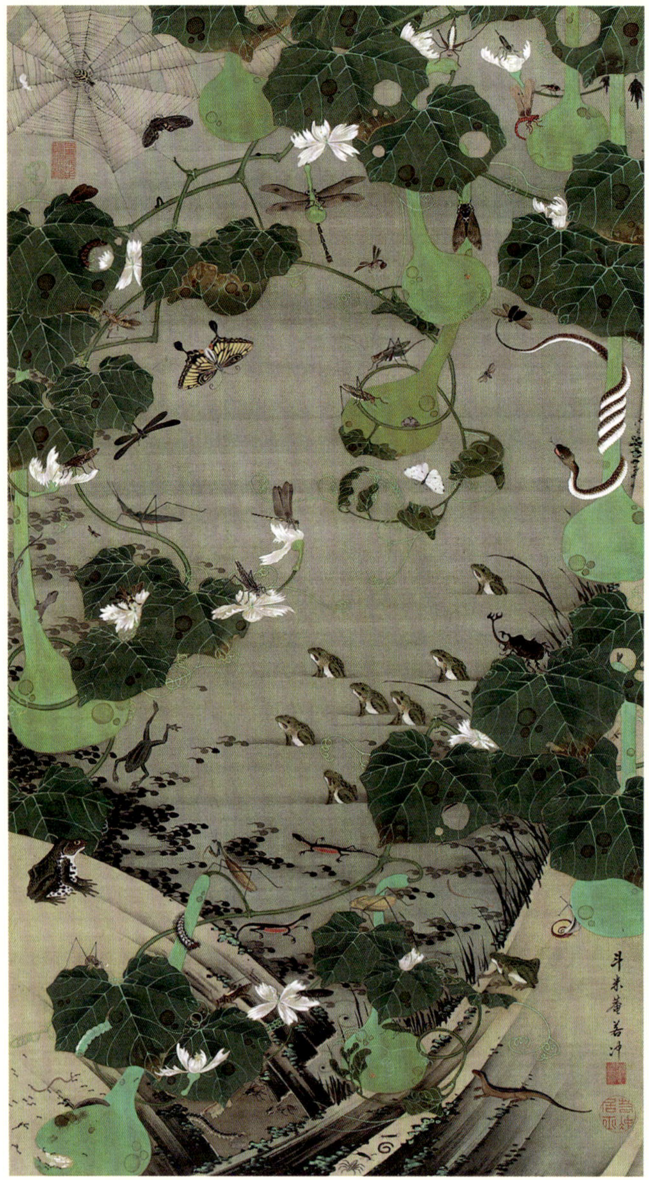

23
Itō Jakuchū (1716–1800)
Insects, Reptiles, and Amphibians at the Edge of a Pond from *Colorful Realm of Living Beings*, Edo period, 18th century

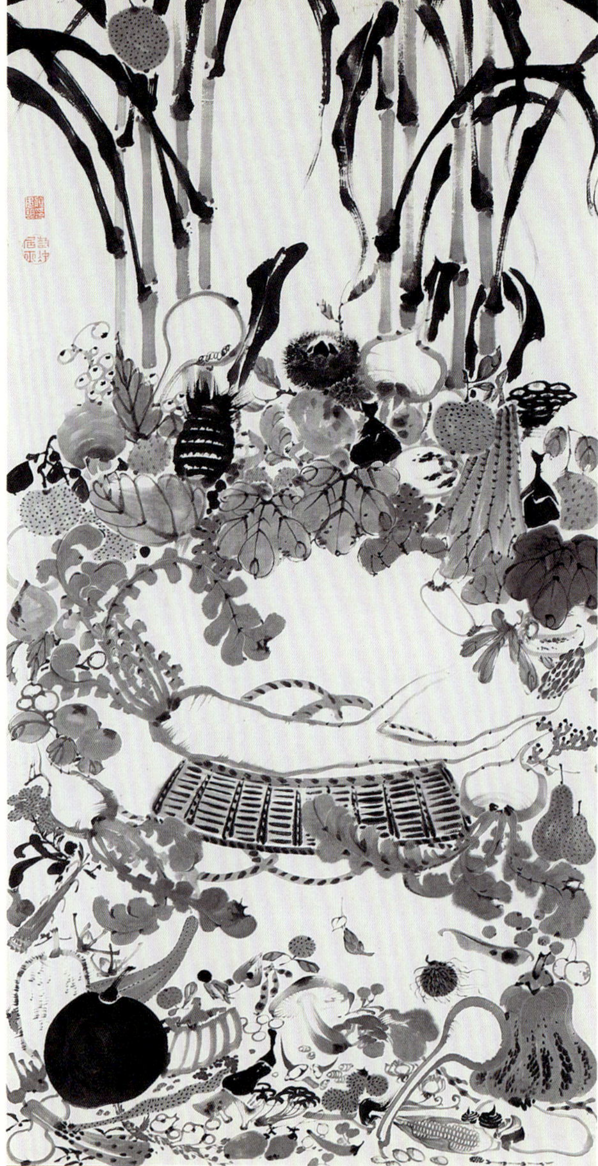

24
Itō Jakuchū (1716–1800)
Vegetable Nirvana, Edo period, 18th century

skills while freely warping traditional motifs and forms, breaking them down, exaggerating them to surprising levels, and rendering them comic, all elements that can be discerned in his own definition of how to paint pictures.

There is a theory that Shōhaku was born in Ise, to the east of Kyoto. While this supposition may be questioned on the basis of information on his gravestone and his death register at Kōshōji in Kyoto, it is true that from the end of his twenties through the first half of his thirties, Shōhaku traveled not once but many times to various parts of the Ise region. The tales of his bohemian goings-on during those trips remained food for talk in the area well into the Meiji era, as noted in memos compiled by the painter Momosawa Nyosui in 1906. The anecdotes are filled with a droll humor, as exemplified by an episode that took place in Ōtsuka Village in Annō County.

Shōhaku stayed with a village official named Kurata for quite a while, but no one ever saw him paint. At one point Kurata was going out and asked Shōhaku, "Since you are staying here for a long time, why don't you paint something on the cedar door at the front of the entrance for me?" It seems that Shōhaku freely promised to paint something. Eventually, when Kurata had finished his errands and returned, he wondered, "When will that lazy teacher paint something for me," and went to look. He found that the entranceway cedar door had been painted all over with black ink, and the image was meant to show a Buddha appearing over the mountains with a halo as big as an umbrella with a bull's eye decoration. In true Shōhaku fashion, he turned to the landlord and said, "So, what do you think? Is it interesting?"

While many of the paintings that Shōhaku created in Ise have been lost, quite a few powerful works remain near Matsusaka in Mie Prefecture. Among them is *Sessan dōji,* a large hanging scroll at Keishōji, painted in fantastically vibrant full colors. The scroll relates a previous life of Shaka, the Historical Buddha, who in the form of a bodhisattva undergoes austerities and who, to learn the truth, sacrifices his body to a demon (fig. 25). This is Shōhaku's interpretation of one of the most famous *jataka* tales, stories that date from the early centuries of the Buddhist faith and describe the previous lives of the Historical Buddha. At Chōdenji there are paintings with heroic brushstrokes of Chinese lions pasted on a wall. Both works are thought to date from the first half of Shōhaku's thirties. All are fully realized, without any sign of Shōhaku lowering his standards because of travel and being away from his studio in Kyoto. His grand *Dragon and Clouds* (now in the MFA), formerly fusuma panels that might have been painted for both sides of the altar of a temple, perhaps in Ise, bears an inscription dating from his thirty-fourth year. In these panels it appears as if a dragon from a Soga Chokuan or Kaihō Yūshō (1533–1615) prototype has been put under Shōhaku's spell and somehow metamorphosed into an outrageous beast. Shōhaku's early thirties can thus be seen as a period in which his extraordinary imagination welled forth. Shōhaku seems to have lived to the age of fifty-two. While the lack of works with dated inscriptions means it is not clear how his painting style developed after his early thirties, his humorous *Lions at Stone Bridge* (now in the Metropolitan Museum of Art) bears an inscription dating it to 1779, when he was fifty years old. This work and several others suggest that Shōhaku maintained his unfettered spirit and superior expressive powers until the end.

Although large numbers of formal landscape paintings remain from Shōhaku's final years, throughout his life the greatest percentage of his oeuvre was dedicated to figure paintings, particularly those of Chinese heroic and legendary subjects. Images of these figures had been widely available in temple elementary

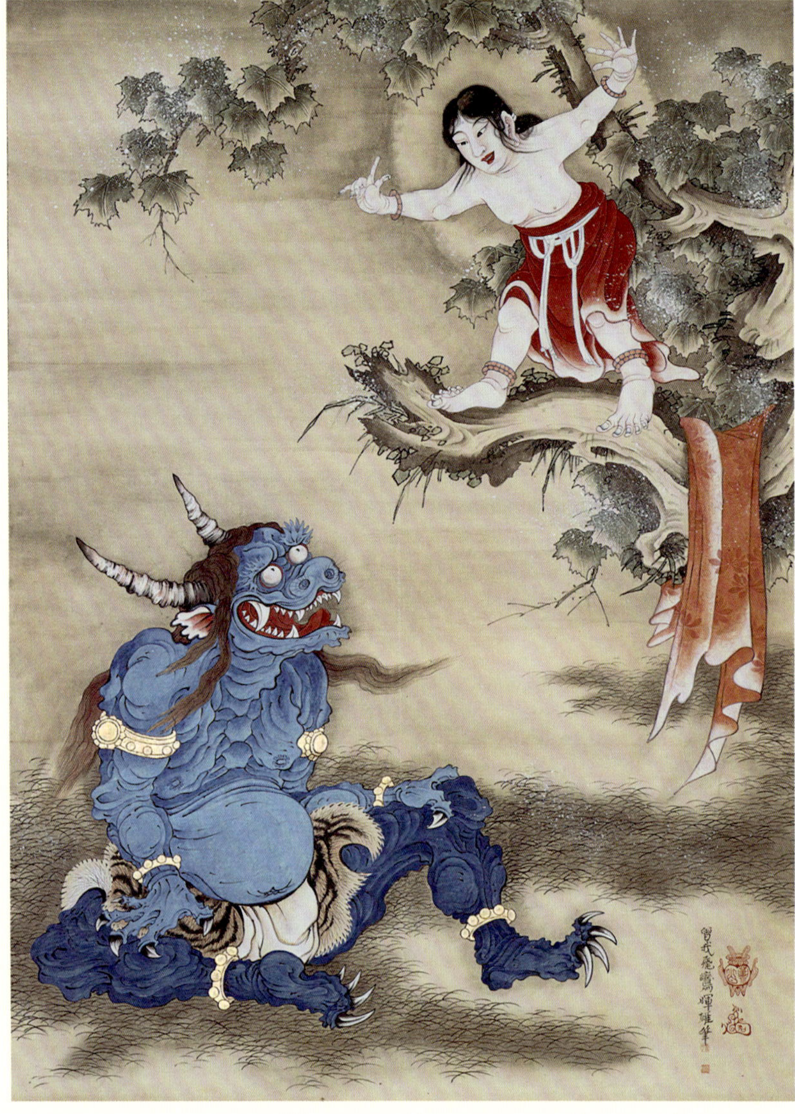

schools and had also been distributed through illustrated books during the Edo period to all segments of society, including commoners. Shōhaku drew upon these sources but then used all manner of devices to make these images more impressive, including evoking fear and surprise, in order to encourage the curiosity of his viewers.

Shōhaku's type of eccentricity reflected a seventeenth-century Chinese literati predilection toward madness, but the bravura required to convey these ideas to a Japanese public could not have been achieved by just any artist. Only an individual like Shōhaku who could recognize the madness and eccentricity in his own character and express them with incredible painting prowess could realize this vision. Thus Shōhaku had the remarkable ability to walk the perilous line between madness and sanity.

25
Soga Shōhaku (1730–1781)
Sessan dōji, Edo period,
18th century

Afterword

I never write my books in English. *Lineage of Eccentrics* is a translation of a book I wrote in Japanese without overseas readers in mind. Most Japanese are not great at foreign languages, and I am a case in point. Okakura, who greatly contributed to forming the foundation of the MFA's tremendous Japanese art collection, devoted his life to sharing Japanese culture and art overseas. He wrote all his books, including *The Book of Tea*, in English, but he was quite an exception to the rule.

My writings printed in English in the preceding pages, therefore, are not something I wrote in English either. Anne Nishimura Morse, who has overseen the collection of Japanese art at the MFA for many years, compiled my past writings as comprehensively as possible, deftly condensed them, added some of her own interpretations, and completed the text. I would like to sincerely thank her for her tremendous efforts here. In addition, I would like to extend my thanks to the other MFA staff members, starting with Anna Barnet, who helped her in this endeavor in their various capacities.

The writings included here are a little different from conventional theories on Japanese art—it might be accurate to call them eccentric. In fact, after many years of my publications and exhibitions, the term *kisō* has practically become a pronoun meaning "me," and indeed, along with that, my image has been set as an eccentric. Even though I am called an eccentric, that does not mean that I am lost in the *kisō* clouds from dawn to dusk, and even though I intend to act in accordance with expected norms, I guess that on some level they had to give me this label to fit in with how various people are organized and labeled by society.

While the quintessential concepts of *wabi* and *sabi* are certainly important in speaking about Japanese aesthetics, I have dared to define them as the aesthetics of "anti-kazari," something that is cognizant of kazari. Fujiwara no Teika, the famous twelfth- and thirteenth-century poet, wrote the following well-known poem, which seems to support this idea. Though this poem appears to be a de-piction of wabi sabi scenery, it ultimately emphasizes kazari concepts such as cherry blossoms and autumn leaves, which evoke bright and festive imagery:

> When I look out,
> There are no cherry blossoms nor any tinted leaves;
> An autumn dusk,
> In the mossy hut by the bay.

Adapted from the following works by Nobuo Tsuji:

ANIMATION

"Ryō nakama to tenrankai." In *Emakimono—Anime no genryū*, edited by Yukari Tai and Tomoko Matsuo.
 Chiba: Chiba City Museum / Studio Ghibli, 1999.
"Early Medieval Picture Scrolls as Ancestors of Anime and Manga." In *Births and Rebirths in Japanese Art*,
 edited by Nicole Coolidge Rousmaniere. Leiden: Hotei, 2001.

KAZARI

"*Kazari*: Decoration in Japanese Art," translated by Lynne E. Riggs. In *Kazari*. Shiga: MIHO Museum, 2016.
"On Kazari," translated by Nicole Coolidge Rousmaniere. In *Kazari: Decoration and Display in Japan,
15th–19th Centuries*, edited by Nicole Coolidge Rousmaniere. London: British Museum Press,
 © The Trustees of the British Museum, 2002.
"The Concept of the Decorative in Japanese Art." In *Japan and Europe in Art History*. Tokyo: Chūo-kōron
 bijutsu shuppan, 1995.
"Ornament (Kazari)—An Approach to Japanese Culture." In *Archives of Asian Art 47* (1994, now published
 by Duke University Press).
"Kazari—Seino akashi toshiteno." In *Kazari no sekai*. Tokyo: NHK Service Center, 1988.

ASOBI

"Element of Play in the Edo Period." *The Asiatic Society of Japan Bulletin* 7 (September 2001).
Playfulness in Japanese Art, translated by Joseph Seubert. Vol. 7 of *The Franklin D. Murphy Lectures*.
 Kansas City: Spencer Museum of Art, University of Kansas, 1986.
"Okoe no sekai." In *Hikaku geijutsu kenkyū II Geijutsu to biishiki*. Tokyo: Bijutsu shuppansha, 1977.

RELIGIOSITY

"Asuka Hakuhō bijutsu" and "Heianjidai no bijutsu." In *Nihon bijitsu no rekishi*. Tokyo: University of
 Tokyo Press, 2005.
"Hen'yō suru shinbutsu tachi." In *Kinsei shūkyōbijutsu no sekai: Hen'yō suru shinbutsu tachi*.
 Tokyo: Shōtō Museum of Art, 1995.
 © 1995 The Shōtō Museum of Art

ECCENTRICITY

Lineage of Eccentrics: Matabei to Kuniyoshi, translated by Aaron M. Rio. Tokyo: Kaikai Kiki, 2012.
 © 2012 by Nobuo Tsuji, © 2012 by Kaikai Kiki Co., Ltd.
Kisō no hakken: Aru bijutsushika no kaisō. Tokyo: Shinchōsha, 2014.
"Kikyō no gaka-ryūha narazaru ryūha." In *Mizue 800* (1971).

---

1   Sergei Eisenstein, "The Cinematographic Principle and the Ideogram," in *Film, Form*, trans. and ed.
     Jay Leyda (New York: Harcourt, Brace, and World, 1949), 28.

2   Tahei Imamura, *Manga eiga ron*, Imamura Tahei eizō hyōron 5 (Kyoto: Daiichi geibunsha, 1941; repr.,
     Tokyo: Yumani shobō, 1991).

3   Isao Takahata, *Jūni seiki no animēshon: Kokuhō emakimono ni miru eiga-teki animeteki naru mono*
     (Tokyo: Tokuma shoten/Studio Ghibli, 1999).

4   Andrew Dudley and Michael Raine, "Japanese Image Culture," *Iris: A Journal of Theory on Image and
     Sound* 16 (Spring 1993): 4.

5   Toyomune Minamoto, "Nihon bijutsu no hi-sanjigensei," in *Bijutsu kōenkai—kōenroku* 3 (Tokyo: Kajima
     Foundation, 1987).

6   Minamoto, "Nihon bijutsu no hi-sanjigensei."

7   Sharon Kinsella, *Adult Manga: Culture and Power in Contemporary Japanese Society* (Honolulu: University
     of Hawai'i Press, 2000), 3.

8   Edwin A. Cranston, trans., *The Glistening Cup*, vol. 1 of *A Waka Anthology* (Stanford: Stanford University Press, 1993), 542–43.

9   Ernest Chesneau, *Les nations rivals dans l'art; l'art japonais; de l'influence des expositions sur l'avenir de l'art* (Paris: Didier, 1868), as translated by Nicole Coolidge Rousmaniere in *Kazari: Decoration and Display in Japan, 15th–19th Centuries* (London: British Museum Press, 2002), 18.

10   Yukio Yashiro, "Shizenbutsu no sōshokuteki henkei," *Nihon bijutsu no tokushitsu*, 2nd ed. (Tokyo: Iwanami shoten, 1965), 260–61.

11   Yashiro, "Shizenbutsu no sōshokuteki henkei."

12   Jianjua Yu, trans., *Xuanhe huapu* (Beijing: Renmin meishu chubanshe, 1964), 213. As cited by John M. Rosenfield in "Ornament (Kazari): An Approach to Japanese Culture," *Archives of Asian Art* 47 (1994): 35n5.

13   E. H. Gombrich, *The Sense of Order: A Study in the Psychology of Decorative Art* (Ithaca, NY: Cornell University Press, 1979), 111.

14   Laurence Binyon, *Painting in the Far East: An Introduction to Pictorial Art in China and Japan* (London: Edward Arnold, 1908), 203.

15   Seiichi Taki, "Nihon bijutsu no tokusei," *Kokka* 133 (June 1901): 4–9. Taki is referring to the *Iris* screens now in the collection of the Nezu Art Museum, Tokyo.

16   Johan Huizinga, *Homo Ludens: A Study of the Play-Element in Culture* (London: Routledge and Kegan Paul, 1949; repr., 1980), 4.

17   Huizinga, *Homo Ludens*, 13.

18   Huizinga, *Homo Ludens*, 186.

19   Narisue Tachibana, comp., *Kokon chomonjū* (Tokyo: Yūhōdō, 1927), 340.

20   Tachibana, *Kokon chomonjū*, 340.

21   *Konjaku monogatari shū*, vol. 28 (Tokyo: Keizo Kondo, 1882), 55.

22   Kunio Yanagita, *Yanagita Kunio shū*, vol. 7 (Tokyo: Chikuma shobo, 1968).

23   O-Young Lee, *Smaller Is Better: Japan's Mastery of the Miniature,* trans. Robert N. Huey (Tokyo: Kodansha International, 1984).

24   Takeshi Umehara, "Animizumu saikō," *Nihon kenkyū* 1 (1989): 13–23.

25   Takeo Izumi, *Ōchō no butsuga to girei* (Kyoto: Kyoto National Museum, 1998), 334.

26   Zennosuke Tsuji, *Kinsei no yon*, vol. 10 of *Nihon bukkyōshi* (Tokyo: Iwanami shoten, 1961), 451–52.

27   I adopted the term *kisō* for the book *Kisō no keifū* (*Lineage of Eccentrics*) from the title of an article by Suzuki Jūzō, "Kuniyoshi no kisō," in the June 1966 issue of the journal *Hōshun*.

28   James Cahill, *Fantastics and Eccentrics in Chinese Painting* (New York: Asia Society, 1967).

29   Fukuchi Mataichi and Okakura Kakuzō, *Kōhon Nihon teikoku bijutsu ryakushi* (Tokyo: Ryūbunkan tosho kabushiki kaisha, 1916). First published in French as *Histoire de l'art du Japon, par la Commission Imperiale du Japon a l'Exposition Universelle de Paris* (Paris: M. du Brunhoff, 1900).

30   For example, the careful observation of an exhaustive array of frogs, tadpoles, snakes, spiders, lizards, centipedes, and crickets can also be seen in sketches by Maruyama Ōkyo and Odano Naotake. In 2012 the National Gallery of Art in Washington, DC, organized the exhibition *Colorful Realm: Japanese Bird-and-Flower Paintings by Itō Jakuchū (1716–1800)*, marking the first time that the entire set of thirty bird-and-flower paintings and the triptych of Shaka, the Historical Buddha, and his attendants had been exhibited outside Japan. During the four-week exhibition over 320,000 people came to view the works.

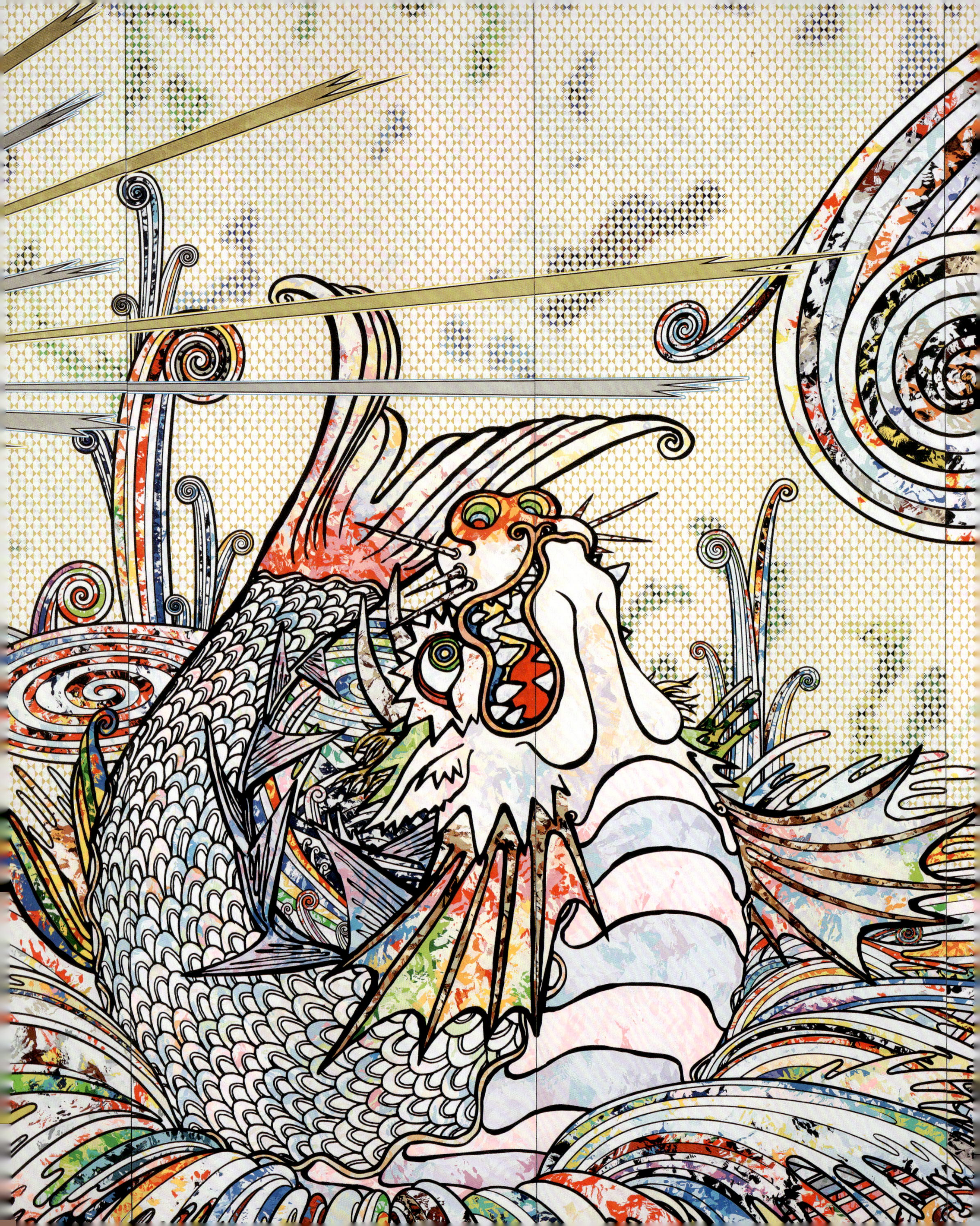

A CONVERSATION WITH TAKASHI MURAKAMI AND NOBUO TSUJI

ANM: In his *Superflat Manifesto* Murakami cited Professor Tsuij's *Lineage of Eccentrics* as being critical to the formulation of his approach to image making. Since that time the two of you have exchanged ideas and collaborated in the series for the art magazine *Geijutsu shinchō*, which has just recently been published in English as *Nobuo Tsuji vs. Takashi Murakami: Battle Royale! Japanese Art History* [fig. 26]. How did your relationship develop?

NT: We first met in 1994 at the Tokyo gallery SCAI the Bathhouse when Murakami was around thirty years old and I was sixty. Murakami is a little different now. Back then he didn't present himself like this. He was more serious, a mild-mannered student.

TM: There was an editor at the publishing firm Iwanami shoten, who had seen this exhibition. Because I was an artist influenced by manga, I didn't have anyone at all to talk with. My friends in contemporary art all hated what I was doing. "That stuff you're doing isn't art," they'd say. I was pretty depressed. But this editor told me, "These works, this style, just may be what the art historian Nobuo Tsuji will be interested in." She had just finished editing the series *History of Japanese Art*, and Tsuji-sensei had contributed the seventh volume. He had written that the one lineage in Japanese art that continues today is manga. At that time Tsuji-sensei alone was saying that. Today there's a whole mass chorus echoing that opinion, and art museums are all holding manga exhibitions. But she told me that then, really only one person was properly doing research on the subject. Feeling I had nowhere else to turn, I began reading Tsuji-sensei's various books. That, come to think of it, was a turning point. Until then I had thought that my way of painting had to be in a style that was influenced by manga artists. And that style had to

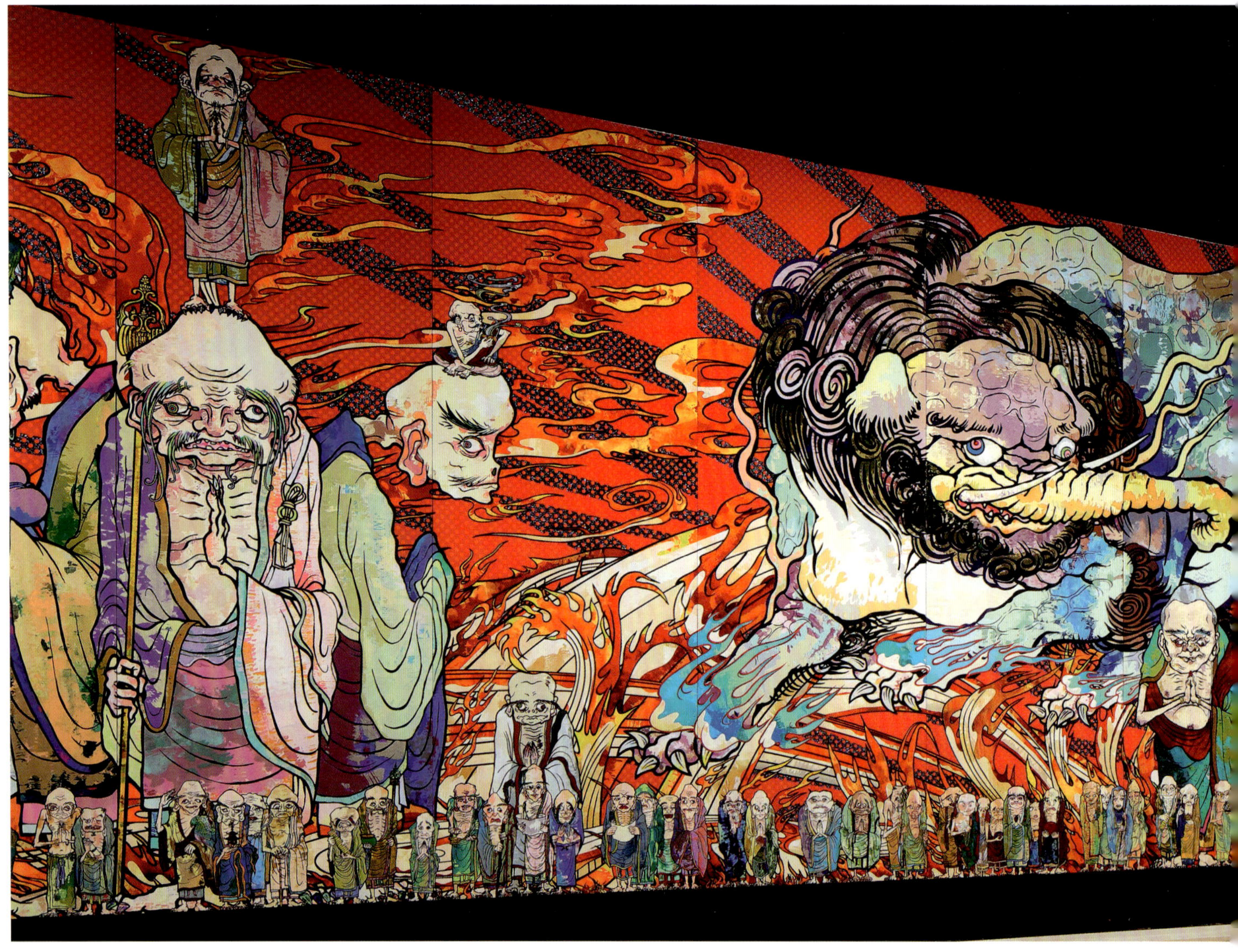

be different from Roy Lichtenstein's and other American pop art. American comics and Japanese manga have completely different roots. I hadn't originally thought of going back into Japanese art history.

Basically, to me, past and present or West and East, these dualities are, well, competing with each other. There's a gap, and my theme had been how to fill in that gap or to build a bridge over it. Tsuji-sensei's writings have taught me all sorts of ways to build that bridge. And that's why I respect him and why I call him my spiritual mentor.

ANM: Flatness has been considered by critics, such as Clement Greenberg, to be a defining element of Western painting in the twentieth century. However, Murakami, in your manifesto you point out that flatness has historically been characteristic of

26

View of *Takashi Murakami: The 500 Arhats*, Mori Museum, Tokyo, 2015

This monumental composition represents the culmination of the exchanges between Tsuji and Murakami in their *Battle Royale!* Murakami drew upon several different works that he had previously explored during the series, including *Dragon and Clouds* by Soga Shōhaku and arhat paintings by Kanō Kazunobu.

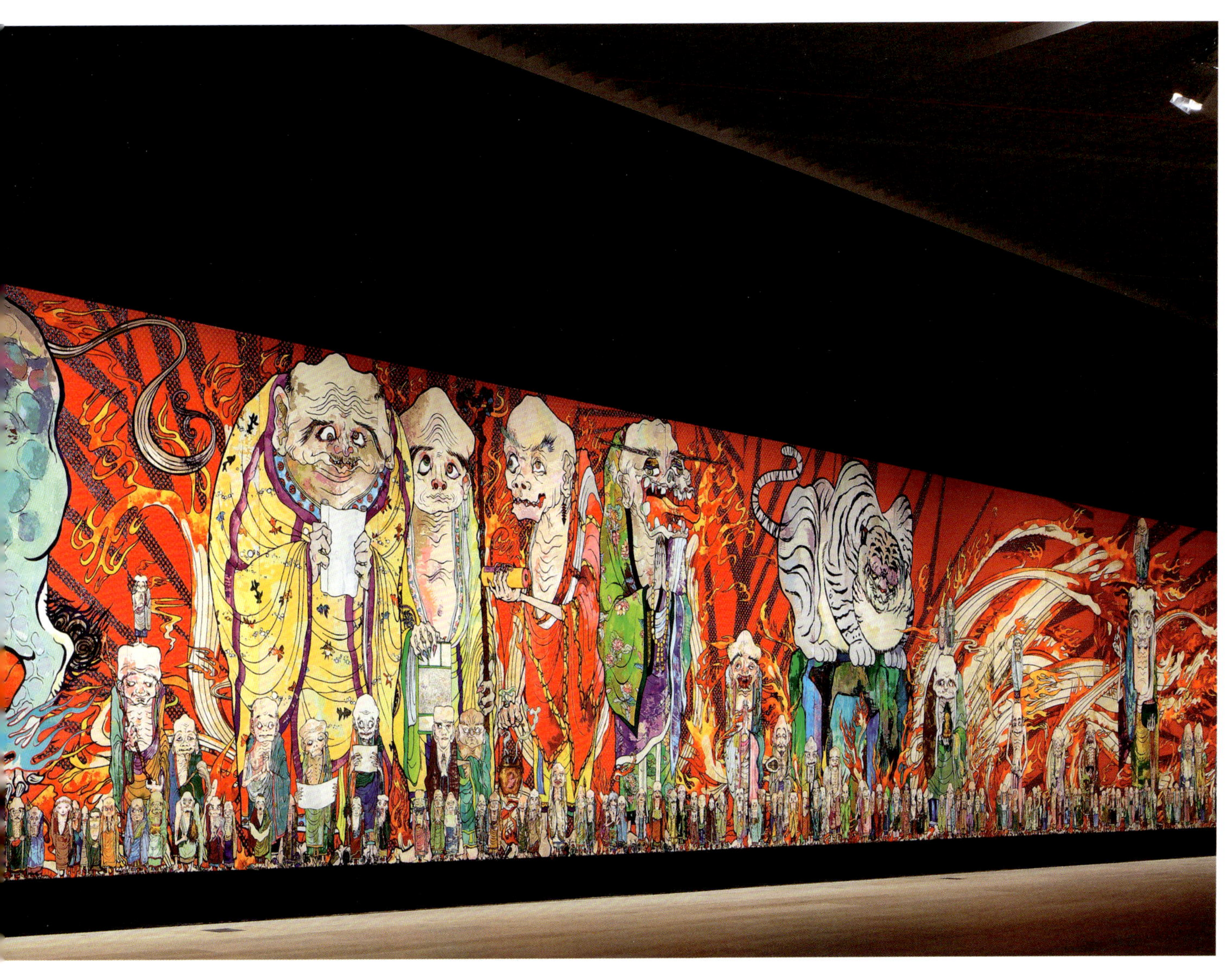

Japanese painting and that there are congruencies between the work of the Eccentrics and contemporary animation artists. What motivated you to write the *Superflat Manifesto*?

TM: Well, *Superflat,* come to think of it, that's a package. In the United States the capital of contemporary art is New York. People in New York think packaging is critical. Without a package, they absolutely will not be receptive to work. That's a historical fact I discovered. Truth or lies, you have to have the package. But Sensei's *Lineage of Eccentrics* is a kind of packaging, isn't it?

NT: Well, I suppose if you put it that way. . . .

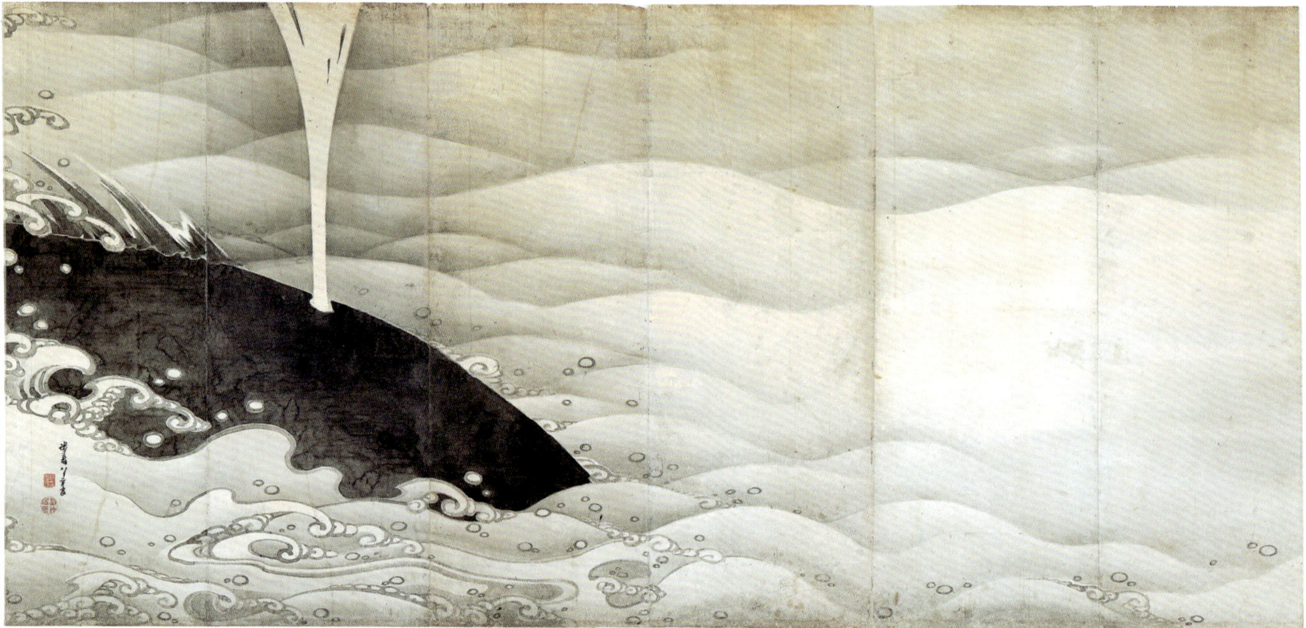

TM: But as for the package, I strongly believed that if you don't do it, people won't understand you. I created the package for my works using the word "superflat" because I thought this word exemplified my works. And thus, in America they were receptive to my work, luckily enough.

ANM: *Superflat* has become a theoretical essay that everyone reads.

TM: But I didn't write a proper theoretical book, you know. I was not up to that. I just put something together that would work as a package. But while I sort of understand what simulationism is, I haven't heard that Jeff Koons has written a book like that.

ANM: Tsuji-sensei's writings have been extremely influential in Murakami's thinking, but how has your relationship affected the development of specific paintings?

NT: We didn't associate with each other right after the meeting at SCAI the Bathhouse. Then after the exhibition *Takashi Murakami: Made in Japan* in 2001 at the Museum of Fine Arts, Boston, I met Murakami for the second time. Murakami had already become quite famous by then, but I did not know what sort of a person he really was until our *Geijutsu shinchō* collaboration.

     That project was a fairly easygoing proposal that came to me, and I agreed to participate in an informal way, then started to write. But as I did so, it was like a fever gradually took over me. Murakami, your paintings grew larger, and finally you painted the *500 Arhats*. The dialogue turned into something we could not have imagined.

TM: I felt that I could confidently get on board with what Tsuji-sensei was writing. Without that, well, I wouldn't have had the courage to do what I have done. But Sensei

27
Itō Jakuchū (1716–1800)
Elephant and Whale Screens,
Edo period, 1797

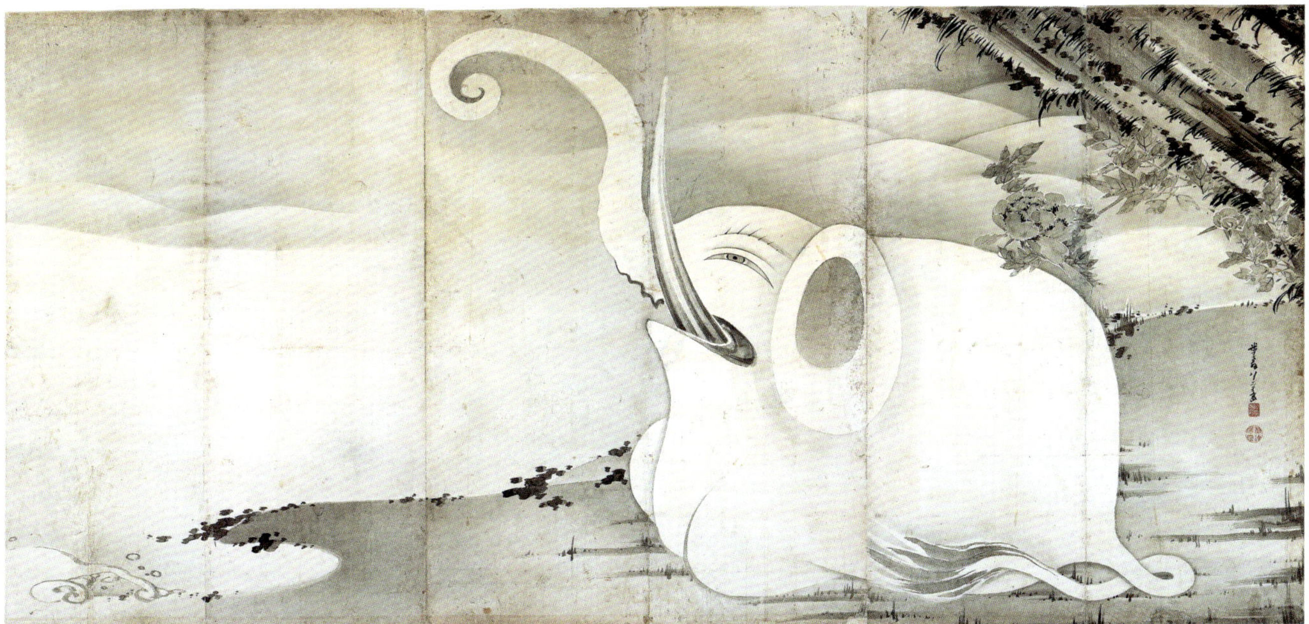

never said positive things, even about my *500 Arhats*. You said all sorts of things. "It's sort of ambiguous," or "This painting does have some amazingly lively parts, but that part's pretty clumsy." [Laughter] Oh, and "In this part, you seem to have run out of material; it's kind of boring." [Laughter]

In the *Geijutsu shinchō* series, you wrote something like, "Murakami, you don't know anything. Instead of yelling at the younger generation, why don't you paint for a change?" And, from my perspective, I thought that anyone who would say that was a complete amateur, but why would you say something so pointless, especially at that time? I was mad. [Laughter] That was when I'd just rented my new studio, and I'd built a huge wall in it. So I thought I'd paint to fill the whole wall, and I first produced the *Elephant and the Whale* in response to Itō Jakuchū's screens in the Miho Museum that you presented as part of the challenge [figs. 27 and 28].

And when I tried, I found I was surprisingly able to paint. I hadn't produced a painting in about ten years. I was just drawing plans. I wish I could paint, I thought. And when I showed them to you, Tsuji-sensei, you just kind of mumbled about them and said they were weak. [Laughter] And I got even angrier, and that's why I painted *Red Dragon* [see pp. 132–34]. But I myself don't think I was painting very well with that one; it didn't work out that great, I think.

NT: There is another red dragon somewhere. I think that one is good.

TM: Well, you see, I painted the not-so-great one. The good one was painted by Yutaka Sugiyama, who was then a graduate student studying Nihonga at Tokyo University of the Arts. [Laughter] And Sugiyama-kun painted the blue one, too. Anyway, Sensei, you lit a fire under me in various ways, and that's why I painted that monumental painting. I had never painted anything so big before.

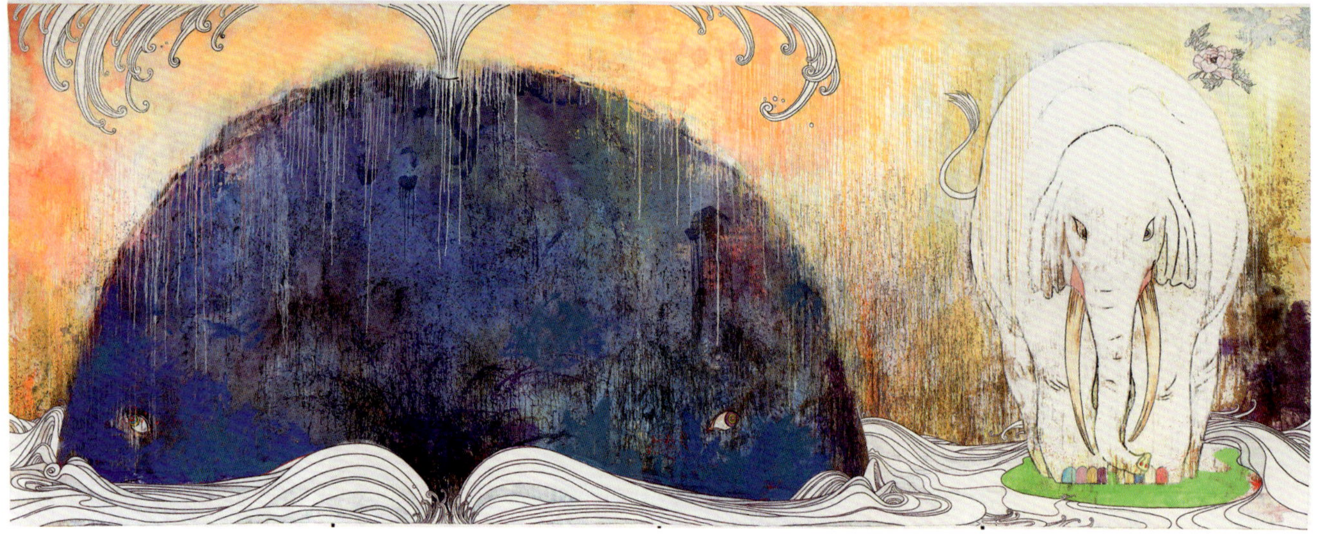

ANM: But I think that the one you painted by yourself is wonderful!

TM: You say that, but right after I painted it, Sensei looked at it and said, "What are you trying to fake over here?" He meant the part that's sort of scribbly and dripping.

NT: It was the first of the paintings. . . . Now I understand. Since it was the first time—we have the word *shohatsusei,* spontaneity, in Japanese. Its appeal lies there.

ANM: Yes, in the *Red Dragon* and some of the small sketches, we can really feel your individual presence and your own personal power.

TM: A museum curator like you can say something like that. But collectors who spend money say, "Oh, this is too easy, too." But you know, when I die, they will say, "Oh, this is precious!" Right? But I'm still alive. That's why, you know I have to construct a very nice surface. That is my being the architect of monumental paintings. But you know the reason that I have been hiding the *Red Dragon* for a long time is because I do understand that this work reflects more than one hundred percent of my passion.

I've complained to Sensei, but his books contain discoveries that startle me and then I start painting. Without an inspiration, something to spur me on, I have a hard time painting. In that sense, a great many of my works could not exist without Sensei's presence in my life. As I said earlier, several of the works that have been turning points for me, including the *500 Arhats* and that huge dragon painting, were influenced by Sensei. In particular, in recent years, they've been increasingly numerous.

So that's how we have gotten to know each other. I didn't have a teacher, a mentor, and Tsuji-sensei has become my sole source of spiritual support, I would say.

ANM: You had not actually seen the Shōhaku *Dragon and Clouds* until several years after you had completed your own painting, when it was on exhibition at the Tokyo National

Museum in 2012. Was the work as you had imagined it from the reproductions in Tsuji-sensei's book?

TM: I went to see it and I was super excited, seeing it for the first time. I was utterly impressed. It was like meeting my father for the first time, Oh, this is my DNA!

ANM: Professor Tsuji, when we first talked about this exhibition, you said to me that you thought Murakami would be more interested in Soga Shōhaku than in Itō Jakuchū. And
I wondered, of the six artists in *Lineage of Eccentrics*, why has Shōhaku been the one with whom you think Murakami has had the most connection?

NT: Murakami and Jakuchū don't fit together well.

TM: Jakuchū wasn't that popular when Tsuji-sensei wrote *Lineage of Eccentrics*, but it seems like Jakuchū is now being acclaimed as Japan's greatest artist. That may be true. Looking at those fascinating stories, including his being from a family of vegetable wholesalers and the letter of appeal that he wrote to the Edo shogunate, I do think Jakuchū was an interesting fellow.

Jakuchū was not a professional artist. He had his business, and he had his prayers, and he created the *Colorful Realm of Living Beings*. The amazing, most profound things he did were, I think, the accomplishments of an amateur, a dilettante. But what he produced after the fire of 1788, which destroyed large sections of Kyoto, is the best. Jakuchū was in a difficult position and produced good things. And it was then, I think, that he became a real artist.

Shōhaku, on the other hand, was an artist from the start. Perhaps Shōhaku was always in less fortunate situations. Coming from the lowest social station, from the counterculture, Shōhaku emerged and had to fight back. Being down on the social ladder and enduring a kind of sorrow can be, I think, extremely good. In my own case, if I look back, I was born in Sakashita (literally the bottom of the slope), in Itabashi Ward in Tokyo. It was a working-class area that often flooded. If you consider Jean-Michel Basquiat, he was a minority artist who had low technique, super, super low technique. But he was also one of the most expressive artists of his generation.

But Jakuchū, he was a bit of the Kyoto gentleman type, a refined fellow. Refinement—that doesn't work for me. Shōhaku was not refined.

NT: No, he wasn't. And you resemble each other in that way. But the amusingness of the unrefined—we see that in Murakami-san's paintings. I, too, was born and raised in a place that wasn't very refined. Perhaps that's the reason I feel an extraordinary empathy with you. [Laughter]

ANM: Let's look at *Transcendent Attacking a Whirlwind*, which you created for the Boston exhibition in homage to Shōhaku's screen by the same title in the MFA collection. [see pp. 39–42].

TM: One of the goals for this work was for Tsuji-sensei to recognize immediately that the painting is derived from Shōhaku compositions. I'm very interested in the whirlwind shape and also the form of the man with the strange long, double-jointed arms; I have included him twice now in my paintings. As for the fish, when I was at the university

I did produce a lot of paintings of fish, big monster fish that looked somewhat like dinosaurs or Chinese mythological creatures.

ANM: Do you see the Shōhaku elements as being part of a narrative, or do you see them as isolated motifs that you work with visually?

TM: For the most part there is no narrative, because I do not have a sense of the context for Shōhaku's works. Basically I love just the shape of the motifs, but there would be a big benefit in understanding the narrative context. As for the shapes, they are a part of a process of misinterpretation. An artist makes a drawing and then other people copy this line or shape over and over so that it becomes a monster. In this new painting, I tried to design something that looks like a misinterpretation, a monster fish. For the figure on the left, I'm extremely interested in the deformed, the skeletally peculiar body. Jean-Auguste-Dominque Ingres's *Odalisque* was like that.

ANM: As you have mentioned, we have seen the same disjointed figure before, specifically in *In the Land of the Dead, Stepping on the Tail of a Rainbow* at The Broad in Los Angeles [see pp. 36–37]. So when you repeat motifs like that or explore motifs, do you think about the connections between paintings?

TM: No, no, no. It's a kind of very playful misinterpretation, breaking through the narrative, the original story. I just want to create a meaningless thing, something that I have been pursuing since my graduate course when I wrote my dissertation, "The Meaning of the Meaninglessness of Meaning."

After American Expressionism, artists lost any reason for including objects in painting. In the 1980s the new painting generation, Julian Schnabel, Jean-Michel Basquiat, and Keith Haring revived the narrative, but this boom was short-lived. Simulationist artists like Jeff Koons and Barbara Kruger cannot create narratives. That's why their ideas come from advertising. Richard Prince turned to Marlboro cigarette ads, and Jeff Koons picked ideas up from Nike posters.

I found my character Mr. DOB in the way that Jasper Johns found the American flag. Somebody asked Johns why he chose the American flag. He answered that in that way he did not have to create designs; he could just make a new painting. In abstract art, just making a painting is great. Since I'm from Japan, from Asia, I decided to take my ideas from Chinese characters and Shōhaku's figures, but they are not necessarily related to historical narratives.

ANM: Does *Transcendent Attacking a Whirlwind* reflect any new approaches to painting?

TM: I've developed a technique where I distract people away from the clumsiness of my drawing by adding more color. It's my new technique!

NT: Unlike what you painted before, the cumulative effect of the color itself in the shape of the lines is very expressive. What progress—you've made wonderful progress.

TM: The director Hayao Miyazaki produces a visual style for each of his anime films. The animation varies due to the changes in his staffing for each project. Similarly the question of whether my staff brings out their talent hinges on the ongoing dialogue we have about the painting at hand and the artwork itself. The selection of colors is very much part of that strategy. That's why I write down the names of all my staff on the back of the paintings.

NT: Just like anime. Film credits are written like this. You're basically making the paintings on a flat surface with an anime feel, with a production process very similar to that of anime!

ANM: Murakami, do you see yourself as part of the Lineage of Eccentrics?

TM: Yes, I feel like I'm part of the Lineage. Sensei, what do you think?

NT: Yes, you're part of it. [Laughter]

TM: Really? That's great! So, at the very last, just before you die, Sensei please add me to the tail end. Just a "There's this artist, too," kind of thing. I really would like you to add me.

NT: Actually, there are lots of painters around, but you're the only one who's said, "Tsuji-sensei, Tsuji-sensei, please mention me." It's really strange and wonderful that such a person exists. Of course, I will be honored to add you to the Lineage.

TM: In a postscript or whatever, you could write something like, "This idiotic, tiresome fellow who's been hanging around me lately is part of the Lineage; his name will be revealed when I die."

NT: Talk about a lineage of eccentrics. . . .

The images on the following pages show views of the exhibition *Takashi Murakami: Lineage of Eccentrics* at the Museum of Fine Arts, Boston, 2017

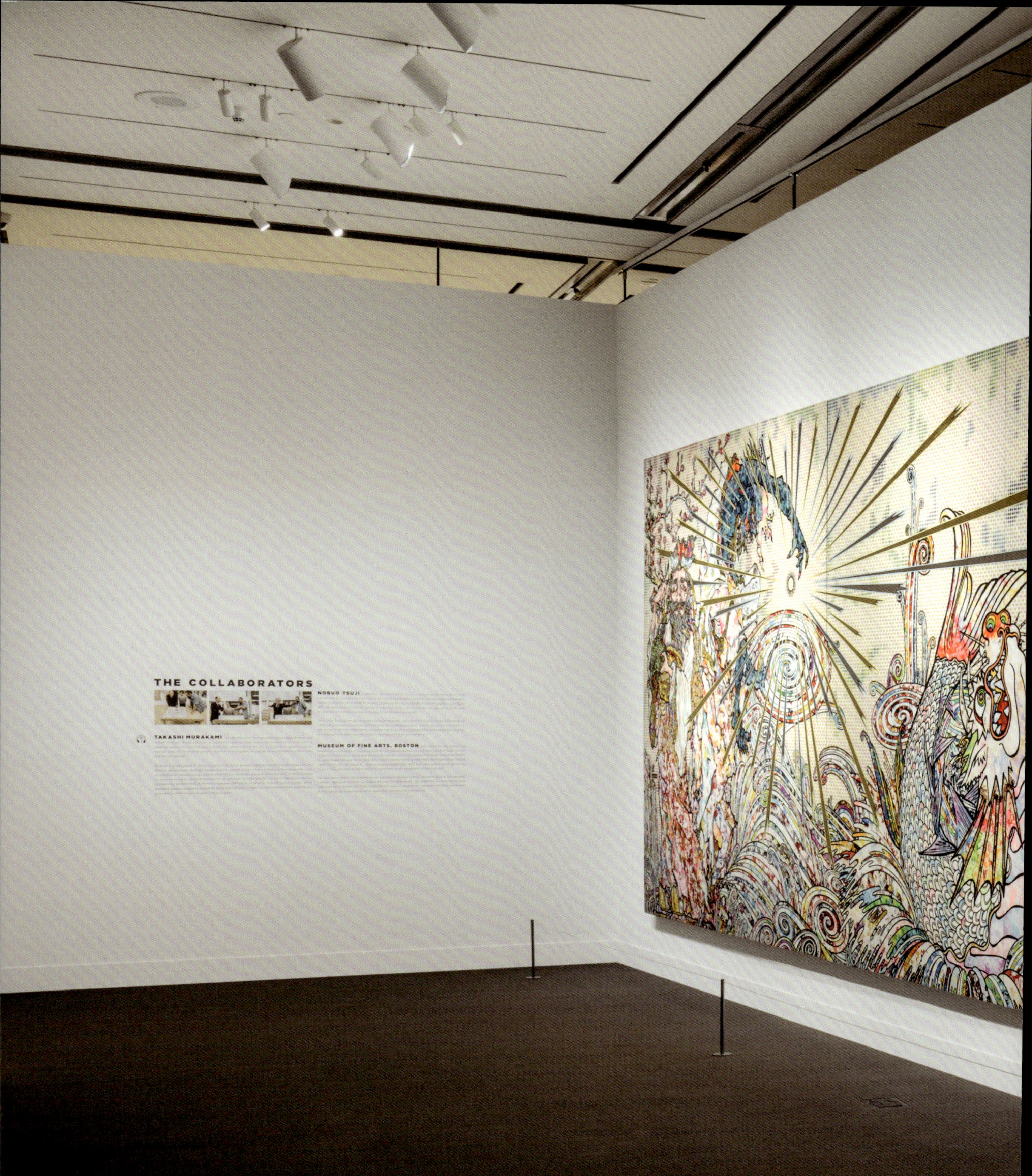
THE COLLABORATORS
TAKASHI MURAKAMI
NOBUO TSUJI
MUSEUM OF FINE ARTS, BOSTON

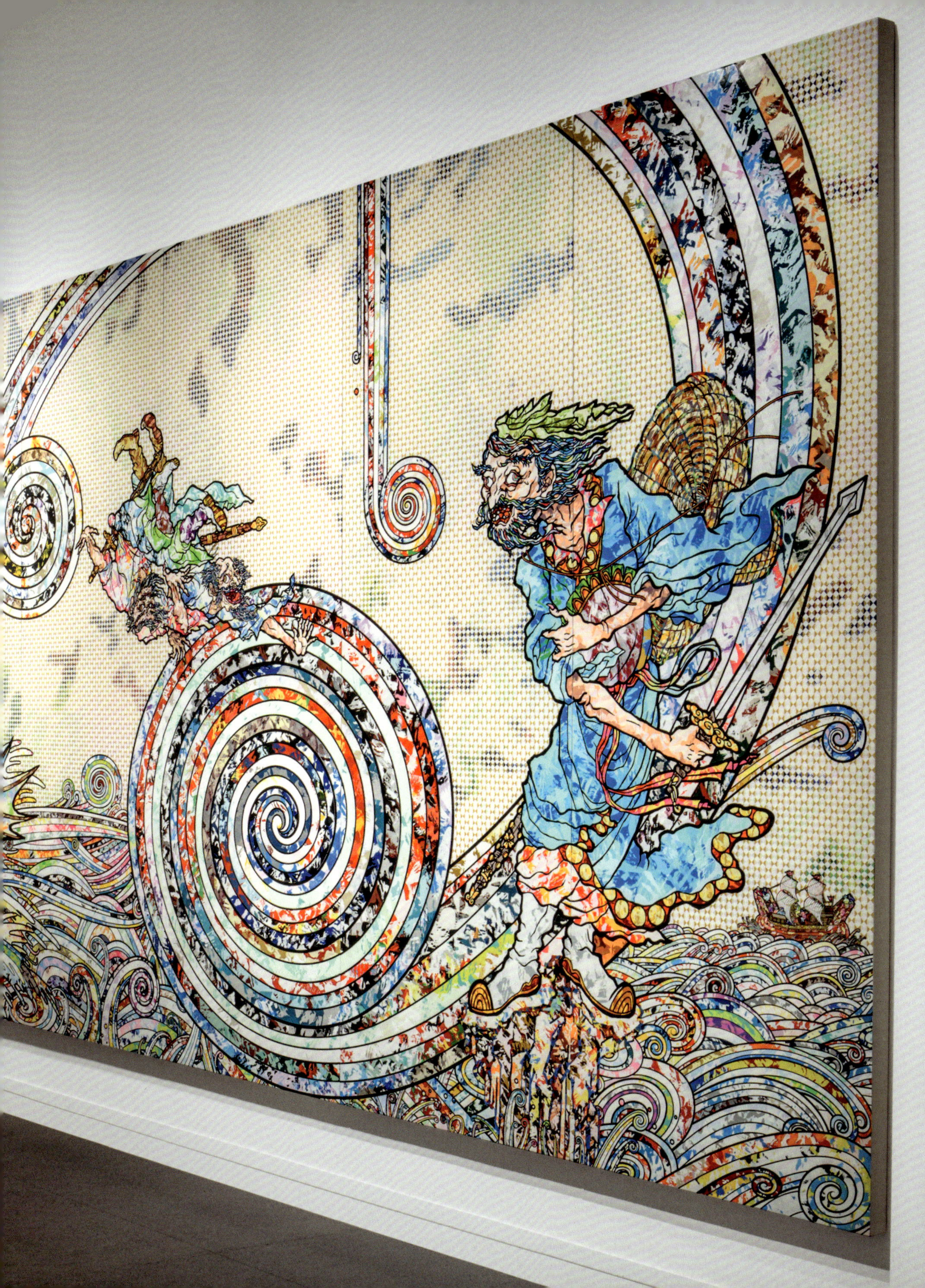

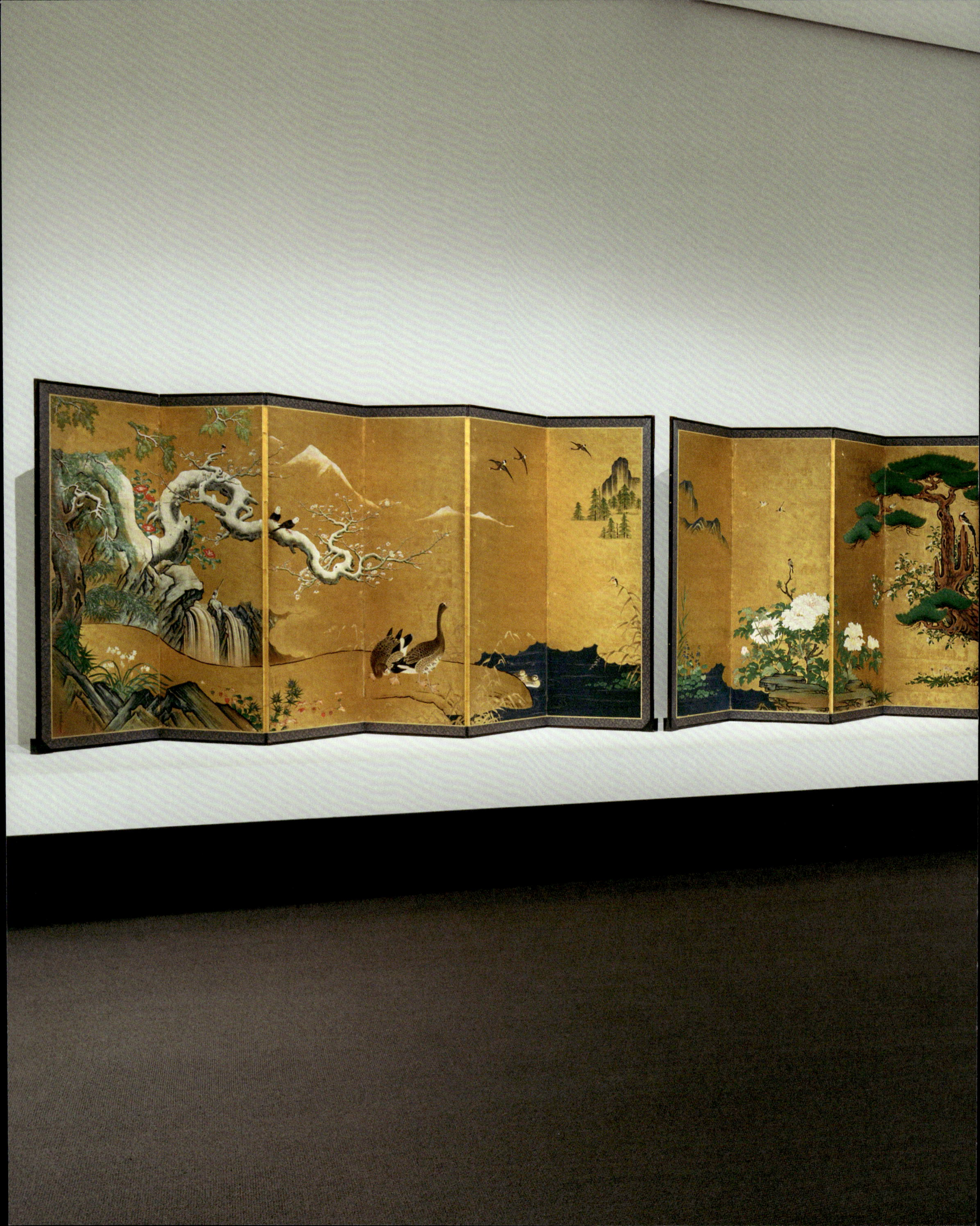

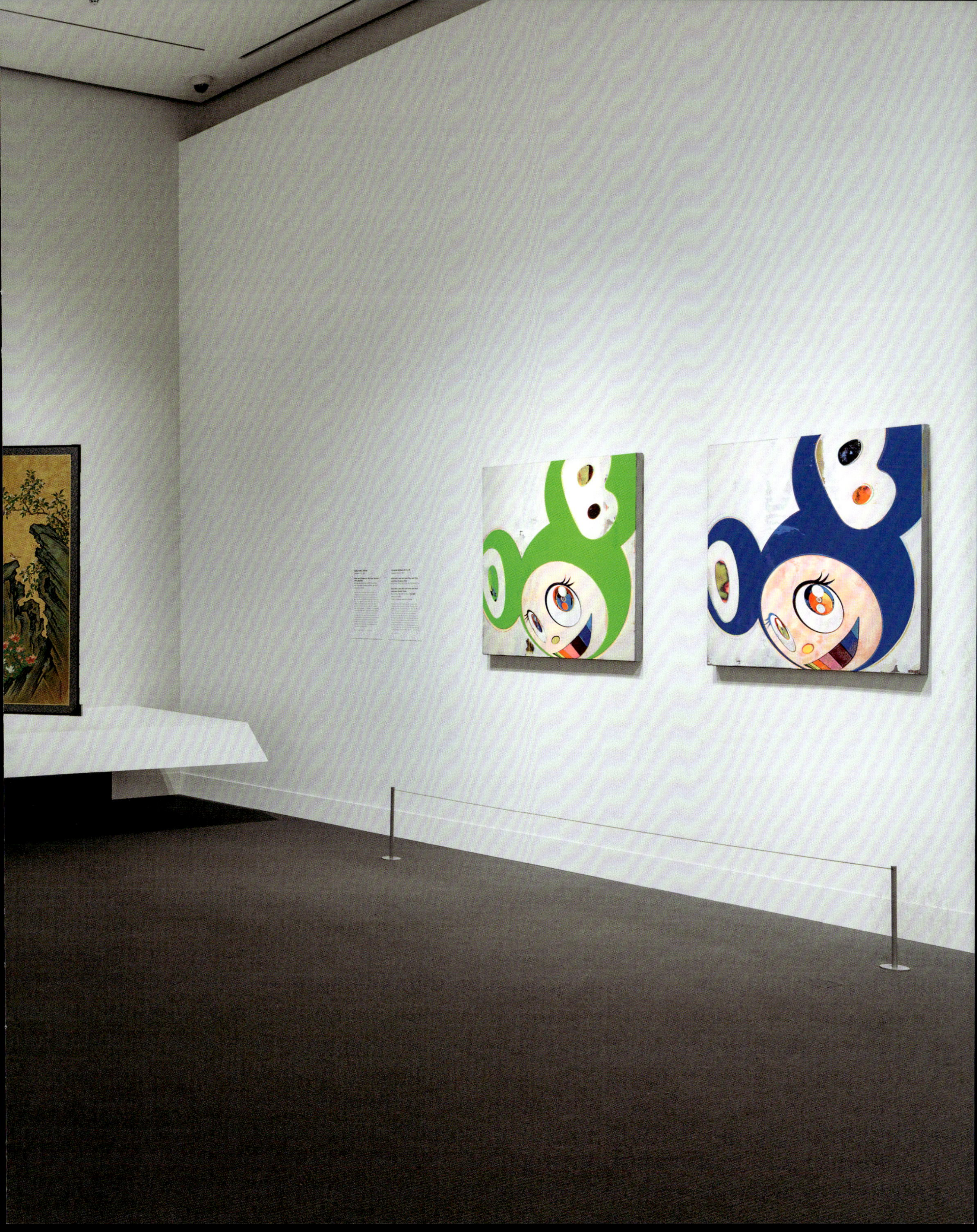

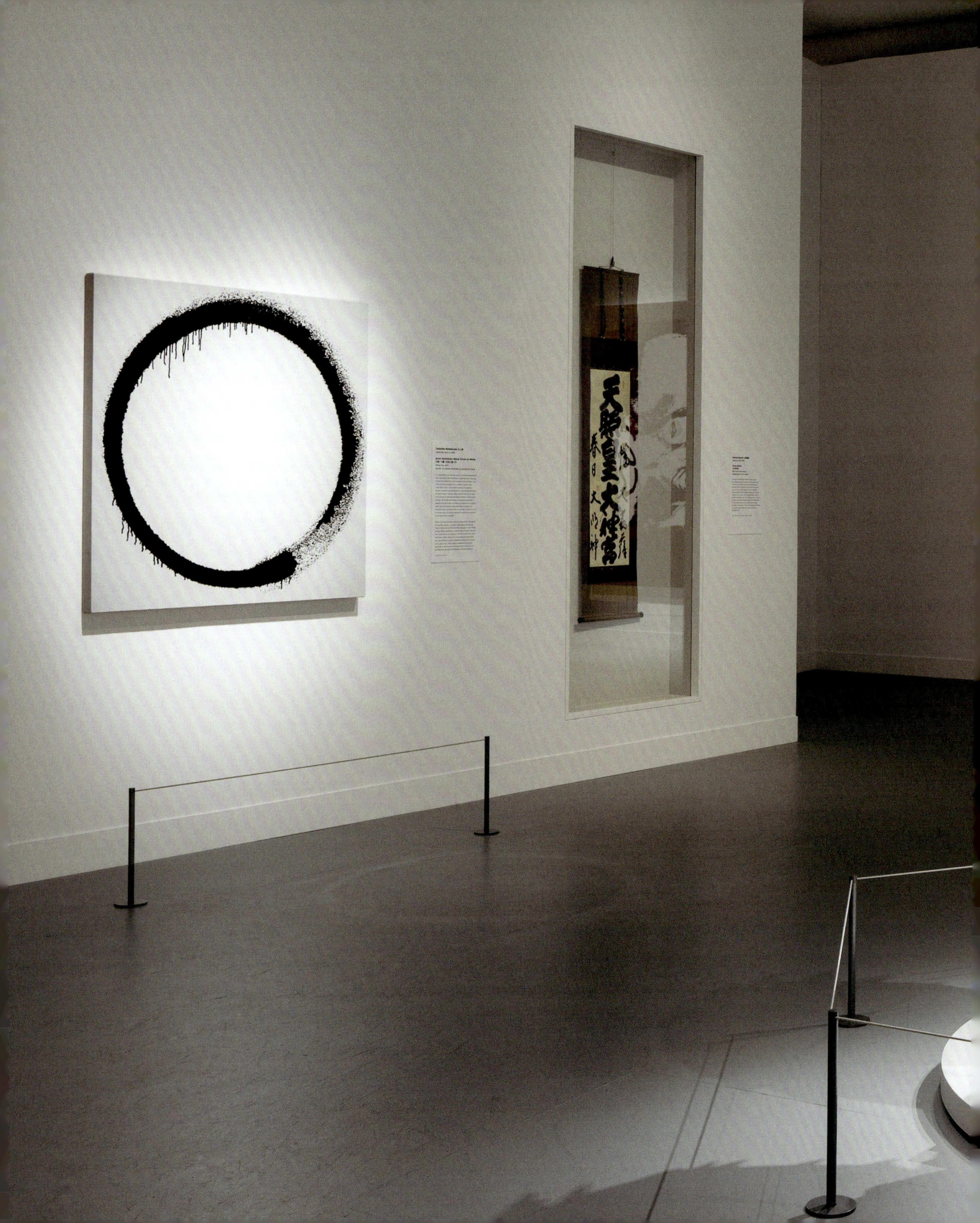

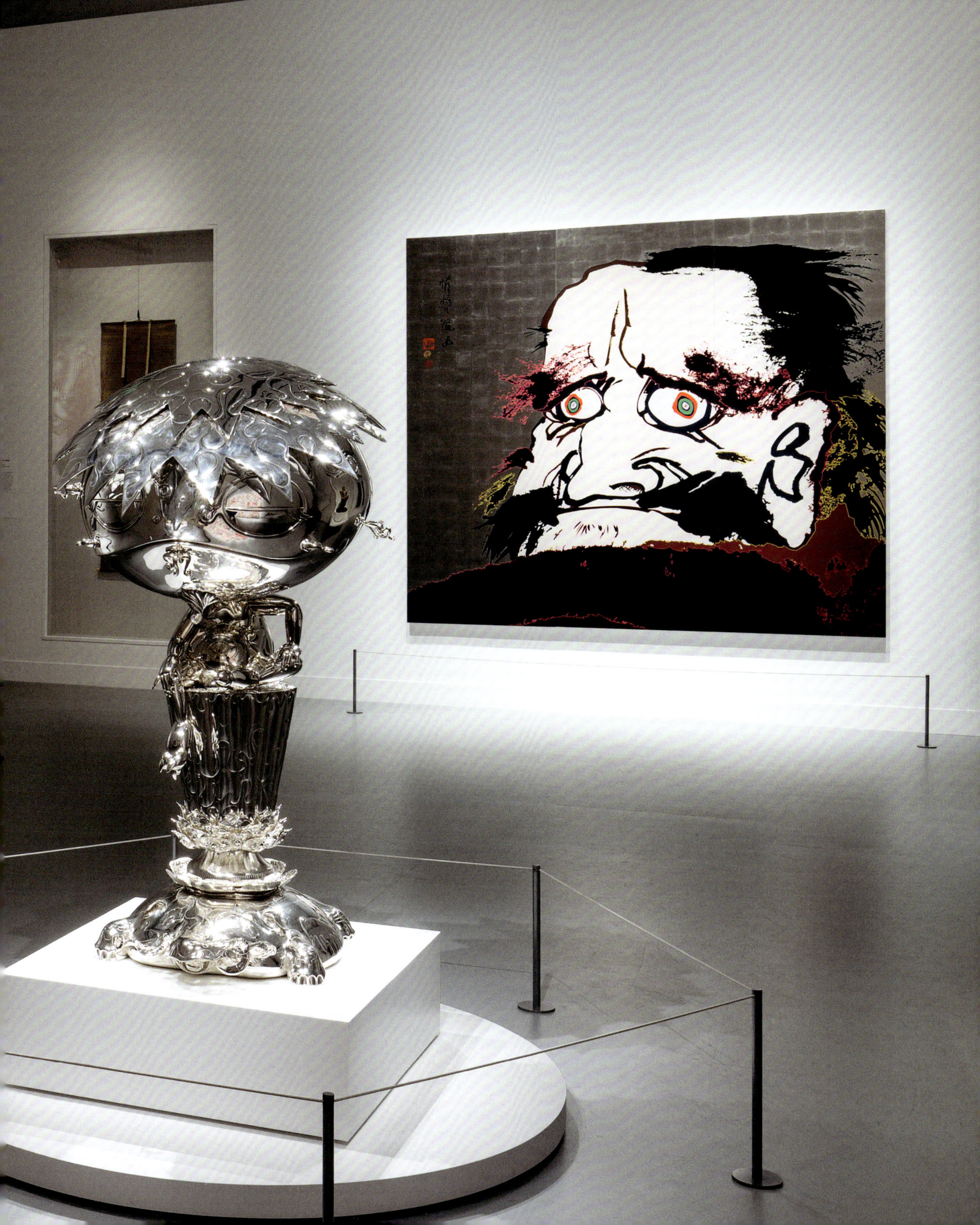

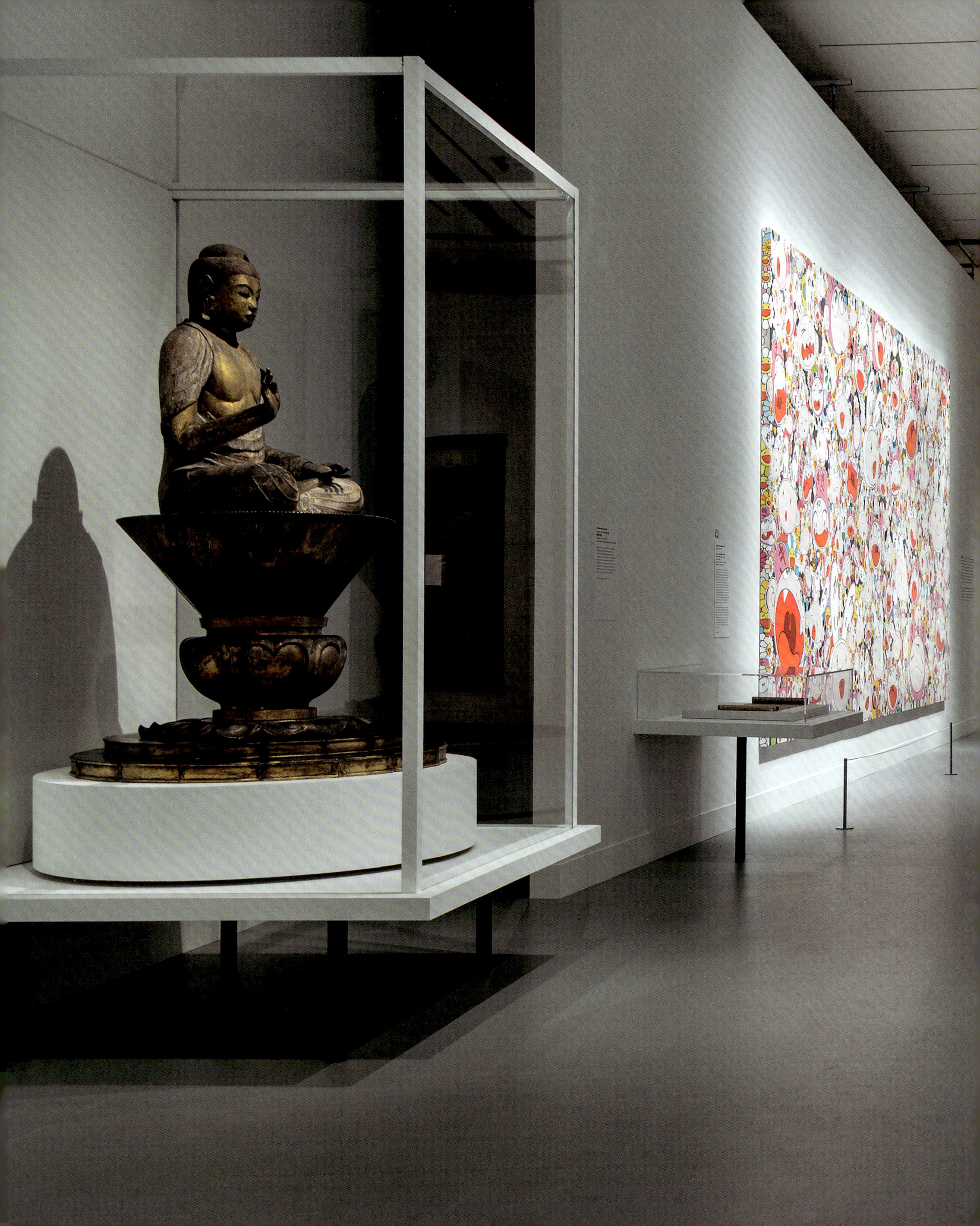

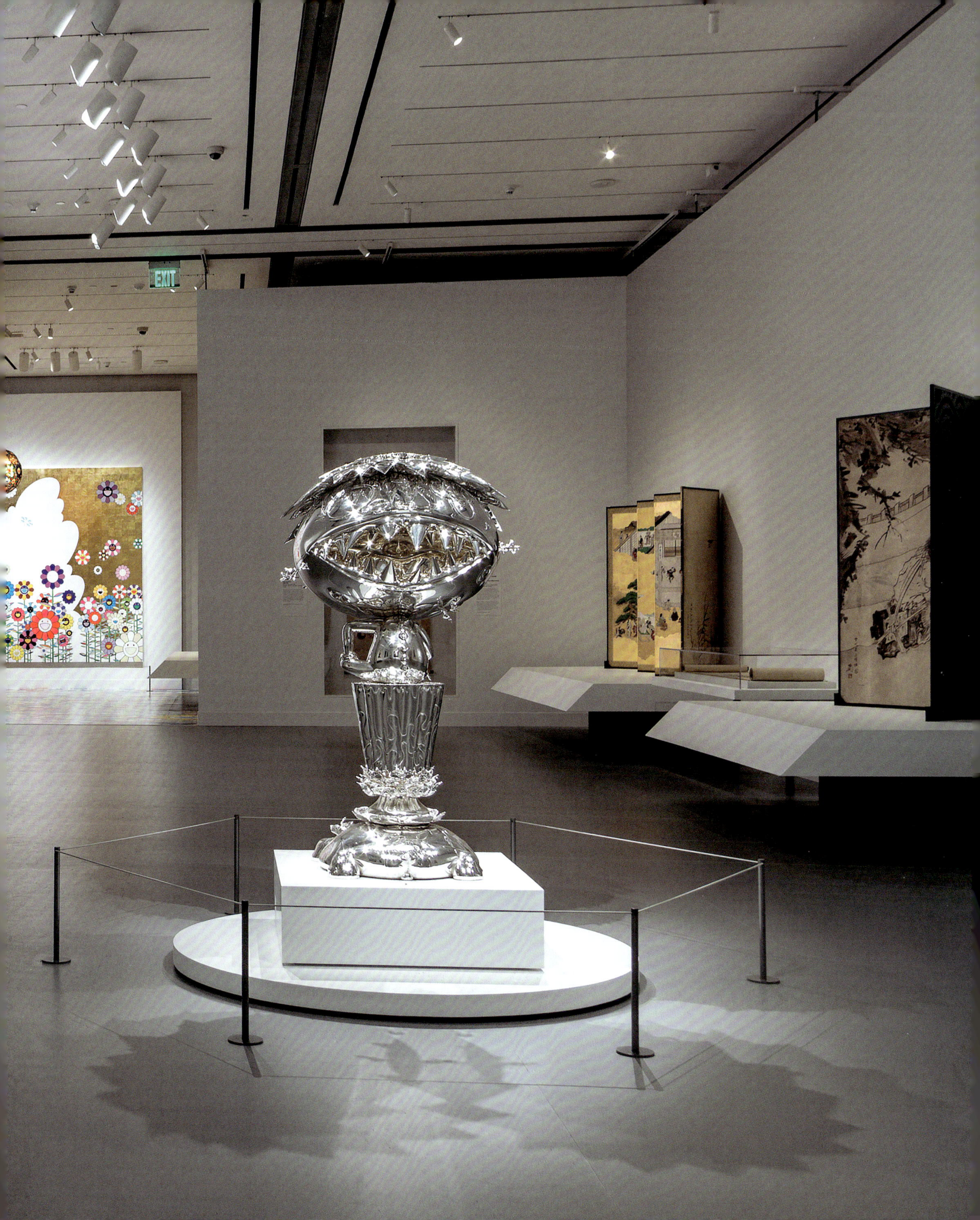

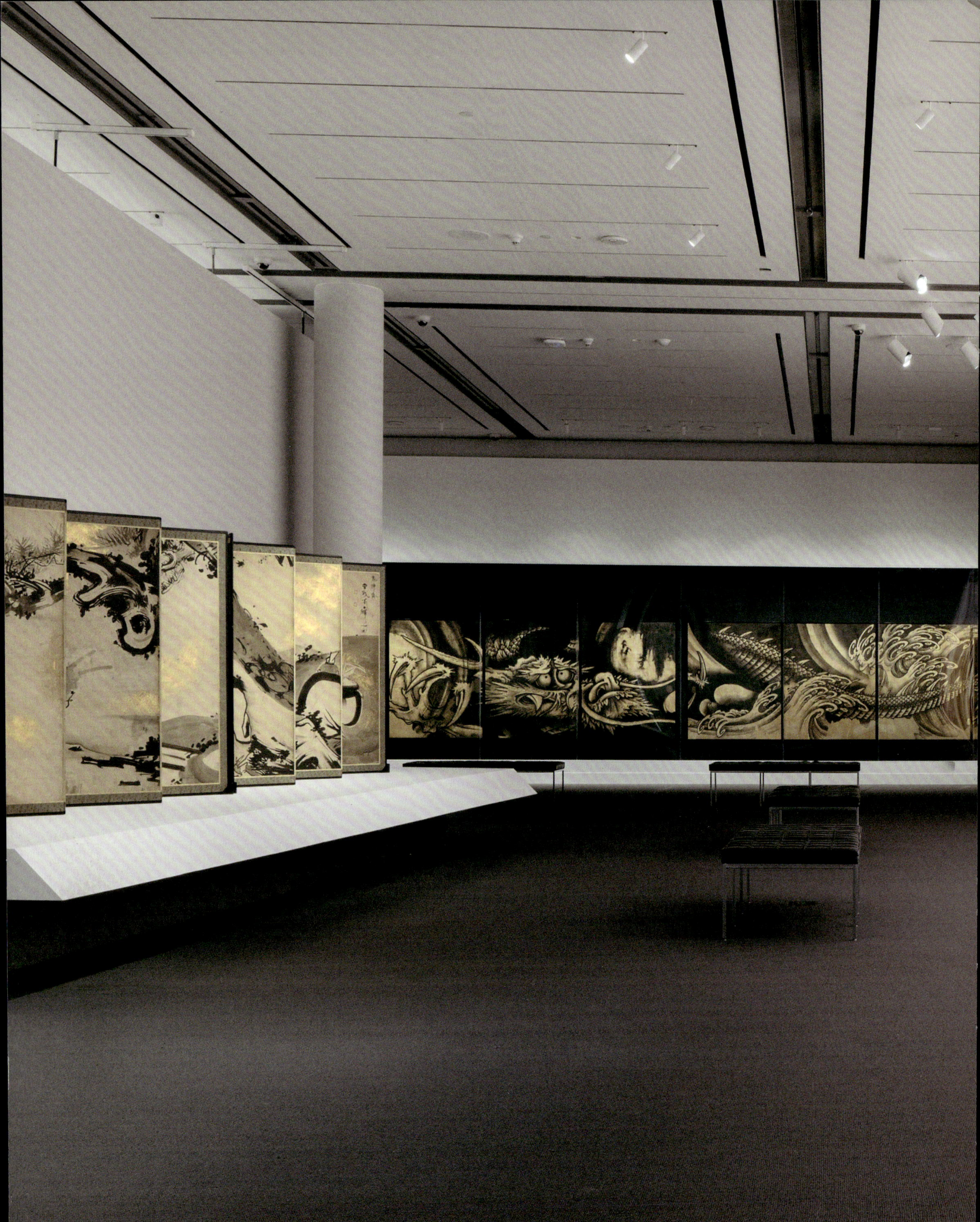

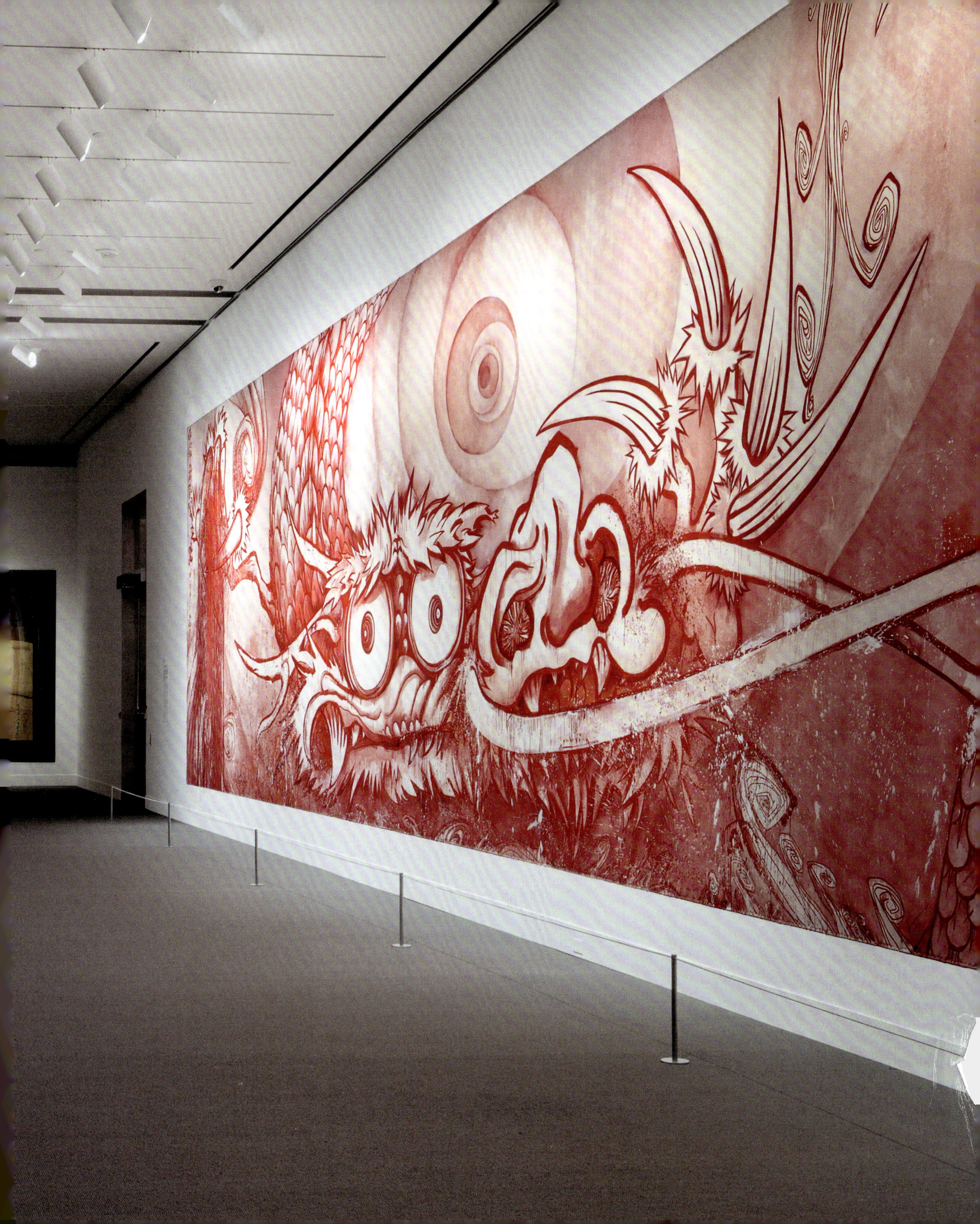

FIGURE ILLUSTRATIONS

1

Original 1970 cover of *Kisō no keifu* (*Lineage of Eccentrics*) by Nobuo Tsuji featuring Soga Shōhaku's *Dragon and Clouds*

2

Takashi Murakami
The Severe Art Critic Redefined: Delighted! Difficult …and Dazed, Heisei era, 2010
Acrylic on canvas mounted on aluminum frame
Set of three paintings, each 75 × 75 cm
(29 ½ × 29 ½ in.)

3

Portrait of Okakura Kakuzō (1863–1913)

4

Takashi Murakami
Nuclear Power Picture, Heisei era, 1988
Straw, cardboard, and silver and gold pigment on canvas
About 2 × 2.6 m (77 in. × 8 ft. 7 in.)

5

Takashi Murakami
Flower Mantango (d), Heisei era, 2001–6, in the Hall of Mirrors, Château de Versailles, 2010
Oil paint, acrylic, fiberglass, and iron
About 3.2 m × 20.5 cm × 2.6 m
(10 ft. 4 in. × 8 ⅟₁₆ in. × 8 ft. 8 in.)

6

Takashi Murakami
727, Heisei era, 1996
Three panels; synthetic polymer paint on canvas board
About 3 × 4.5 m (9 ft. 10 in. × 14 ft. 9 in.)
The Museum of Modern Art, Gift of David Teiger

7

View of the exhibition *Takashi Murakami: Made in Japan*, Museum of Fine Arts, Boston, 2001

8

Takashi Murakami
Crucified Upside Down, Heisei era, 2010
Photographer: Kentaro Hirao
Stylist: Kazuki Yunoki
Art Director: Aki Kasai
Special Effects Makeup: JIRO
Production Coordinator: Kaikai Kiki

9

Battle pennant of Ochiai Saheiji Michitsugu, Momoyama period, 16th century
Painted banner; color with ink on silk
145× 133 cm (57× 52 ⅜ in.)
Collection of the Historiographical Institute, The University of Tokyo

10

Takashi Murakami painting *Dragon in Clouds—Red Mutation: The version I painted myself in annoyance after Professor Tsuji told me, "Why don't you paint something yourself for once?"* in 2010

11

Takashi Murakami
In the Land of the Dead, Stepping on the Tail of a Rainbow, Heisei era, 2014
Acrylic on canvas
About 3 × 25 m (9 ft. 10 in. × 82 ft.)
Collection of The Broad, Los Angeles, California

12

Soga Shōhaku (1730–1781)
Transcendent Attacking a Whirlwind, Edo period, about 1764
Six-panel folding screen; ink and light gold on paper
About 1.6 × 3.6 m (61 ¼ in. × 11 ft. 11 in.)
Museum of Fine Arts, Boston, Fenollosa-Weld Collection, 11.4510

13

Takashi Murakami
Transcendent Attacking a Whirlwind, Heisei era, 2017
Acrylic, gold leaf, and platinum leaf on canvas mounted on wood panel
About 3 × 10 m (9 ft. 10 in. × 32 ft. 10 in.)

14

Detail from *Miraculous Tales of Mount Shigi* (*Shigisan engi emaki*), scroll 1, Heian period, 12th century
Handscroll; ink and color on paper
About 31.7 cm × 2.3 m (12 ½ × 91 ⅝ in.)
Collection of Chōgosonshiji Nara Prefecture

15

Detail from *The Tales of the Major Counselor Ban* (*Ban dainagon ekotoba*), scroll 2, Heian period, 12th century
Handscroll; ink and color on paper
About 31.4 cm × 8.5 m (12 ⅜ in. × 27 ⅞ ft.)
Collection of Idemitsu Museum, Tokyo

16
Round mirror with animals and flowers,
China, Tang dynasty, 8th century
Bronze with mother-of-pearl and coral
Diam. 27.2 cm (10 ¾ in.)
Collection of Shōsō-in, Tōdaiji, Nara

17
Five Poems from the *Lady Ise Volume* (*Ise-shū*) of
the *Sanjūrokunin-shū* (Collection of Thirty-Six Poets)
known as *Ishiyama-gire*, Heian period, about 1112
Book page mounted as a hanging scroll; ink and
gold and silver pigments on dyed, collaged paper
Image 20.2 × 16 cm (7 ⁵⁄₁₆ × 6 ⁵⁄₁₆ in.)
Museum of Fine Arts, Boston
Gift of Sylvan Barnet and William Burto, 2014.1506

18
Ogata Kōrin (1658–1716)
Red and White Plum Screen, Edo period, 18th century
Pair of two-panel folding screens; ink, color, and
gold leaf on paper
156 × 172.2 cm (61 ⅜ × 67 ¾ in.) each
Collection of MOA Museum of Art, Atami

19
Torii Kiyonobu I (1664–1729)
Detail from *Erotic Contest of Flowers*, Edo period,
early eighteenth century
Handscroll; ink, color, gold, and silver on paper
Image about 34.8 cm × 5 m (13 ¹¹⁄₁₆ in. × 16 ⅔ ft.)
Museum of Fine Arts, Boston
William Sturgis Bigelow Collection, RES.09.234

20
Boar, Kofun period, 6th century
Unglazed earthenware
H. 50.2 cm, l. 58 cm (H. 19 ¾ in., l. 22 ⅞ in.)
Collection of Tokyo National Museum

21
Main altar in the Golden Hall, Chūsonji, Hiraizumi,
Iwate Prefecture, constructed in the Heian period,
1124

22
Hakuin Ekaku (1685–1768)
Giant Bodhidharma, Edo period, 18th century
Hanging scroll; ink on paper
130.8 × 55.2 cm (51 ½ × 21 ¾ in.)
Gitter-Yelen Collection, New Orleans

23
Itō Jakuchū (1716–1800)
*Insects, Reptiles, and Amphibians at the Edge of
a Pond* from *Colorful Realm of Living Beings*,
Edo period, 18th century
Hanging scroll; ink and color on silk
142.3 × 79.7 cm (56 × 31 ⅜ in.)
Museum of the Imperial Collections, Tokyo

24
Itō Jakuchū (1716–1800)
Vegetable Nirvana, Edo period, 18th century
Hanging scroll; ink on paper
181.7 × 96.1 cm (71 ⁹⁄₁₆ × 37 ¹³⁄₁₆ in.)
Collection of Kyoto National Museum

25
Soga Shōhaku (1730–1781)
Sessan dōji, Edo period, 18th century
Hanging scroll; ink and color on paper
170.3 × 124.6 cm (67 ¹⁄₁₆ × 49 ¹⁄₁₆ in.)
Keishōji, Matsuzaka, Mie Prefecture

26
View of *Takashi Murakami: The 500 Arhats*,
Mori Museum, Tokyo, 2015

27
Itō Jakuchū (1716–1800)
Elephant and Whale Screens, Edo period, 1797
Pair of six-panel screens; ink on paper
About 1.6 × 3.5 m (62 ¾ in. × 11 ft. 7 ¾ in.) each
Miho Museum, Shiga Prefecture

28
Takashi Murakami
Study of Jakuchū's Elephant and Whale Screens,
2009–10
Acrylic on canvas
About 3.7 × 9.4 m (12 ½ ft. × 30 ft. 8 in.)

IMAGE CREDITS

Details

pp. 1, 10: Takashi Murakami, *"I open wide my eyes but see no scenery, I fix my gaze upon my heart"* (pp. 124–25)

pp. 2, 100: Takashi Murakami, *Lots, Lots of Kaikai and Kiki* (pp. 98–99)

p. 3: Hishikawa Moronobu, *Fantastical Scenes* (p. 104)

pp. 4, 22, 182: Takashi Murakami, *Transcendent Attacking a Whirlwind* (pp. 40–42)

p. 5: Soga Shōhaku, *The Daoist Immortal Li Tieguai (Tekkai)* (p. 149, right)

p. 6: Takashi Murakami, *Crucified Upside Down* (p. 34, left)

p. 7: Soga Shōhaku, *Asahina in a Tug-of-War with a Demon* (p. 107)

p. 8: Takashi Murakami, *Oval Buddha Silver* (p. 117)

p. 9: Shaka, the Historical Buddha (p. 118)

p. 11: Bodhidharma (Daruma) on a Reed (p. 123)

p. 12: Takashi Murakami, *Kawaii–Vacances: Summer Vacation in the Kingdom of the Golden* (pp. 86–87)

p. 14: School of Tawaraya Sōtatsu, *Poppies* (pp. 90–91)

p. 16: Soga Shōhaku, *Dragon and Clouds* (pp. 138–39)

pp. 18–19: Takashi Murakami and Nobuo Tsuji photographed in the exhibition *Takashi Murakami: Lineage of Eccentrics* at the Museum of Fine Arts, Boston, 2017

p. 152: Takashi Murakami, *The Severe Art Critic Redefined: Delighted! Difficult . . . and Dazed* (p. 24)

TAKASHI MURAKAMI, NOBUO TSUJI, AND ANNE NISHIMURA MORSE THANK:

Museum of Fine Arts, Boston

Ann and Graham Gund Director:
Matthew Teitelbaum

Curatorial:
Yuiko Hotta, Kelsey Mallet, Tomoko Nagakura

Education:
Adam Tessier, Lynn Courtney, Brooke DiGiovanni Evans, Abby McBride

Exhibitions:
Anne Silk, Edward Saywell, Patrick McMahon

Design:
Keith Crippen, Jennifer Liston Munson, Damon Bishop, Cyrille Conan, Eben Haines, Neal Johnson, Cara Kuball, Quinn Papazian, Nick Pioggia, Olsen Images Inc.

Registrar:
Jill Kennedy-Kernohan

Conservation:
Matthew Siegal, Michiko Adachi, Brett Angell, Caitlin Breare, Frank Egloff, Ales Hlousek, Abigail Hykin, Irene Konefal, Adeline Lutts, Annette Manick, Kim McParland, Richard Newman, Louise Orsini, John Robbe, Gerri Strickler, Tanya Uyeda, Dante Vallance

Publications:
Anna Barnet, Anne Levine, Terry McAweeney, Hope Stockton, Emiko Usui, Lesley Chi (Goto Design), Takaya Goto (Goto Design), ProGraphics, Graphicom, Dalia Geffen, Martha McClintock, Ruth S. McCreery, Yuiko Kimura

Intellectual Property:
Katherine Campbell, Greg Heins, Valentine Lescar, Maggie Loh, Jared Medeiros, John Woolf

Facilities:
Mark Kerwin, Tom Carey, Scott Cina, Lawrence Gibbons, Karen Haley, Ralph LaVoie, Jose Benitez, John Botelho, Dan Burke, Bryan Campbell, Luke Cannon, Sean Cooper, Fred Curtis, Chris Daunais, Matthew Davidson, John Doyle, Aaron Kakos, Brian LeBlanc, Aaron Luckman, Robert Meighan, Joe Morgan, Paul Picardi, Antonio Pires, Robert Taylor, Antonello Verdiglione, Mike Wals, Jason Whelan, David Willcutt

Communications:
Katie Getchell, Karen Frascona, Dawn Griffin, Gary Mak, Janet O'Donoghue, Jill Bendonis, Ashley Bleimes, Amelia Kantrovitz, Olga Khvan, Audrey Rodriguez, Michael Roper, Natalie Rosen, George Scharoun, Caroline Washburne, Connelly Partners, Wondriska Russo, Richard Lewis Media Group

Retail:
Ellen Bragalone, Sean Halpert, Donna Kent, Denis McGrath, Michael Mirarchi, Christina Murphy, Bill O'Connor, Ginger Shannon

Opening Events:
Linda Chernoff, Linda Apple, Meghan Sundermier, Kate Hannigan, Kristen Hoskins, Jen Leclerc, Kelly O'Hara

Development:
Cynthia Glott, Cynthia O'Brien, Susan Veroff, Christopher Barberesi, Patty Doyle, Rachel Harrington, Stephanie Heinbeck, Blair Hollis, Emma Rose Rainville, Lucinda Zuniga

Protective Services:
Nicki Luongo, Jeremy Lehane, Brandon Perigard

Member and Visitor Services:
Matt Murphy, Jeremy Gotsch

Kaikai Kiki

Executive Manager:
Chiaki Kasahara (Kaikai Kiki Co., Ltd. (KKJP))
Yuko Sakata

Exhibition Production Director:
Shinichi Kitahara

Painting Directors:
SHISHO, Ayako Funakoshi, Yoichi Ishikawa (KKJP)

Data Chief Staff:
Kazami Suzuki, Sayo Yoshida, (KKJP)

Painting Chief Staff:
Haruka Tajiri, Minako Kurasawa, Rentaro Murachi,
Keisen Tamada, Taiga Takegawa (KKJP)

Painting Consultants:
Yoshikazu Hirata, Tomoko Sugimoto

Data Staff:
Nozomi Ikuyama, Shun Kaneko, Mayumi Kobayashi,
Chieri Nakano, Hazuki Kibe, Sayaka Inoue,
Yoshihiro Takeuchi, Tomoyo Arato, Motomi Hirose,
Ayumi Tanaka, Makoto Namikawa (KKJP)

Painting Staff:
Kazuko "Ninja" Suzuki, Masayo Yakushi,
Haruka Oyaizu, Toshiyuki Maeda, Ryosuke Mitsuta,
Ayana Koga, Hiroaki Konaka, Yu Tanaka,
Tomohiro Fuchiwaki, Takaaki Yamabe, Sakiko Miura,
Mei Nakamura, Takeru Kageyama, Hiroki Mano,
Yukino Nagasawa, Tatsumi Takahashi, Takuma Wada,
Yoshito Nakamura, Emamiyeh Mohammad,
Akiho Suzuki, Ayaka Sako, Sho Natsume,
Kazuki Maeda, Shinya Yamada, Tamaki Ishii,
Shinichiro Takeura, Yukino Mizushima,
Maki Nakamura, Yuka Hamamoto, Akiho Yamamoto,
Takane Matsushita, Chika Kameyama,
Chihiro Obayashi, Ami Tsukamoto, Toshihiko Fujisaki,
Natsumi Ashida (KKJP), Stephen Michael,
Brandon Loyd, Ema Chen, Joseph Regan,
Branche Coverdale, Brian Byun, Jennifer Tong,
Adrienne Arredondo, Amelia Hirschauer,
Vladan Sibinovic, Nicholas Madonia, Melissa Garvin,
Lucas Perez, Ly Bui (Kaikai Kiki New York, LLC
(KKNY))

Exhibition Production:
Jun Tagawa, Koichiro Endo, Yuki Morimoto,
Tomoyuki Mitani, Goro Ishimori, Yuma Shimazaki
(KKJP) Paatela Fraga, Chandler Meyers (KKNY)

Legal:
Masako Iida (KKNY), Daisuke Murakoshi (KKJP)

Project Management:
Miwa Takahashi, Reiko Anzaki, Ayane Nakajima,
Aki Kono (KKJP), Michael Choi, Yoshimi Sanada,
Shinnosuke Seto, Sayaka Toyama (KKNY)

Accounting:
Miki Hara (KKJP)

Personal Assistant:
Shoko Suzuki (KKJP)

Merchandise:
Mitsuru Oguma, Teppei Yamazki (KKJP)

Stylist:
Kazuki Yunoki

Sculpture Production:
Lucky Wide Co., Ltd., Kurotani bijutsu,
Hirohisa Yoshizawa, Hiroki Iijima,
Makoto Dohi, Takeshi Nagata,
Fumito Kobayashi, Rideaworks Inc.

Other Operations:
Yamato Logistics Co., Ltd. (Shipping)

Special Thanks:
Emmanuel Perrotin (Perrotin)
Etsuko Nakajima (Perrotin)
Reona Takayama (Geijutsu Shincho)

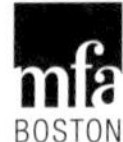

MFA Publications
Museum of Fine Arts, Boston
465 Huntington Avenue
Boston, Massachusetts 02115
www.mfa.org/publications

Published in conjunction with the exhibition *Takashi Murakami: Lineage of Eccentrics, A Collaboration with Nobuo Tsuji and the Museum of Fine Arts, Boston*, organized by the Museum of Fine Arts, Boston, from October 18, 2017, to April 1, 2018.

The exhibition was generously supported by the Carl and Ruth Shapiro Family Foundation. Additional support was provided by Davis and Carol Noble, and Peggy Koenig. The media sponsor was *The Boston Globe*.

Generous support for this publication was provided by the Andrew W. Mellon Publications Fund.

Jacket: Takashi Murakami, *Dragon in Clouds—Red Mutation: The version I painted myself in annoyance after Professor Tsuji told me, "Why don't you paint something yourself for once?"* 2010 (detail, pp. 132–34)

Cover: Takashi Murakami, *Lots, Lots of Kaikai and Kiki*, 2009 (detail, pp. 98–99)

Edited by Anna Barnet
Editorial assistance by Tomoko Nagakura
Translations by Martha McClintock, Ruth S. McCreery, Yuiko Kimura, Yuiko Hotta, and Yuko Sakata
Copyedited and proofread by Dalia Geffen

Designed by Takaya Goto, Lesley Chi, and Sho Momma, Goto Design, New York
Production by Terry McAweeney
Photography research and permissions by Anne Levine

Printed on 150 gsm Perigord
Printed and bound at Graphicom, Verona, Italy

Distributed in the United States of America and Canada by
ARTBOOK | D.A.P.
75 Broad Street, Suite 360
New York, New York 10004
www.artbook.com

Distributed outside the United States of America and Canada by
Thames & Hudson, Ltd.
181A High Holborn
London WC1V 7QX
www.thamesandhudson.com

SECOND PRINTING
Printed and bound in Italy
This book was printed on acid-free paper.